MADE IN CHINA

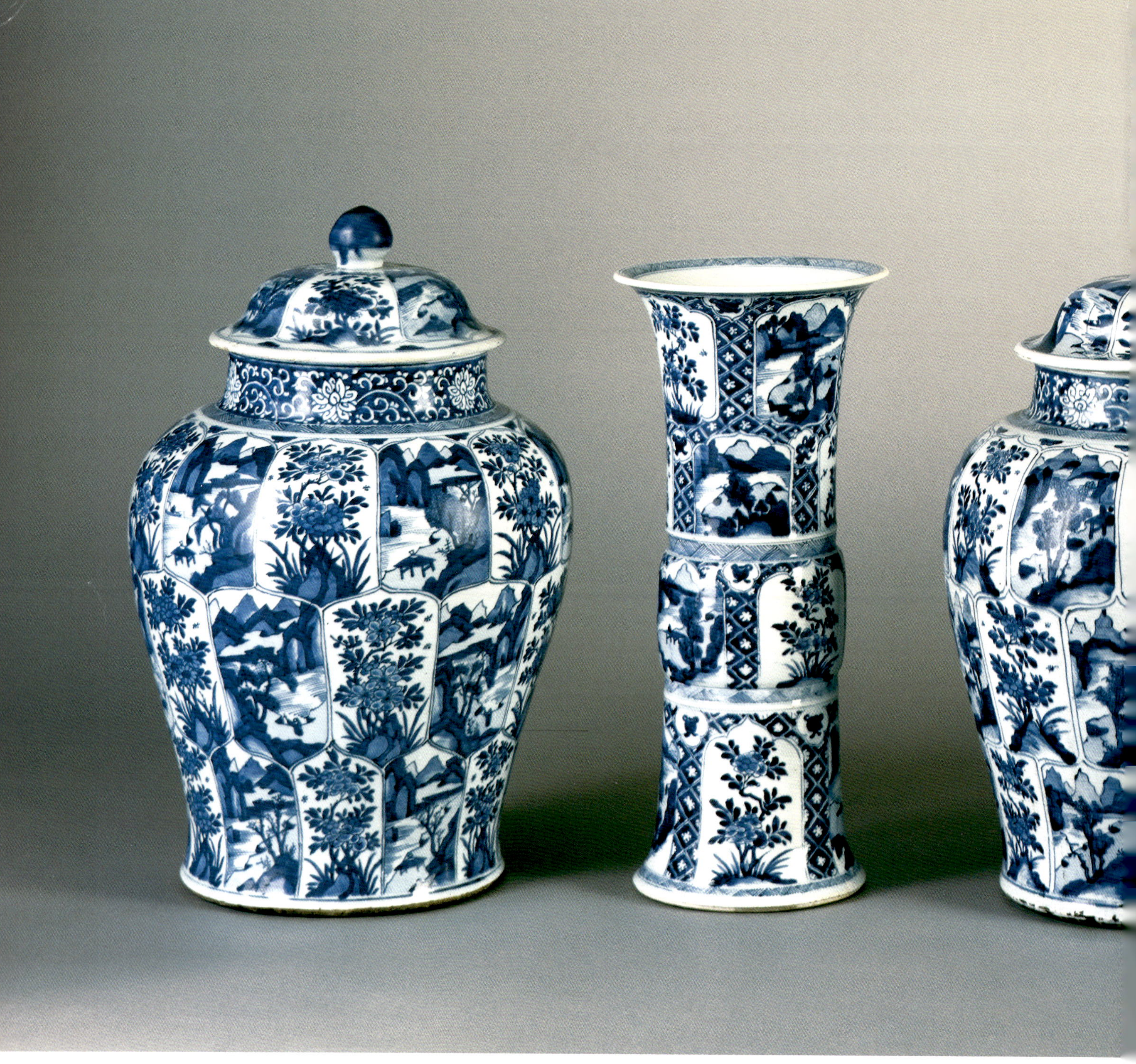

Made in China

Ronald W. Fuchs II

in collaboration with

David S. Howard

Photography by Gavin Ashworth

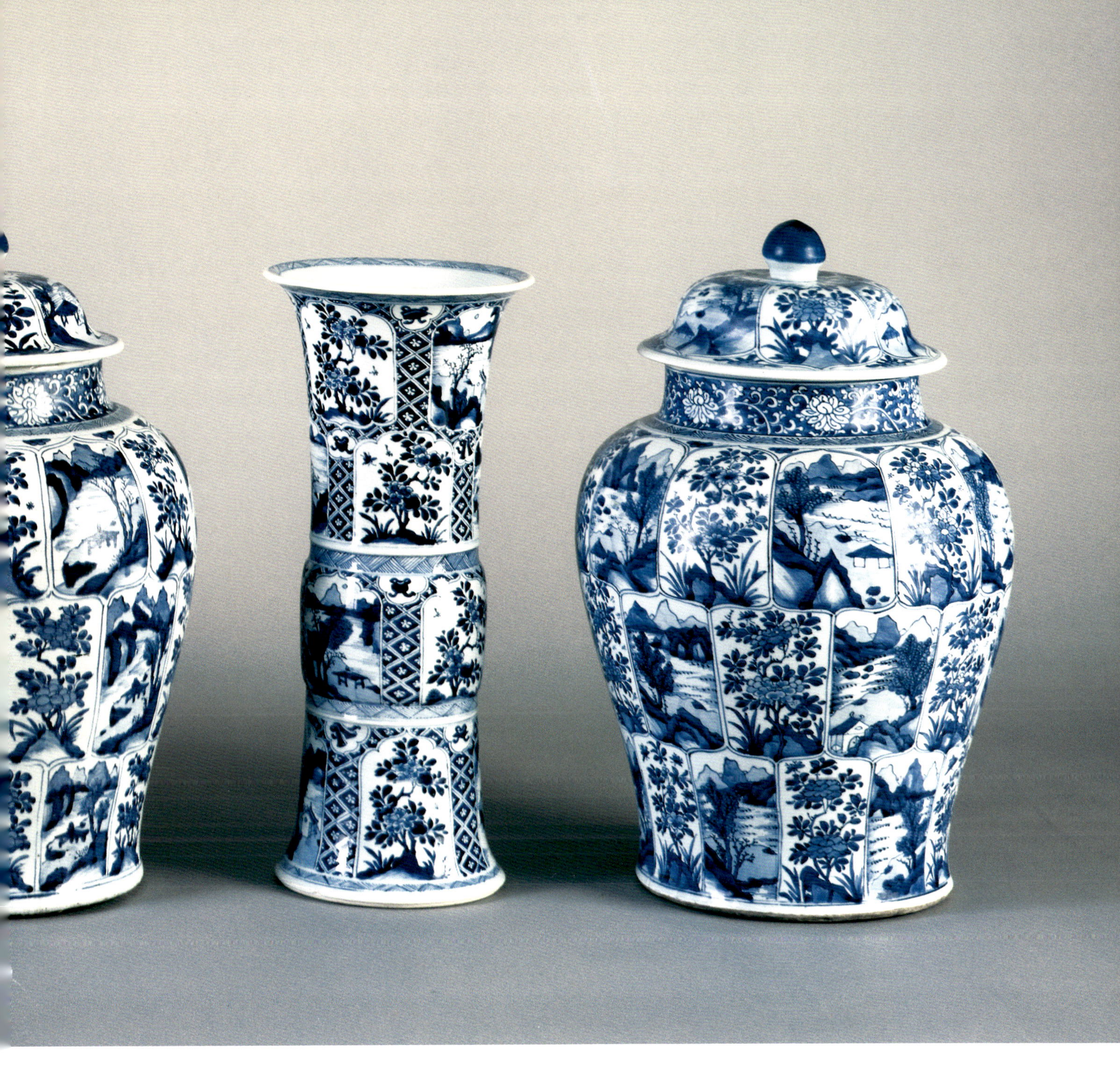

EXPORT PORCELAIN FROM THE LEO AND DORIS HODROFF COLLECTION AT WINTERTHUR

A Winterthur Book

Distributed by University Press of New England

Funding for this catalogue and the exhibition that it accompanies is made possible through the generosity of Leo and Doris Hodroff.

Library of Congress Cataloging-in-Publication Data

Fuchs, Ronald W.
Made in China : export porcelain from the Leo and Doris Hodroff collection at Winterthur / Ronald W. Fuchs II in collaboration with David S. Howard ; photography by Gavin Ashworth.
p. cm. — (A Winterthur book)
Includes bibliographical references and index.
ISBN 0-912724-64-1 (alk. paper)
1. China trade porcelain—Catalogs. 2. Porcelain, Chinese—Ming–Qing dynasties, 1368–1912—Catalogs. 3. Hodroff, Leo—Art collections—Catalogs. 4. Hodroff, Doris—Art collections—Catalogs. 5. Porcelain—Private collections—Delaware—Catalogs. 6. Porcelain—Delaware—Catalogs. 7. Henry Francis du Pont Winterthur Museum—Catalogs. I. Howard, David Sanctuary. II. Ashworth, Gavin. III. Henry Francis du Pont Winterthur Museum. IV. Title. V. Series.

NK4565.5.F83 2005
738.2'0951'0747511—dc22 2004021323

Distributed by
University Press of New England

Page 1: Plate (see cat. 44)
Pages 2–3: Garniture (see cat. 104)
Page 10: Watercolor (see fig. 8)
Page 12: Soldier vase (see cat. 107)

Edited by Onie Rollins
Proofread by Laura Iwasaki
Typeset by Marissa Meyer
Designed by John Hubbard
Color separations by iocolor, Seattle
Produced by Marquand Books, Inc., Seattle
www.marquand.com
Printed and bound by CS Graphics Pte., Ltd., Singapore

Contents

Director's Foreword

For more than fifty years, Leo and Doris Hodroff, of Minneapolis and Palm Beach, have been enamored of Chinese and Japanese export porcelain, building one of the largest and finest collections in existence. Their passion for porcelain is matched only by their commitment to sharing that collection with the public. The Hodroffs have generously donated to museums, supported the publication of what has become one of the standard references in the field—David S. Howard's *Choice of the Private Trader: The Private Market in Chinese Export Porcelain Illustrated from the Hodroff Collection*—and have recently established the Leo and Doris Hodroff Collection at Winterthur.

One of the most magnificent gifts to come to the museum since its founding, the Hodroff donation joins the already impressive holdings of Chinese export porcelain amassed by founder Henry Francis du Pont, allowing the institution to tell the full story of export porcelain made for Europe and America between 1550 and 1850. Winterthur is deeply honored by the opportunity to share such outstanding objects with our visitors, and we are deeply grateful for the Hodroffs' extraordinary support. Indeed, the extent of their support and desire to widen an understanding of the field of export porcelain represents the perfect fulfillment of the educational mission of the museum as set forth by H. F. du Pont.

Great collectors have often been aided by great scholars. Such is the case in this instance. For more than twenty years, Leo and Doris Hodroff have worked with one of the world's leading experts, David S. Howard, to build and refine their export porcelain collection. It was David who brought Winterthur and the Hodroffs together in 2000, recognizing a mutual dedication to excellence and to education. For this we offer our sincere thanks. We extend our gratitude to David as well for his time and knowledge and for freely sharing both, especially with Ron Fuchs, Assistant Curator of the Leo and Doris Hodroff Collection at Winterthur, with whom he authored this catalogue. This exquisite volume, the fruit of their collaboration, stands as a testament to not only the superb quality of the collection but also the sustained dedication and generosity of Leo and Doris Hodroff to sharing the wonders of export porcelain—its incredible beauty and history—with the public.

Leslie Greene Bowman
Director

Foreword

Having been fortunate to have been involved in the preparation of this book has made me appreciate the very exceptional circumstances that have led to its publication. I think it only right to draw attention to them here, for they could be regarded as a blueprint for future planning, for both collectors and museums.

Over many years, the generosity of American collectors in particular has enabled numerous museums to receive gifts of the widest range in both the fine art and antique fields. Although much welcomed, this has sometimes turned into an embarrassment for the museums themselves, where the generosity of donors has exceeded the display areas in the museum—leaving in its wake two consequences that should always be taken into account. One is the consigning of large numbers of objects to a more-or-less permanent condition of storage (euphemistically referred to as "reserve collections"), and the other is the unnecessary depletion of the flow and availability of interesting objects in the marketplace, sometimes creating a corresponding rise in the apparent value of such objects that are still available for purchase but also a reason to deflect interest from the subject itself because too few objects of merit are available for purchase by collectors and enthusiasts. (It is possible that such situations may one day be eased by a universal accessibility of illustrations and information worldwide on the Internet, but this is still a long way ahead and does not cater for the natural desire of collectors to own and study.)

However, it is clear that with its exceptional founding by Henry Francis du Pont, its curatorial excellence, and, above all, its commitment to education and the guiding of future generations of curators through its postgraduate programs, Winterthur Museum itself is a unique institution and fully able to support a worthwhile initiative.

In this case it has been possible for Winterthur to bond with an exceptional collector, Leo Hodroff, who, having enjoyed creating the largest collection of Chinese export porcelain in the world, has significantly turned to museum donations and long-term education, first by encouraging the book *The Choice of the Private Trader* (which I had the pleasure of writing a decade ago) and then by making a far-sighted gesture of funding a curatorship at Winterthur. He has then given a substantial number of his most interesting pieces to the museum so that they would provide long-term security for study in the future and act as a tool in the strengthening of curatorial knowledge on the subject, and to the benefit of the public who can see so much at Winterthur.

Using these ideas to widen understanding of the subject, and for the benefit of other museums, a traveling exhibition has now been planned by Winterthur which it is hoped will eventually reach any area in which there is interest. Not only did this require considerable organization by Winterthur but a far-sighted dedication by the collector to ensure that a representative but highly interesting range of pieces should be permanently available so that the Hodroff curator could use these assets in the foreseeable future to enhance study as broadly as possible.

To support the traveling exhibition, it was essential to plan a new book, largely written by the Hodroff curator, who would also be available to lecture. This would describe and provide an ordered catalogue and history of all those pieces which have been donated for the traveling exhibition—and this has resulted in this volume with its broad-based title *Made in China,* which provides a most useful sequel with many other fascinating examples of the trade.

The curator of the Leo and Doris Hodroff Collection at Winterthur, Ron Fuchs, has been able to make a number of journeys to select porcelain that will make up the traveling display and which will undoubtedly please audiences wherever it appears. For me, it has been a gratifying experience to see this cooperation flourish while also being able to take part in the preparation of the catalogue at a number of stages—seeing it as a logical follow-up to *The Choice of the Private Trader.* It is always pleasing when it is possible to link the best of a number of worlds, as has been achieved in this case—with *this* museum, *this* donor, and *this* curator.

What is particularly encouraging about this collaboration is the effect it will have on the understanding of the China Trade, which was perhaps the first major international trade undertaken by the new United States. By advancing the study of Chinese export porcelain and its considerable influence in the field of decorative arts, there is little doubt in my mind that the Hodroff initiative follows in the footsteps and long-term vision of Henry Francis du Pont.

I feel that one can look to this book and the traveling exhibition it will accompany not only as a permanent record of excellent cooperation on many fronts in the art and museum worlds but also as an exceptional display of the subject itself, providing a real and important reflection on a specialist aspect of development in the United States through its links to the China Trade.

David S. Howard
Wiltshire, England

Acknowledgments

I am profoundly grateful to the many people who have helped make this exhibition catalogue possible. First and foremost, my thanks go to Leo and Doris Hodroff for the opportunity they have given me to work with their incomparable collection. Without their vision and generosity in building this collection and creating the Leo and Doris Hodroff Collection at Winterthur, this catalogue and the exhibition that it accompanies would simply never have happened. Heartfelt thanks also go to my collaborator, David S. Howard, for his extensive knowledge, advice, and guidance and to Angela Howard as well. I offer praise and gratitude to Gavin Ashworth for the magnificent photography that fully highlights the beauty of each object herein.

Numerous colleagues at Winterthur have also had a hand in the production of this volume. I extend my thanks to Bruce Perkins, Chairman, Board of Trustees; Leslie Greene Bowman, Director; Pat Halfpenny, Director of Collections; and Leslie Grigsby, Curator of Ceramics and Glass, for their advice and support and to Onie Rollins, Editor, for her superb work. Thanks also to Cheryl Payne, Anne Verplanck, Don Fennimore, Wendy Cooper, Linda Eaton, and Katherine Hunt in the Curatorial Department; Shannon Schuler, Grace Eleazer, and Molly Greenfield in the Registration Office; Bruno Pouliot, Mark Bockrath, Adam Nesbit, and Margaret Little in the Conservation Department; Susan Randolph, Susan Newton, and Jim Schneck in the Department of Communications; Cate Cooney, Kathy Coyle, Dot Wiggins, and Jeanne Solensky in the Library; and volunteer Joyce Longworth.

In addition, I am most appreciative of the contributions of those outside Winterthur as well, including John Hubbard at Marquand Books for the stunning design of this catalogue; William Sargent at the Peabody Essex Museum; Christiaan Jörg at the Groninger Museum; John Finlay at the Norton Museum of Art; Helen Espir of London; and Johan de Haan of the Netherlands.

Finally, sincere thanks are due my family, friends, and especially Mike for all their encouragement, support, and patience.

Ronald W. Fuchs II

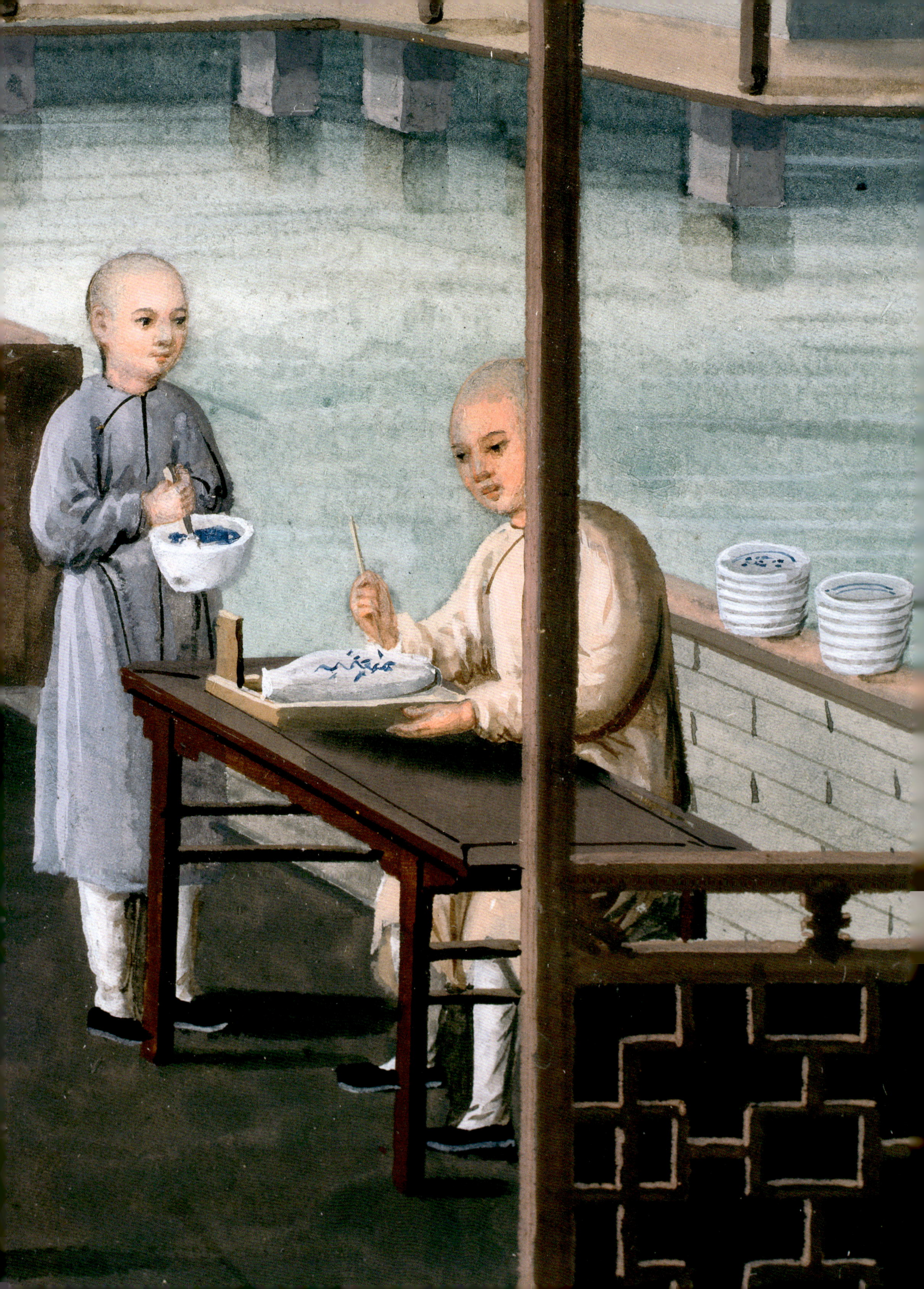

Notes to the Catalogue

Made in China: Export Porcelain from the Leo and Doris Hodroff Collection at Winterthur accompanies the exhibition of the same name and is also a partial catalogue of the Leo and Doris Hodroff Collection at Winterthur. It follows, and is greatly indebted to, David S. Howard's excellent 1994 catalogue entitled *The Choice of the Private Trader: The Private Market in Chinese Export Porcelain Illustrated from the Hodroff Collection*. A number of objects published in that volume are included in this exhibition and therefore appear in this publication.

The catalogue opens with an introductory essay that provides an overview of the manufacture of porcelain, the history of the China Trade, and export porcelain's place in European and American history and material culture. The introduction is followed by individual catalogue entries grouped into four sections according to function: dining wares, drinking wares, household and personal utensils, and decorative wares. Each grouping is preceded by a short essay that places the objects within an historical context. Within the groupings, objects are arranged according to form and date.

Each entry includes the object's name, place and date of manufacture, dimensions, accession number, and essential information about its design, history, and original function. A Literature listing, which is by no means comprehensive, then notes where an object has previously been published. For especially rare or unusual objects, references to similar or related objects are included in an endnote. Unless specified, those references are to page numbers, not entry or plate numbers.

Two appendixes follow the entries. The first is an explanation of how to "read" an achievement of arms. The second is a listing of Chinese dynasties covered in this volume.

Unless otherwise noted in a credit line, all objects form part of the Hodroff Collection.

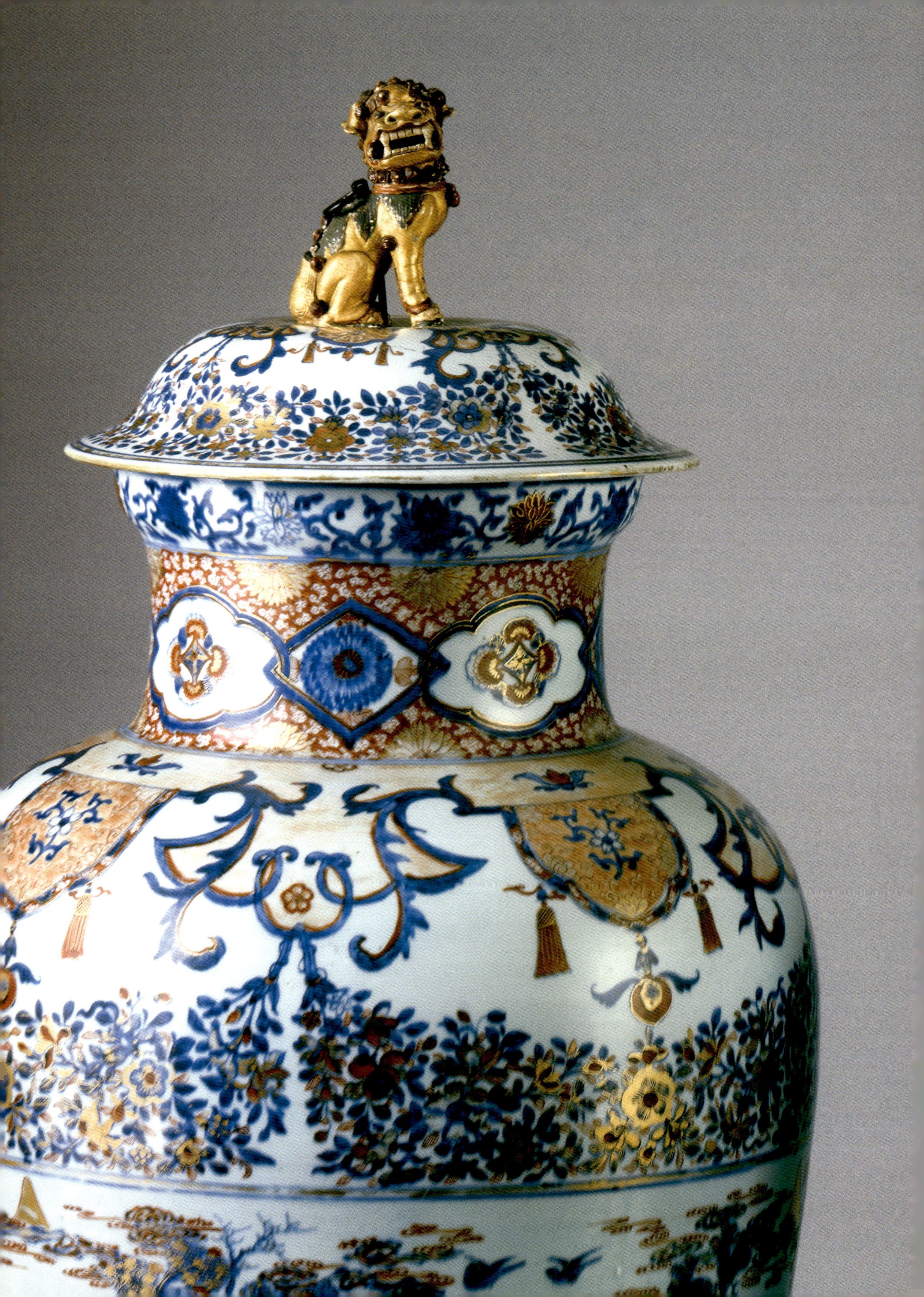

Introduction

Chinese export porcelain has long been prized in Europe and America. With its fine white body, delicately painted decoration, and associations with the exotic and mysterious world of Asia, porcelain has symbolized wealth and refinement from the time it was introduced to the West during the Middle Ages.[1] Since then, as many as 100 million pieces of "china," as it became known, have been transported to Europe and America—encouraging the development of international trading networks linking Asia and the West; inspiring major developments in the European ceramics industry; and revolutionizing the way people drank, dined, and decorated their homes.

CHINESE PORCELAIN

What is it about porcelain that so captivated Europeans and Americans? The most basic answer is the material itself. "There is nothing like it in European pottery," admitted one Jesuit missionary in the 16th century, acknowledging that Chinese porcelain was superior to the crude earthenwares and stonewares made in Europe at the time.[2]

Porcelain was developed by the Chinese more than 1,000 years ago, during the Tang Dynasty (618–906). It is a highly fired ceramic with a bright white body that is strong, translucent, and sonorous, producing a bell-like tone when struck. These special qualities that set porcelain apart from earthenware and stoneware result from the two main ingredients: china clay, which is also known as kaolin, and china stone, which is also known as petunse.

Although both china clay and china stone are formed from decomposed granite, the two have different properties. China clay is a fine white clay that is rich in alumina. It can be fired at a very high temperature without melting, and it is relatively plastic, meaning that it can be shaped easily but will not hold that shape well. China stone is a feldspathic rock that is rich in silica. China stone is less plastic, meaning that it is harder to shape but holds that form better. It also fuses into a sort of natural glass when fired. Thus the combination of china clay and china stone creates a material that molds easily, holds its shape, and tolerates firing at such a high temperature (up to 1350°C/2462°F) that the body becomes vitrified, or glasslike, and therefore translucent. Since neither

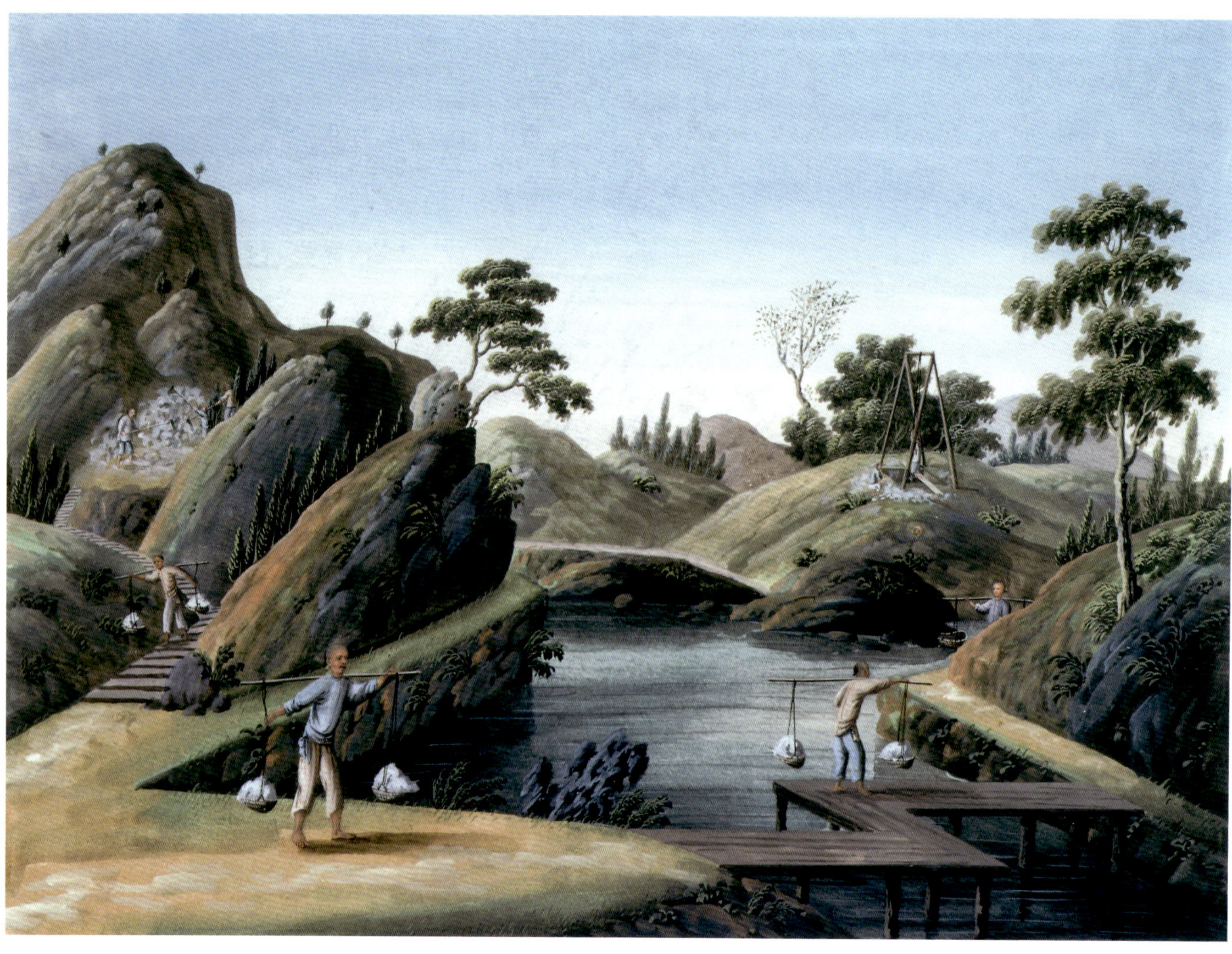

Figs. 1–10.
Set of paintings showing the manufacture of porcelain
China; about 1820
Watercolor on paper
2003.47.14.1–.10

1. *Digging the clay*
Clay was excavated from mines in the mountains surrounding Jingdezhen.

china clay nor china stone contains much iron, the mineral that gives most clays their reddish color, porcelain is white.[3]

Surprisingly, the word *porcelain* comes not from Chinese but from the Italian *porcellana,* meaning little pig. The term was first applied to cowrie shells, which have a glassy, bright white body that resembles a recumbent pig. Such shells were used as currency in parts of Asia, India, and Africa. The Venetian explorer Marco Polo, who traveled to China between 1271 and 1295, was one of the first Europeans to come in contact with Chinese porcelain and is thought to have coined the word to describe both the shells and the glassy, white, shell-like ceramic wares.[4]

The Chinese produced porcelain in an almost assembly-line fashion, with the different tasks—mining and refining the clays, forming and decorating the pieces, and firing the kilns—subdivided among a number of different craftsmen. "A Piece of China-ware, after it is baked [fired in the kiln], has passed the hands of seventy Workmen," wrote Père d'Entrecolles, a Jesuit missionary who toured the pottery-producing center of Jingdezhen in 1712 and 1722.[5] Sets of watercolors produced in China for export document the stages of porcelain production (figs. 1–10). First the clays were mined, washed, and refined; then they were worked into the desired shapes—either thrown on a wheel

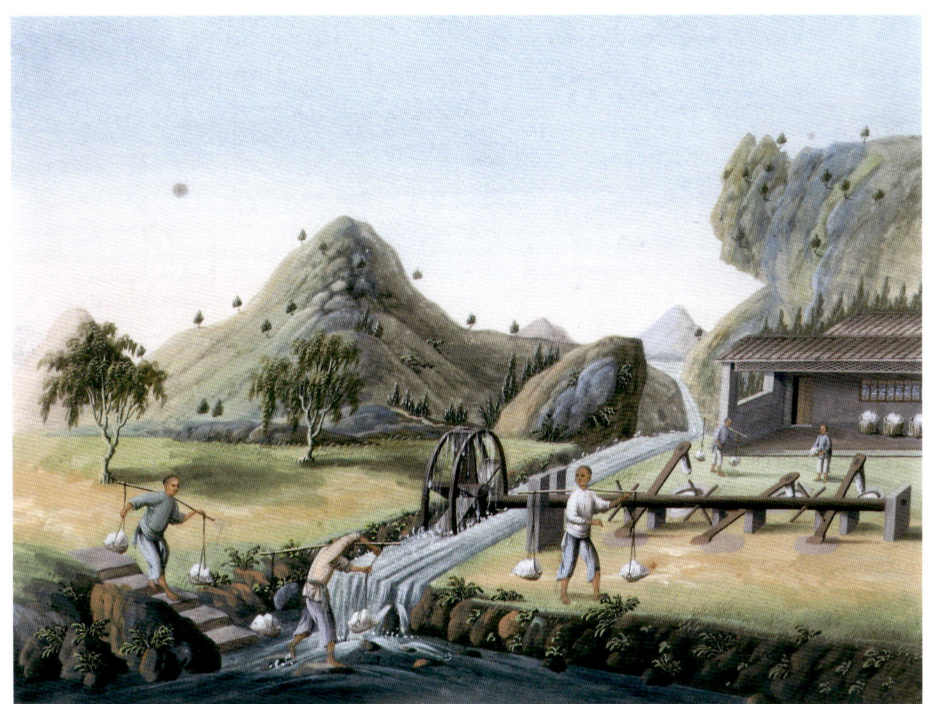

2. *Breaking up the clay*
Once mined, the clays were pulverized into a fine powder by water-powered trip hammers.

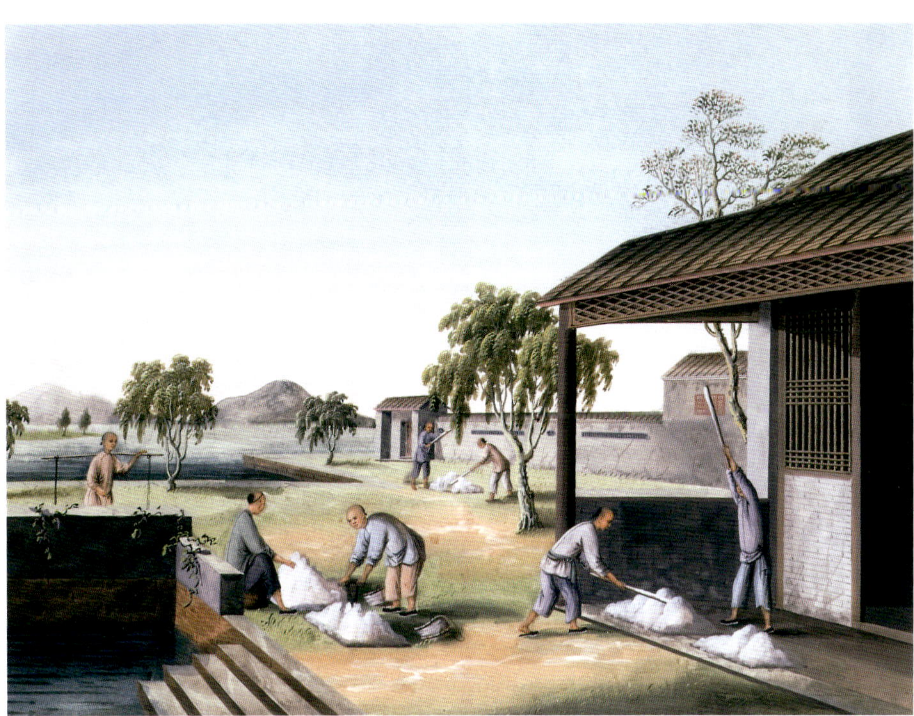

3. *Pounding the clay*
The pulverized materials were washed repeatedly to remove impurities. They were then mixed, beaten, and kneaded to drive out excess water and air.

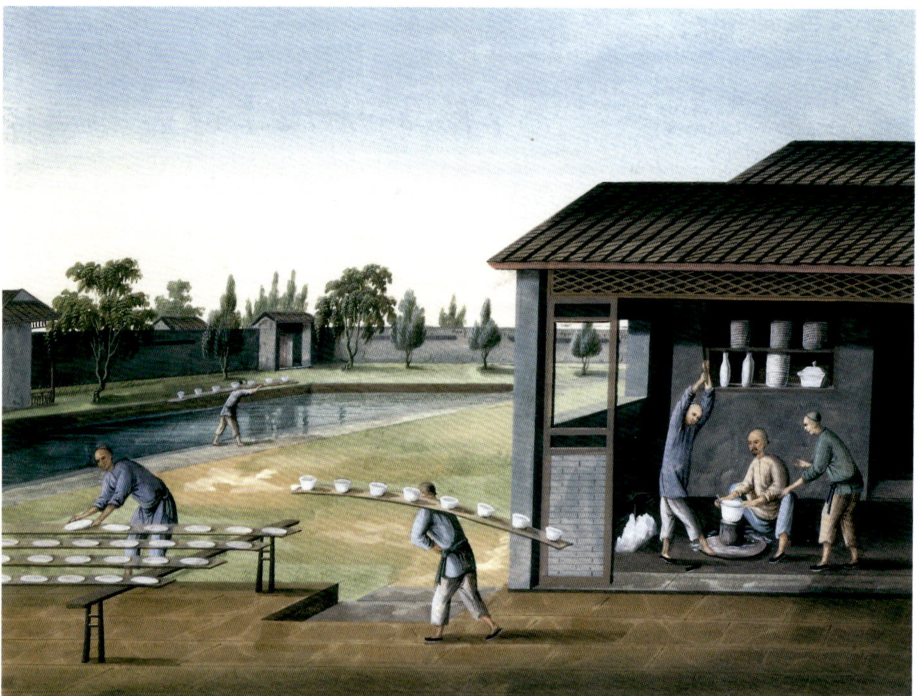

4. *Throwing a bowl*
Circular and symmetrical vessels were thrown on a kick wheel, here powered by a man who steadies himself by holding onto a rope while kicking the wheel with one foot. Vessels were then air-dried on long racks.

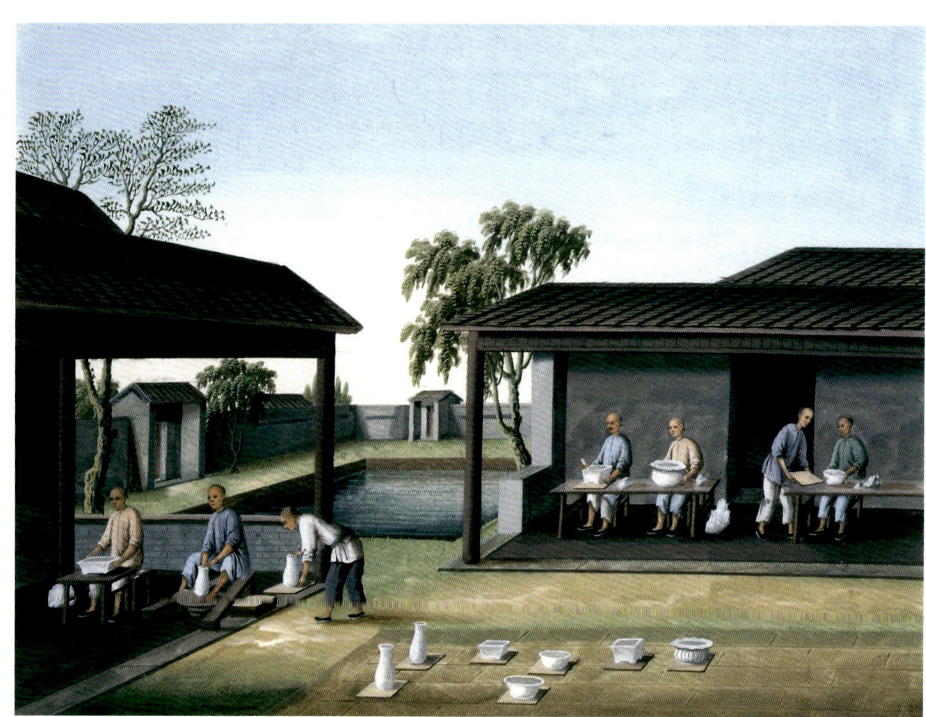

5. *Shaping and modeling vases and pots*
Asymmetrical shapes could not be thrown; they were either made in molds or formed and carved by hand, as is seen here.

6. *Finishing a foot on a bowl and glazing the porcelain*
Once thrown or molded, vessels were finished by polishing and tooling details such as foot rims, as seen on the left. They were then dipped into vats of glaze, as is seen on the right. Glaze is made of porcelain stone mixed with water and smaller amounts of limestone and the ashes of burned ferns.

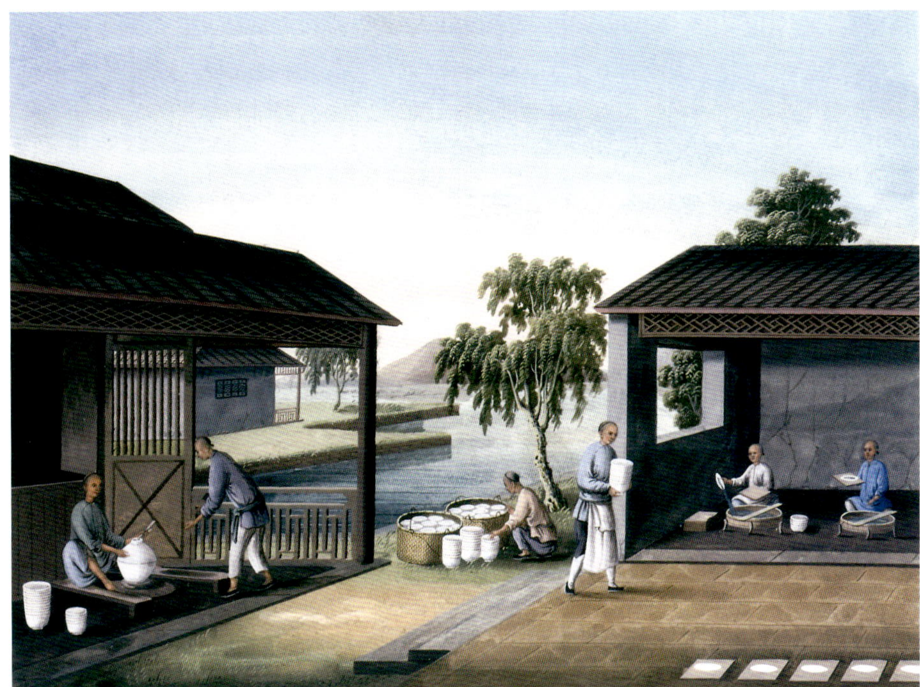

7. *Firing the porcelain in a kiln*
Glazed wares were packed into saggars (ceramic containers that protect the porcelain from the direct heat of the kiln) and placed into kilns, which were then closed and fired. Despite a potter's best attempts, pieces were often damaged during firing and had to be discarded.

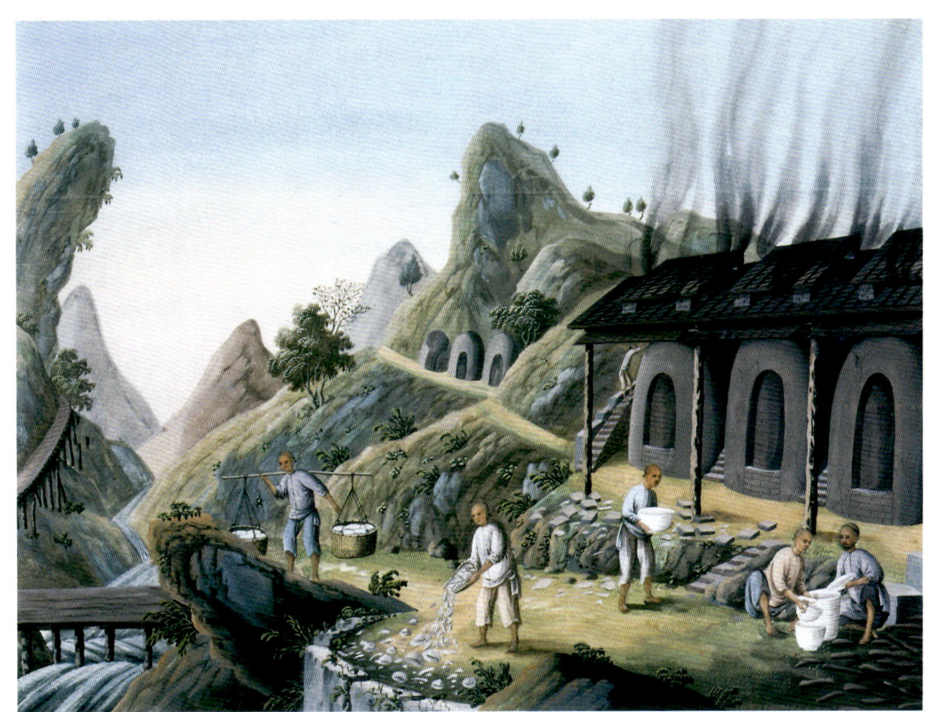

8. *Decorating the porcelain*
Almost all porcelain was embellished with underglaze blue or overglaze enamel colors. The decorating was done in assembly-line fashion. The four painters seen in the background each may be working on a different element of the same design.

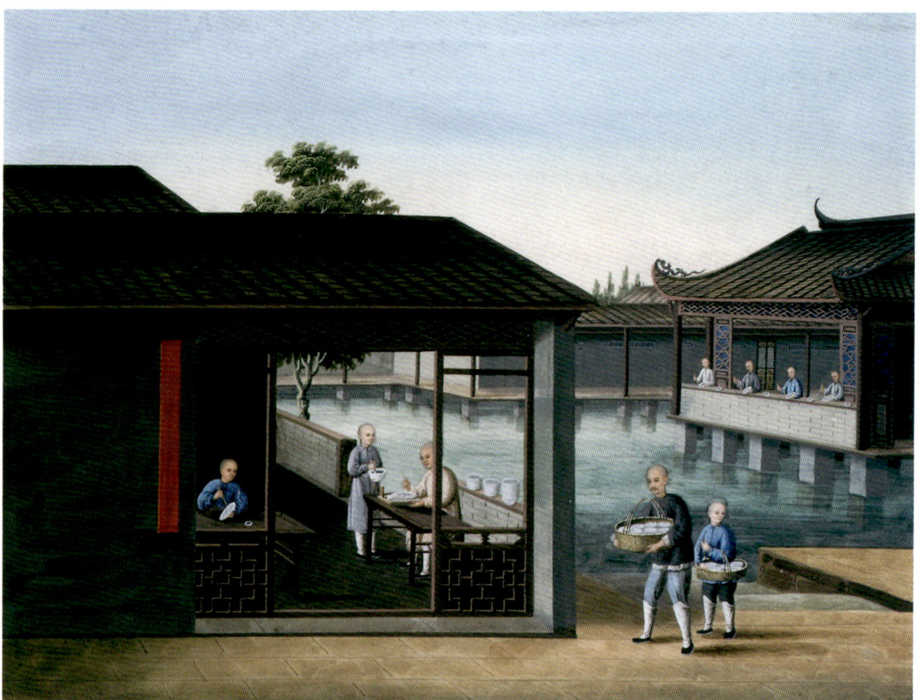

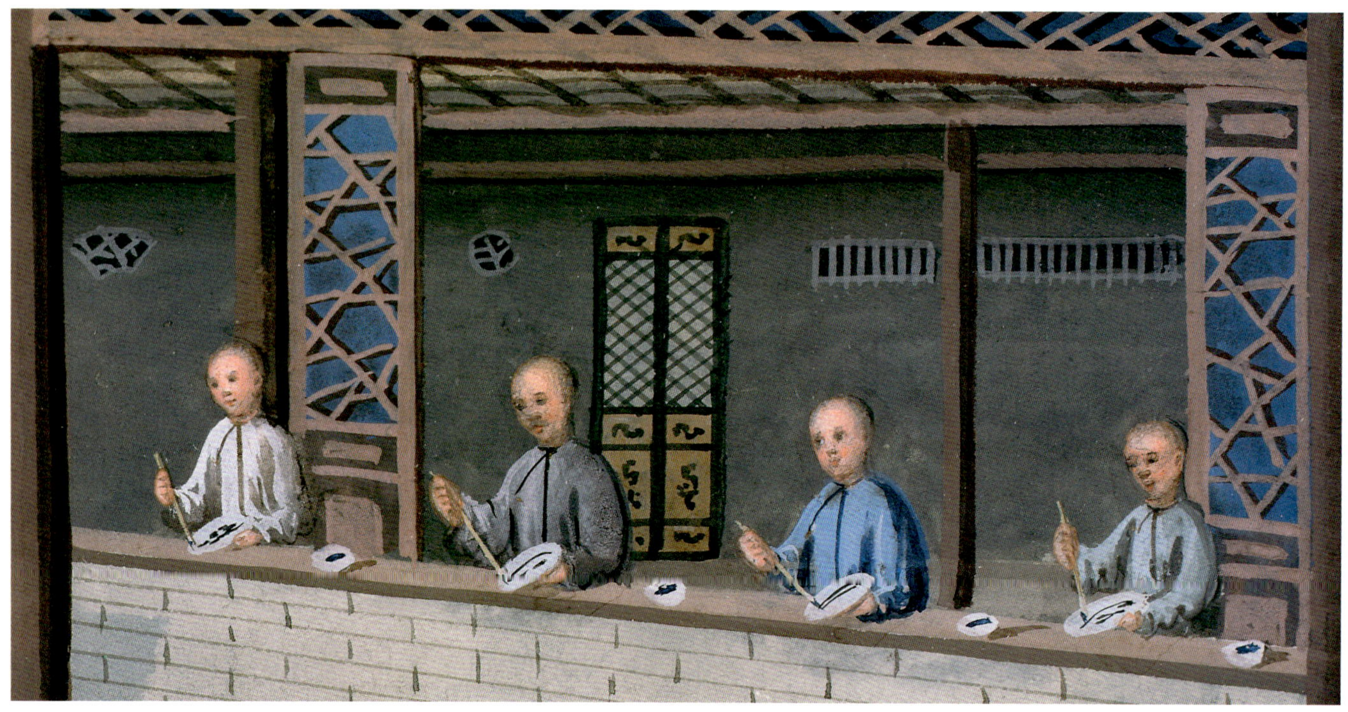

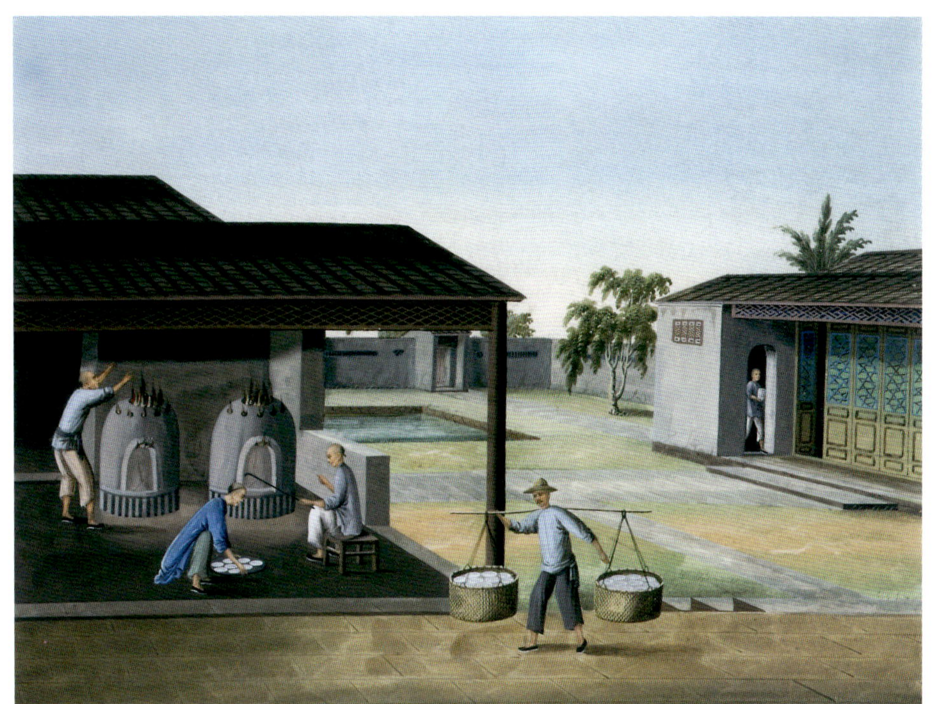

9. *Firing the decorated porcelain in a muffle kiln*
Once decorated, the porcelain was fired a second time at a lower temperature in a muffle kiln.

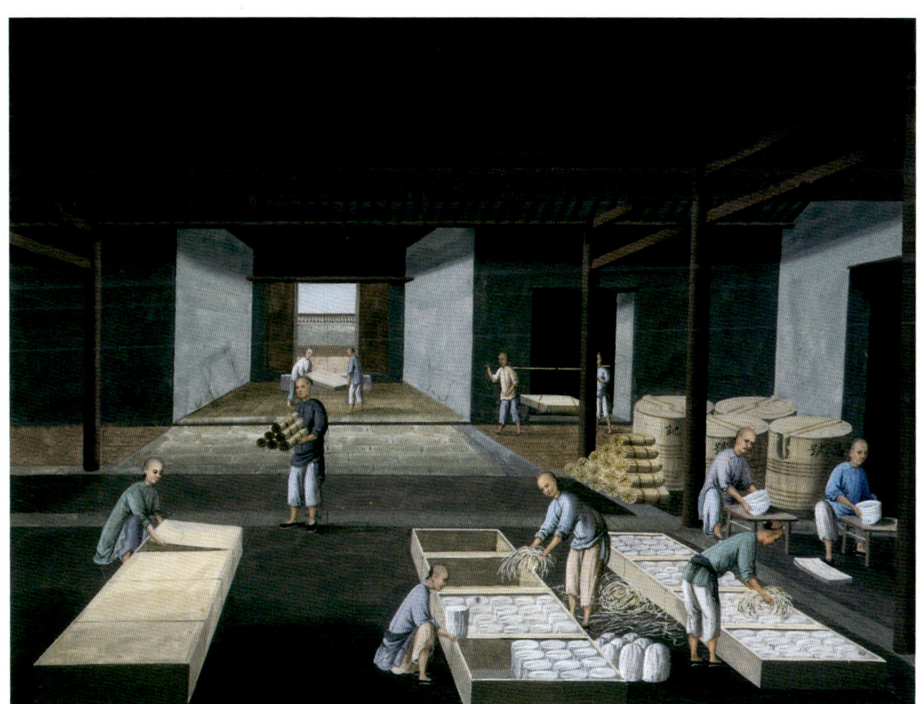

10. *Packing the porcelain*
Once completed, the porcelain was wrapped in straw and packed in tubs and boxes for shipment.

(for circular, symmetrical objects) or pressed into a mold (for oblong or asymmetrical objects); then the objects were glazed and fired.

Though porcelain was prized because of its white body, it was almost always decorated. The colors used were derived from minerals: cobalt for blue, iron for red, gold for pink, lead stannate for yellow, copper for green, manganese for purple, and lead arsenic for white.[6] Colors were applied at different stages of manufacture. Only cobalt was strong enough to withstand the high heat necessary to fire porcelain, so it was the only color painted on the body before it was glazed and fired in the kiln and is therefore known as underglaze decoration. Other, more delicate colors that could not survive the high temperature of the kilns were applied to an already glazed and fired object. Known as overglaze enamels, these were then fixed and hardened by firing the piece again, but at a lower temperature (about 800°C/1472°F), in a smaller kiln known as a muffle kiln.

The blue and white palette, developed in the 14th century probably for the Middle Eastern market, was the most popular type of decoration on export porcelain from the 16th through the 19th century (fig. 11). Overglaze enamels were introduced on export porcelain in the late 17th century and quickly captured the upper end of the market. The most popular color combinations were Imari (blue, red, and gold), popular from about 1675 to 1750 (fig. 12); *famille verte* (bright, translucent green, yellow, and purple), popular from the 1680s until the 1730s (fig. 13); and *famille rose* (soft, opaque pink, white, yellow, green, and blue), popular from about 1725 through the 1850s (fig. 14). Like potting, decorating was also an assembly-line process. According to d'Entrecolles, "The Labour of Painting is divided in the same Laboratory between a great number of Workmen: it is the business of one to make the coloured Circle, which is near the Edges of China-ware; another traces the Flowers, which are painted by a third; it belongs to one to make Rivers and Mountains, to another Birds and Animals."[7]

The vast majority of porcelain made for export was manufactured in the city of Jingdezhen in southcentral China (fig. 15). Blessed with rich sources of china clay and china stone, a large and skilled population, and proximity to waterways that linked the city to the rest of the country, Jingdezhen was the undisputed center of porcelain production for the entire world. In the early 18th century, the city's population was estimated at more than one million, and there were so many kilns that at night "one thinks that the whole city is on fire, or that it is one large furnace with many vent holes."[8]

In addition to Jingdezhen, export porcelain was also made in Dehua, in southern China. Known in the West as *blanc-de-chine,* that porcelain had a dense, highly translucent body and a soft, milky white glaze. Dehua potters specialized in producing highly modeled figures (fig. 16). This was due in part to the fact that the clays in that region were rich in china stone, which, although difficult to throw on a wheel, is easy to mold. Unlike the porcelain of Jingdezhen, *blanc-de-chine* was almost never decorated, so as not to obscure the brilliant white surface.[9]

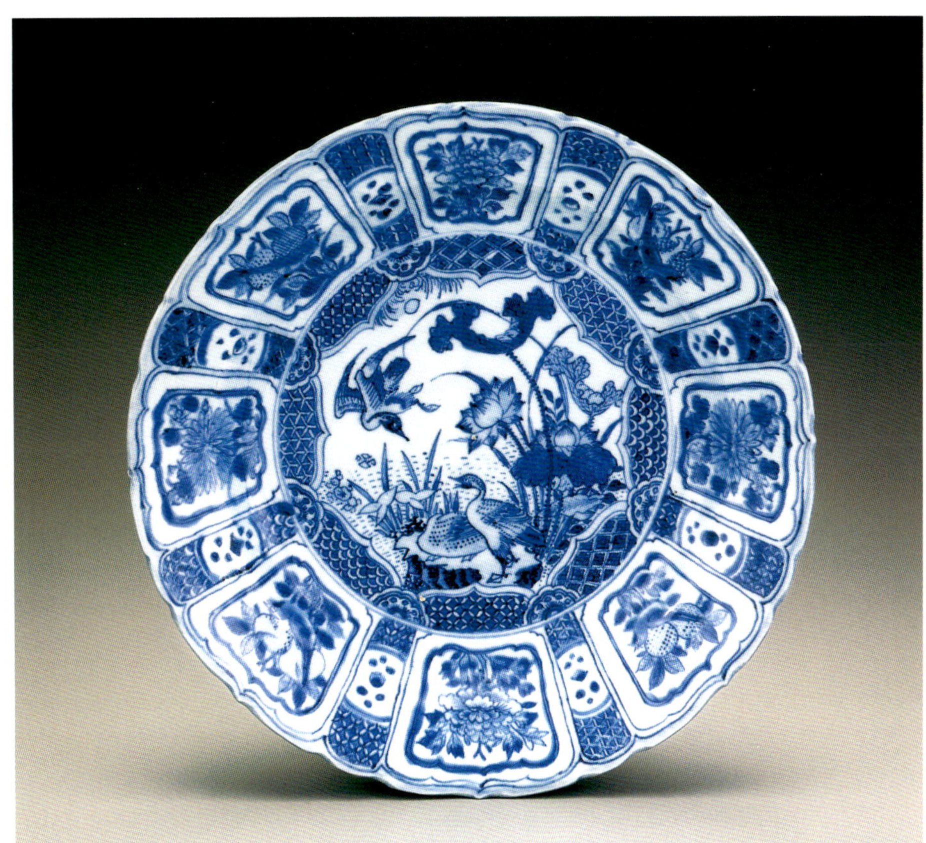

Fig. 11.
Dish with blue and white decoration
Jingdezhen, China; 1640–44
Diameter: 11.5 in. (292 mm)
2000.61.2

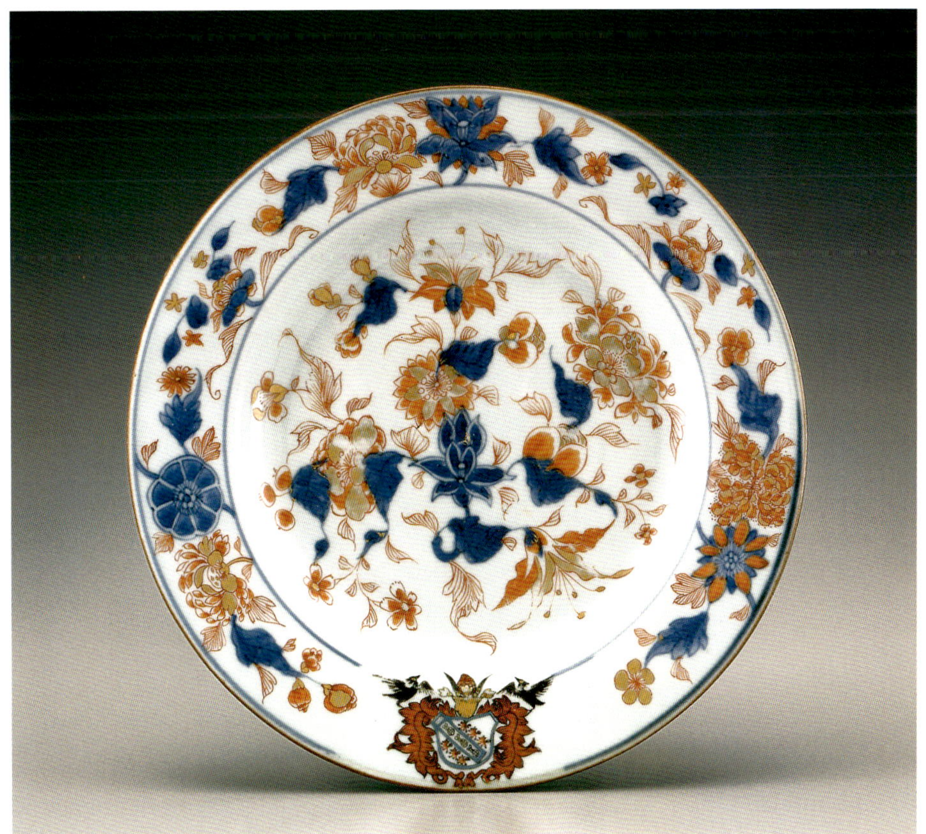

Fig. 12.
Plate with Imari decoration
Jingdezhen, China; about 1720
Diameter: 8.75 in. (222 mm)
L03.2775.103

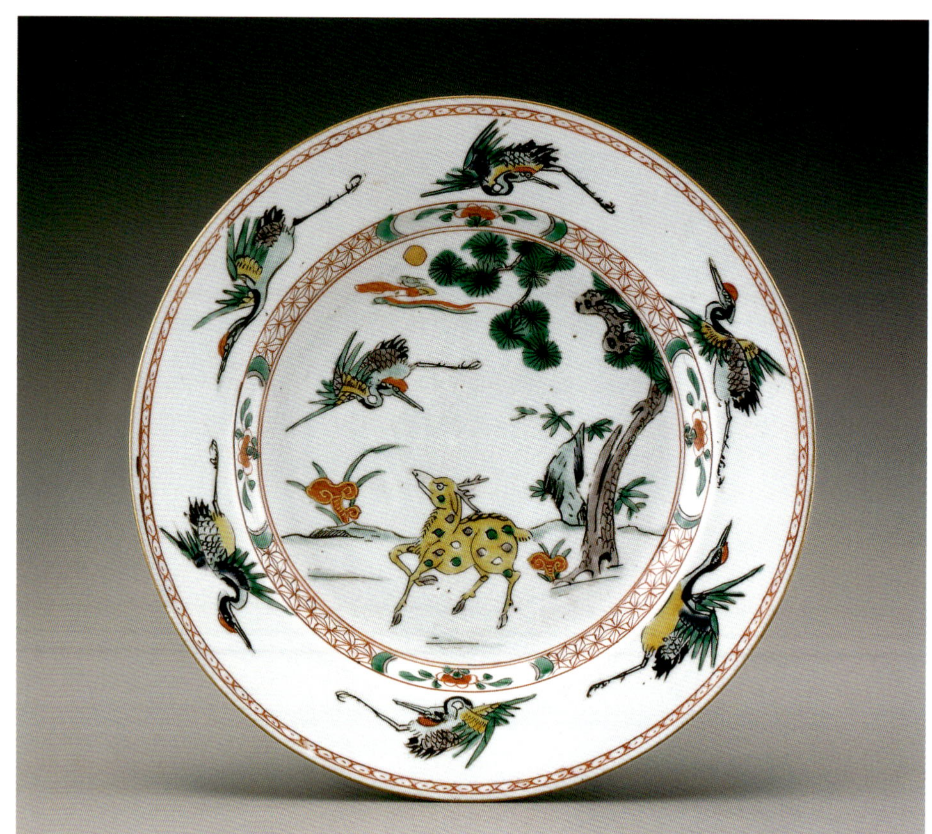

Fig. 13.
Plate with *famille verte* decoration
Jingdezhen, China; about 1715
Diameter: 8.625 in. (220 mm)
2000.61.7

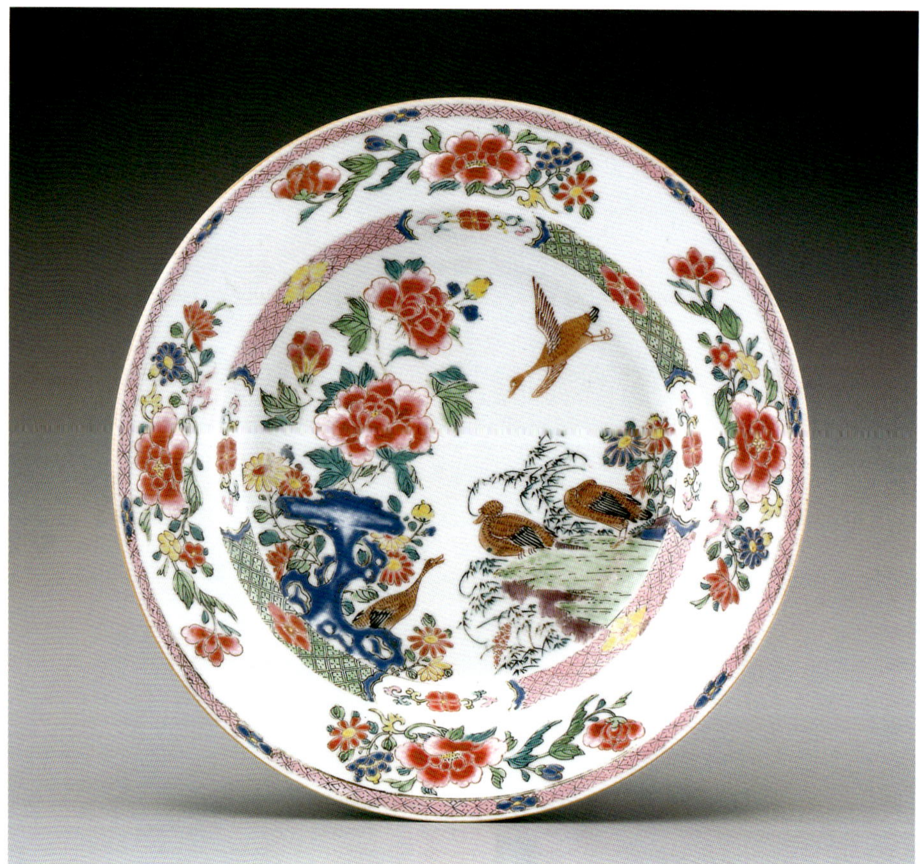

Fig. 14.
Plate with *famille rose* decoration
Jingdezhen, China; 1730–50
Diameter: 8.875 in. (225 mm)
2003.47.1

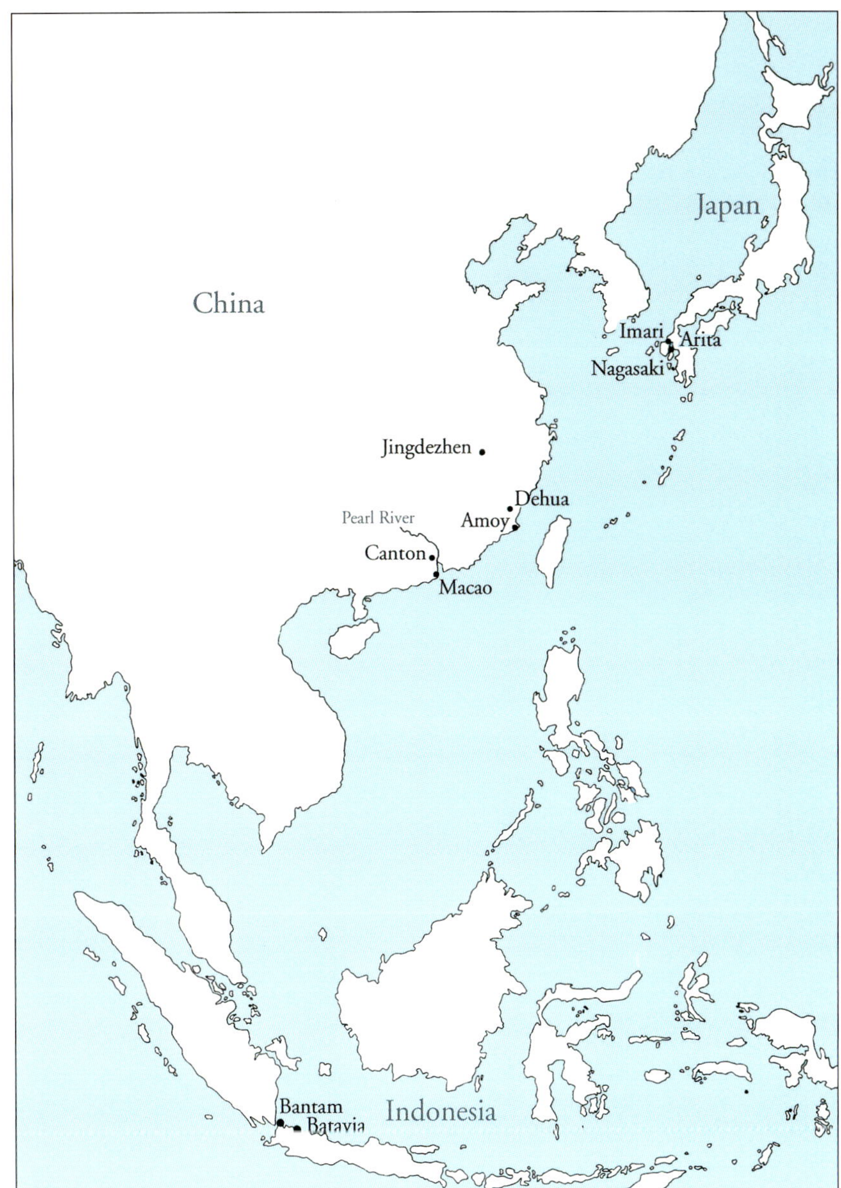

Fig. 15.
Map highlighting the Asian porcelain-producing cities as well as ports and trading centers.

Fig. 16.
Figure of Guanyin
Dehua, China; 1680–1720
Height: 10.25 in. (262 mm)
2000.61.89

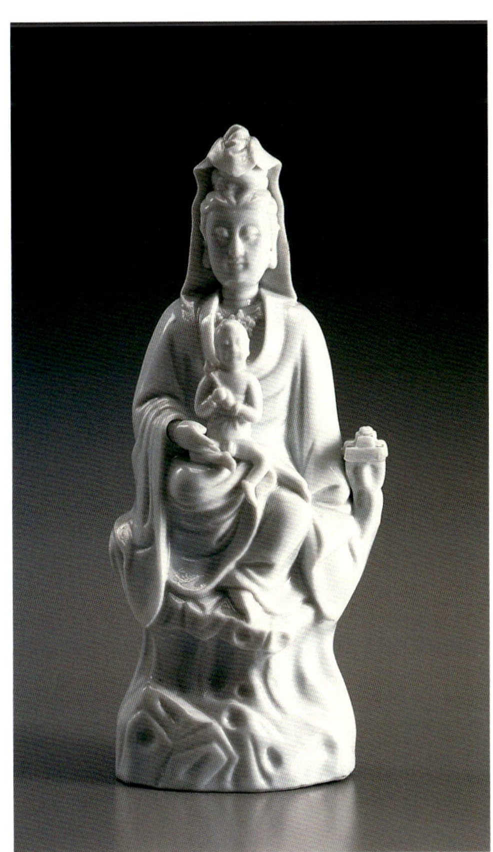

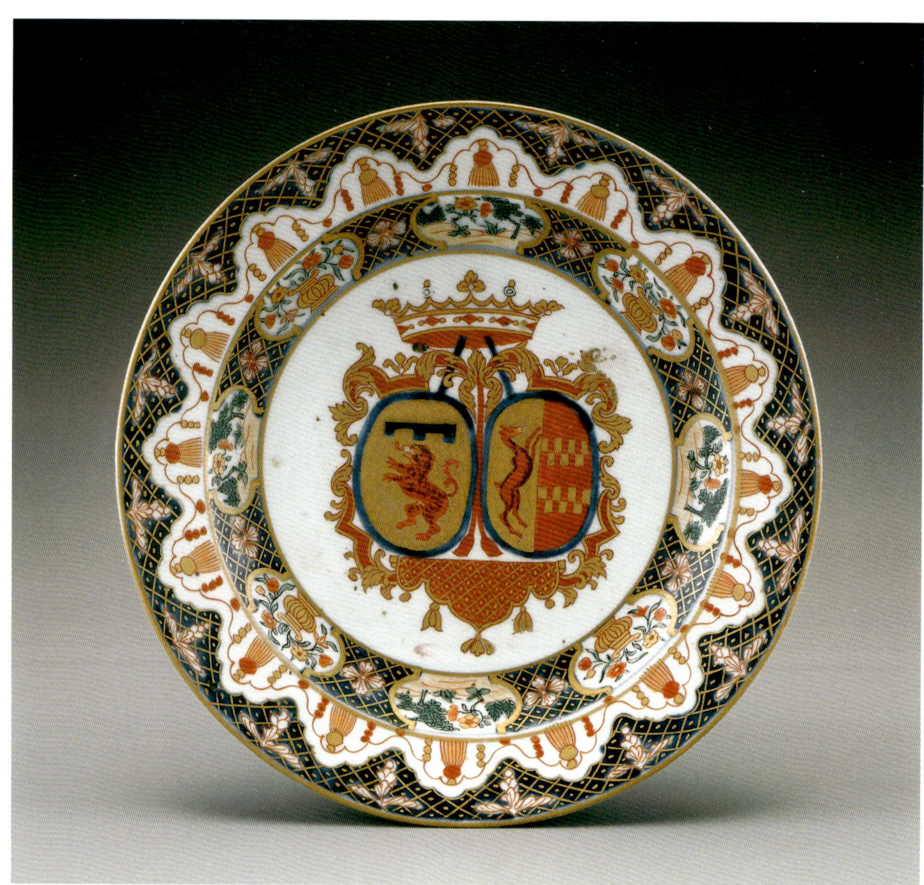

Fig. 17.
Plate
Arita, Japan; 1702–10
Diameter: 10 in. (254 mm)
L03.2775.99

Porcelain was also produced in Japan beginning in the early 17th century, primarily in the city of Arita, on Kyushu, the southernmost of the country's large islands. This porcelain was initially rather simple in form and decoration and was designed primarily for the domestic market. That situation changed, however, in the 1650s when the Dutch East India Company sought a new source of export porcelain after the supply from China ceased because of the civil war there. The Japanese porcelain industry grew to fill the need, imitating Chinese blue and white porcelain and introducing its own styles, such as Imari, which combined underglaze blue and overglaze red and gold (fig. 17) and was subsequently copied by the Chinese. Japanese porcelain was shipped to Europe from the 1650s until the 1740s, when cheaper Chinese products drove it out of the export market.[10]

THE CHINA TRADE

Export porcelain was prized in Europe and America not just because of its physical properties but also because it came from the exotic world of Asia. China, Japan, India, and Southeast Asia, collectively known in Europe as "The Indies," were the source of a wide range of luxury goods such as tea, spices, silks, and porcelain, which made life more comfortable and attractive. It was a desire for these goods and for the wealth that could be made by selling them that led first Europeans and later Americans to enter the China Trade.

The China Trade was a vast and complex network that linked Asia and the West. Chinese goods first reached the West during the Roman Empire, and the volume grew throughout the Middle Ages and the Renaissance. They were carried overland along the Silk Road through Central Asia and the Middle East or shipped via the Indian Ocean, the Red Sea, and the Mediterranean to the Italian ports of Genoa or Venice. Starting in the early 1400s, adventurous and avaricious Europeans looking for a way to cut Middle Eastern merchants out of the lucrative spice trade began to search for a direct sea route to the fabled Indies. Some sailed east like Portuguese explorer Vasco da Gama, who rounded the Cape of Good Hope in Africa in 1497 and reached India in 1498. Others sailed west like Spanish-sponsored Christopher Columbus, who inadvertently stumbled on the Americas in 1492.

The Portuguese were the first to trade directly with China, arriving in 1517 and establishing a permanent trading settlement in Macao in 1557. Although focused on the spice trade, they were the first to import porcelain directly into Europe, and by 1580 there were a half dozen shops in Lisbon selling "extremely fine porcelain of very varied shapes." The Portuguese were also the first Europeans to order porcelain with Western decoration, commissioning pieces displaying the Portuguese royal arms and emblems of Catholic monastic orders by the mid-16th century. Portugal's early dominance of the China Trade had begun to fade in the late 1500s, however, when it was annexed by Spain, which was already shipping Chinese goods to Europe via the Philippines and Mexico. Competition also came from the Netherlands, whose merchants began to trade directly with China after the Portuguese ports were closed to Dutch traders in 1595.[11]

In 1602 the Dutch founded the Verenigde Oost Indische Compagnie (V.O.C.), or Dutch East India Company, which dominated the China Trade during that century. The Dutch government granted the V.O.C. a monopoly on trade with the East as well as the authority to establish colonies, raise armies, and attack the trading vessels of competitors. Operating out of Batavia (modern-day Jakarta, Indonesia), the trading base set up by the company, the Dutch soon wrested control of the China Trade from Portugal and Spain. They even came to dominate the inter-Asian trade among China, Japan, Southeast Asia, and the Middle East that had previously been controlled by Asian, Indian, and Middle Eastern merchants. The Dutch, like almost all Westerners who came east, did not make a favorable impression on the Chinese. According to one 18th-century Chinese source, "The people which we call Red-hair or Red barbarians are the Dutchmen. . . . They are covetous and cunning and have good knowledge of valuable commodities and are clever in seeking profits. They spare not even their lives in looking for gain."[12]

Encouraged by the highly profitable sale of porcelain from captured Portuguese ships in 1602 and 1604, the Dutch were the first to import large quantities of export porcelain into Europe—an estimated three million pieces between 1604 and 1657. They were also the first to commission practical European forms, asking the Chinese as early as 1608 for Western-style saltcellars, butter dishes, and mustard pots "if they can make them."[13]

Although the Dutch dominated the China Trade during the 17th century, they were not without competition. The English had founded their first East India Company in 1600, two years before the V.O.C., and their presence grew slowly through the 1600s. In 1708 the two leading British East India companies merged to form the Honorable East India Company, which became probably the largest corporation the world has ever known, not only dominating the China Trade but also controlling most of the subcontinent of India and boasting an army and navy that rivaled those of many European nations. In 1715 the English founded the first permanent European trading post, or factory, in the Chinese port of Canton (modern-day Guangzhou), and it is from there that increasing amounts of porcelain were exported over the course of the 18th century. Between 1720 and 1770 the British are estimated to have imported thirty to thirty-five million pieces to Britain, her colonies, and continental Europe.[14]

The Dutch and British were not the only Europeans to found East India companies. The Compagnies des Indes, a French concern, was in operation between 1664 and 1769. The Swedish East India Company existed from 1731 to 1806, led primarily by Scottish expatriates. Less successful were the Generale Keijserlyche Indische Compagnie (General Imperial India Company, also known as the Ostend Company), which was chartered by the Emperor of Austria and traded from 1722 until 1734, and the Königliche Preussische Asiatische Companie zu Emden (Prussian East India Company), established by Frederick the Great of Prussia and in existence from 1751 to 1757.[15]

America was a latecomer, not trading directly with China until after establishing its independence from Great Britain. Prior to that, the colonies were part of the British mercantile system, which was designed to filter all trade through the mother country. Americans were so eager to join the lucrative China Trade that the ship *Empress of China* left New York bound for Canton in February 1784, less than a year after the ratification of the Treaty of Paris had ended the American Revolution.

The Americans received a relatively warm welcome in China; according to Samuel Shaw, the supercargo on the *Empress of China,* "Ours being the first American ship that had ever visited China, it was some time before the Chinese could fully comprehend the distinction between Englishmen and us. They styled us the New People, and when, by the map, we conveyed to them an idea of the extent of our country, with its present and increasing population, they were not a little pleased at the prospect of so considerable a market for the productions of their own empire."[16] Known to the Chinese as the flowery-flag devils (after the field of stars on the American flag), American merchants sailed out of port cities including Salem, New York, and Philadelphia. Their trade with China peaked in the early years of the 1800s but declined after 1830.

Although situations varied during the three centuries of the China Trade, in general the average voyage of a European or American China Trade vessel proceeded as follows. Ships sailed from their home ports—Lisbon, Amsterdam, London, or New York—down the west coast of Africa, sometimes stopping at the Azores or Cape Verde Islands for fresh water, food, or repairs. They then rounded the Cape of Good Hope and proceeded across the Indian Ocean. Ships sometimes called at European trading posts in India or Southeast Asia before continuing up to the southern coast of China. The voyage could last up to six months.

Prior to 1729, ships might proceed to one of several ports: Macao, Amoy (modern-day Xiamen), or Canton. After 1729 the Chinese attempted to control Western contact with China by restricting traders to Canton. Vessels sailed first to Macao, the Portuguese settlement at the mouth of the Pearl River, where the merchants would negotiate with customs officials and hire a Chinese pilot to guide the ship upriver through the Boca Tigris (or Tiger's Mouth, where the Pearl River narrows) and on to the anchorage at Whampoa, which was the farthest upriver that ocean-going ships could reach. The officers and crew remained in Whampoa while the supercargoes, merchants, and cargo were transferred to Chinese junks that ferried them the final twelve miles of shallow water to Canton (figs. 18–21).

In Canton, trading offices known as hongs or factories served as home, workplace, and warehouse for European and American traders. Built in a Western style and leased from Chinese merchants, these long, narrow buildings were located on a quarter-mile strip of land along the waterfront outside the city walls. Hongs were identified by their occupants' national flags, which were flown from poles in front of the structures. Behind the hongs were narrow streets that were, in the words of one late 18th-century visitor, "filled with storehouses for the reception of European goods until they are disposed of to the natives, or Chinese goods for exportation until shipped. The front of almost every house is a shop; and the shops of one or more streets are laid out chiefly to supply the want of strangers [foreign merchants]."[17]

Few Westerners (all of whom were male, as Western women were not allowed in Canton) were permitted any farther into China than this small strip of land. Shaw, one of the first Americans to reach Canton, noted with some disappointment that "Europeans, after a dozen years' residence, have not seen more than what the first month presented to view." During this period the

Figs. 18–21.
Set of paintings showing Macao, Boca Tigris, Whampoa, and Canton
China; about 1805
Oil on canvas
1959.1871.1–.4 Gift of Henry Francis du Pont.

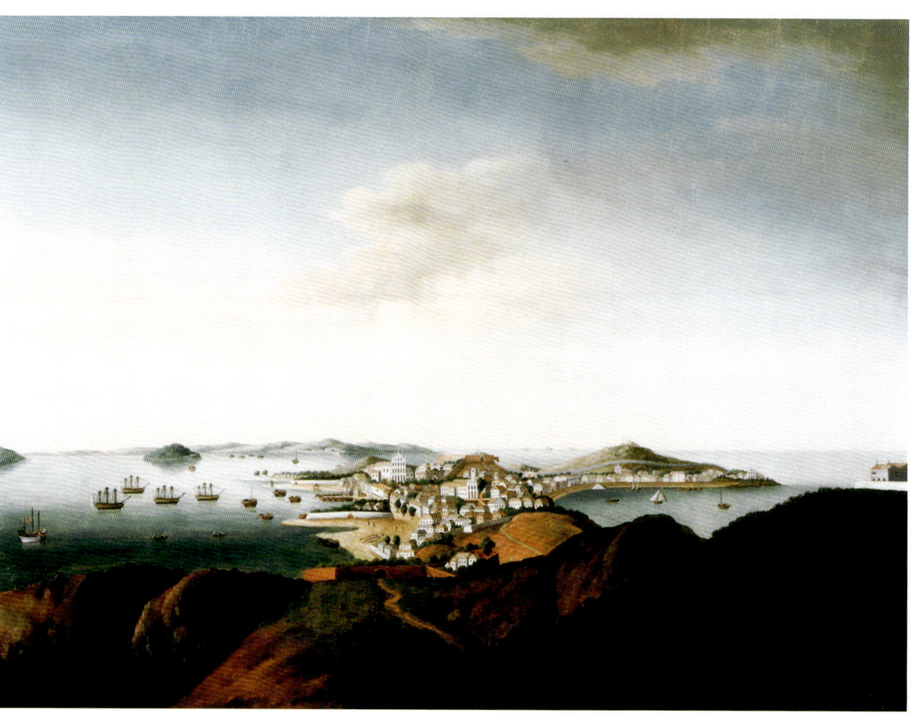

18. Macao

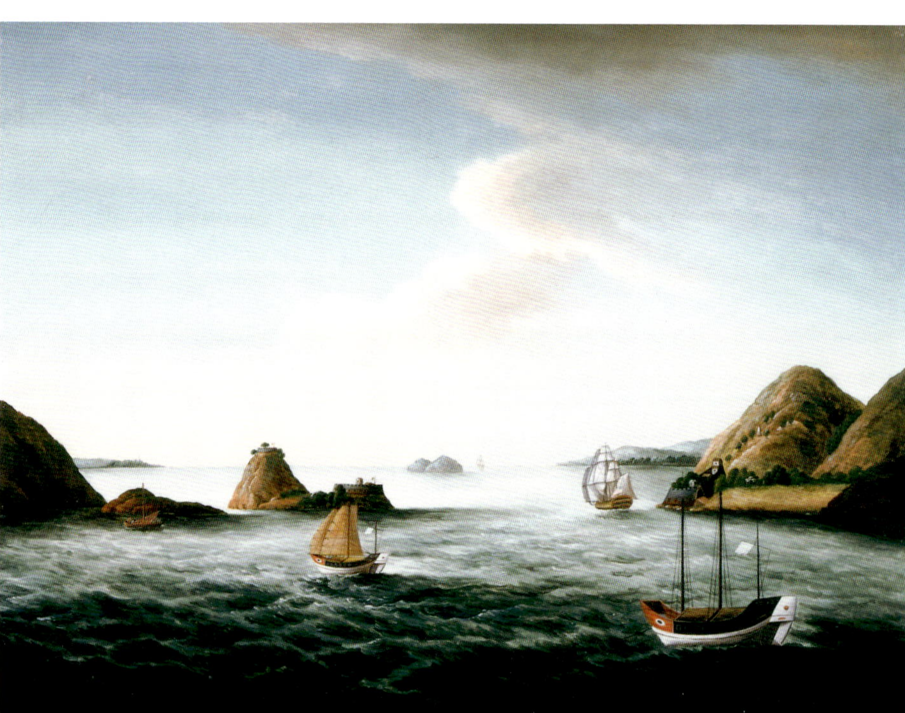

19. Boca Tigris

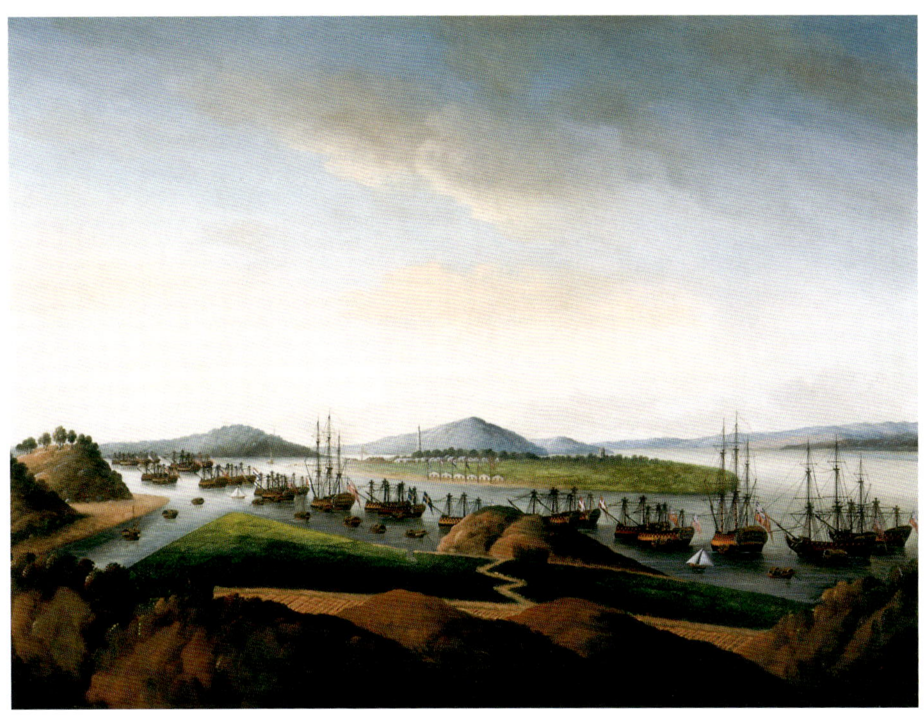

20. Whampoa

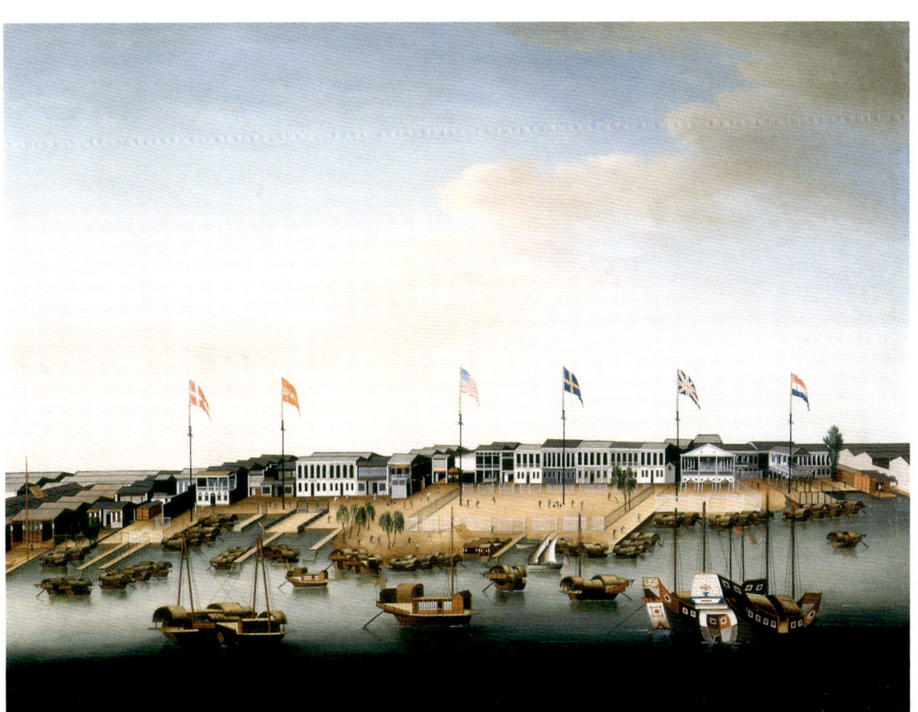

21. Canton

Chinese government generally practiced a policy of isolation. It did allow trade with European and American merchants but restricted their contact with the general population in order to minimize the impact on Chinese culture.[18]

In Canton, trade was conducted between supercargoes and hong merchants, who purchased the right from the Chinese government to trade with Westerners. Hong merchants were also responsible for the Westerners' good behavior while in Canton. Life for the supercargoes was far from pleasant; according to Shaw, "Considering the length of time they reside in this country, the restrictions to which they must submit, the great distance they are at from their connections, the want of society, and of almost every amusement, it must be allowed that they dearly earn their money." Supercargoes stayed in Canton from three to six months, unloading and selling their incoming cargo and purchasing and loading their outgoing supplies of tea, silk, porcelain, and other goods. Tea was by far the most important commodity, accounting for up to 70 percent of the total value of a ship's load. Porcelain was a relatively minor concern, making up only 5 to 10 percent of an average cargo.[19]

Porcelain could be purchased from general merchants or from specialist porcelain dealers, either from stock or specially commissioned. Most were bulk orders that were then sold wholesale to European and American merchants. The amounts could be enormous; the Dutch East Indiaman *Geldermalsen* was carrying approximately 239,000 pieces of porcelain when she sank en route from China to the Netherlands in 1752. The size of this cargo was typical. In fact, the Dutch East India Company bought almost 500,000 pieces in that year alone.[20]

These bulk orders for porcelain were drawn up by East India Company officials at home and were often quite specific, noting in detail the form, decoration, and number of pieces that were to be purchased. Rarely could these orders be filled exactly, as the range of forms, the supply, and the price of porcelain available in Canton varied from year to year. Supercargoes were therefore given a degree of latitude; the 1712 instructions for the supercargo on the British East Indiaman *Loyal Bliss* realistically advised that "if you can't get all the sorts of China ware or the full quantities of each sort above mentioned, get as many of them as you can. If you can't get the sorts exactly according to the Patterns get them as near as you can."[21]

Generally, porcelain purchased by the East India companies for resale consisted of practical and relatively simple blue and white wares for drinking and dining. The majority of items on the *Geldermalsen* were plates (14,315); tea cups and saucers (63,623); and bowls (25,921). The variety of designs was also limited; in 1774 the British East India Company requested only two designs for an order of more than 100,000 pieces of enameled porcelain and only four designs for a far larger order of blue and white porcelain. Some of this could be purchased from stock, but new forms and styles of decoration had to be specially ordered. These requests took longer to fill, as they were forwarded more than 500 miles to Jingdezhen, where they were executed and then returned to Canton. The process took time, so orders were normally placed one year and delivered the next. According to American China Trade merchant John Latimer, "To have china ware according to pattern as it respects shape it is necessary it should be engaged 12 months before wanted."[22]

Pieces that were more elaborate were generally acquired through what was known as the Private Trade, which was conducted by supercargoes and sea captains. The large East India companies had no desire to bother with the small, complex orders for extremely specialized shapes and personalized decoration. They therefore allowed their officials to handle these relatively lucrative deals as one of the perks of employment. An individual in Britain, continental Europe, or America could give a pattern and instructions to a supercargo or sea captain to take to China. The order was then entrusted to a Chinese merchant who translated the instructions into Chinese and forwarded the information to the potters or decorating studios where the order was to be executed.[23]

By the mid-18th century, enameling workshops had been established in Canton so that special orders could be filled more quickly. Coats of arms, initials, portraits of ships, and other personal or topical images were painted onto ready-made porcelain blanks by decorators working for merchants like Yam Shinqua, "China Ware Merchant at Canton," who advertised "All sorts of Chinaware, Arms etc., Painted on the most reasonable Terms." According to one American China Trade merchant, decorating took several weeks: "If this article (porcelain) is to be ship'd orders ought to be given the first thing . . . as the Patterns are all painted after order & requre three to four weeks to compleat."[24]

One of the biggest issues that faced Western traders was what "currency" to use to purchase the porcelain and other Chinese goods they so desired. Europe and America had little to offer that the Chinese wanted. Emperor Gaozong (r. 1127–63) voiced an opinion long held when he proclaimed, "China's territory produces all goods in abundance, so why should we buy useless trifles from abroad?"[25] Westerners marketed lead, wool cloth, fur, mirror glass, clocks, ginseng (a medicinal root), and other items with some success, but for most of the period they bartered with silver that came from mines in colonial South America. Starting in the late 18th century, European and American traders also began to smuggle opium into China, reversing the balance of trade and leading to enormous social problems in the country.

The Chinese produced porcelain for a variety of markets. First and foremost, they made porcelain for themselves, with the finest pieces reserved for the Imperial household. They also created porcelain for a wide range of export markets, including Japan, Southeast Asia, India, the Middle East, Europe, and America. Chinese potters easily adapted their wares to produce forms and types of decoration that appealed to the needs and tastes of different customers. Western traders found that merchants and potters were happy to make porcelain that was tailored to their wishes. From the early 17th century onward, European traders sent drawings, turned wooden models, and even Western metal, glass, and ceramic objects to be copied. They also specified what kinds of designs were to appear on the porcelain. Chinese floral and figural designs were always popular, but by the turn of the 18th century, Western designs were being copied from numerous sources, including drawings, prints, cartoons, book illustrations, armorial bookplates, trade cards, newspapers, and even coins. The Chinese had little difficulty in executing such requests, and although mistakes did appear, such as incorrect armorials, those were exceedingly rare.[26]

CHINESE EXPORT PORCELAIN IN EUROPE AND AMERICA: AN OVERVIEW

When the first rare pieces of Chinese porcelain arrived in Europe during the Middle Ages and Renaissance, they were treated as near-miraculous objects. Often given precious silver, gold, and even jeweled mounts, they were, in the words of one 16th-century Portuguese friar, "esteemed by the greatest princes for their delight and curiosity." Over the next few centuries, the flow of porcelain increased from a trickle to an eventual flood. By the end of the 16th century, Chinese export porcelain dishes were a necessity for the royalty and nobility of Europe. "The most expensive and rare salads, fruits, and preserves count for nothing," wrote a French observer, "if they are not served in porcelain."[27]

During the 17th century, as the Dutch began importation on a large scale, porcelain became more common; by 1640 English diarist Peter Mundy noted that even in rural Cornwall, "any house of indifferent quality was well supplied with Chinese porcelain." The statement is an exaggeration, but Mundy was observing the movement of porcelain down the social ladder, from royalty to the aristocracy and eventually to the gentry. Export porcelain became the "currency of social emulation," as aspiring individuals sought to improve their place in life by copying the lifestyles of those above them.[28]

Philadelphia printer Benjamin Franklin provides a rare glimpse of this phenomenon in his account of how

> being call'd one Morning to Breakfast, I found it in a China bowl with a Spoon of Silver. They had been bought for me without my Knowledge by my Wife, and had cost her the enormous Sum of three and twenty Shillings, for which she had no other Excuse or Apology to make, but that she thought *her* Husband deserv'd a Silver Spoon and China Bowl as well as any of his Neighbours. This was the first Appearance of Plate and China in our House, which afterwards in a Course of Years as our Wealth encreas'd augmented gradually to several Hundred Pounds in Value.

New developments, such as the introduction of practical shapes in the early 17th century and the widespread introduction of Western designs later in the century kept demand for export porcelain high. Around the turn of the 18th century, coats of arms and other personal devices on porcelain became popular among the aristocracy, who used them to display familial pride and to set their dishes apart from simple blue and white and enameled wares. It has been estimated that over the course of the 18th century some 8,000 armorial porcelain services were ordered for European, British, and American families, with more than 6,000 of those being for the British.[29]

By this time, porcelain had come to symbolize luxury, refinement, and good taste. It could be found throughout continental Europe, Britain, and even in colonial outposts in North America. The young Virginia planter George Washington assured his place as a member of the gentry class by purchasing in 1758 a "Compleat sett fine Image china [a tea set decorated with Chinese figures]" for entertaining in his new home, Mount Vernon. So popular was Chinese decoration that Europeans imitated it, developing a style called chinoiserie. Designers looked to Chinese porcelains, silks, lacquer, and other objects as well as their own fertile imagination to create exotic and often fanciful designs of fantastic landscapes, Chinese figures, pagodas, and dragons.[30]

By the mid-18th century, Chinese export porcelain was facing competition from new types of European ceramics. When first introduced, export porcelain was seen as vastly superior to earthenwares and stonewares, and European potters strove to replicate porcelain's fine white, translucent body or at least to create a tolerable imitation. The tin-glazed earthenware (delftware) industries of the Netherlands and Great Britain responded in the early 17th century by producing blue and white dishes decorated with chinoiserie scenes. But ambitious potters, supported by noblemen who wanted the prestige and income that a successful rival to Chinese porcelain would bring, continued to search for the secret to making true porcelain. It was in 1708 that Johann Friedrich Böttger, an alchemist working for Augustus the Strong of Saxony, succeeded in creating the first European pieces of true porcelain, in Meissen, Germany.

During the 18th century, the secret to making true porcelain spread throughout Europe, and porcelain made in Germany, France, and England captured the attention of the upper classes in Europe as well as in America. Chinese export porcelain also faced competition from new and improved stonewares and earthenwares made by English potters such as Josiah Wedgwood, and by the second half of the 18th century, European ceramics had replaced Chinese porcelain as the most fashionable type of tableware. It was now the Chinese who were copying Meissen figures and creamware tureens. Wedgwood was so confident of the superiority of his own earthenwares that he boasted, "Don't you think we shall soon have some Chinese Missionaries come here to learn the art of making creamcolour?"[31]

Although private orders for export porcelain continued—placed mostly by Europeans and Americans who were involved in the China Trade—by the end of the 18th century, bulk importation had ceased everywhere but the United States. What had been prized more highly than silver and gold for some three centuries was now beginning to fade from fashion. But in doing so, it was taking on a new life—for the commodity once revered solely for its unique and rare qualities was being sought for its historical associations as well. And it remains so today. Chinese export porcelain continues to be highly collectible, providing an unending source of both education and delight.

A Dinner Dreſt May 15th.

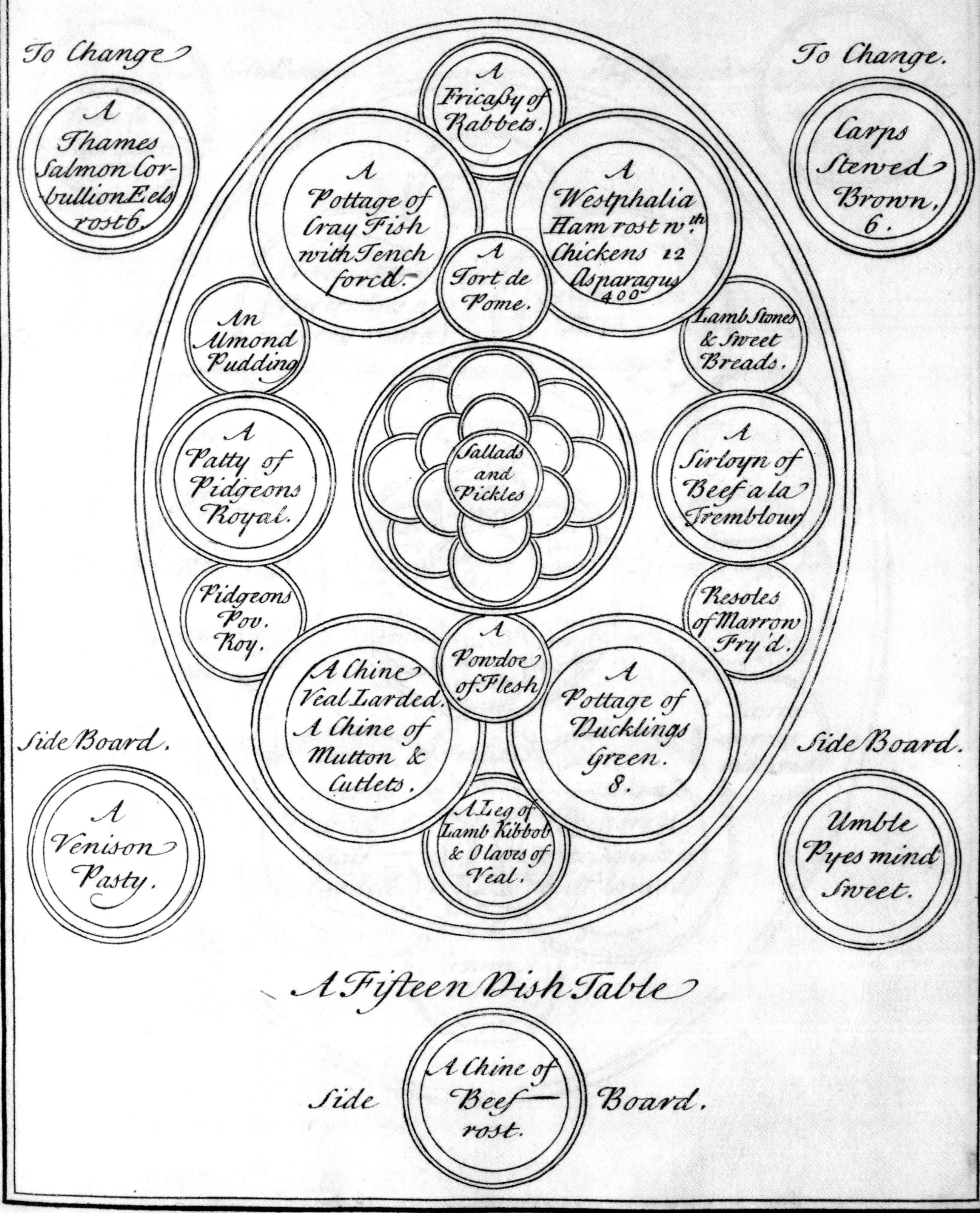

Dining Wares

Between 1500 and 1850, dining habits changed dramatically, and Chinese export porcelain played a role in those changes. Medieval-style dining, which emphasized lavish displays of highly spiced and decorated foods, was gradually replaced with a new style that emphasized simpler, more subtly flavored foods. A greater variety of meats, vegetables, and fresh fruit was served, and new types of cuisine such as soups, salads, and sauces were developed. This change was first seen in Italy during the 16th century and then spread to the rest of Europe.[32]

Along with a change in cuisine came a change in how food was served. During medieval times, people dined communally, sharing trenchers (usually of bread), cups, and even spoons. Food was presented on unadorned platters and dishes, with the standing salt being the only real decorative piece of tableware. New ideas of refinement arose during the Renaissance, however, and meant that diners now needed their own plates, cutlery, and drinking vessels. Also, new foods called for specialized containers; hence, elaborate forms such as tureens, sauceboats, and cruets were created.[33]

One of the most dramatic changes in dining habits was the development of the dinner service, consisting of a matched set of plates and serving dishes. Those made of ceramic appeared in early 16th-century Italy, but until the late 17th century the elite still used silver, and the rest of the population ate off pewter or wooden dishes. At first, Chinese export porcelain seems to have been reserved for the "banquet," or dessert, course of a meal; in 1681 cookbook author Hannah Woolley advised that sweetmeat plates "should be either of Silver or China."[34]

Around the turn of the 18th century, porcelain began to replace silver on the dinner table proper, and by 1750 fashion dictated that tables be decorated with a "choice collection of porcelane" and "only a few pieces of plate." These services ranged in size from modest, with a dozen plates and a few serving dishes, to enormous collections of more than 500 pieces. But a typical example can be found in the seven blue and white octagonal "table sets" purchased by the British East India Company in 1755, which included 60 plates, 24 soup plates, 13 serving dishes, 8 salad dishes, 1 saucer dish, 2 tureens and stands, 2 sauceboats, and 4 salts.[35]

A table setting illustrates the large number of dishes needed for a proper 18th-century meal. Plate 30 from Charles Carter, *The Complete Practical Cook* (London: Printed for W. Meadows, C. Rivington, and R. Hett, 1730). Printed Book and Periodical Collection, Winterthur Library.

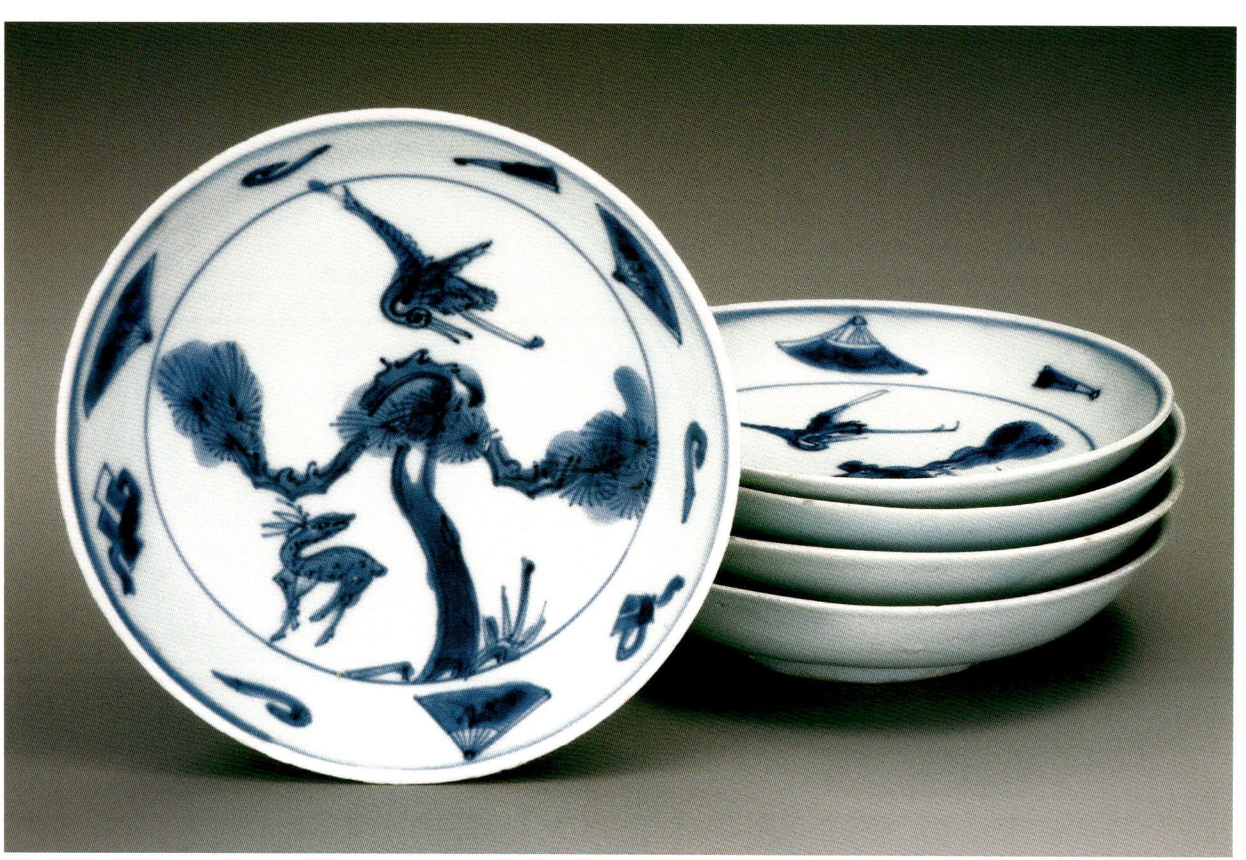

1 SET OF FIVE DISHES

Jingdezhen, China; 1620–40
Diameter: 6 in. (152 mm)
2000.61.109.1–.5

These five small dishes were made for export to Japan, where they were used in formal tea ceremonies.[36] Such sets were designed specifically for the Japanese market; the odd number of pieces and the asymmetrical nature of the decoration would have appealed to those consumers but would have been totally foreign to their Chinese makers.

Known as *ko-sometsuke,* or old blue and white, Chinese porcelain was prized at the very highest levels of Japanese society. Japan was one of the earliest places to which Chinese porcelain was exported, arriving as early as the 9th century. By the 12th century, the Chinese were designing porcelain specifically for that market.[37]

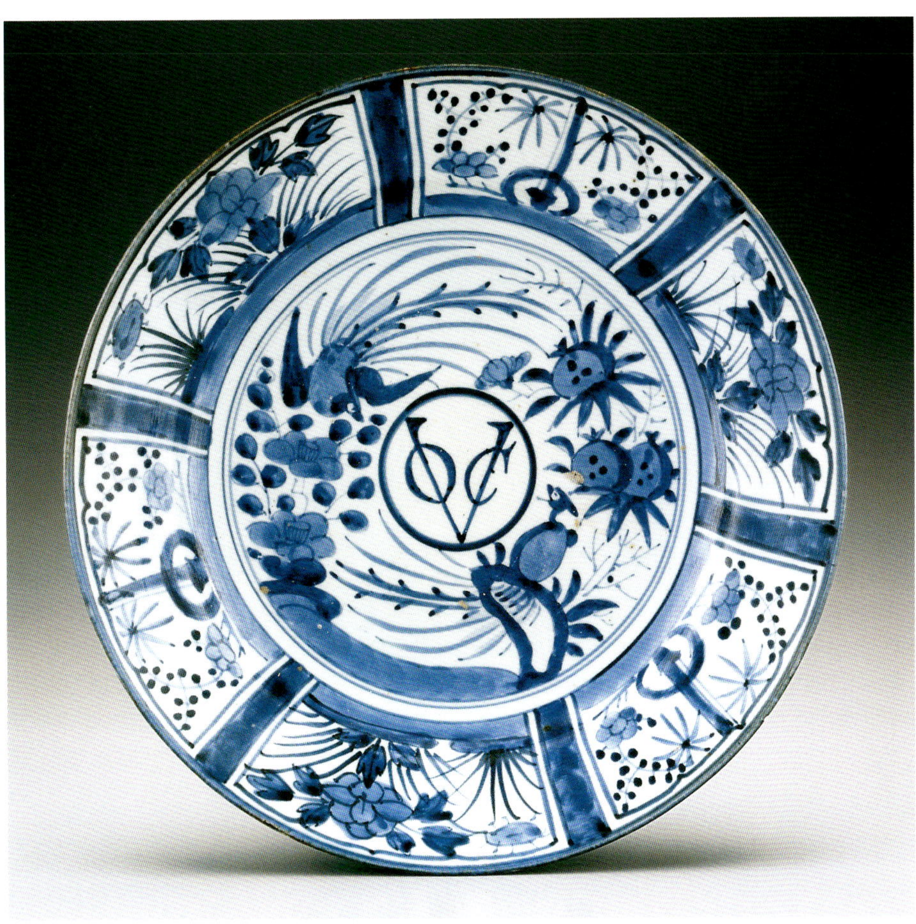

2 CHARGER

Arita, Japan; 1670–1720
Diameter: 14.25 in. (366 mm)
2000.61.3

The monogram of the Verenigde Oost Indische Compagnie (V.O.C.), or Dutch East India Company, adorns this charger.[38] It appeared on all sorts of goods belonging to the company and was a mark of both identification and pride.

Dishes like this charger were for the company's use and could have been found at its settlements in Asia, on board ships, and at its offices in the Netherlands. Fragments of V.O.C. dishes have been excavated at Deshima, the site of the V.O.C. trading post in Nagasaki, Japan. V.O.C. dishes are also known to have graced the governor's table in Batavia; in 1686 officials there ordered "2,400 pieces . . . all painted inside and outside with the mark of the Company." Both chargers and plates are known and were made by at least three kilns in Arita.[39]

LITERATURE
Illustrated in Howard, *Choice of the Private Trader,* p. 39; Howard and Ayers, *China for the West,* 1:123.

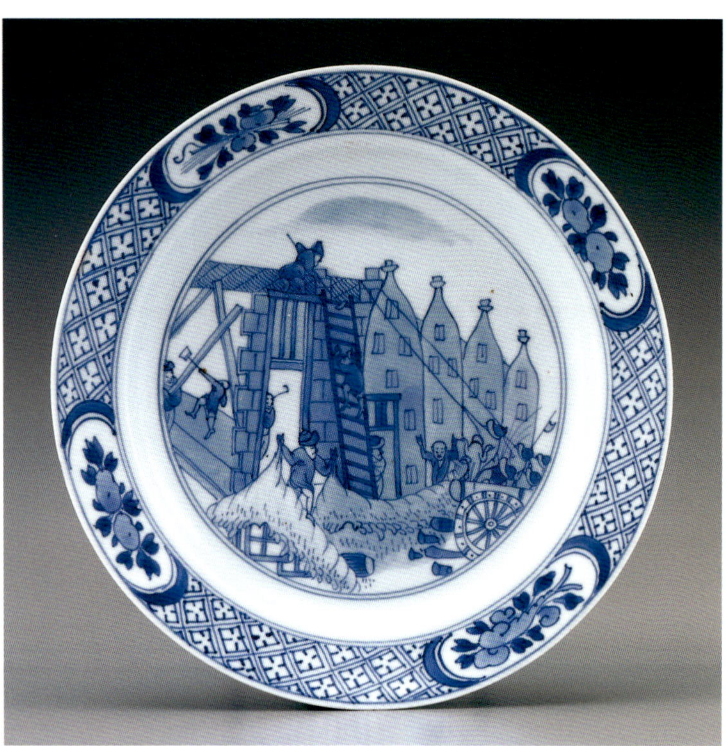

3 PLATE

Jingdezhen, China; 1690–95
Diameter: 8 in. (203 mm)
L03.2731.16

This plate portraying a riot that took place in Rotterdam, the Netherlands, in 1690 is the earliest known example of Chinese export porcelain to depict a specific, contemporary event. The scene shows the destruction of Chief Bailiff Jacob van Nyevelt's house by rioters on the night of October 4, 1690. Van Nyevelt was blamed for the death of Cornelis Kosterman, a guard at Rotterdam's city hall who was accused of killing a clerk during a fight. Kosterman was tried and convicted, and his execution on September 16 touched off demonstrations by townspeople convinced of his innocence. The disturbances lasted several weeks, culminating in the destruction of Van Nyevelt's house and ending only when town officials agreed to appoint a more acceptable bailiff.[40]

The riots were commemorated in poems and prints and on a medal that served as the model for this plate. Struck in silver by Dutch engraver Jan Smeltzing, it illustrates the destruction of Van Nyevelt's house on one side and Kosterman's severed head on the other. Both plates and cups were decorated with scenes from the medal (the cups were further embellished with a view of Kosterman's head in the bottom of the vessel), and the number that survive suggests that quite a few were ordered. One appeared in the collection of Augustus the Strong of Saxony, and seventeen plates decorated with the "Uproar of Rotterdam" were sold at an auction in Amsterdam as late as 1754, indicating that they were popular items.[41]

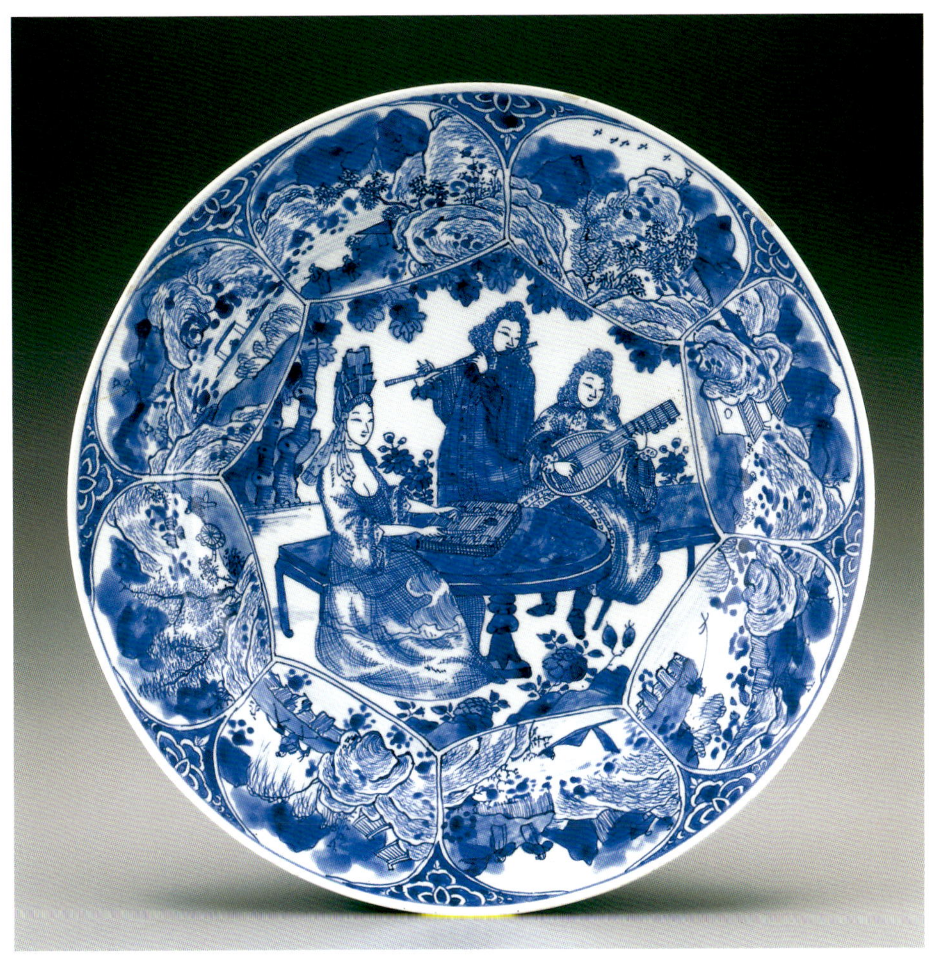

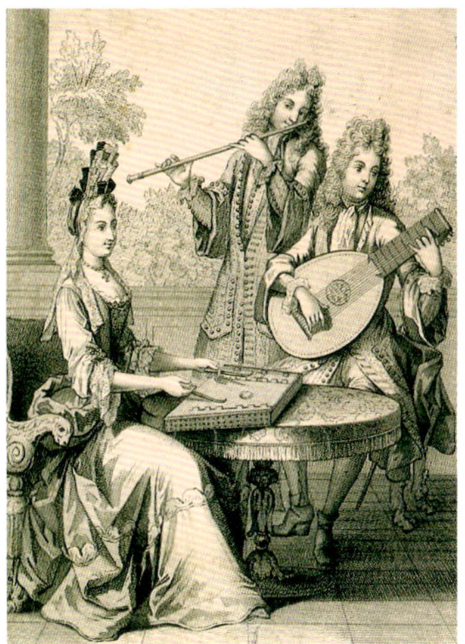

Nicholas Bonnart, *Symphonie du Tympanum, du Luth, et de la Flûte d'Allemagne,*
Paris, France, about 1700.
Etching; H. 9 in., W. 6.75 in.
L03.2775.45

4 CHARGER

Jingdezhen, China; about 1700
Diameter: 13.375 in. (349 mm)
L03.2775.44

The images of musicians that decorate this charger were copied directly from a French print entitled *Symphonie du Tympanum, du Luth, et de la Flûte d'Allemagne* (also known as *The Music Party*). It was engraved about 1700 by Nicholas Bonnart and is based on a painting or drawing by his brother Robert. The print illustrates a short poem comparing the inferior pleasure of music to the superior pleasure of love.

Starting in the late 17th century, merchants took European prints to China to be reproduced on export porcelain. French fashion prints such as the one seen here were especially popular at the turn of the 18th century, and many showing aristocratic men and women engaged in genteel pastimes such as playing music or relaxing outdoors were copied onto porcelain.[42]

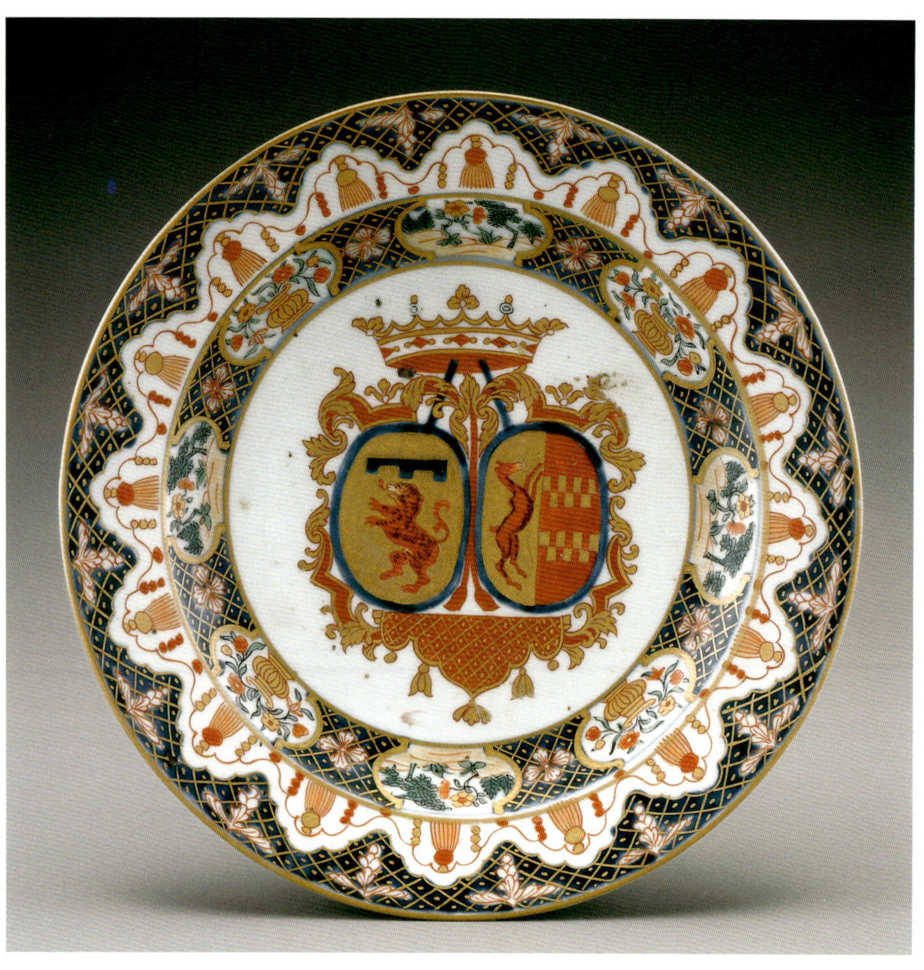

5 PLATE

Arita, Japan; 1702–10
Diameter: 10 in. (254 mm)
L03.2775.99

This plate is from a dinner and tea service made for Ida Marie van Buren and Joan van Brederode, who married in 1702. One of the earliest known armorial services for a Dutch family, it is decorated with an elaborate baroque-style border of drapery and tassels. Another member of the Van Buren family, perhaps Arend van Buren, also ordered an armorial service. Arend was a rear admiral in the Dutch Navy and would have had contacts in Japan able to procure a service for him. The borders on the two services are identical, suggesting that they were ordered at the same time.[43]

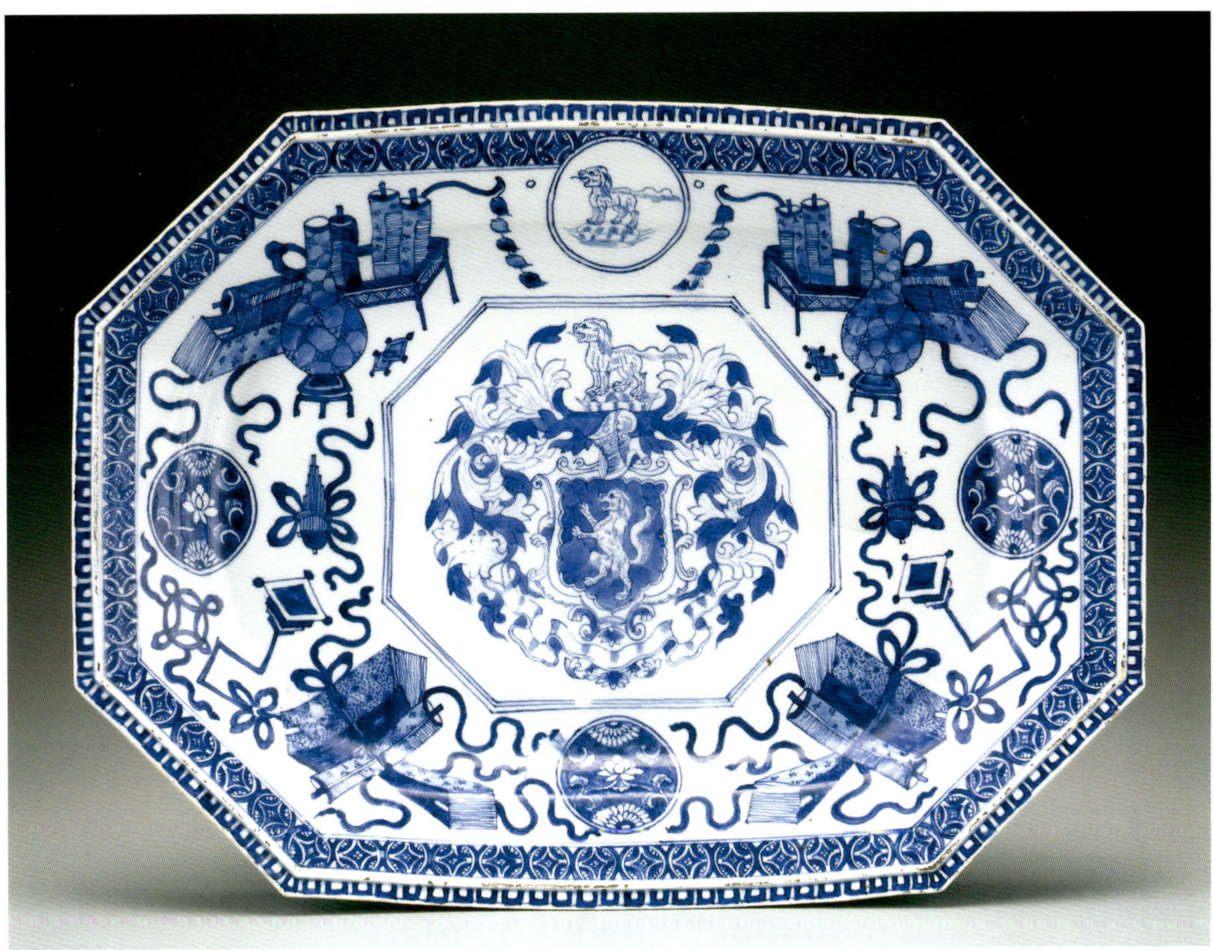

6 PLATTER

Jingdezhen, China; about 1705
Length: 20.5 in. (521 mm)
L03.2775.98

Created for Rev. William Talbot of England, this platter is from the earliest known Chinese armorial dinner service made for the British market. Talbot, who was a member of the House of Lords, served in turn as the bishop of Oxford, Salisbury, and Durham.[44] He was known for his extravagance, which is certainly borne out by the fact that he was among the first Englishmen to own porcelain decorated with his coat of arms.

A number of members of the Talbot family served in the British East India Company, and it was almost certainly through one of them that Reverend Talbot ordered his service. Most of the other early examples of armorial porcelain were made for families that were in some way connected to the China Trade, such as the plant pots made about 1695 for Sir Henry Johnson, one of the company's primary shipbuilders, or the service made for Thomas Pitt, governor of Fort St. George in India.[45]

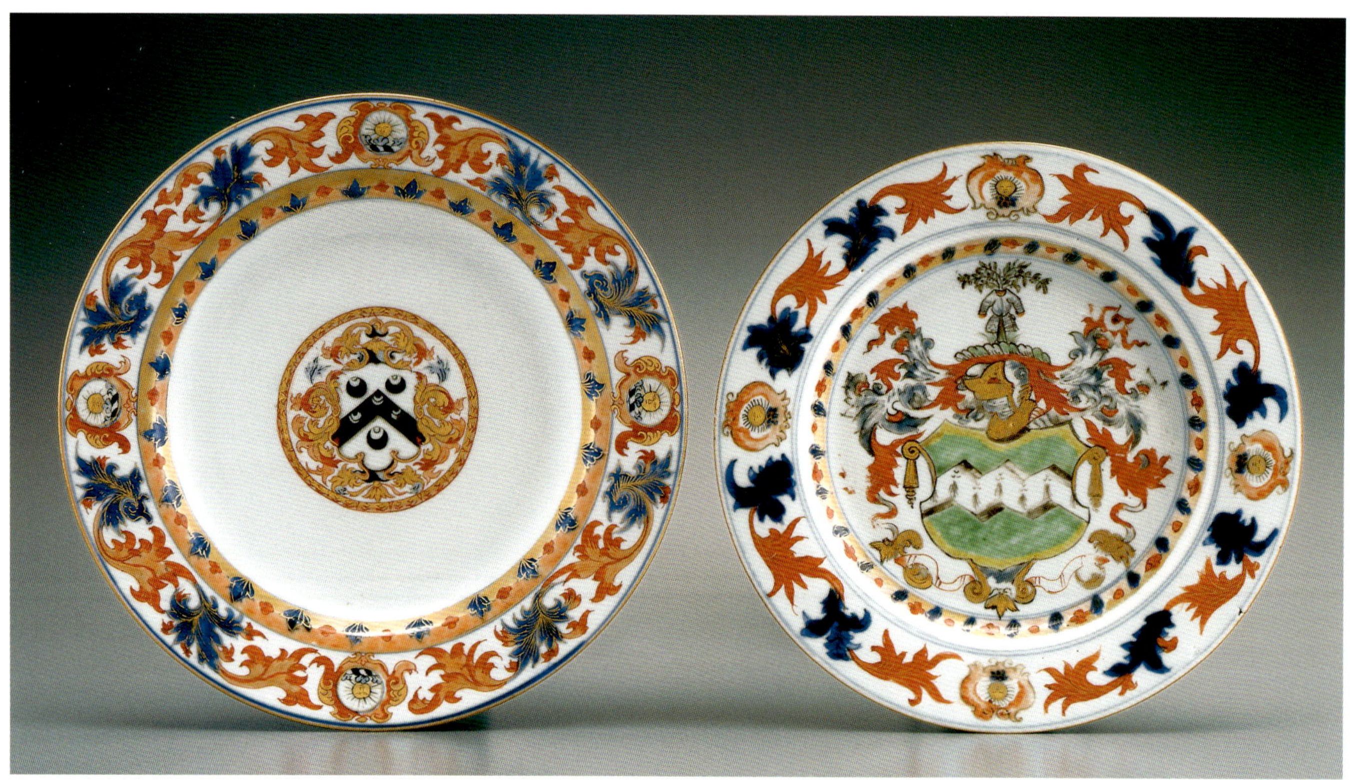

7 TWO PLATES

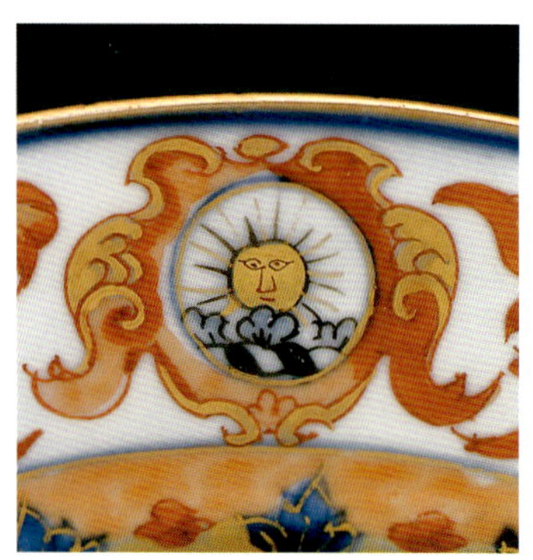

Jingdezhen, China; about 1712 *(left),* about 1715 *(right)*
Diameter: 9.5 in. (241 mm), 8.875 in. (225 mm)
L03.2775.80, .81

Chinese porcelain painters were remarkably adept at reproducing the complex armorial designs they were sent, but sometimes they did make mistakes. The plate on the left was made for William Walker, a doctor of law and judge advocate. It bears his coat of arms in the center; his crest, which is a rising sun, is repeated four times between baroque scrollwork on the rim of the plate. The plate on the right was made for Lord Somers, lord chancellor of England, and bears his coat of arms in the center. However, it is not his crest on the rim; it is Dr. Walker's.

How did this happen? Somers and Walker were both high-ranking officials in the government and probably knew each other socially. Somers probably saw Walker's new service, wanted to keep up with his stylish friend, and copied the design. The esoteric detail of whose crest was whose was lost somewhere in translation, and Walker's crest remained on the rim. The influence of Walker's design spread even further, as Robert Walpole, later prime minister of England, found an identical crest on the rim of the dinner service he acquired about the same time.[46]

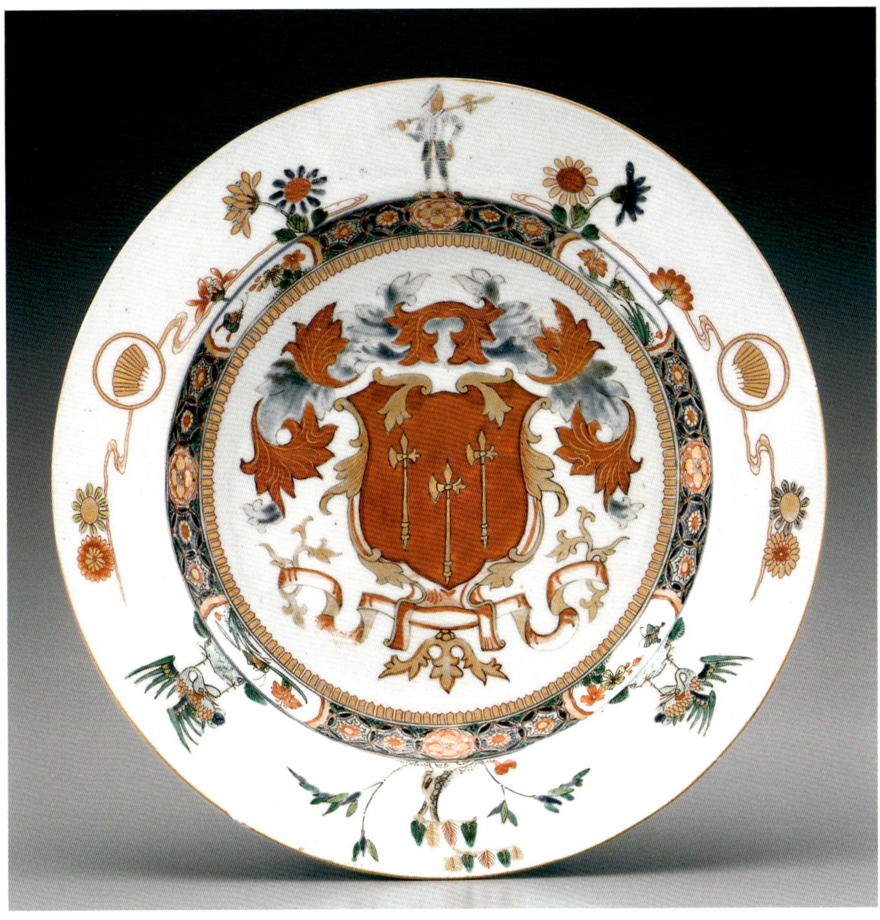

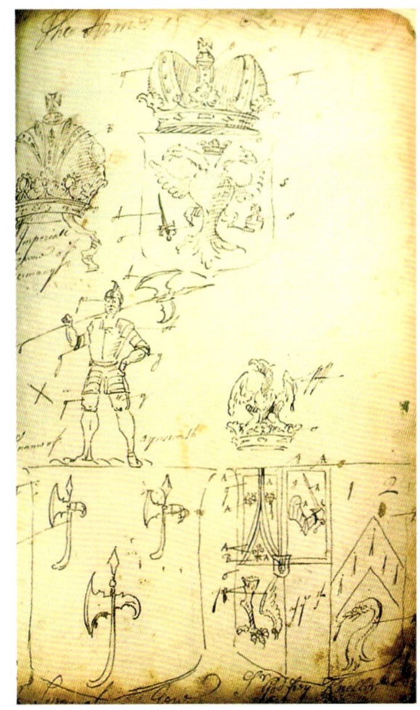

Coach painter's order book, London, England, about 1715. Photo, courtesy of David S. Howard.

8 PLATE

Jingdezhen, China; about 1718
Diameter: 10 in. (254 mm)
L03.2775.92

Coats of arms were a source of great pride, and few families were shy about advertising the fact that they were members of the aristocracy. Arms were carved into the facades of homes, engraved on silverware, printed on bookplates, enameled on porcelain, and painted on the doors of horse-drawn coaches.

Coaches were a mark of status, just as armorial porcelain was, and titled individuals often ordered theirs decorated with their arms. Stephen Ainsworth, an Englishman who lived in Madras, India, did exactly that. At about the same time he ordered the dinner service from which this plate comes, he had the doors of his coach emblazoned with his coat of arms. Ainsworth was in good company; his order is listed on the same page of a coach painter's order book as those of both Sir Godfrey Kneller, the noted English portrait painter, and Peter the Great, the "Czar of Muscovy."[47]

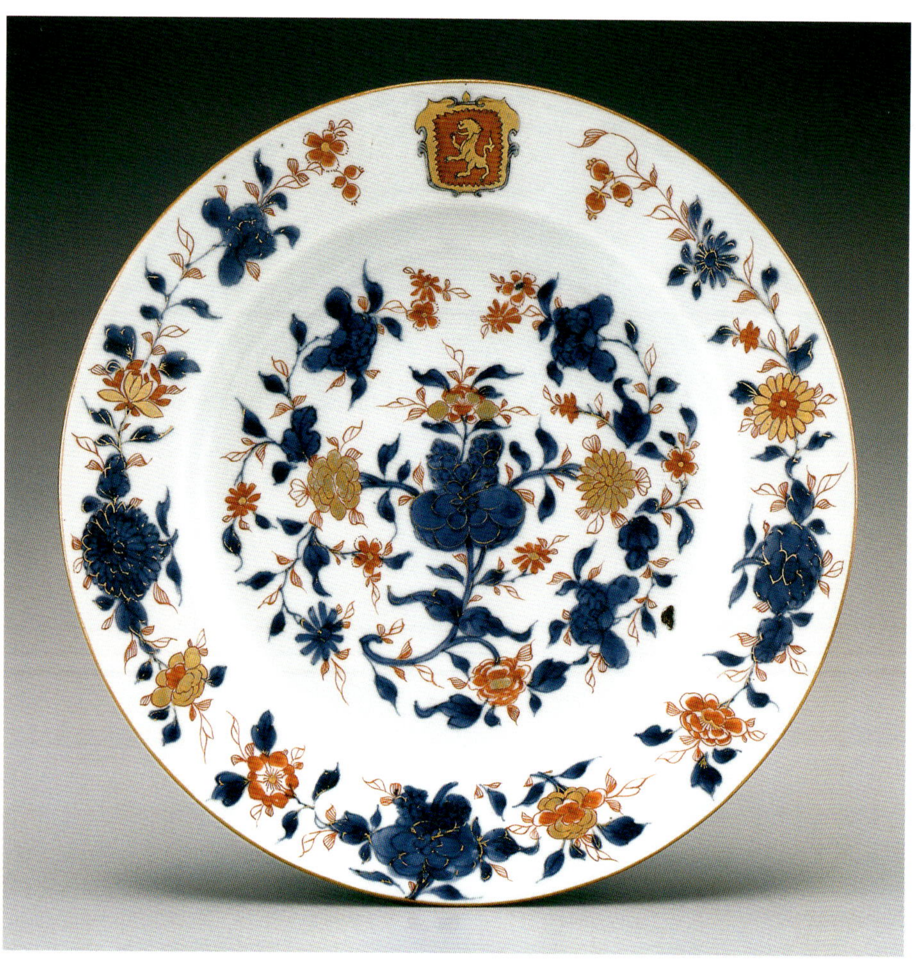

9 PLATE

Jingdezhen, China; about 1720
Diameter: 9.75 in. (248 mm)
L03.2775.64

This elaborately decorated plate with floral sprays in the Imari palette is from a service made for a member of the Talbot family of England. It possibly belonged to Rev. William Talbot, who commissioned the earliest known Chinese armorial dinner service for the British market (see entry 6) and was a member of the House of Lords as well as bishop of Oxford, Salisbury, and Durham. Clearly a man of fashion, Talbot possibly ordered the Imari service after his earlier blue and white had become passé. The service might also have been for Talbot's son, Charles, a London barrister who could have been influenced by his father's earlier purchase.[48]

LITERATURE

Illustrated in Howard, *Chinese Armorial Porcelain,* 2:135.

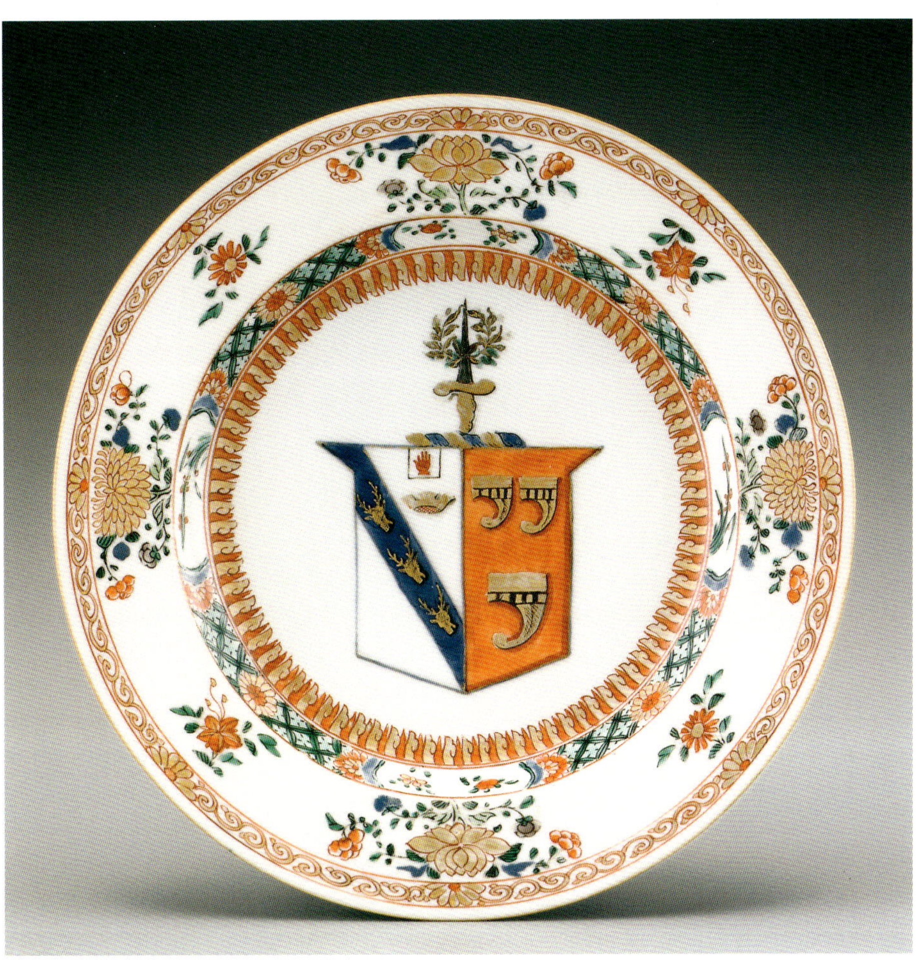

10 PLATE

Jingdezhen, China; about 1720
Diameter: 9 in. (229 mm)
L03.2775.104

The delicate floral sprays and intricate lattice border on the rim of this plate, painted in *famille verte* enamels, were popular from about 1715 to 1720. Surprisingly enough, *famille verte* enamels were rarely used on porcelain decorated with Western designs. The reason for this is not known. It may be that *famille verte* colors were used in only a few decorating shops in Jingdezhen, and those shops may not have filled orders for the West. This plate is from a service made for Sir John Stanley and his wife, Anne Granville, who lived at Grange Gorman near Dublin, Ireland.[49]

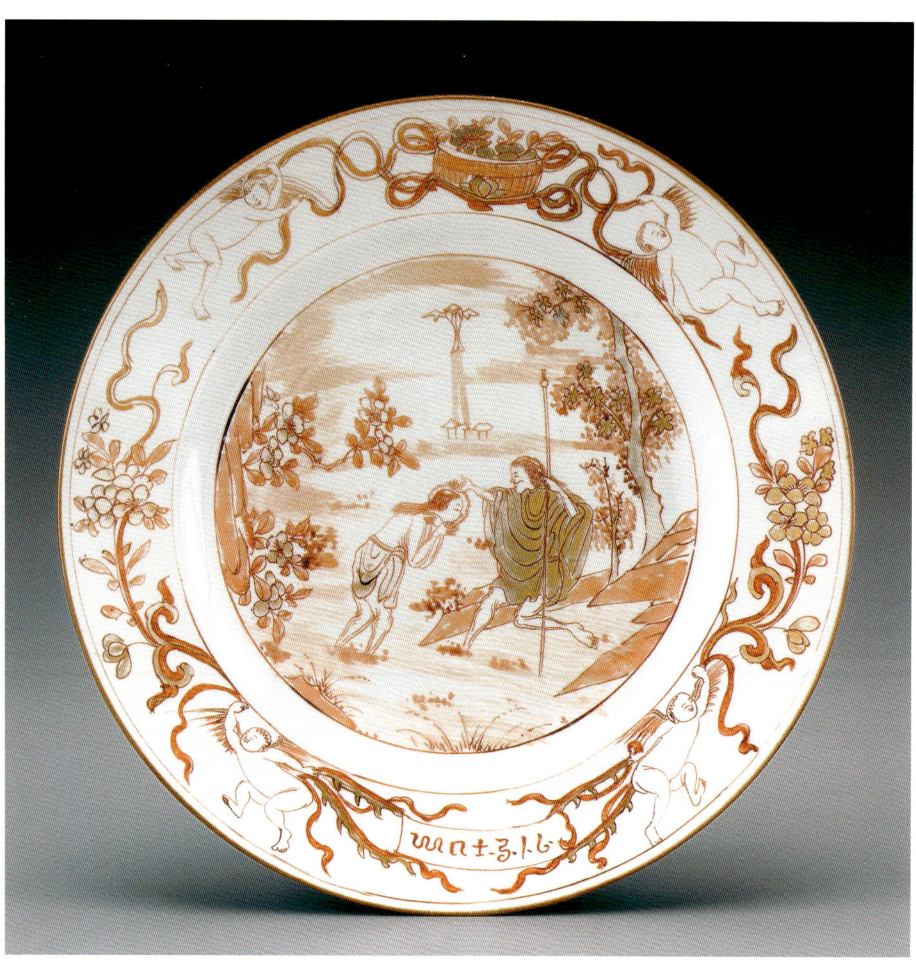

11 PLATE

Jingdezhen, China; 1720–30
Diameter: 10.875 in. (276 mm)
L03.2731.17

The scene on this plate shows Jesus being baptized in the River Jordan by John the Baptist, illustrating the biblical passage Matthew 3:16: "And Jesus, when he was baptized, went up straightaway out of the water: and, lo, the heavens were opened unto him, and he saw the Spirit of God descending like a dove, and lighting upon him."[50] The reference is inscribed on a banner held by two putti on the lower rim of the plate.

A number of plates decorated with the baptism of Jesus survive from this period. They were possibly inspired by images taken to Asia by Jesuit missionaries, who were active in China and Japan from the 16th century onward. The border also suggests that a European tin-glazed earthenware (delftware) plate may have been the model. These and similar plates decorated with the Anointing of Saul may have been designed for newly converted Chinese or Japanese Christians and may have been sent back to Europe as evidence of the success of missionaries in Asia.[51]

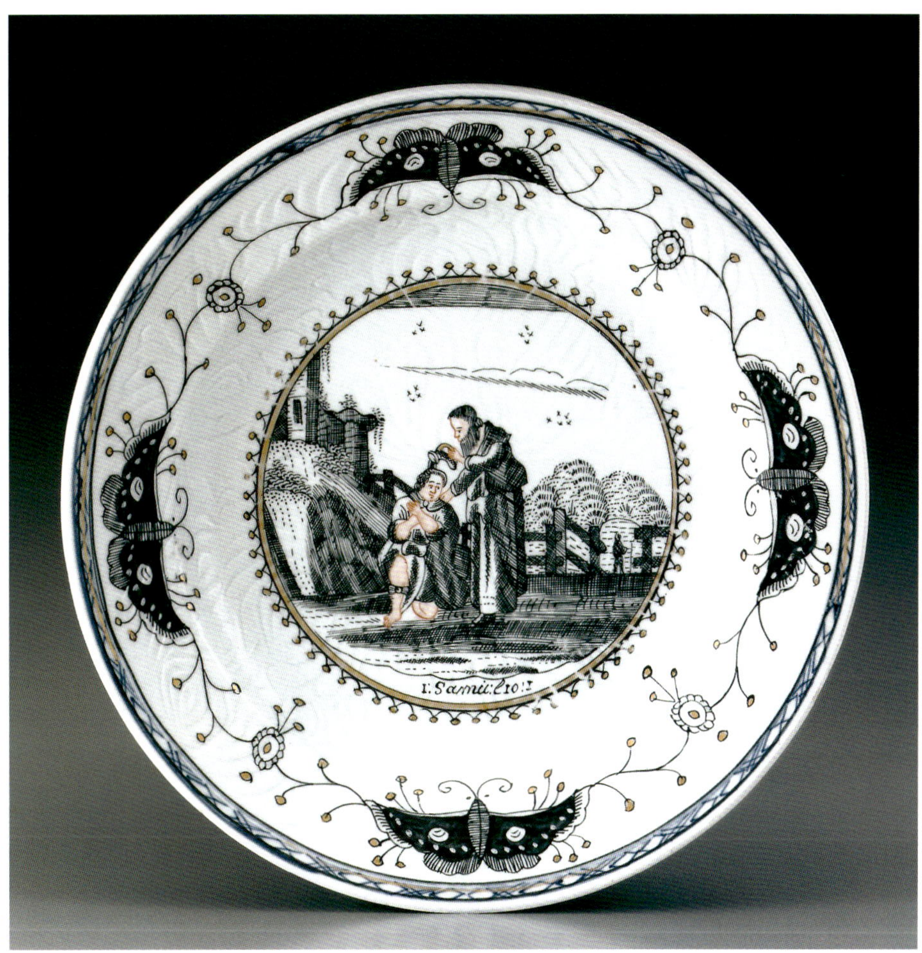

12 PLATE

Jingdezhen, China; 1720–40
Decorated in the Netherlands; 1730–50
Diameter: 9.25 in. (235 mm)
L03.2775.26

The scene on this Dutch-decorated plate shows Samuel, one of the judges of the Israelites, anointing Saul, the first king of the Israelites: "Then Samuel took a vial of oil, and poured it upon his head, and kissed him, and said, Is it not because the Lord hath anointed thee to be captain over his inheritance?"[52] The biblical reference is inscribed beneath the image.

This design was popular and appears on porcelain decorated in China (sometimes with the biblical passage misspelled) as well as in Europe. During the first decades of the 18th century, Europeans imported undecorated white porcelain that was intended to be over-decorated, which is what occurred with this plate. It was imported into the Netherlands and painted there, probably by someone who normally worked with earthenwares.[53]

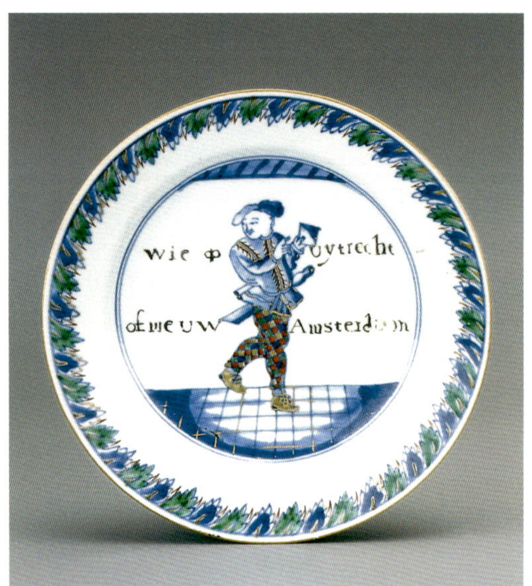
wie op uytrecht
of neuw

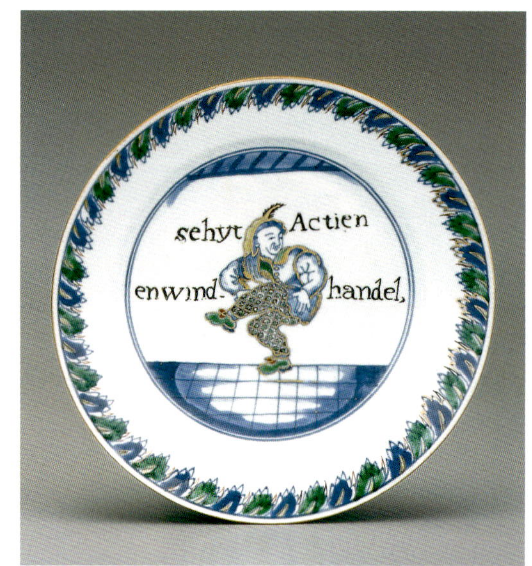
schyt Actien
en wind- handel,

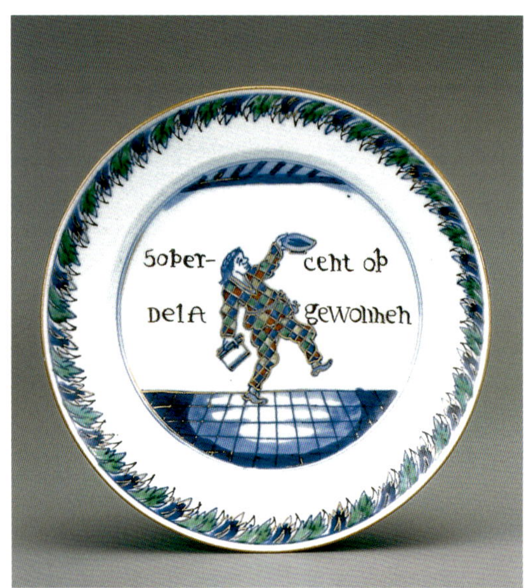
Sober- cent op

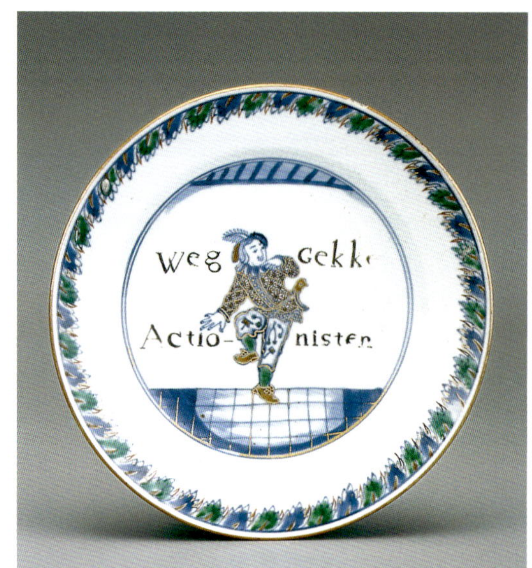
Weg
Actio- nisten

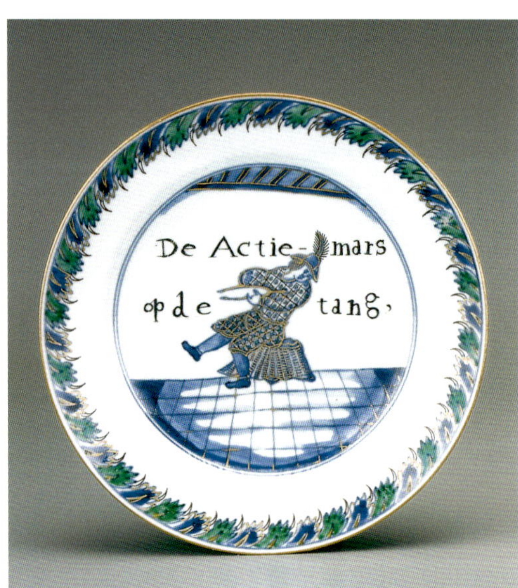
De Actie- mars
op de tang,

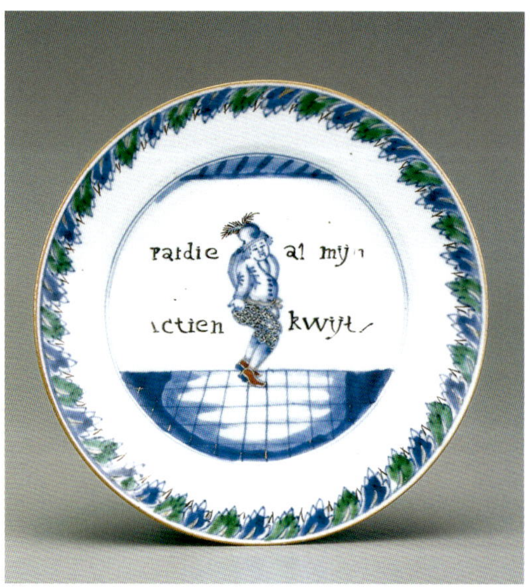
Pardie al

13 SET OF SIX PLATES

Jingdezhen, China; 1721–25
Diameter: 6.25 in. (159 mm)
2000.61.11.1–.6

This set of six plates satirizes the South Sea Bubble, the name given to the financial collapse of the South Sea Company in 1720. The company was founded in 1711, ostensibly to trade with the South Seas and the West Indies, but in reality, it was more of a financial management organization than a commercial trading enterprise. The company did not conduct any real trade but depended instead on rising share prices for profit. Vast fortunes were made as the company's stock rose, leading to speculation in even riskier companies; eventually, confidence evaporated, and the bubble burst, leading to a recession.

Characters from the commedia dell'arte can be seen cavorting across the plates. The characters, including Harlequin in his checkered pants, were an improvisational group that integrated current events into their sarcastic, satirical performances. These plates were made for the Dutch market and are inscribed:

Wie op Uytrecht of Nieuw Amsterdam
(Who wants to speculate on Utrecht or New Amsterdam?)
Sehÿt Actien en windhandel
(Shares and swindle)
50 percent op Delft Gewonnen
(Fifty percent profit on Delft)
Weg Gekke Actionisten
(Away foolish shareholders)
De Actiemars op de tang
(The march of the share values played on the tuning fork)
Pardie al myn actien kwyt
(By God, lost all my shares)

Relatively few Dutchmen lost money in the collapse of the South Sea Company, but there was a general concern that risky speculative investments could ruin the hard-won wealth of the Dutch Empire. A number of cartoons, prints, playing cards, and sets of plates were made to satirize the event and to serve as a cautionary tale.[54]

LITERATURE
Illustrated in Howard, *Choice of the Private Trader,* p. 54.

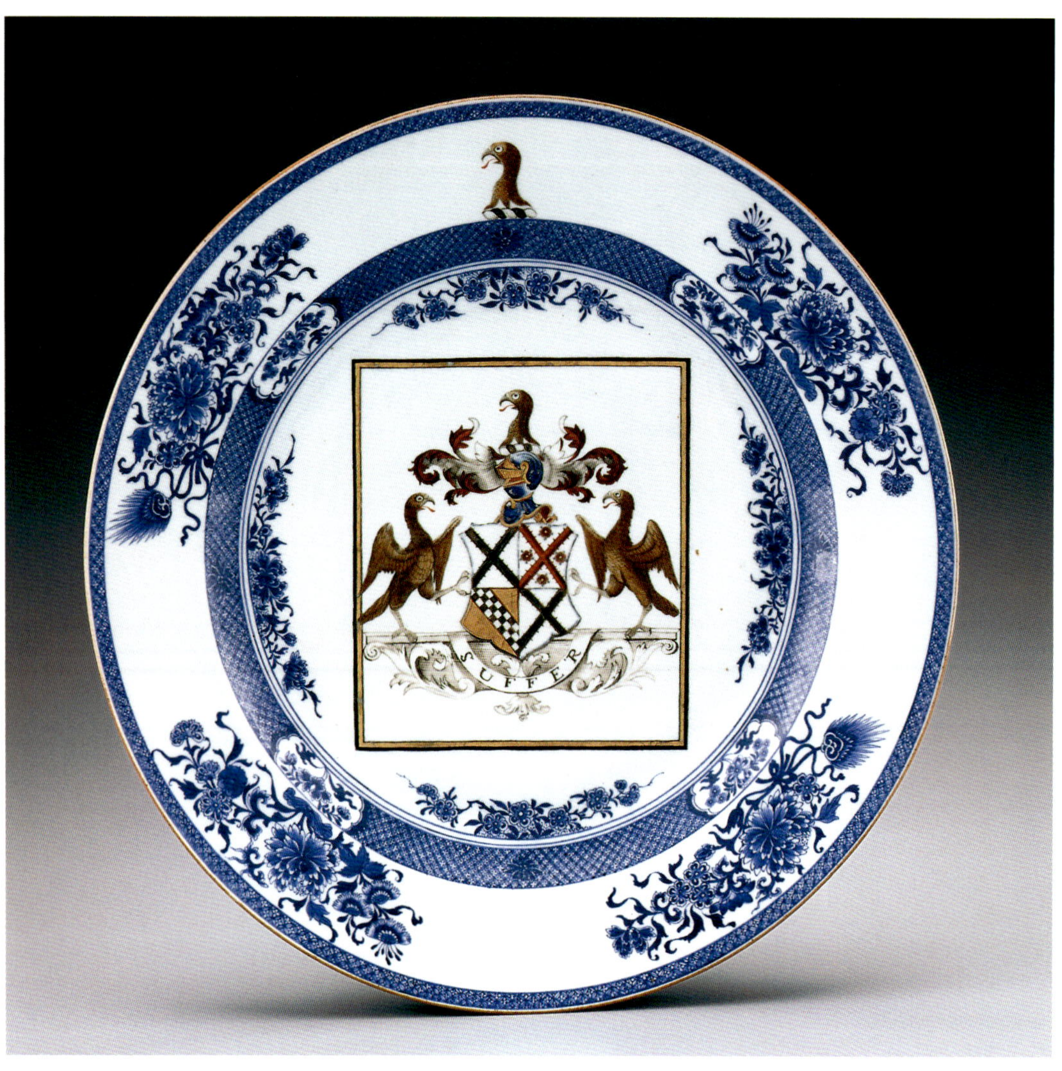

14 CHARGER

Jingdezhen, China; about 1725
Diameter: 14.25 in. (362 mm)
L03.2775.30

Bookplates were commonly sent to China to be used as models for the coats of arms on porcelain. They were readily available, easily colored, and the perfect size for copying onto porcelain. This particular charger, decorated with the arms of John Haldane of Gleneagles, Scotland, is the earliest documented example of an armorial porcelain design based on a bookplate. The service is unusual in that the arms are surrounded by a frame, suggesting that the Chinese painter may not have realized that it was not part of the arms. The bookplate was one of two designed in 1707 for Haldane, but the service was probably made for one of his four sons.[55]

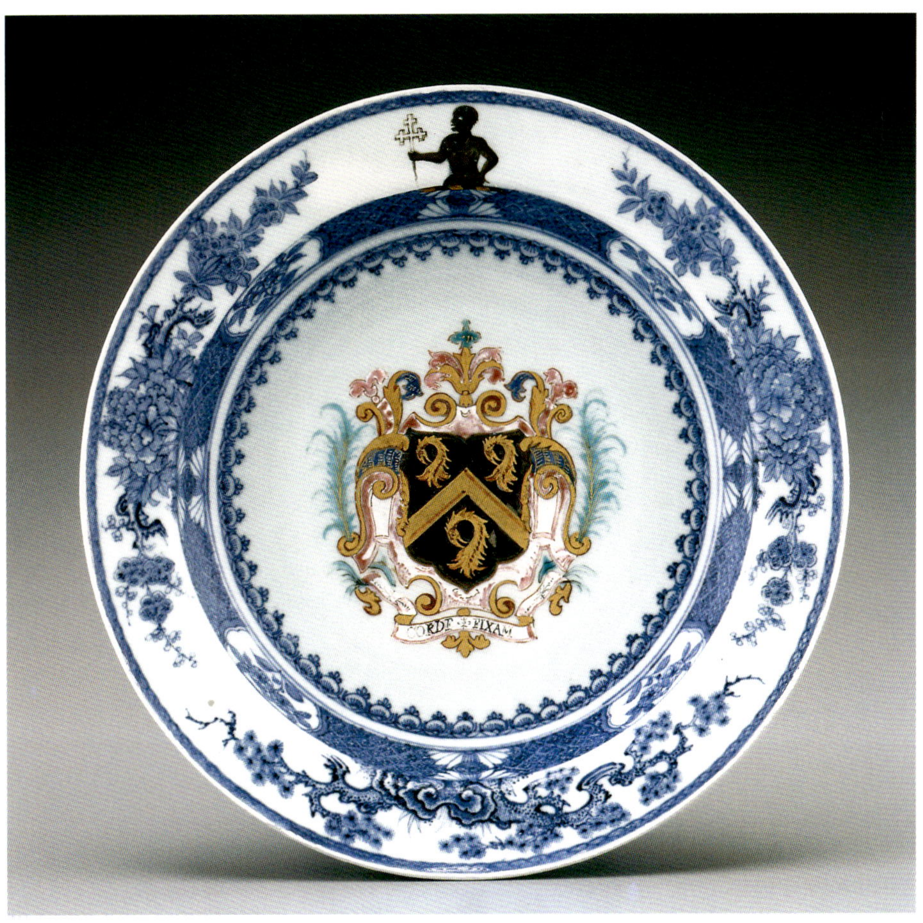

15 SOUP PLATE

Jingdezhen, China; about 1725
Diameter: 8.625 in. (219 mm)
L03.2775.25

This soup plate is decorated with an elaborate floral and latticework border painted in underglaze blue with the arms and crest painted in overglaze polychrome enamels—a pattern popular in the 1720s. It is from a service made for a member of the Godfrey family of England, which commissioned four armorial porcelain services in the 1720s. They may have been ordered by Peter Godfrey, a supercargo for the British East India Company who was known to have traveled to Canton in 1728.[56]

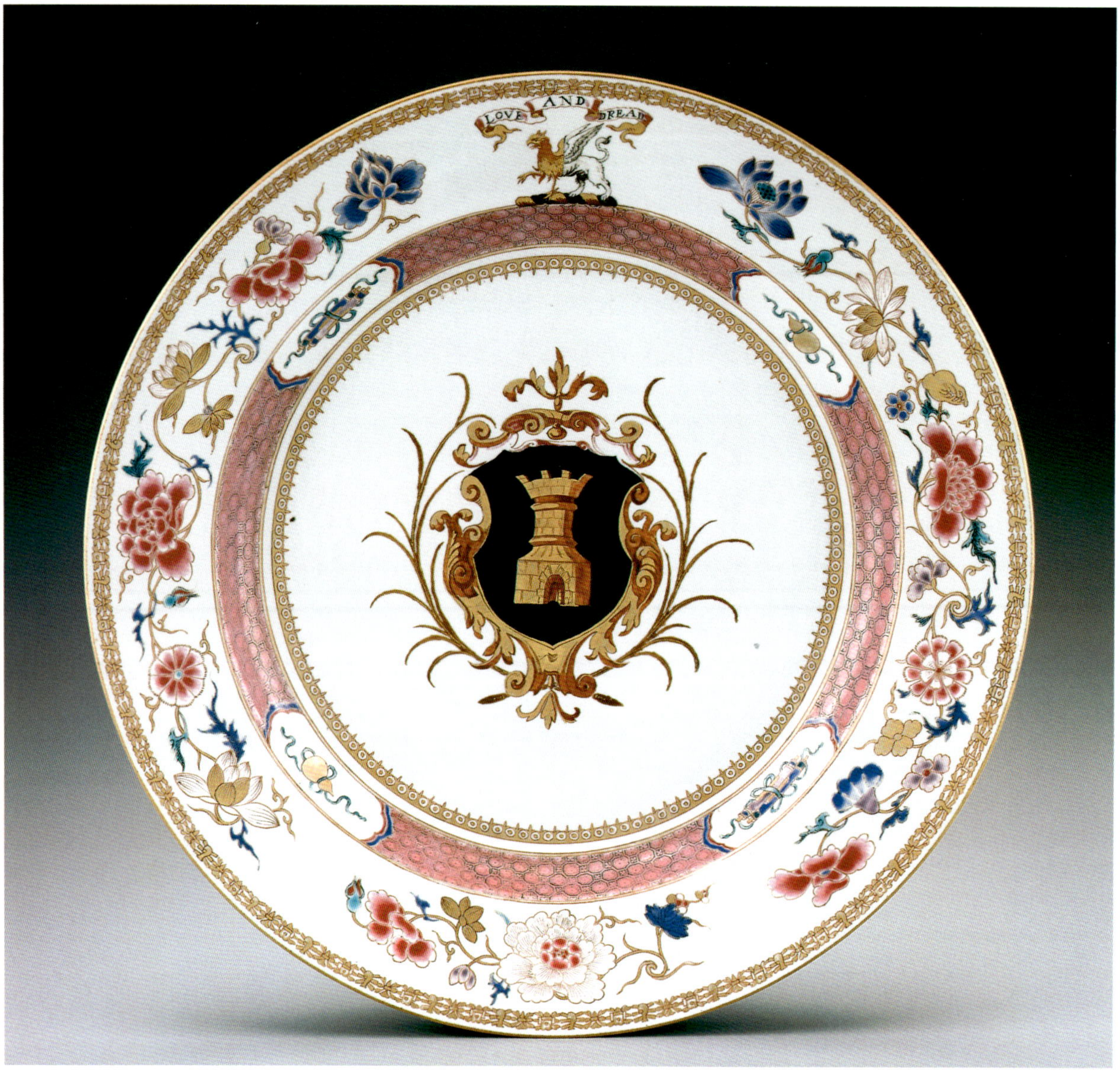

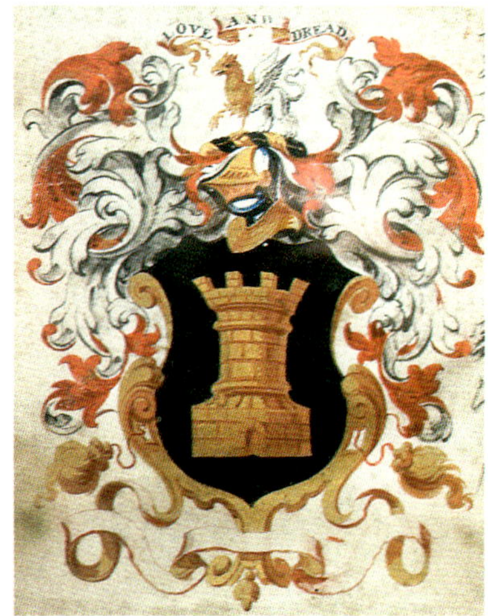

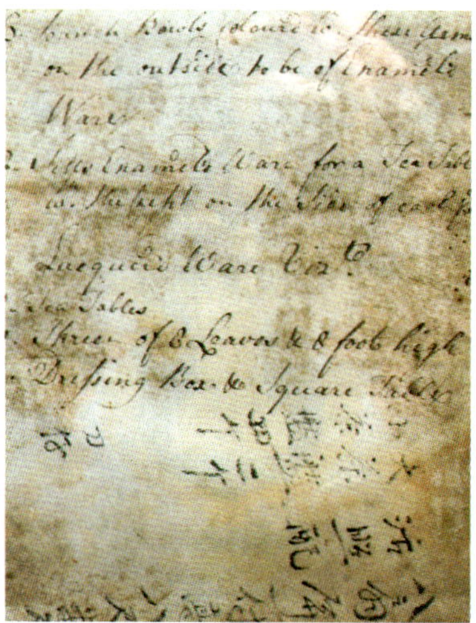
on the outside to be of Enamelled
Ware
Lacquered Ware Viz.
Three of 8 Leaves & 8 foot high
Dressing Box & Square Table

Painted armorial pattern and order, England, about 1728. Oil on vellum; H. 4⅜ in., W. 5⅜ in. Photo, courtesy of the Tower Trust.

16 CHARGER

Jingdezhen, China; about 1728
Diameter: 15.375 in. (390 mm)
L03.2731.15

What is extraordinary about this charger is that part of its original order and painted pattern survives. That order, which is for armorial porcelain and lacquered furniture, is a sheet of vellum with the arms of Christopher or Thomas Tower painted on one side and a list of objects wanted on the reverse:

> 6 Punch Bowls Colourd to these Arms
> on the outside to be Enameld
> Ware
> 2 Setts Enameld Ware for a Tea Table
> w. the Crest on the side of each pc.
>
> Lacquerd Ware Vizt.
> 2 Tea Tables
> 1 Skreen of 8 leaves and 8 foot high
> 1 Dressing Box & Square Table

Also on the reverse is a Chinese translation of part of the order (the rest was probably lost when the vellum was framed in the 19th century):

> one screen of 8 leaves and 8 foot high,
> with all the accessories
> two big plates
> four smaller saucers[57]

The Chinese order is signed by Dao Zai, probably a merchant in Canton specializing in porcelain. His shop would have been located on Thirteen Factory Street, which ran behind the hongs, or on one of the alleys such as Hog Lane or Old China Street, which ran perpendicular to the river. Dao Zai would have received the Tower order from a supercargo or captain and conveyed it to Jingdezhen, where the porcelain would have been manufactured and decorated.

Christopher and Thomas Tower were joint auditors of His Majesty's Revenue and members of Parliament; Thomas was a trustee of the colony of Georgia. This charger is from one of five services of armorial porcelain ordered by the brothers between 1720 and 1730.[58]

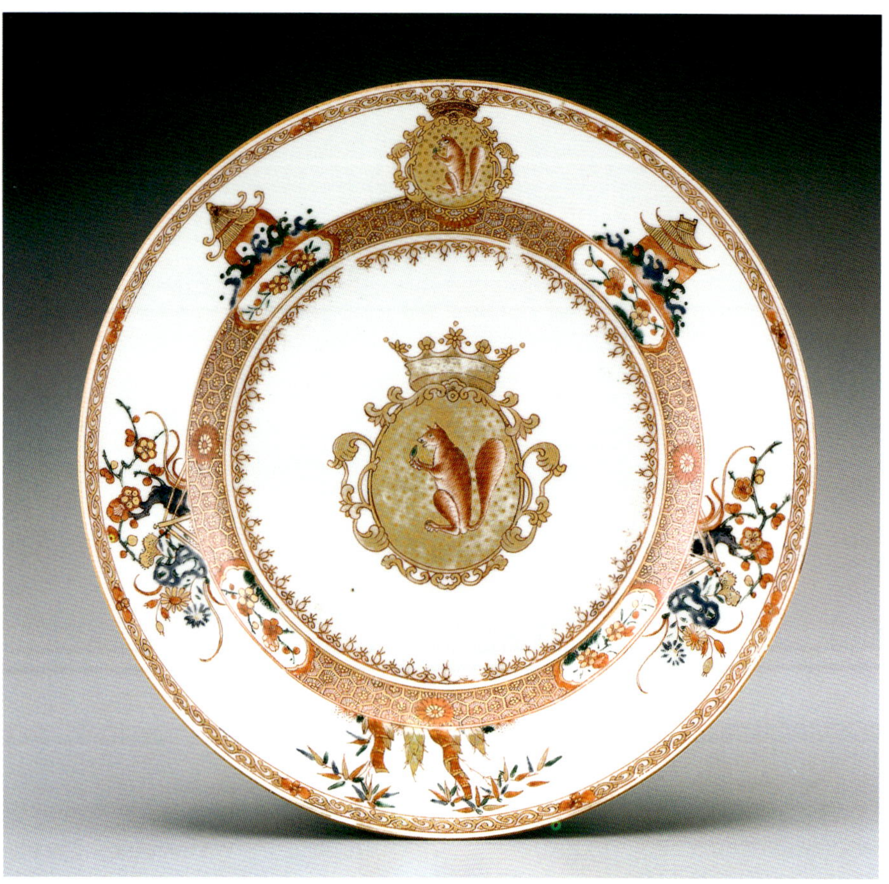

17 PLATE

Jingdezhen, China; 1730–40
Diameter: 9.125 in. (232 mm)
2003.47.3

An enormous armorial service made for Jan Albert Sichterman of the Netherlands includes the plate seen here. Sichterman worked for the Dutch East India Company and was based in the East from 1716 until 1745. He had a seemingly insatiable appetite for porcelain, building a collection of at least 3,000 pieces over the course of his lifetime, including an unbelievable 10 dinner services and 41 tea services.[59]

While based at the Dutch trading centers of Batavia and Bengal, Sichterman ordered at least three armorial services, one decorated in blue and white, one in red and gold, and one in black and gold. They were among the largest ever commissioned, containing rare and unusual forms such as garnitures, cisterns, candlesticks, and shaving bowls as well as the more typical platters and plates. In 1745 Sichterman returned to his hometown of Groningen, in the northern Netherlands, where he built one of the most elaborate and elegant houses in town. His estate was so grand that upon his death it took three sales to dispose of his possessions; the house was then split into two smaller, more manageable dwellings.[60]

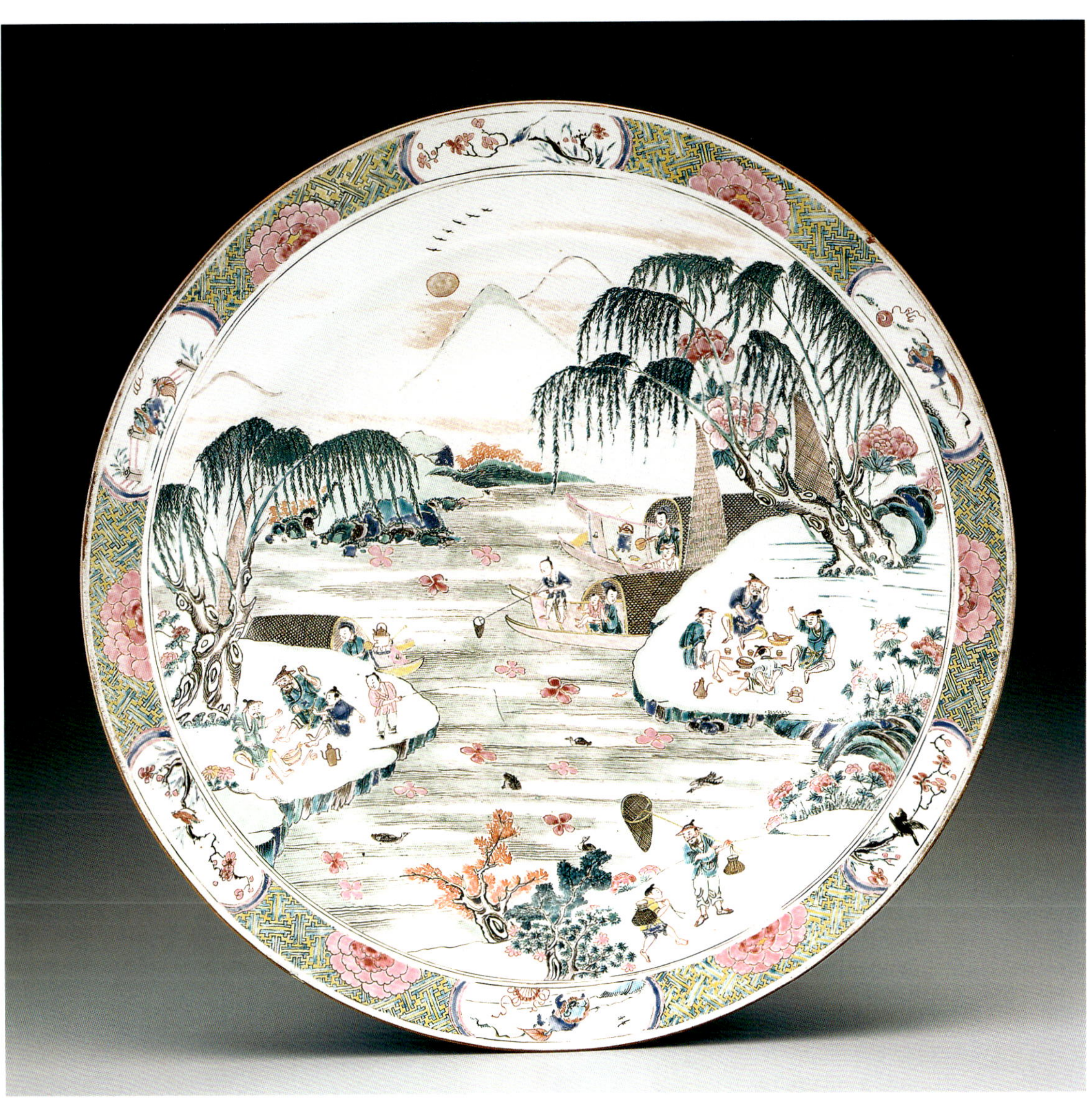

18 CHARGER

Jingdezhen, China; about 1730
Diameter: 22 in. (558 mm)
2000.61.19

The elaborate landscape design on this massive charger depicts Chinese men and women picnicking by a river. Probably created for display rather than use, the charger shows an idyllic, if unrealistic, view of life in China. Such images fit the preconceived notions that Westerners had about the country, and designs "according to the genius of the Chinese" were among the most popular found on export porcelain.[61]

LITERATURE
Illustrated in Howard, *Choice of the Private Trader,* pp. 64–65.

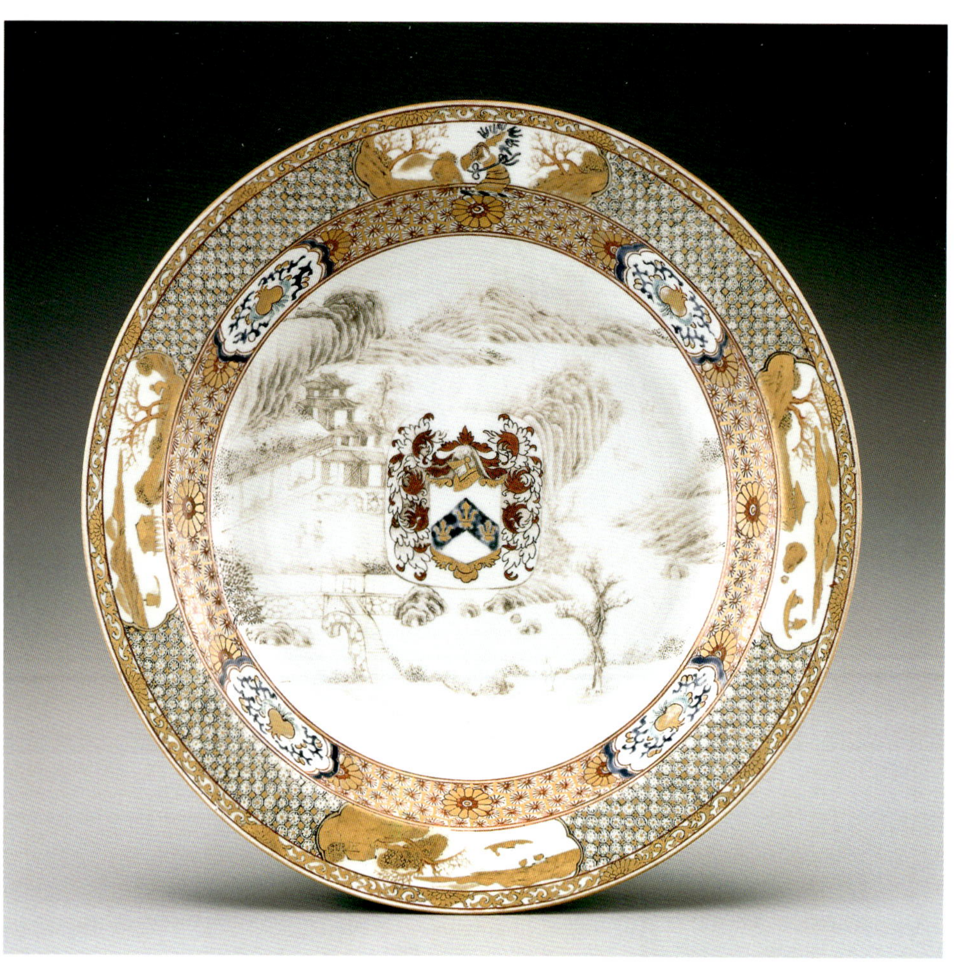

19 DISH

Jingdezhen, China; about 1730
Diameter: 12.25 in. (310 mm)
L03.2775.106

This dish is the earliest datable example of porcelain decorated *en grisaille*—in tones of gray. Inspired in part by black and white prints taken to China by missionaries and traders, the palette was developed sometime in the 1720s.

Developing the *grisaille* color had not been easy; according to Père d'Entrecolles, a Jesuit missionary who toured Jingdezhen in 1712 and 1722, "They [the Chinese] have attempted to paint some China-Vessels black, with the finest China-Ink, but without success, for when the Vessels were baked they were found to be very white; for which reason it was supposed that the black Colour, not being substantial enough, was dissipated by the Action of the Fire, or else they had not sufficient Strength to penetrate the Lay of Varnish [glaze], or produce a Colour different from Varnish alone."[62]

This dish is part of a service made for John Elwick, who was a director of the British East India Company from 1713 to 1720. He probably ordered the service just before his death in 1730.[63]

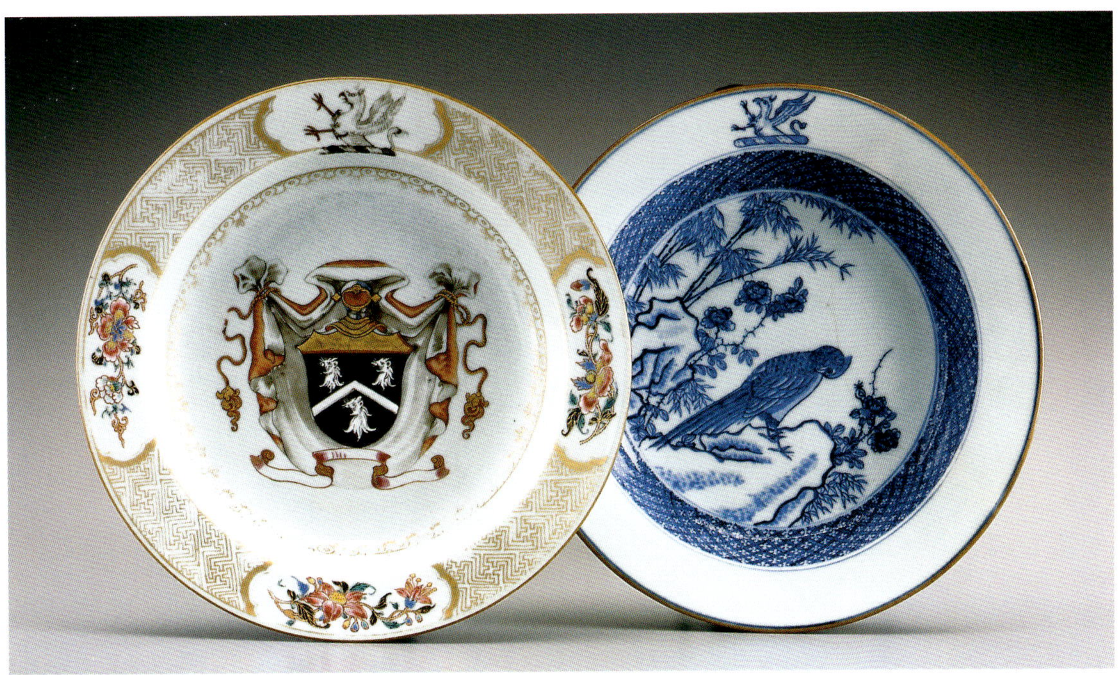

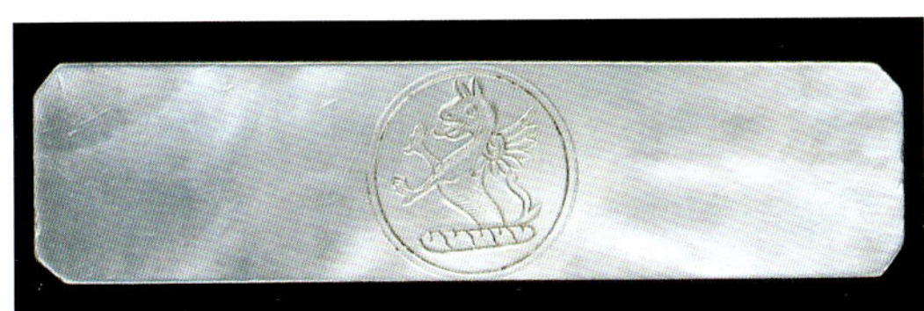

Gaming counter, China, 1730–31. Mother of pearl; L. 2.25 in. 2004.10 Gift of David S. Howard.

20 TWO SOUP PLATES

Jingdezhen, China; 1730–31
Diameter (each): 8.5 in. (217 mm)
L03.2775.16, .17

These two soup plates come from perhaps the best-documented services of Chinese export porcelain known. The original invoices survive, telling us who ordered the services, how many pieces there were, how much they cost, and how they were shipped.[64]

Both services were made for the Peers family of Oxfordshire, England. On November 19, 1731, the blue and white service was loaded in Canton and was described in the invoice as "two chests of China ware, Laden on board the ship *Canton Merchant.* Capt. Timothy Tullie, Commander, bound to the Port of Madras and consigned to the Nicholas Morris Merchant there on account and risque of Charles Peers, Esq." The shipment contained 255 pieces "of China Ware blue and white painted with a crest," including 100 plates, 60 soup plates, 6 soup serving dishes, 4 sets of bowls, 12 sauceboats, and 12 salts. The cost was £13. The second, polychrome service was considerably more expensive; it included some 450 pieces and cost £76. That shipment was loaded on the *Harrison* on December 10, 1731.[65]

In addition to porcelain, two sets of mother-of-pearl gaming counters decorated with the family's arms were ordered at the same time. It has been estimated that at least one-third of all orders of armorial porcelain were accompanied by requests for gaming counters.[66]

LITERATURE
Illustrated in Howard, *Choice of the Private Trader,* p. 67 *(right).*

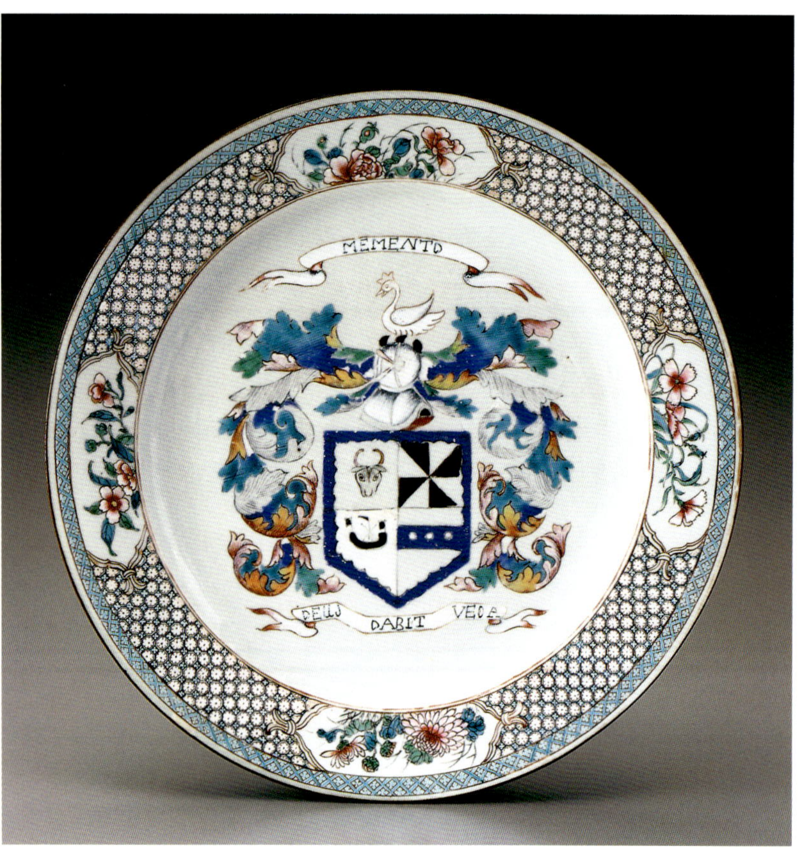

21 PLATE

Jingdezhen, China; about 1732
Diameter: 11.25 in. (285 mm)
L04.1027

This plate is part of a dinner service made for Colin Campbell, a Scottish-born merchant who was one of the founding directors of the Swedish East India Company. Created in 1731 with a royal charter from King Frederick I, the company operated out of the port of Gothenburg. There was a sizable Scottish expatriate community in Sweden at the time, and many were involved in the China Trade.[67]

Campbell had a checkered employment history, to say the least. He started at the British East India Company but moved to the South Sea Company, where he was implicated in the financial scandals that led to the company's collapse in 1720. He fled England in 1723, for Ostend in Belgium, where he worked for the Austrian East India Company until it was shut down in the late 1720s. In 1730 he moved to Sweden, where his experience with the China Trade led to his elevation to the nobility. Campbell traveled to China as the senior supercargo on the first voyage of the *Fredericus Rex,* arriving in Canton in 1732. There he oversaw the purchase of 2,000 chests of tea; 23,355 pieces of silk; and 499,061 pieces of Chinese export porcelain. For himself, he purchased the armorial service from which this plate comes.[68]

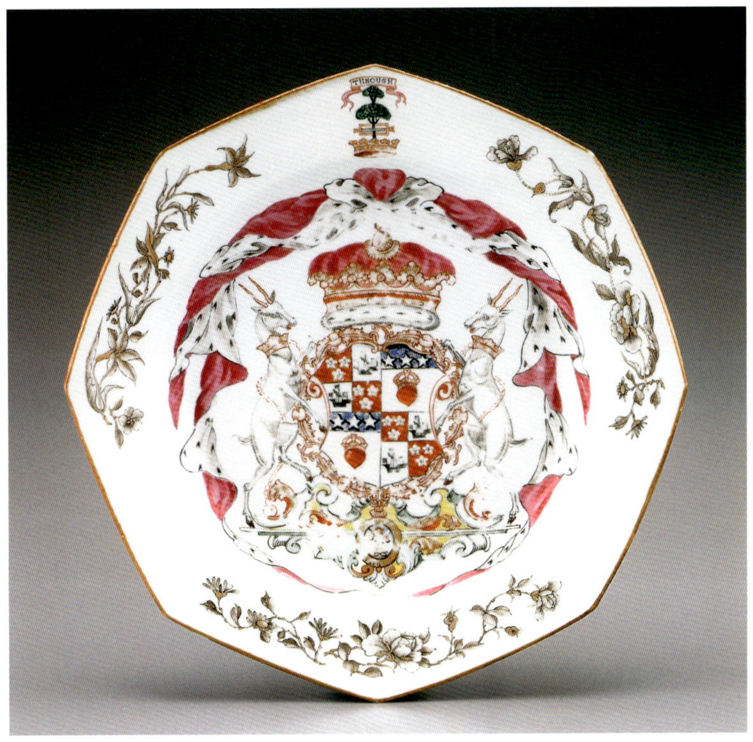

22 PLATE

Jingdezhen, China; about 1733
Diameter: 9 in. (230 mm)
2003.47.7

This plate, made for James, the 5th Duke of Hamilton, of Scotland, has one of the most elaborate coats of arms (more accurately known as an achievement of arms) to be found on Chinese export porcelain.

The shield bears James's coat of arms; it is quartered, with each quarter containing the arms of one of his noble ancestors. Hamilton's arms are in the shield's upper left and lower right quadrants, as viewed; the arms of Douglas (another ancestor) are in the upper right and lower left quadrants. Above the shield is a duke's coronet, which is surmounted by the crest and motto "Through," on the rim of the plate. (Scottish families usually displayed their mottoes above the shield; English families displayed theirs below.) Below the shield is the medallion of the noble Order of the Thistle. Flanking the shield are two antelope, which are supporters that mark the head of a family; draped around the achievement is the duke's ermine mantling.[69]

Hamilton was clearly proud of his noble heritage and eager to display his honors. The service from which this plate came was ordered after he became a Knight of the Thistle in 1726. In 1737 Hamilton married his third wife, Anne Spencer. Despite the fact that his armorial service was relatively new, he ordered another identical to this one except that the coat of arms contains a tiny shield in the center bearing the Spencer arms, ensuring that this marriage would be noted by his dinner guests.[70]

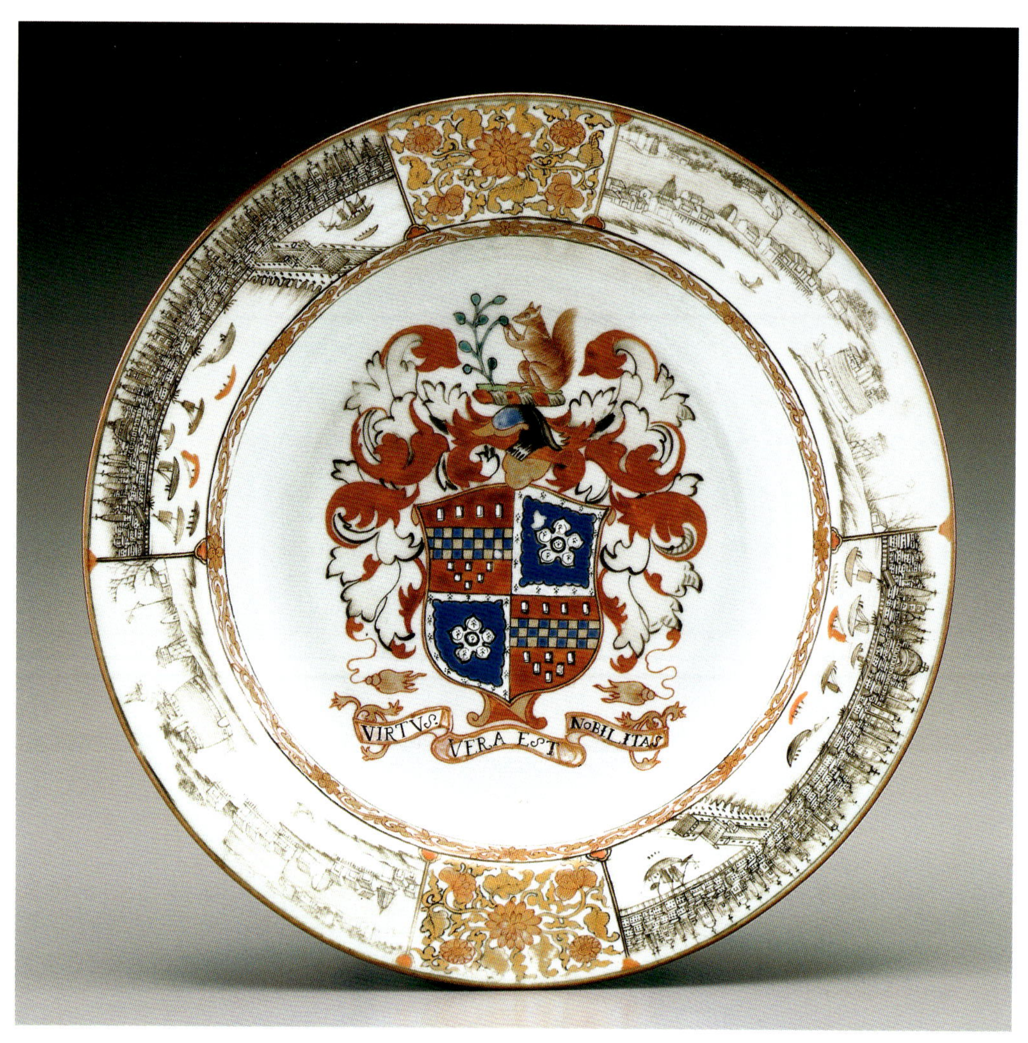
VIRTUS VERA EST NOBILITAS

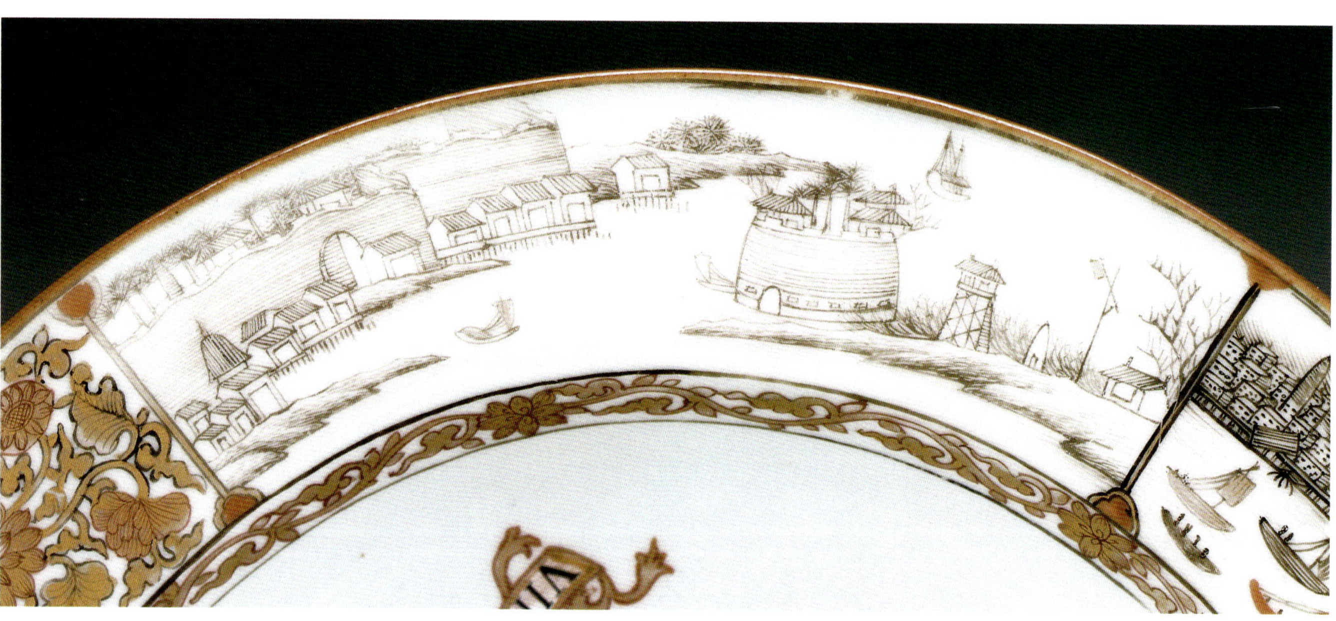

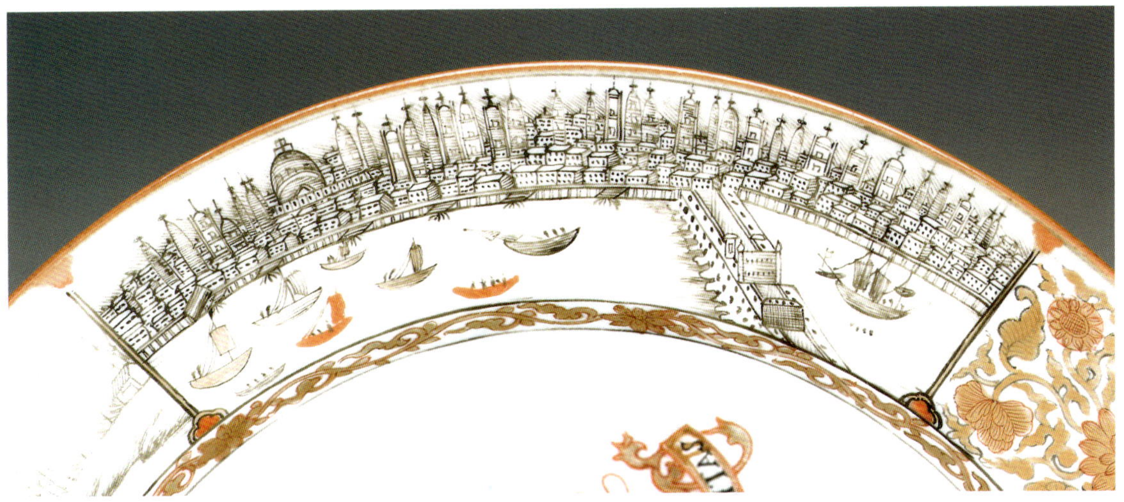

23 SOUP PLATE

Jingdezhen, China; about 1733
Diameter: 9 in. (230 mm)
2001.61.20

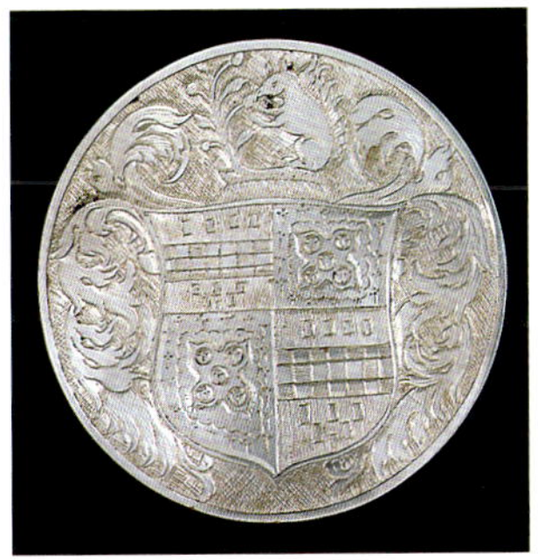

Gaming counter, China, about 1733. Mother of pearl; Diam. 1.375 in. 2004.9 Gift of David S. Howard.

Scenes of London and Canton, two of the most important China Trade ports of the 1700s, decorate the rim of this extraordinary soup plate. The cities represent the beginning and end of the long voyage from Europe to China. The view of the River Thames with London Bridge, the dome of St. Paul's Cathedral, and spires of the city's many churches was probably based on a panoramic print. The image of Canton, showing the city walls, one of its gates, and one of the folly forts in the Pearl River, is the earliest known depiction of the city on porcelain. Its format and painting style suggest that it was probably based on a Chinese hand scroll.[71]

Views of Canton began to appear on porcelain in the early 18th century, reflecting the increasingly prominent role that city played in the China Trade. The port's success was due in part to its proximity to both the coast and the tea-, silk-, and porcelain-producing regions of central China, but the primary reason centered on the fact that after 1729 foreign trade was restricted to Canton.

This plate is from one of three armorial services made for the Lees of Coton, in Shropshire, England. In addition to their armorial porcelain, the family also commissioned mother-of-pearl gaming counters decorated with their arms. This particular service was probably for Eldred Lancelot Lee (who died in 1734) or for one of his two sons, Lancelot and Harvey.[72] These Lees were cousins of the American branch of the family, who were ancestors of Confederate general Robert E. Lee.

LITERATURE
Illustrated in Howard, *Choice of the Private Trader,* p. 68.

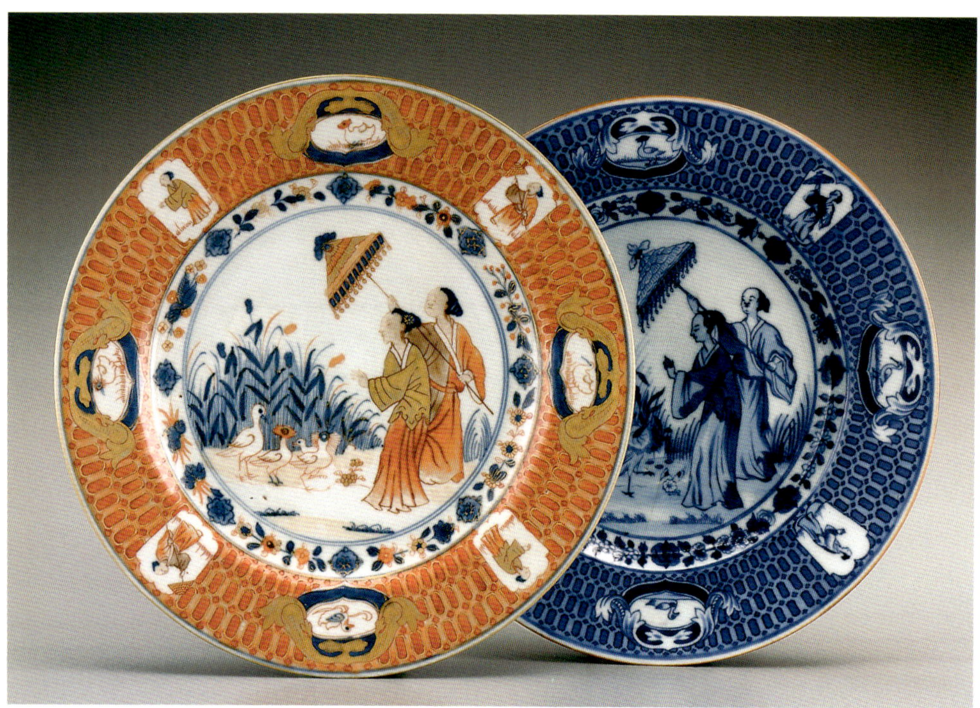

24 TWO PLATES

Jingdezhen, China; 1736–40
Diameter (each): 9 in. (230 mm)
2000.61.124, .21

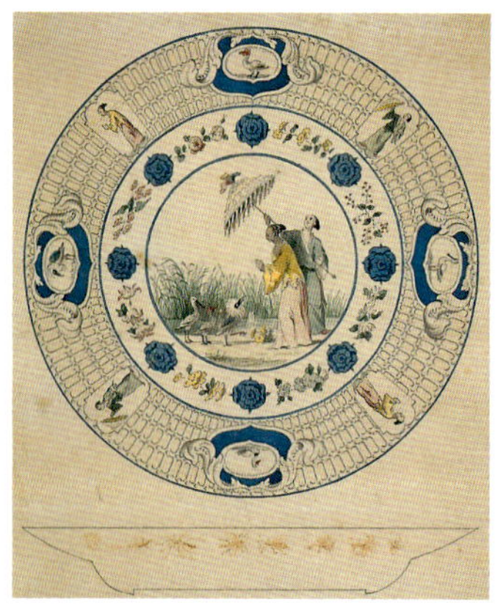

Cornelis Pronk, design for plate, Netherlands, 1734–38. Paper; H. 7.5 in., W. 6.25 in. Photo, courtesy of the Rijksmuseum, Amsterdam.

Although the ladies on these two plates are Asian in appearance, the design is by a Dutch artist, Cornelis Pronk, who was hired by the Dutch East India Company in 1734 "to make and deliver all the drawings and models to our satisfaction of such porcelains as shall from time to time be required from the Indies, with the colors duly set down, whether blue, gilt or other colors, and in all sorts of fashions."[73]

Four of Pronk's designs survive, all of them examples of chinoiserie—a Western adaptation of Chinese design. Pronk most likely relied on Chinese and Japanese porcelain, lacquerwork, and scroll paintings for inspiration, adapting them to create something more suitable to Western taste. In the design seen here, the Asian women are surrounded by European birds (spoonbills and thrushes) and European bulrushes.[74]

The drawing, marked "A" and known as *The Lady with the Parasol,* is thought to be the first of Pronk's designs executed in export porcelain. It was made in blue and white and Imari colors (as seen here) as well as in *famille rose* enamels and even in Japanese Imari porcelain. Plates are the most common pieces, but entire dinner services, tea services, fountains and cisterns, and vases were also created.

LITERATURE

Illustrated in Howard, *Choice of the Private Trader,* p. 73 *(right).*

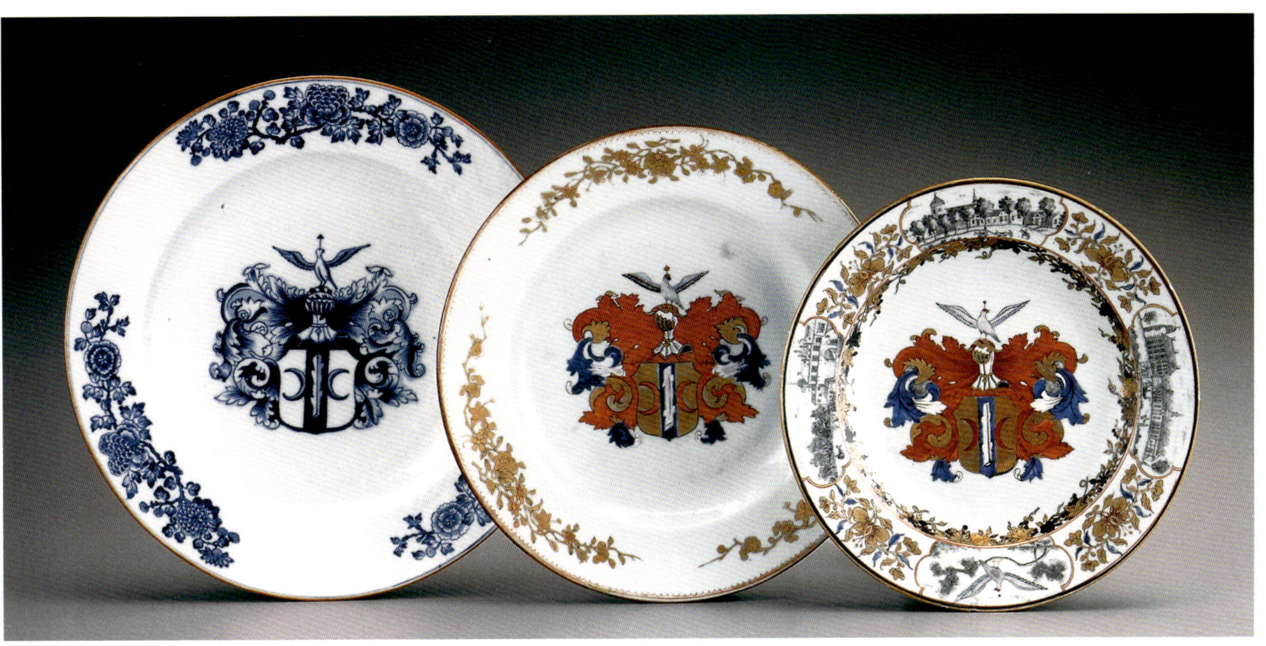

25 THREE PLATES

Jingdezhen, China; about 1738
Diameter: 11.125 in. (283 mm), 10.25 in. (257 mm), 9 in. (230 mm)
L03.2775.7, 2000.61.120, L03.2731.19

Despite the cost and difficulty of obtaining custom-made designs, some individuals were not content to own just one service of export porcelain. Adriaan Valckenier, the probable owner of these three plates, was one such person. Each of his services is decorated with his coat of arms, with the simplest in underglaze blue, the next in overglaze enamels and gilt, and the finest in overglaze enamels and gilt with an elaborate border embellished with *grisaille* landscape panels. The panel to the left of the arms has been identified as the King William Gate at Cleves.[75]

It is not known how Valckenier used his multiple services. The simplest may have been for everyday use or perhaps for a country estate, with the more elaborate ones reserved for special occasions or a more formal town residence. Possibly the finest pieces were designed just for decoration—speculation borne out by the absence of any real wear to the fragile overglaze enamel decoration.

A native of Amsterdam, Valckenier worked for the Dutch East India Company and was governor-general of the Dutch trading settlement of Batavia, providing him with ample opportunity to acquire as much porcelain as he desired. He may have been influenced by other Dutch East India Company officers who purchased multiple services or even by his ancestors, one of whom commissioned a set of Japanese export porcelain jugs decorated with the family's arms in the late 17th century.[76]

LITERATURE
Illustrated in Howard, *Choice of the Private Trader,* p. 79 *(right).*

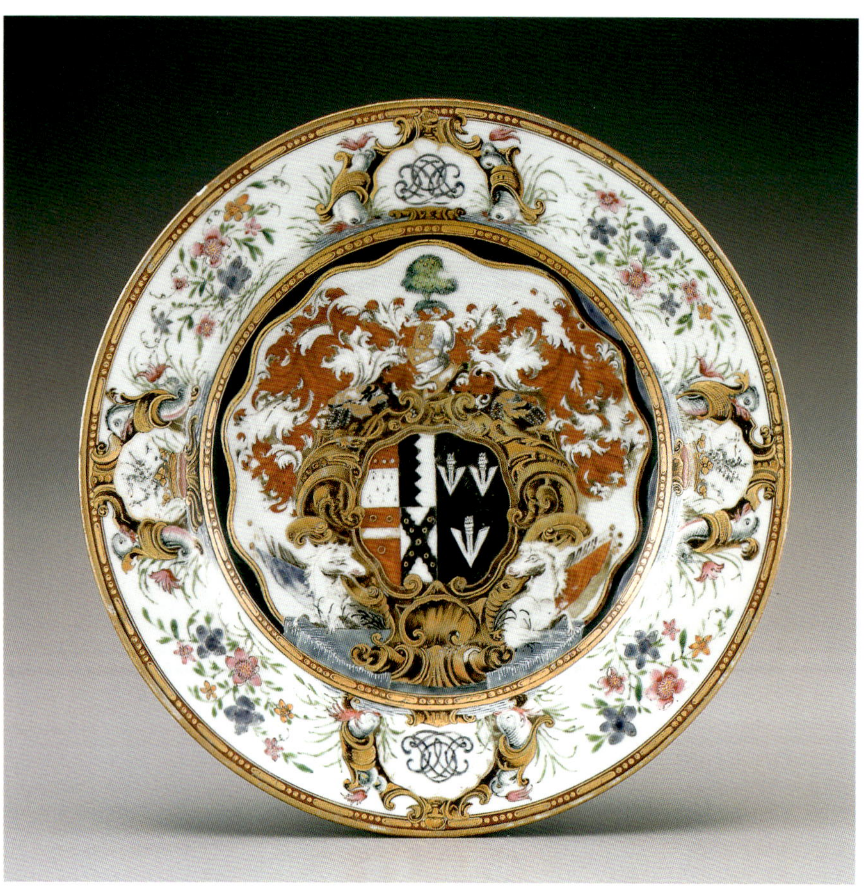

26 PLATE

Jingdezhen, China; 1739–42
Diameter: 9 in. (230 mm)
2000.61.24

This plate, made for Leake and Mary Okeover, is part of what is arguably the most elaborately decorated export porcelain dinner service ever created. Okeover ordered the service about 1738, sending to China a painted pattern with the instructions "The Arms of Leake Okeover, Esqre. Of Okeover near Ashbourn in the Peak in the County of Derbyshire—a pattern for China plate. Pattern to be returned." That request was fulfilled on January 16, 1740, when 70 plates and 30 dishes were delivered. The cost was £99.11.10, an astronomical sum given that a much larger service of 450 pieces made for Charles Peers in 1731 cost only £76.[77]

Clearly pleased with his purchase, Okeover ordered additional pieces and in 1743 received at "ye Jerusalem Coffee House, Change Alley, a consignment of fifty plates and four large dishes with your arms" from Joseph Congreve, commander of the ship *Prislowe.*[78]

LITERATURE
Illustrated in Howard, *Choice of the Private Trader,* p. 80.

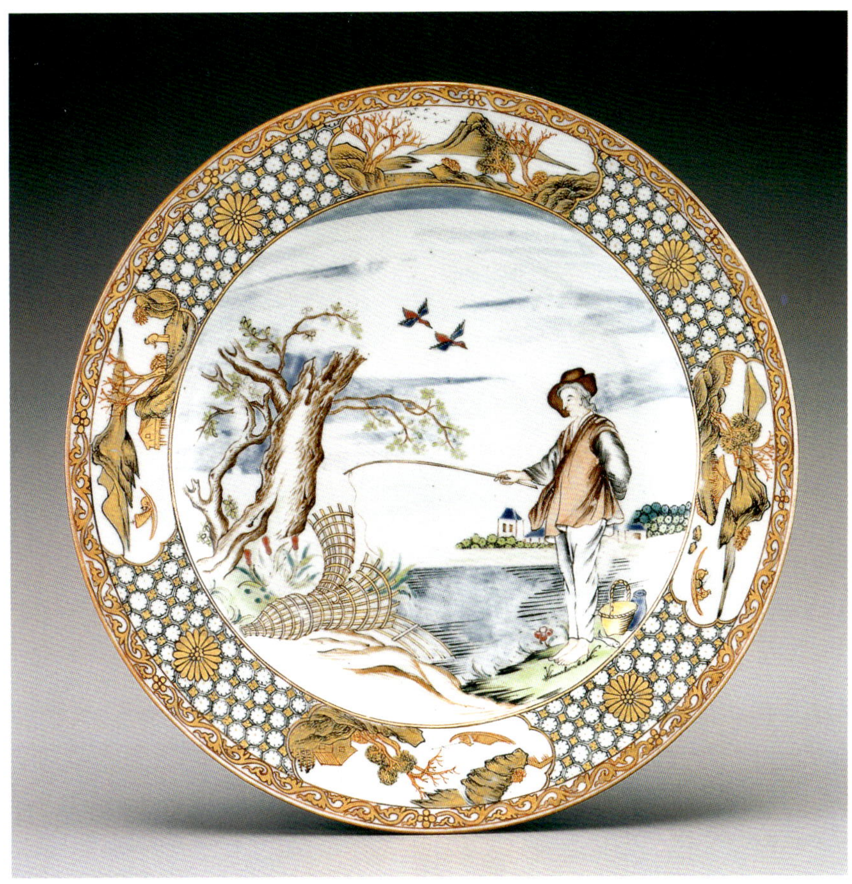

27 PLATE

Jingdezhen, China; about 1740
Diameter: 8.75 in. (223 mm)
2000.61.25

A delicately painted scene of a man fishing, based on a print called *Le Pêcheur* (The fisherman) by the 16th-century Dutch artist Abraham Bloemaert, adorns this plate. The image was clearly a popular one; the print was reproduced throughout the 17th and 18th centuries, and at least three different versions of the image appeared on export porcelain. The one seen here, with the elaborate *grisaille* and gold diaperwork border that was popular in the 1730s and 1740s, is thought to be the earliest.[79]

LITERATURE

Illustrated in Howard, *Choice of the Private Trader,* pp. 82–83.

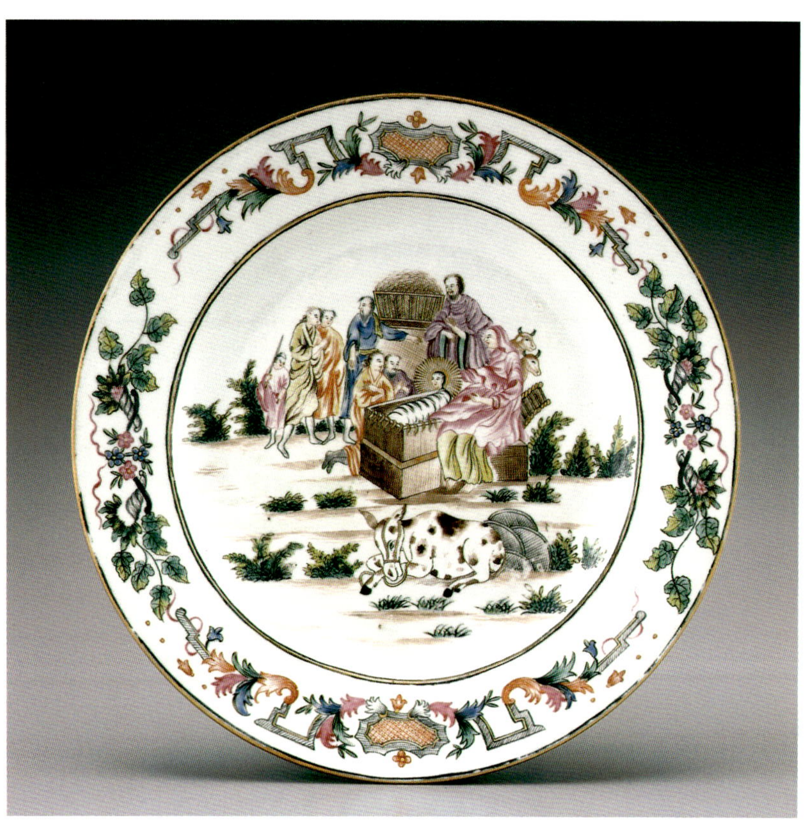

28 PLATE

Jingdezhen, China; about 1740
Diameter: 9.125 in. (232 mm)
L03.2775.36

This plate, depicting the birth of Christ, is part of a group of four decorated with the Nativity, Crucifixion, Resurrection, and Ascension. All are based on engravings by Dutch artist Jan Luyken. The images were originally part of a series of twenty-four prints illustrating the New Testament published in 1680. They were later included in a Lutheran Bible, the *Nederduytse Bijbel,* first published in Amsterdam in 1734. The title page of this Bible includes a portrait of Martin Luther that was also reproduced on Chinese export porcelain, suggesting it was the illustrations from this volume that were copied in China. Bibles were a common part of a ship's furnishings, and the small octavo-size edition of the *Nederduytse Bijbel* would have been especially convenient.[80]

A large number of these plates survive as do wares for tea, coffee, and chocolate that carry simplified versions of the scenes. Those decorated *en grisaille* are most common; polychrome examples, like this one, are rare. There is almost no wear on any of the plates, suggesting that they were designed primarily for display. They may have been used occasionally on Christian feast days or during periods of mourning, as the traditional Dutch name for the *grisaille* versions of these plates is *rouwgoed,* or mourning wares.[81]

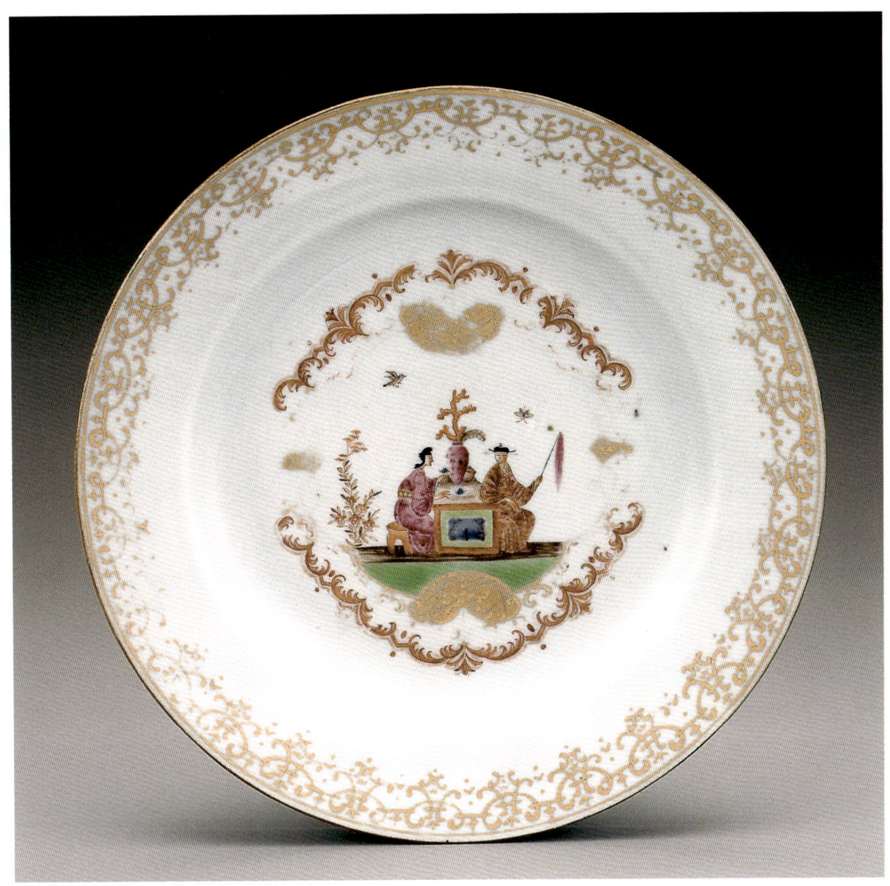

29 PLATE

Jingdezhen, China; about 1740
Diameter: 9 in. (230 mm)
L03.2775.20

The whimsical scene and elaborate gilt border on this plate are based on porcelain made at the Meissen factory in Germany in the 1720s and 1730s. Under the direction of Meissen's artistic director, Johann Gregor Höroldt, fanciful interpretations of designs found on Chinese porcelain and lacquer became popular. Known as chinoiserie, these designs appeared on a wide range of European-made objects and were even sent to China to be copied onto export porcelain. Plates such as the one shown here were made to compete with those from Meissen—which was making inroads into the export market—and may have been sold as true Meissen porcelain, which, by this period, was more expensive than Chinese export porcelain.[82]

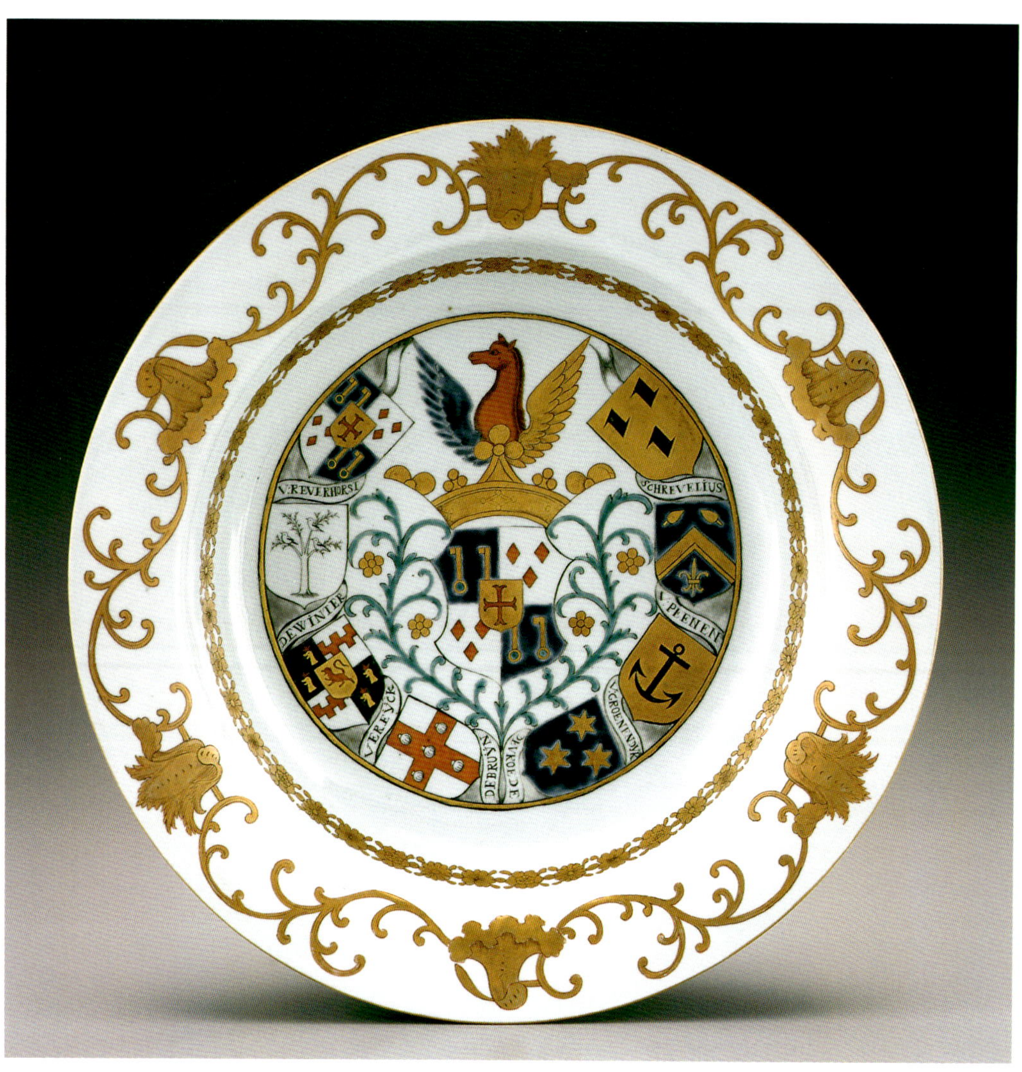

30 BASIN

Jingdezhen, China; about 1745
Diameter: 14.25 in. (362 mm)
L03.47.17

This basin is part of a service that represents the ultimate expression of familial pride found on Chinese export porcelain. The central arms, of Theodorus van Reverhorst or his brother Adriaan, are surrounded by the arms of their eight great-grandparents. It was rare for an individual to be able to say that all eight great-grandparents were "gentlemen" (and therefore possessed coats of arms).[83]

Like most Dutchmen who ordered armorial porcelain, the brothers were active in the Dutch East India Company; Adriaan was a merchant in Canton, and Theodorus served on the Court of Justice in Batavia.

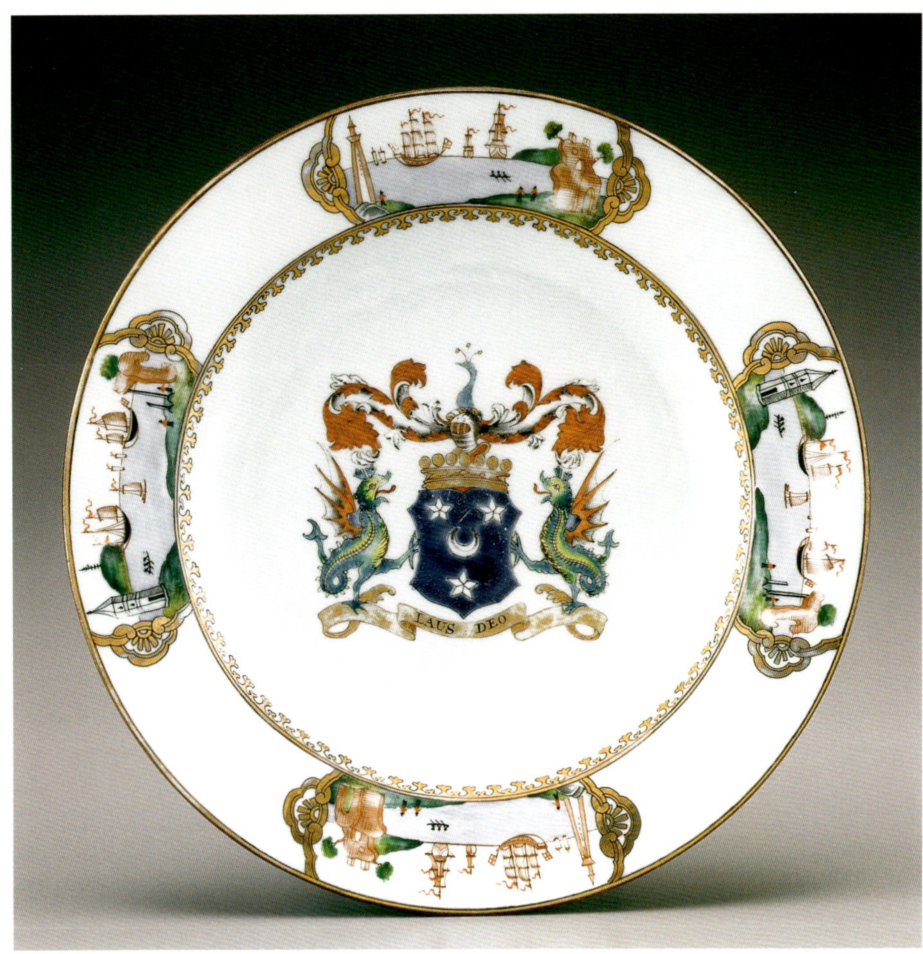

31 PLATE

Jingdezhen, China; about 1745
Diameter: 8.75 in. (222 mm)
2000.61.106

The vibrantly painted coat of arms in the center of this plate is surrounded by four panels on the border containing alternating views of Plymouth Sound, on the southwest coast of England, and the anchorage at Whampoa on the Pearl River in China. The brown tower is the Eddystone Lighthouse near Plymouth; the gray tower is one of the pagodas, possibly the Yellow Pagoda, near Canton. The views were based on more detailed and accurate images that appeared on a service made for William Anson, an English admiral. Chinese decorators integrated a simplified version of these panels into their repertoire and used them to ornament a number of armorial services throughout the 1740s. This plate is from a service made for John, 5th Viscount Arbuthnott, of Scotland. Arbuthnott and his wife, Jean Morrison, ordered two armorial services, of which this is the more elaborate.[84]

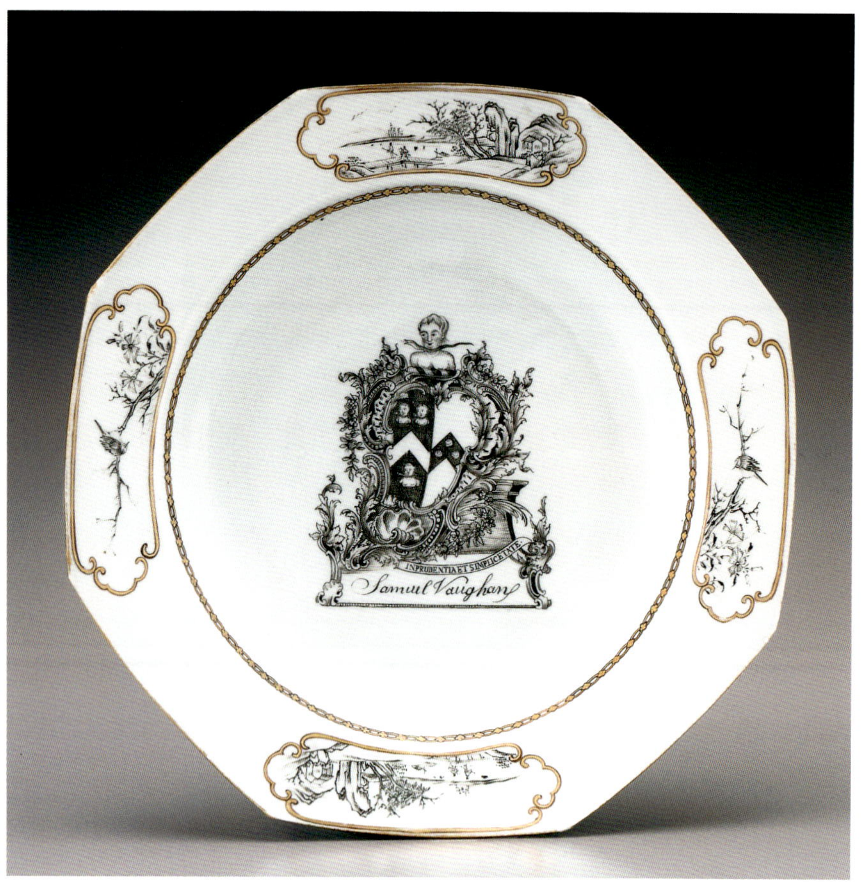

32 SOUP PLATE

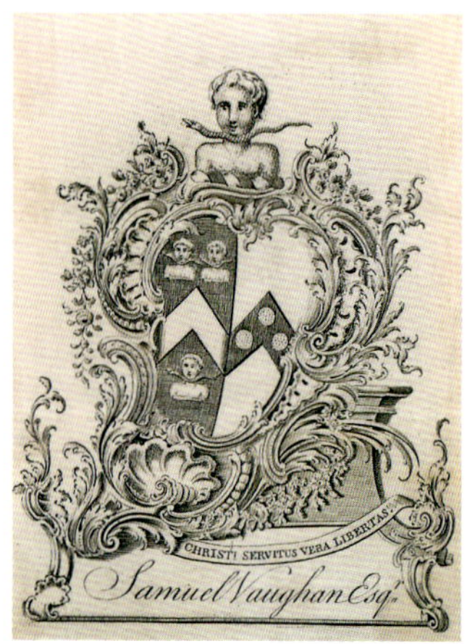

Bookplate of Samuel Vaughan, Esq., probably England, 1747–50. Ink on paper; H. 4.125 in. 00x126.165 Winterthur Library, gift of Martha Gandy Fales.

Jingdezhen, China; 1747–55
Diameter: 8.875 in. (225 mm)
L03.2775.57

This soup plate is from one of at least three armorial services made for Samuel and Sarah Vaughan. Vaughan was an English merchant who married Sarah Hallowell of Boston in 1747. They ordered their armorial porcelain soon after, making this one of the earliest Chinese armorial services with an American connection. The coat of arms is copied directly from the Vaughans' bookplate, which was probably engraved shortly after their marriage.[85]

Vaughan owned estates in England, Jamaica, and America, and in 1783 he and his family took up residence in Philadelphia. Ardent supporters of American independence, the Vaughans were friends of Benjamin Franklin and George Washington and even commissioned a portrait of Washington from Gilbert Stuart. Vaughan was vice president of the American Philosophical Society (founded by Franklin) and designed the garden at the Pennsylvania State House (now Independence Hall).[86]

LITERATURE

Illustrated in Howard and Ayers, *China for the West,* 2:486–87.

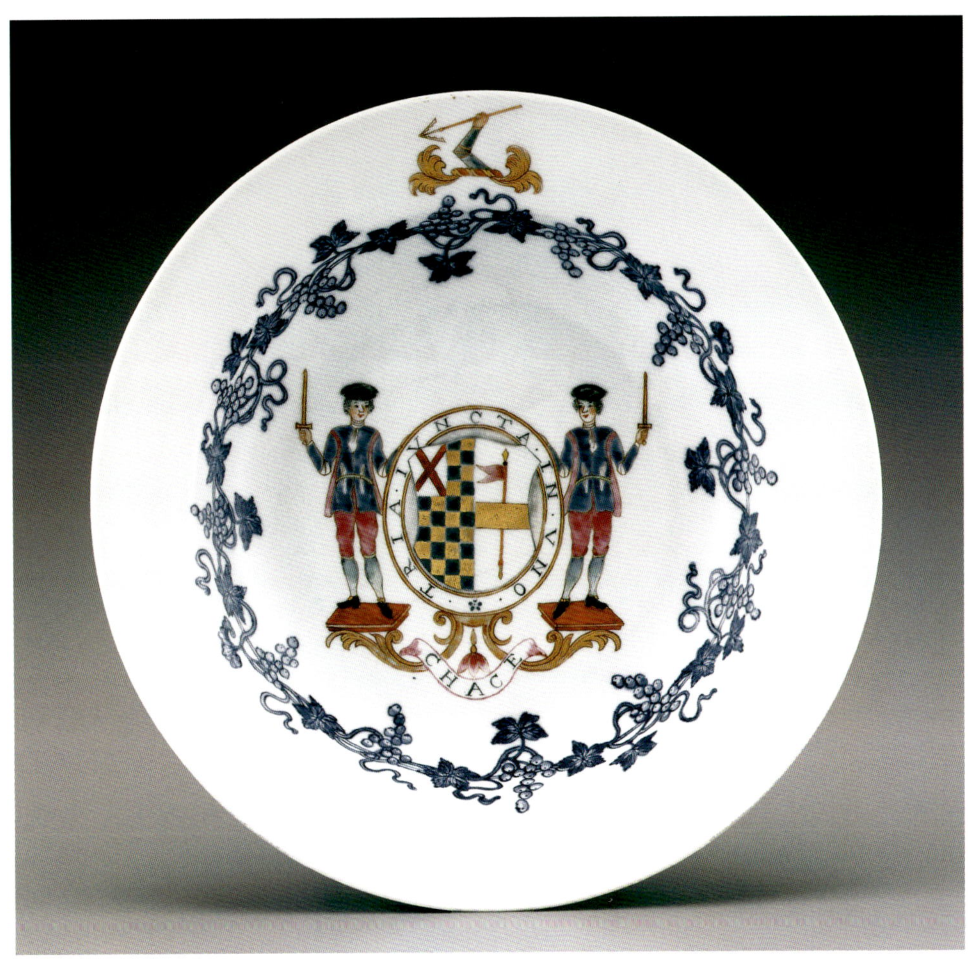

33 PLATE

Jingdezhen, China; about 1750
Diameter: 8.875 in. (225 mm)
L03.2775.62

An unusual and rare underglaze-blue border decorates this dish from a service made for Sir Peter Warren, a vice admiral in the British Navy, and his wife, Anna Susanna De Lancey, daughter of Stephen and Anne van Cortlandt De Lancey of New York. It was not uncommon for English and American families to intermarry in the 18th century; after all, the colonies were part of Britain. Warren had considerable estates in America—in particular, Johnson Hall in upstate New York, which he gave to his nephew Sir William Johnson—but is not known to have actually lived here.[87]

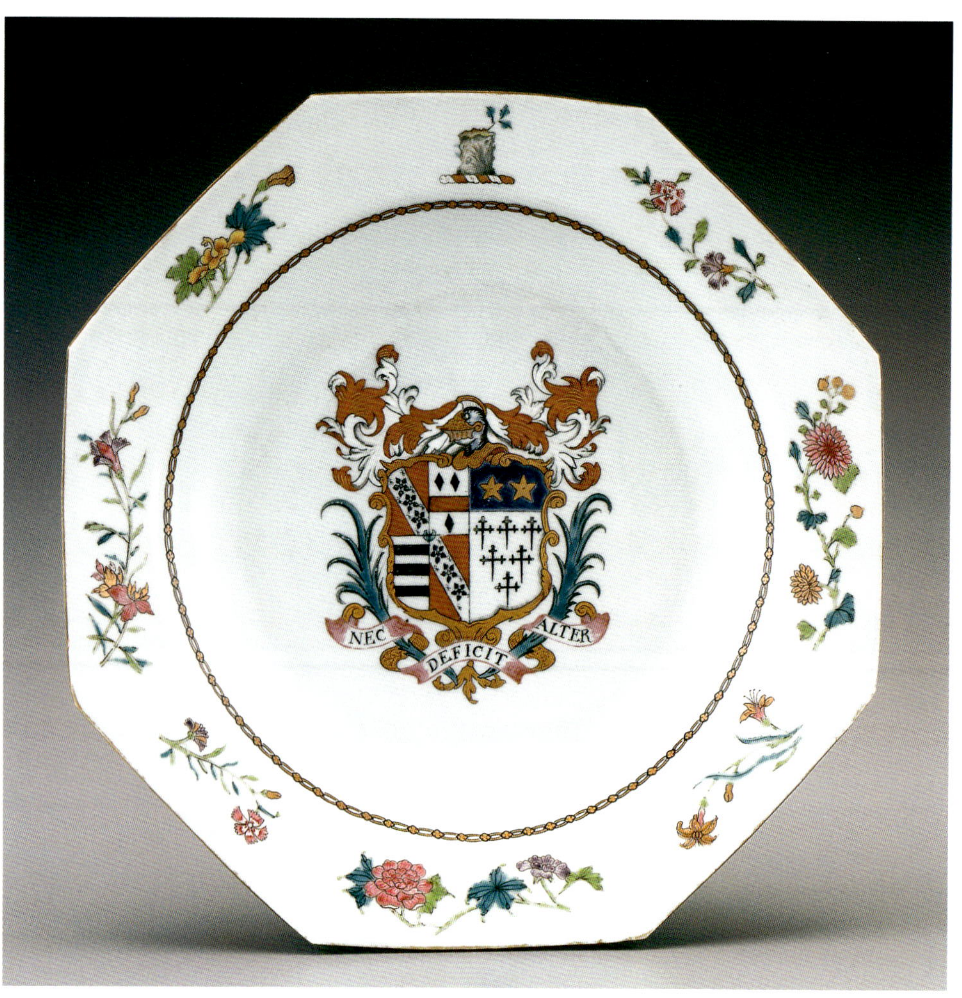

34 SOUP PLATE

Jingdezhen, China; about 1750
Diameter: 8.625 in. (219 mm)
L03.2775.65

This soup plate is decorated with a chain border around the well and simple floral sprays on the rim—one of the more popular designs on export porcelain made about 1750. Octagonal plates were also popular at that time. This particular plate is from a service belonging to Robert Roddam, a captain in the British Navy, and his wife, Lucy Clinton, daughter of Henry Clinton of New York. The service was almost certainly ordered between 1749, the year they were married, and 1750, the year Lucy died in childbirth.[88]

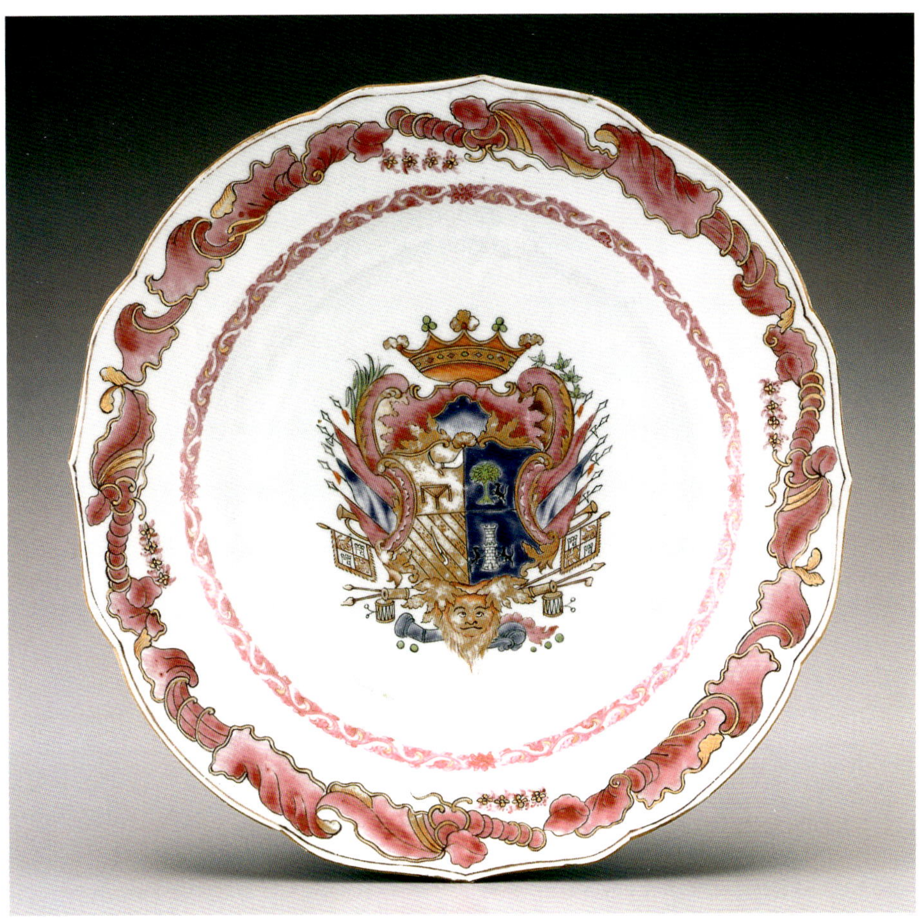

35 PLATE

Jingdezhen, China; about 1750
Diameter: 9 in. (230 mm)
L03.2775.6

This plate, made for a Spanish count, is decorated with elaborate rococo-style leafy scrolls and shells, which were popular as border decoration from about 1740 into the 1760s. The border was favored not just in Spain; it also appears on a service made for the Pignatelli family of Italy, and simplified versions were used on porcelain made for the Dutch and English.[89]

Export porcelain was created for the Spanish market beginning in the 16th century. Although Spain had lost its position of dominance in the 17th century, it continued to be active in the China Trade into the 19th century. While other Europeans reached China by sailing south and then east around Africa and through the Indian Ocean, Spanish traders sailed west to the coast of Mexico, traveling overland to the Pacific and then by ship to the Philippines. There they acquired goods from Chinese merchants who brought items from the mainland.

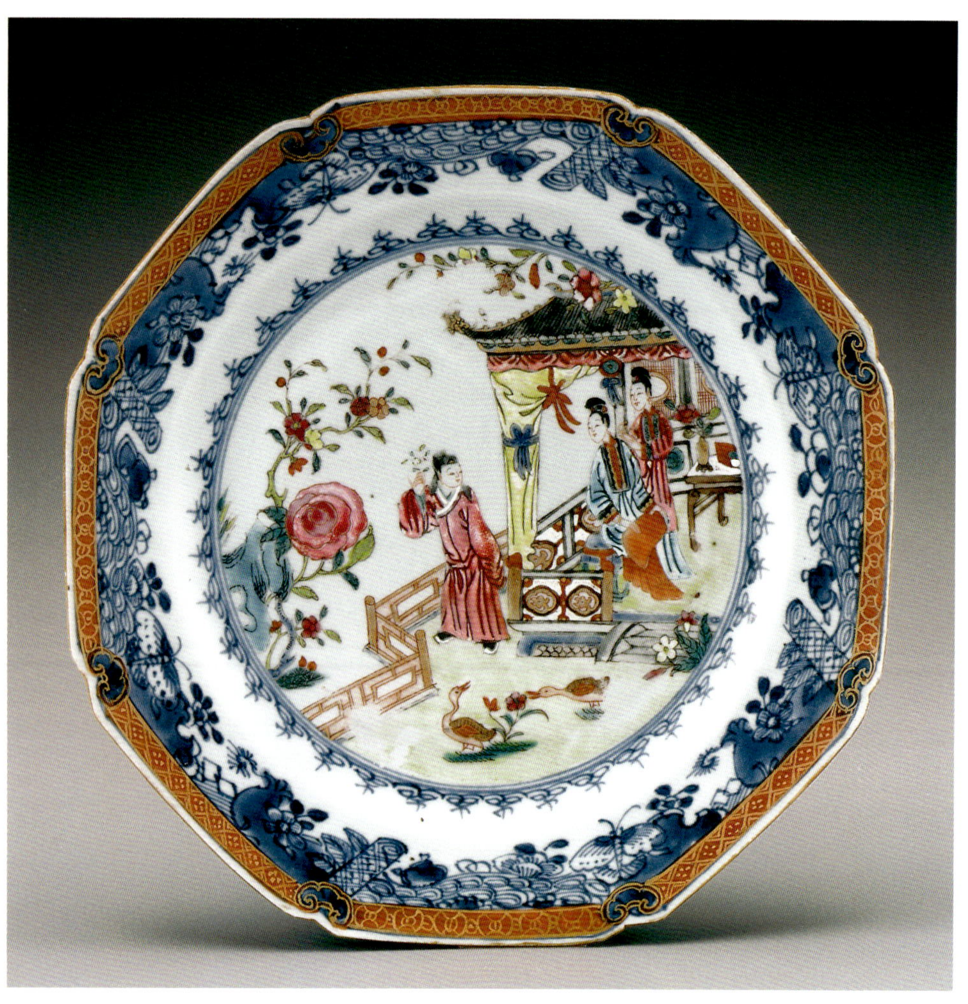

36 PLATE

Jingdezhen, China; about 1755
Diameter: 9 in. (230 mm)
2000.61.104

Porcelain decorated with large, central scenes was popular from the 1740s to the 1770s. Chinese views were especially favored, and those of Chinese men and women in gardens and pavilions were often known in the period as Mandarin or Image ware. In 1757 a young George Washington ordered a "Compleat sett fine Image china" that was decorated with scenes of Chinese men, women, and children in a garden.[90]

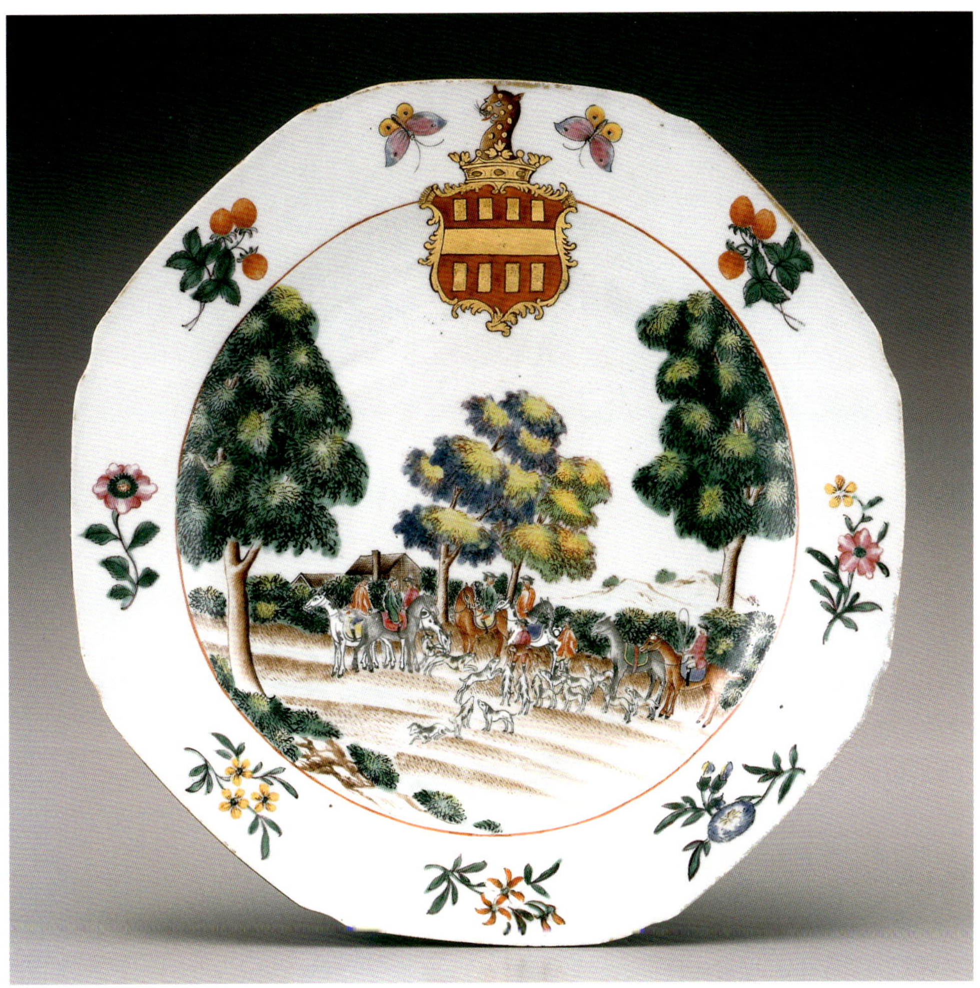

37 PLATE

Jingdezhen, China; about 1755
Diameter: 8.75 in. (224 mm)
2003.47.23

The foxhunting scene on this plate is based on a print—probably by Anthony Walker—of a painting entitled *The Death of the Fox,* by Englishman James Seymour. The image is the last in a set of four depicting the stages of a hunt: *Going Out in the Morning, Brushing into Cover, In Full Chase,* and *Death of the Fox.*[91]

Foxhunting was a popular sport among the gentry of 18th-century England, and Seymour's paintings were well regarded. They were reproduced as prints that were then copied onto export porcelain. In addition to this service, created for the May family of London and Sussex, a number of punch bowls decorated with similar images were produced during the third quarter of the 18th century (see entry 87).

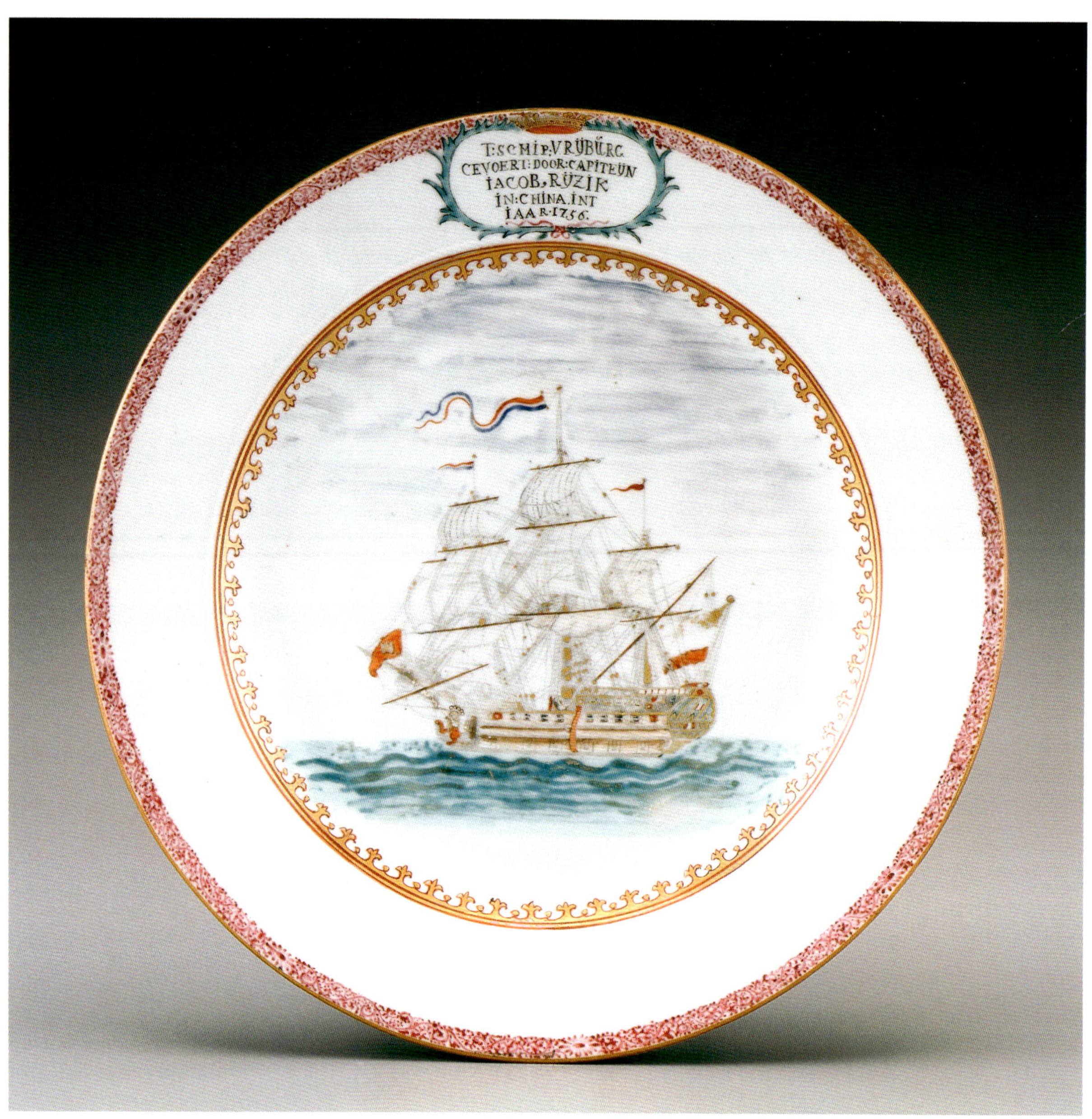
T:SCHIP:VRŸBŰRG
CEVOERT:DOOR:CAPITEUN
IACOB.RŸZIK
IN:CHINA.INT
IAAR.1756.

38 PLATE

Jingdezhen, China; 1756
Diameter: 9 in. (230 mm)
2003.47.6

Captains and crewmembers often purchased porcelain decorated with ships as souvenirs of their voyages to China, but few ordered any as specific as this example commissioned in 1756 by Capt. Jacob Ryzik of the Dutch East Indiaman *Vryburg.* The plate is decorated with a view of the ship and the inscription in Dutch "Portrait of the Ship *Vryburg,* Captain Jacob Ryzik in China in 1756."[92]

The *Vryburg* was a typical Dutch East Indiaman. Built in 1748, she weighed 1,150 tons, measured more than 140 feet long, and enjoyed a relatively long life for a ship active in the China Trade—remaining in service until 1771. During the typical round-trip voyage from the Netherlands to China and back, which could have lasted as long as two years, the vessel would have been home to more than 100 seamen, merchants, and soldiers.[93]

This plate was almost certainly decorated in an enameling workshop in Canton. Although most depictions of ships on export porcelain were based on prints, this one may actually be a portrait of the *Vryburg.* The inclusion of a gangplank suggests that the image was made when the ship was anchored at Whampoa, near Canton. Surprisingly, Captain Ryzik was not alone in commemorating his voyage; his first mate, Christiaan Schoonman, also commissioned similar plates.[94]

LITERATURE

Illustrated in Howard, *Choice of the Private Trader,* p. 99; Howard and Ayers, *China for the West,* 1:222.

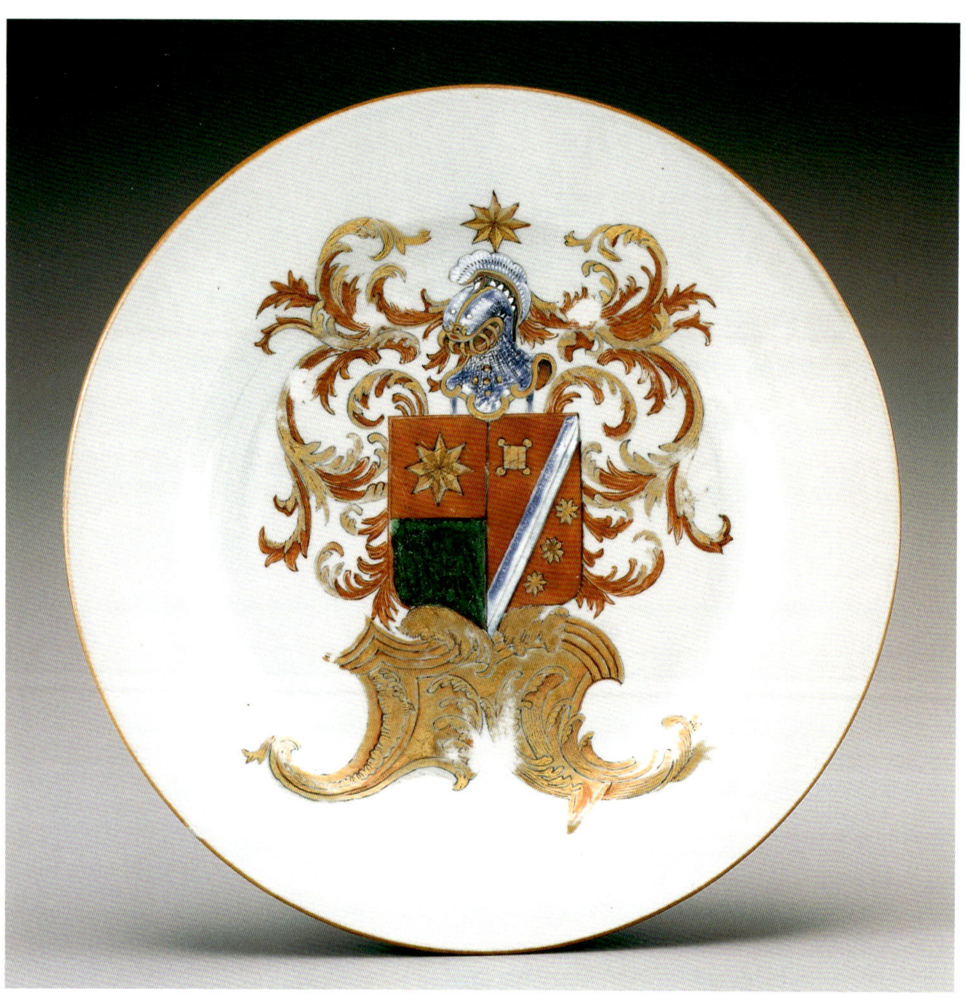

39 PLATE

Jingdezhen, China; 1760–65
Diameter: 9 in. (230 mm)
L03.2775.67

This plate is unusual in that the coat of arms is its only decoration. Armorial porcelain was normally highly decorated, and the lack of ornament, even a border at the rim, is rare. The arms, with an elaborate rococo-style plinth, belong to the De Heere family of the Netherlands. The service may have been made for Huijbert Johan de Heere, who served in the Dutch East India Company and spent time in the East in the 1740s and 1750s, returning to the Netherlands in 1763.[95]

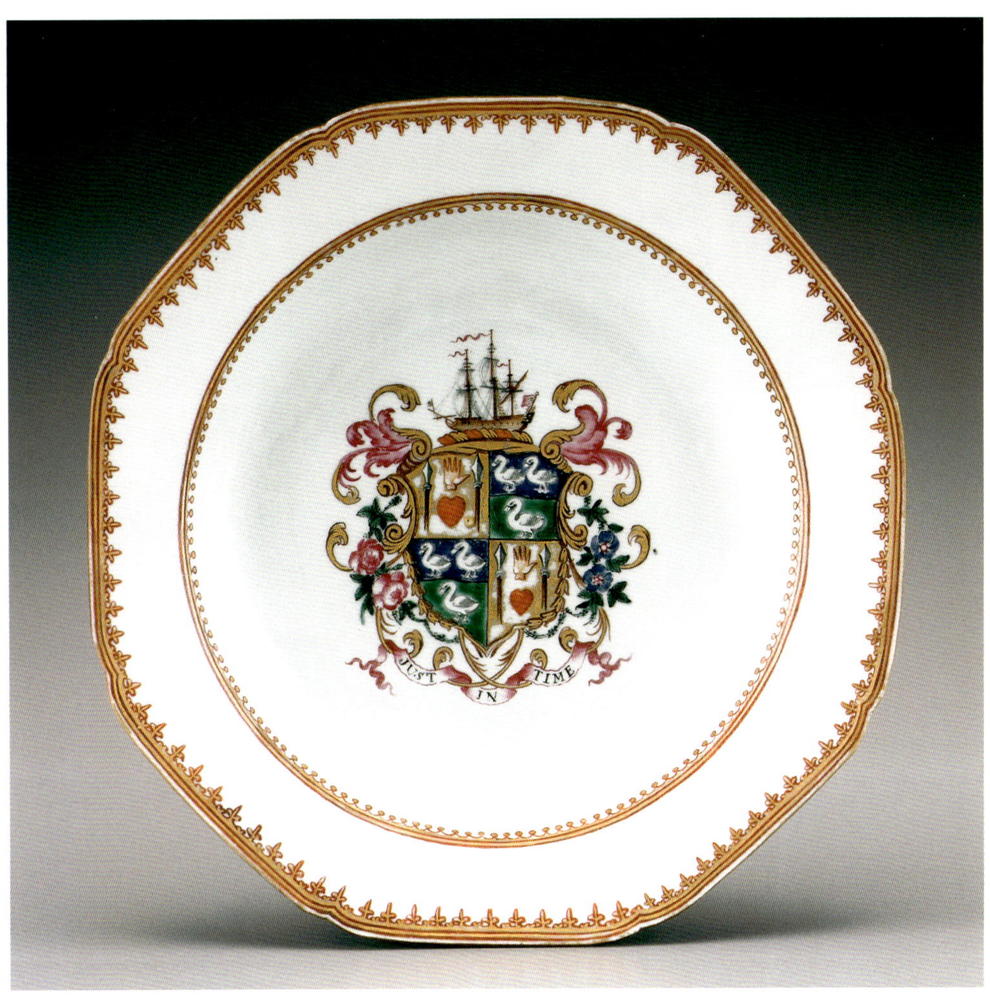

40 SOUP PLATE

Jingdezhen, China; about 1770
Diameter: 8.625 in. (219 mm)
L03.2775.70

This soup plate is decorated with a gilded spearhead border, which was among the most popular border designs from about 1735 to 1790. The plate carries the arms of the Milligan family of Ireland and England and was probably made for London merchant David Milligan. The crest is a merchant ship flying the flag of the British East India Company, which may be a reference to Milligan's livelihood. Other members of his family are known to have been involved in overseas trade; his brother and heir, Robert, was chairman and a founder of the West India Dock Company, which built an enormous dock complex in London to handle trade with the West Indies.[96]

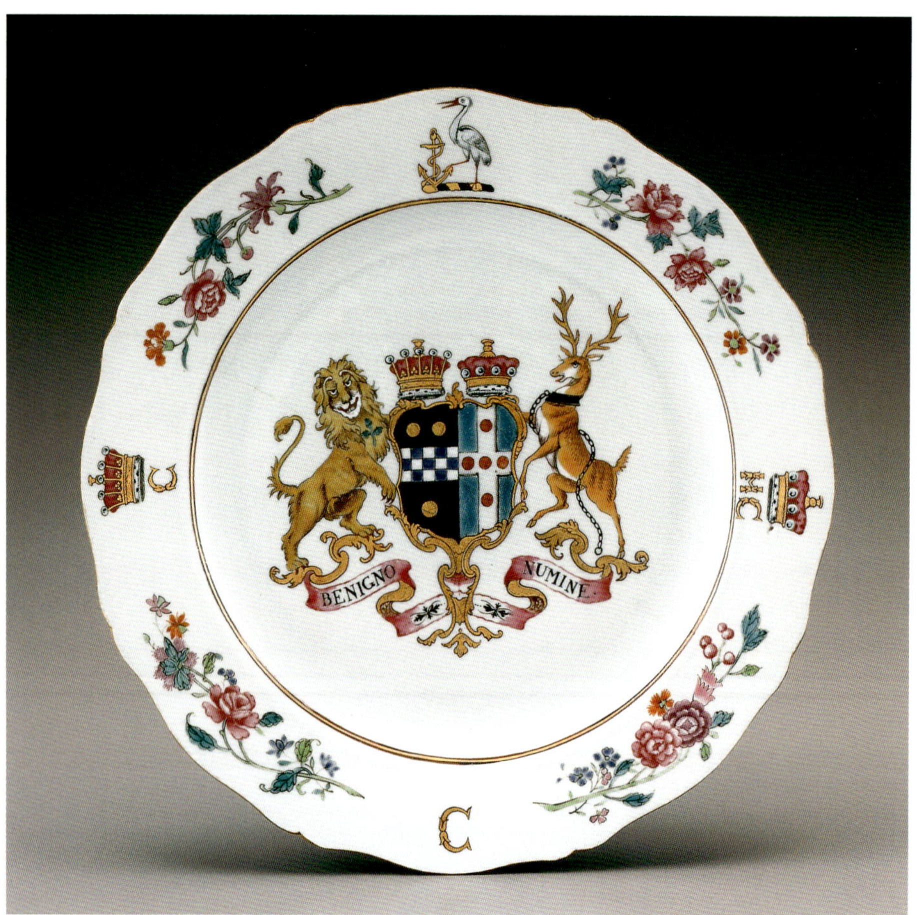

41 PLATE

Jingdezhen, China; 1772
Diameter: 9 in. (230 mm)
L03.2775.66

This plate is part of a large service that was a gift from the British East India Company to William Pitt, prime minister of Great Britain and one of 18th-century England's most able statesmen. Pitt entered Parliament in 1735 and rose to become prime minister, first from 1757 to 1761 and then again from 1766 to 1768. He is best known for his leadership during the Seven Years' War and for his opposition to harsh British policies toward the American colonies in the 1760s and 1770s.

Pitt was the son of a member of Parliament and the grandson of Thomas Pitt, an East India Company officer who built the family fortune by purchasing a diamond in India that he resold for great profit to the French royal family, who placed it in the crown of France. Despite his great wealth, William Pitt was known as the Great Commoner and remained in the House of Commons for much of his career. His wife, Hester Grenville, was made Baroness of Chatham in 1761, but Pitt himself was not created a peer until 1766, when he received the title Viscount Pitt and Earl of Chatham.[97]

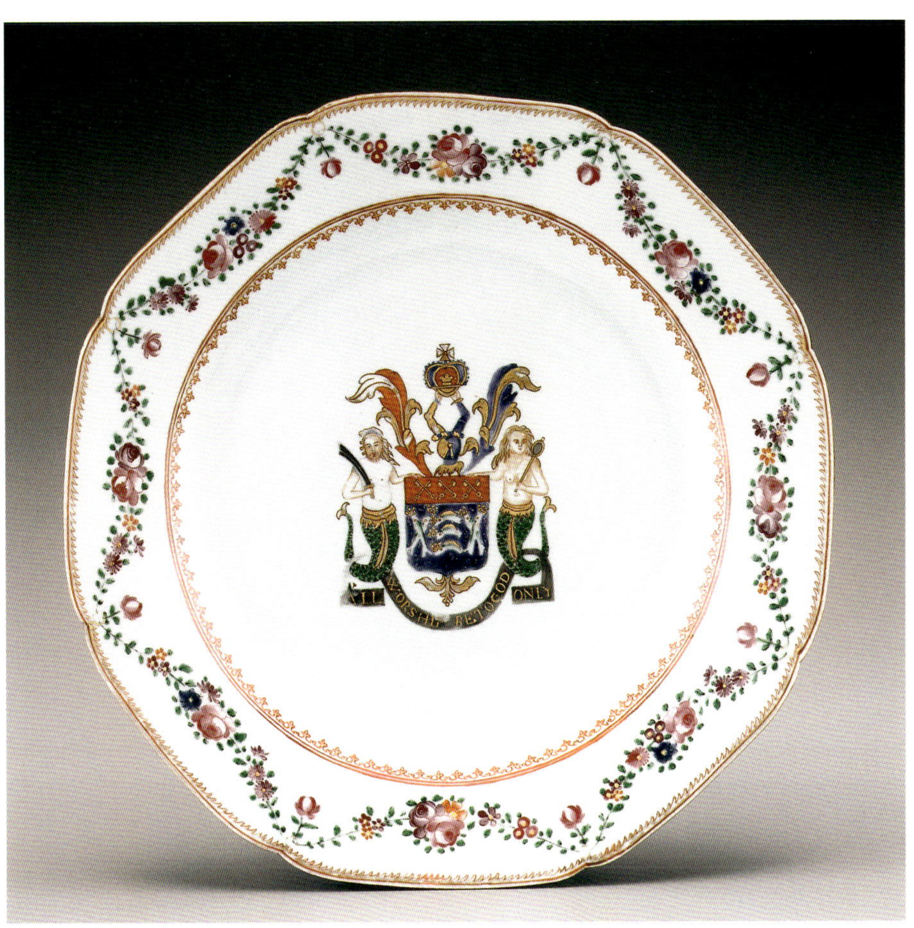

42 PLATE

Jingdezhen, China; about 1775
Diameter: 9 in. (230 mm)
L03.2775.42

Although most armorial porcelain was made for families, some was created for organizations, such as this plate from a dinner service decorated with the arms of the Fishmongers' Company, one of the guilds of London. Like many arms, this one contains visual references to the Fishmongers' source of income; the supporters are a merman and a mermaid, and three dolphins decorate the shield. The plate is from one of three export porcelain services made for the company and would have been used at ceremonial dinners held at their hall in London. The floral swags on the rim were copied from engraved decoration on silver and were popular as a border design in the 1770s.[98]

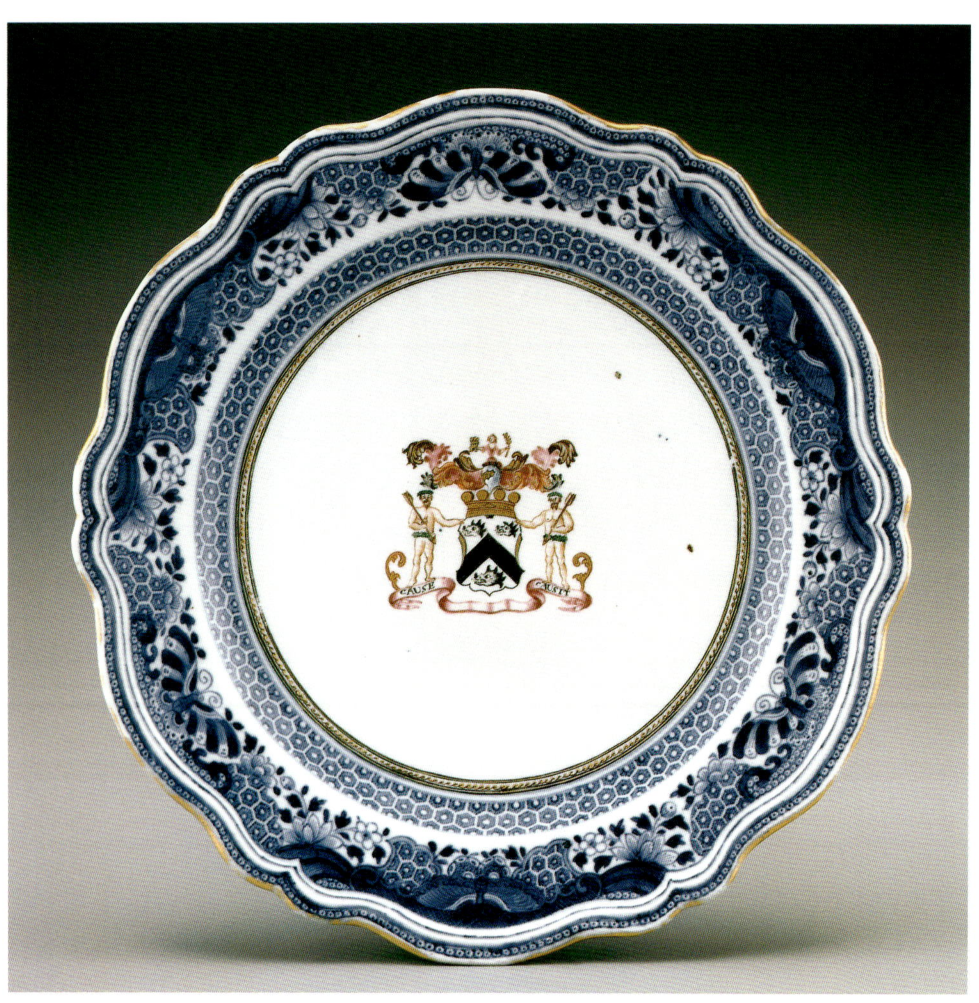

43 PLATE

Jingdezhen, China; about 1780
Diameter: 9.5 in. (241 mm)
L03.2775.10

The elaborate latticework border on this plate, with butterflies painted in underglaze blue, is known as the Fitzhugh border and was popular on export porcelain made in the 1780s. The name, however, is inaccurate. Although it comes from the Fitzhugh family of England, who ordered blue and white porcelain about 1780, this border did not appear on that service although later services with the Fitzhugh central design and this border were made about 1800. The term *Fitzhugh* was eventually applied to this border design in the early 20th century by ceramics manufacturers, collectors, and curators. This plate is from a service made for Baron Elphinstone of Scotland, either Charles, 10th Lord Elphinstone, who died in 1781, or his son, John, who was the 11th Lord Elphinstone.[99]

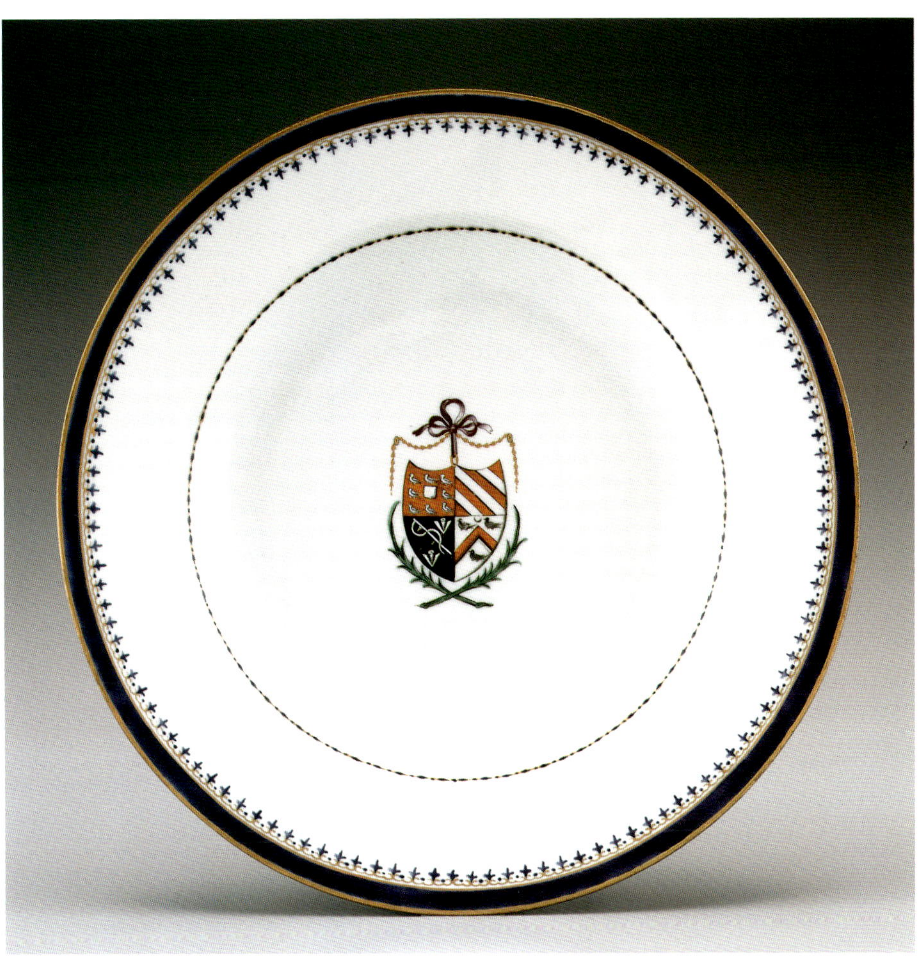

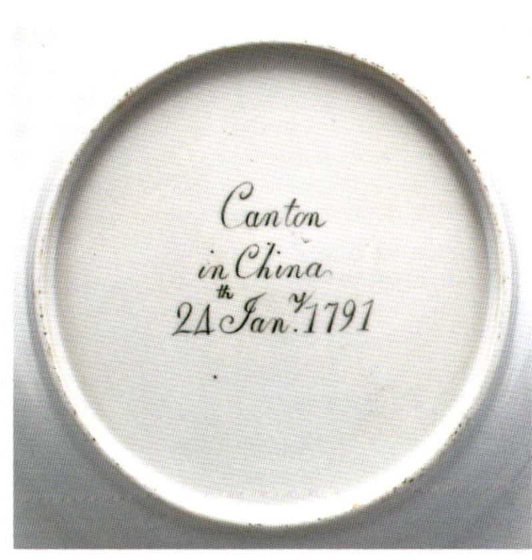

44 PLATE

Jingdezhen, China; 1791
Diameter: 10 in. (254 mm)
L03.2775.105

Each piece of porcelain in this service is marked on the back with the inscription "Canton in China 24th Jany. 1791." This rare inscription provides evidence of how porcelain was ordered. The service was made for a member of the Chadwick family of Staffordshire, England.[100]

By the mid-18th century, porcelain-enameling workshops had been established in Canton, allowing armorials and other specially commissioned designs to be executed far more quickly and cheaply than before, when all work was done in Jingdezhen. This meant that special orders could be filled during one voyage; previously, an order was placed one year and delivered the following year. This particular service seems to have been a last-minute request in Canton; generally ships arrived in China in late summer or early fall and departed in December or January, meaning this service was probably one of the last things loaded on board the vessel before its departure on the voyage to England.

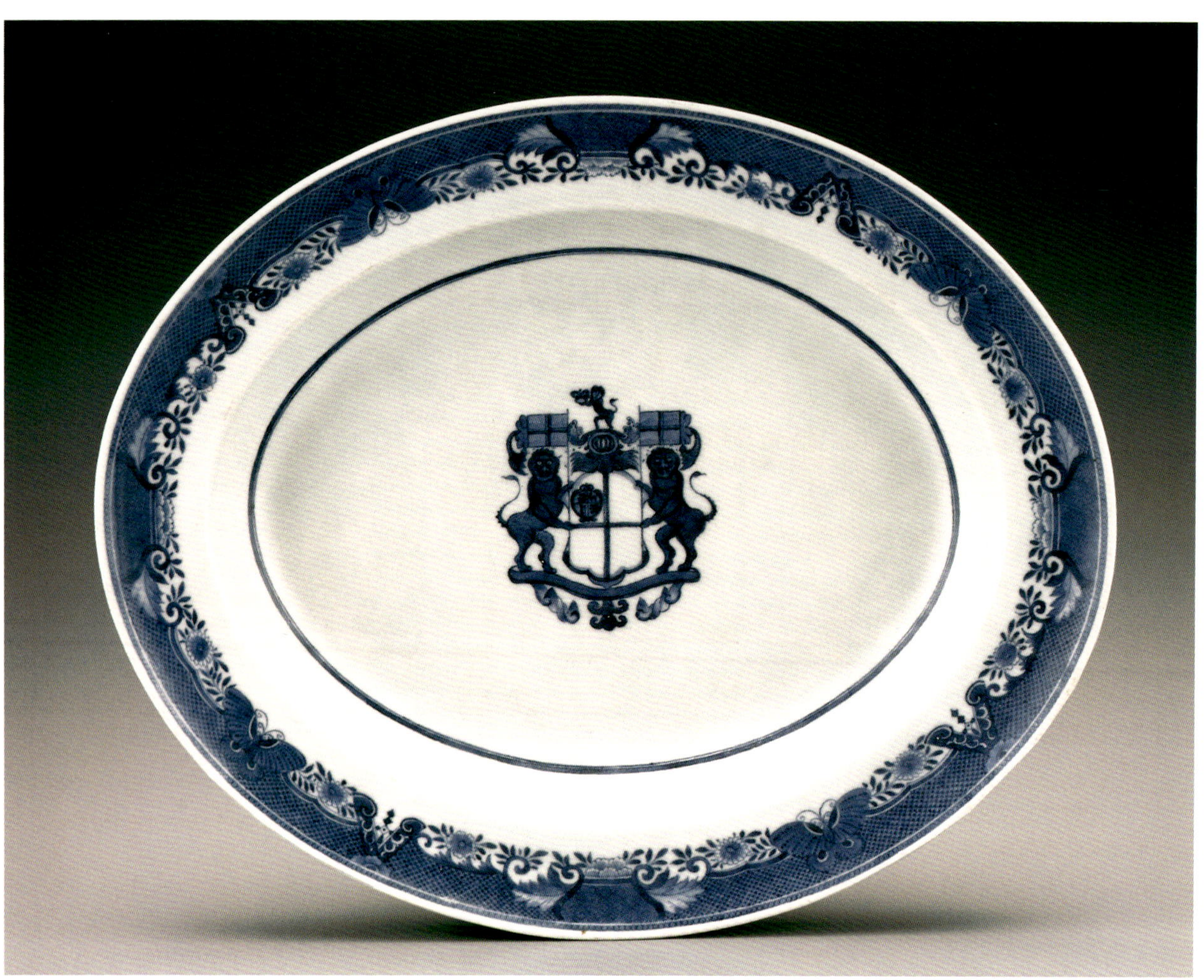

45 PLATTER

Jingdezhen, China; about 1800
Length: 14.625 in. (372 mm)
L03.2775.114

This platter bears the arms of the Honorable East India Company of England, which was arguably the largest trading company the world has ever known. Formed in 1708 by the merger of two rival British companies, the concern controlled trade between Britain and India, Indonesia, and China from the time of its founding until its eventual demise in 1833. This blue and white service, with a design based on the company's bookplate, was made for one of the their trading settlements in the East. Other overglaze-enamel services were also made for use on company ships or in their trading settlements.[101]

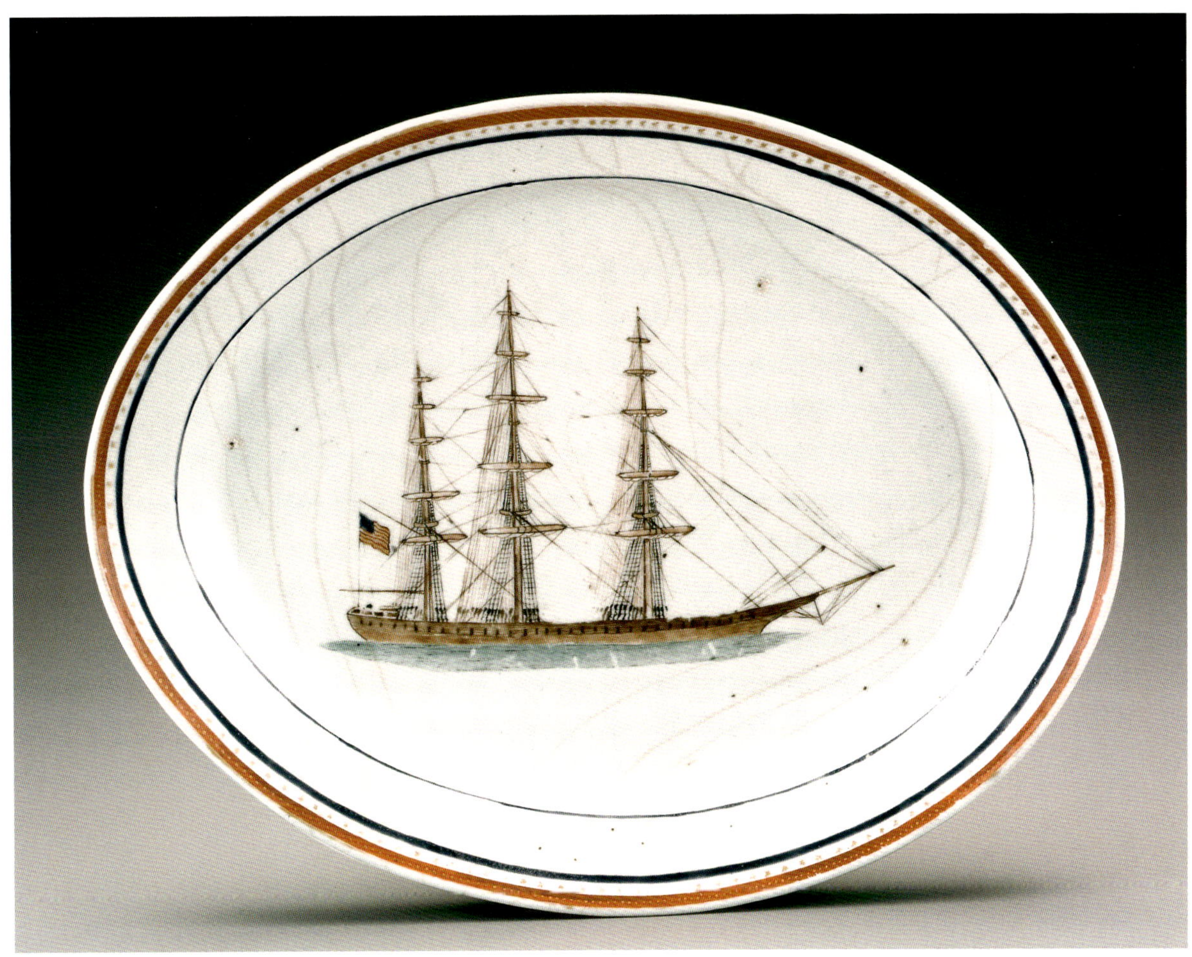

46 PLATTER

Jingdezhen, China; about 1850
Length: 14.625 in. (372 mm)
L03.2775.59

In the 19th century, America dominated the China Trade with sleek, fast ships like the one depicted on this dish. The vessel, with its raked bow and heavy rigging, probably dates to the 1850s; the image was most likely copied from a print.[102] The thick body of the plate, which has cracked and become stained, is typical of the inexpensive porcelain made for export in the mid-19th century.

LITERATURE
Illustrated in Howard and Ayers, *China for the West,* 1:229.

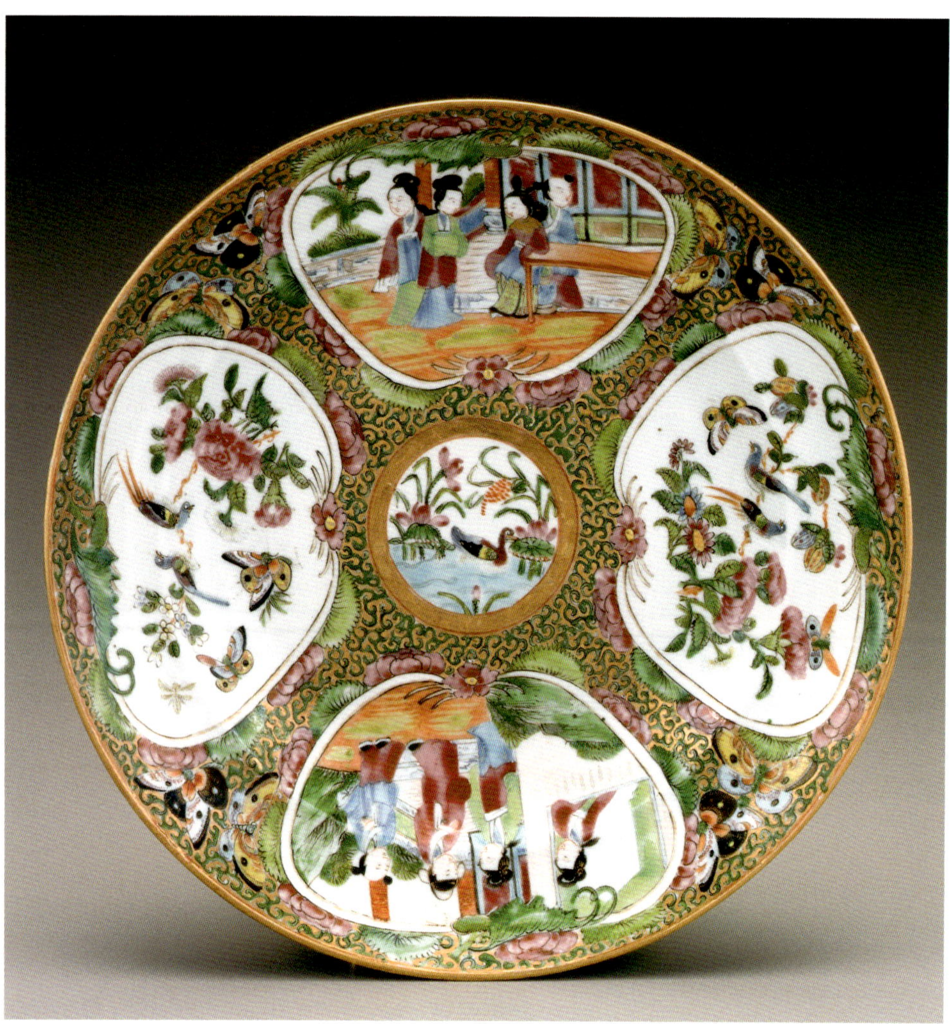

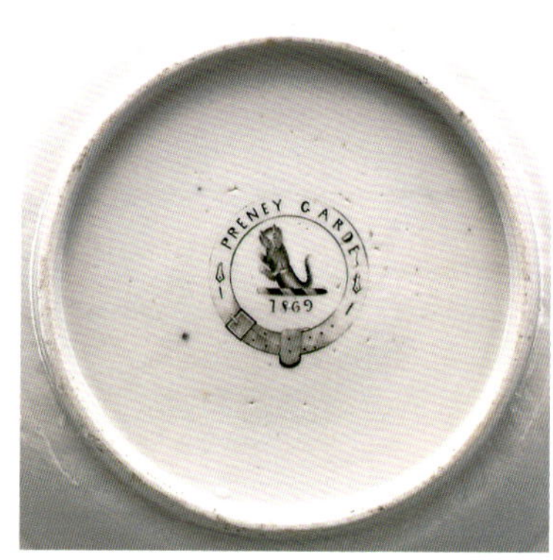

47 DISH

Jingdezhen, China; 1869
Diameter: 10 in. (254 mm)
L03.2775.24

This dish is decorated in an elaborate floral and figural design known as the rose medallion pattern, which was popular in the mid-19th century. The name refers to the central medallion surrounded by four quadrants containing floral and figural scenes.

This dish is part of a tea service made for a member of either the Mackintosh or Rickard families, whose crest and motto as well as the date 1869 are painted on the underside. The families had branches in both Britain and America, and it is likely that the dish was made for an American member of the family.[103]

LITERATURE

Illustrated in Howard, *Chinese Armorial Porcelain,* 2:702.

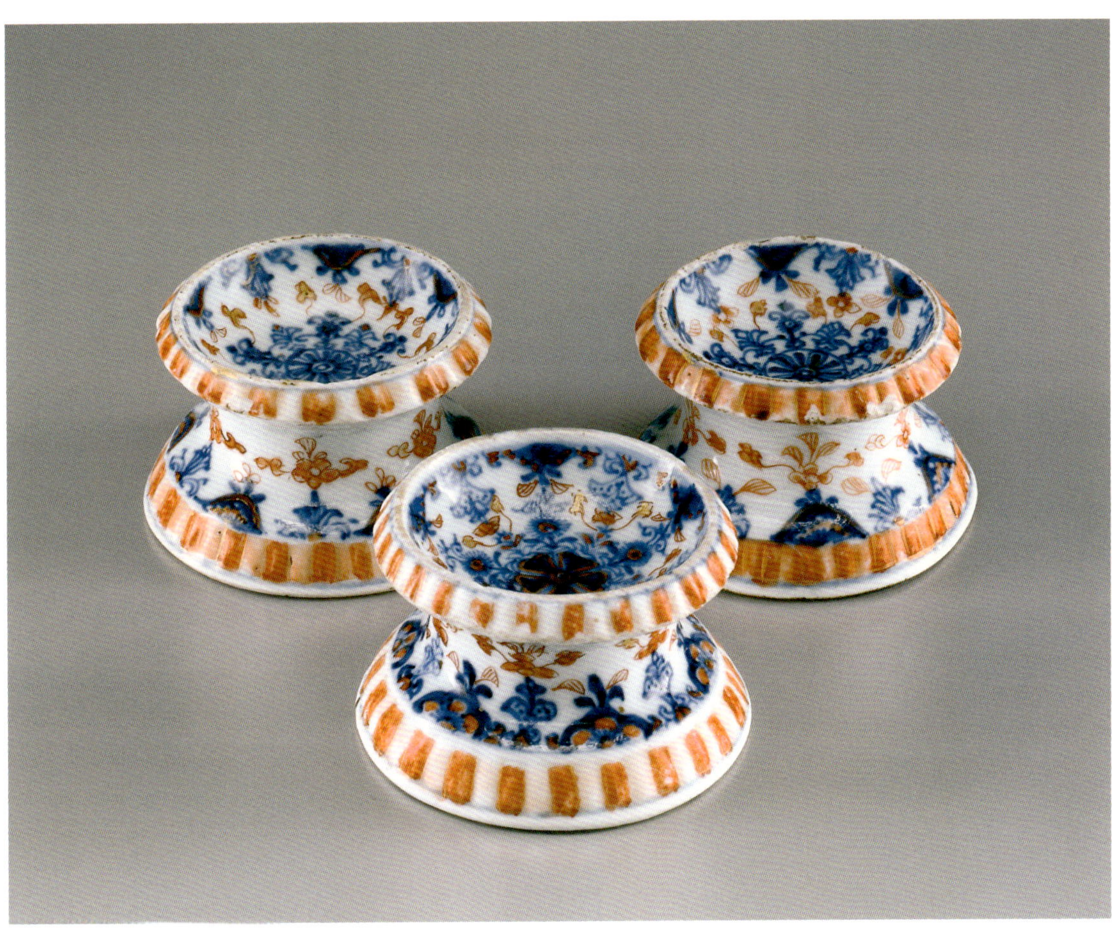

48 SET OF THREE SALTS

Jingdezhen, China; 1720–50
Diameter (each): 3.25 in. (82.5 mm)
L03.2775.85.1–.3

These small saltcellars are known as trencher salts because they were meant to be placed on the table next to each place setting, or trencher. This particular design, with a circular body and gadrooned edge, was almost certainly copied from a silver example made at the turn of the 18th century. Some of the red and gold decoration may have been added in Europe.[104]

Salt, a popular and common condiment, has long had specialized containers from which it was dispensed. During the Middle Ages and Renaissance, salt was held in a single large, monumental vessel that served as the centerpiece of the table. These grand, standing salts began to fade from fashion in the mid-17th century and were replaced by multiple smaller salts such as those shown here. A standard 18th-century dinner service would have had four salts.[105]

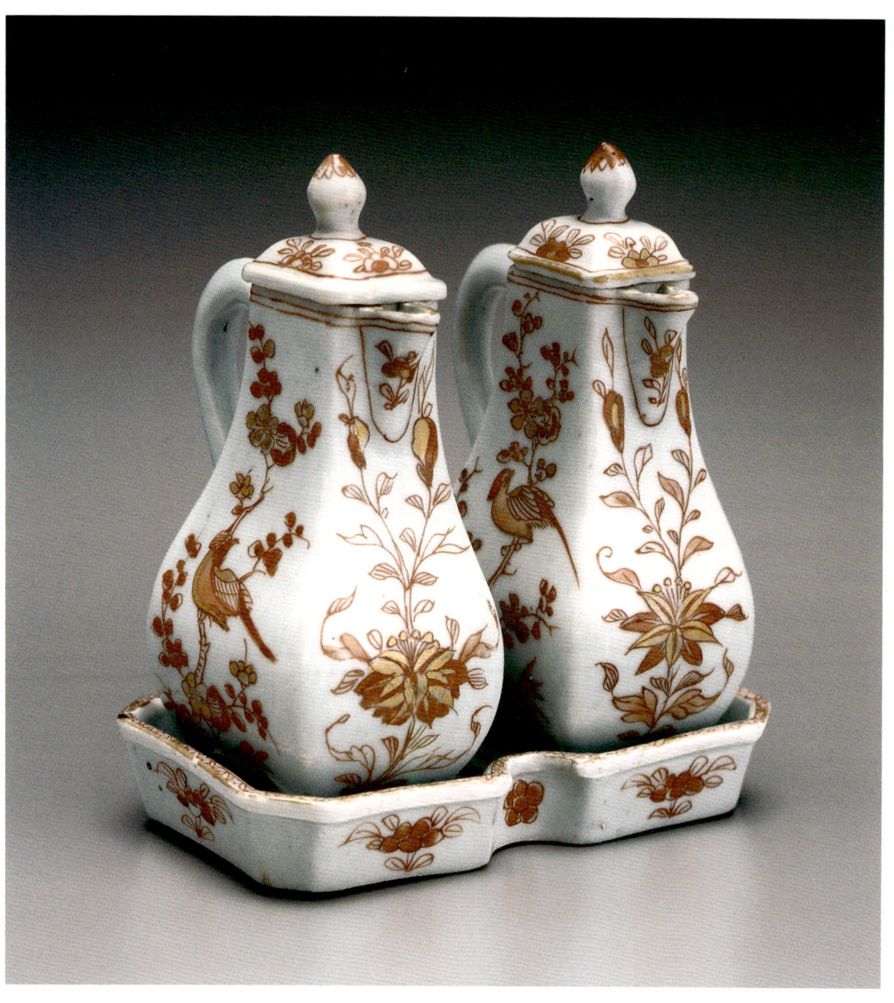

49 CRUET SET

Jingdezhen, China; 1725–50
Length (stand): 5.5 in. (133 mm)
L03.2775.91a–e

These cruets were designed to hold oil and vinegar for dressing salads. Recipes for salads appeared in Italian cookbooks as early as the 15th century, and it is likely that cruets for oil and vinegar were developed in Italy at that time and spread from there throughout Europe. As early as 1612, the Dutch East India Company ordered "small oil and vinegar jars," and they continued to be made throughout the 17th and 18th centuries.[106]

This particular set is rather simple, having only two bottles. More elaborate cruets included additional bottles—for flavored vinegars, ketchups, and even soy sauce—as well as saltcellars and castors for pepper, sugar, and dry mustard.[107] The red and gold decoration was most popular during the second quarter of the 18th century and was sometimes known as blood and milk.

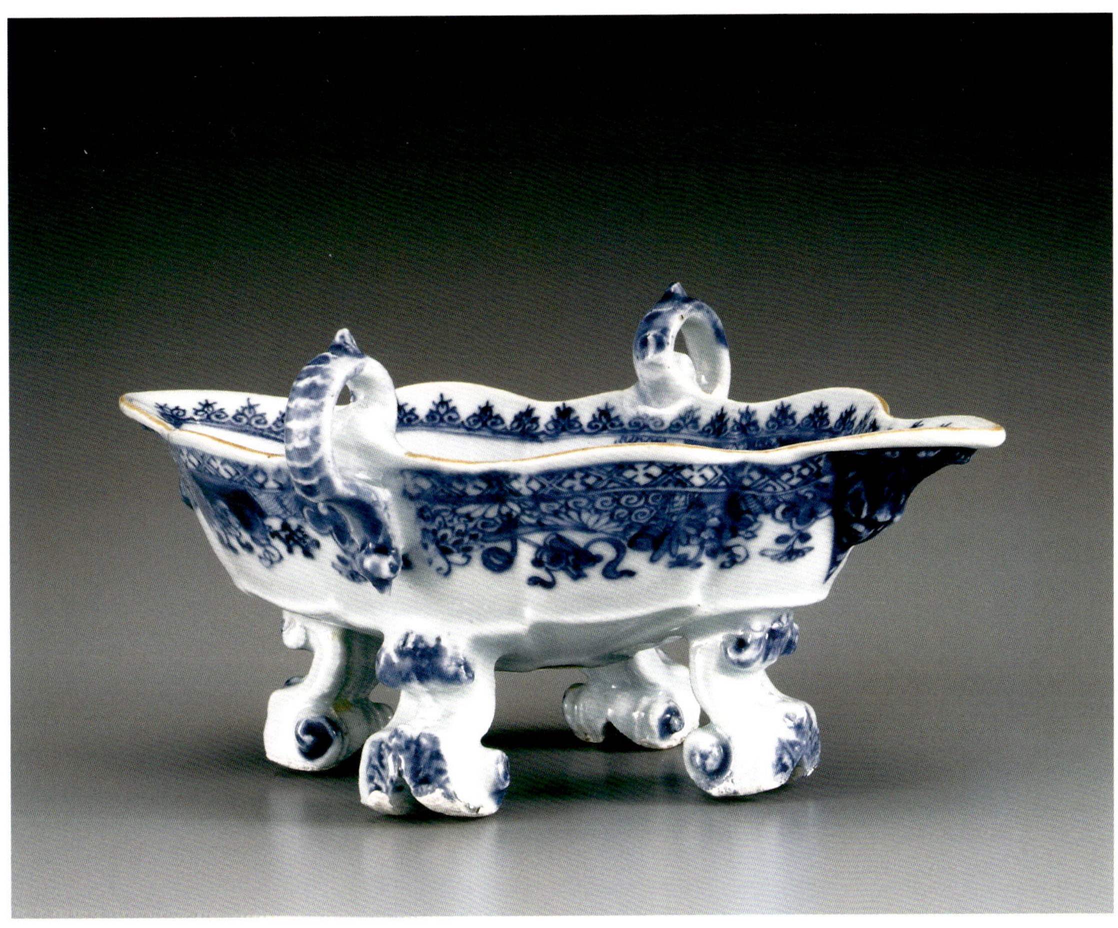

50 SAUCEBOAT

Jingdezhen, China; 1730–50
Length: 9.5 in. (241 mm)
L03.2731.11

The design of this sauceboat was probably copied from a silver example made in the second quarter of the 18th century; it may originally have been one of a pair. The shaped lip, "C" scroll handles, and scrolled feet make it a fine example of baroque design translated into export porcelain.

Sauces were an increasingly important part of the high-style cuisine that emerged in France in the late 17th century at the court of Louis XIV. They were originally served in shallow, circular dishes called saucers. The double-lipped, double-handled form of sauceboat was developed in France in the 1690s and spread quickly throughout Europe. Such sauceboats remained popular until the 1740s, when they were replaced by those having a single spout and handle.[108]

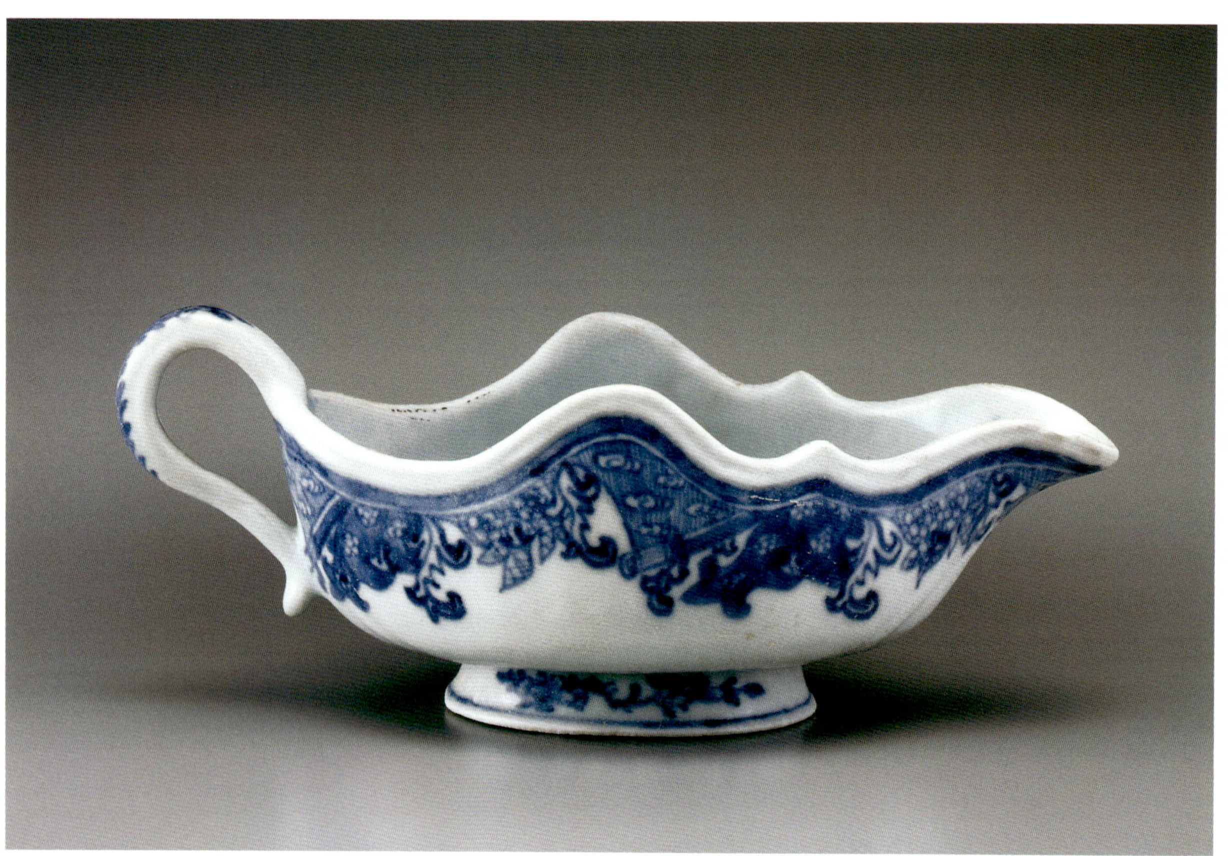

51 SAUCEBOAT

Jingdezhen, China; about 1750
Length: 8.25 in. (210 mm)
2000.61.43

This sauceboat was recovered from the wreck of the Dutch East India Company ship *Geldermalsen,* which sank in 1752 en route from Canton to the Netherlands. The ship was carrying approximately 239,000 pieces of porcelain, the majority of it relatively basic blue and white dining and drinking wares that would have found a ready market among the middle classes of Europe and America. This porcelain was ordered in bulk by the East India companies, who chose pieces that were inexpensive, readily available, and easy to pack as opposed to the more elaborate and expensive special pieces that were acquired through the Private Trade.[109]

This is one of three types of sauceboats recovered from the *Geldermalsen.* Since no sauceboats were listed in the ship's cargo manifests, they were perhaps part of the 171 dinner services on board. The form is probably based on a single-handled silver sauceboat, a style that emerged in the 1740s, replacing the double-handled versions that had been in favor earlier.[110]

LITERATURE

Illustrated in Howard, *Choice of the Private Trader,* pp. 122–23.

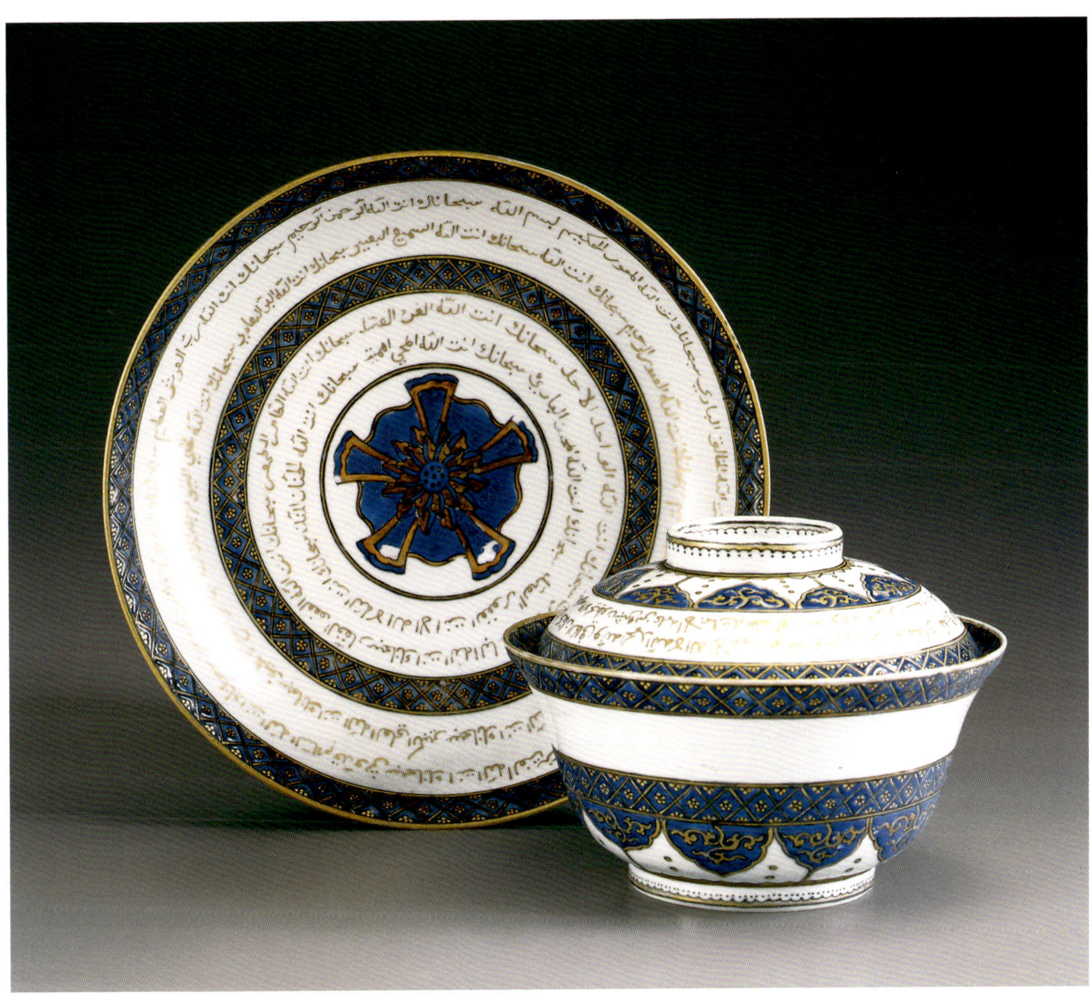

52 COVERED BOWL AND DISH

Jingdezhen, China; about 1770
Diameter (dish): 7.75 in. (197 mm)
L03.2775.13a–c

This covered bowl and dish, decorated with *ayahs* (verses) from the *Qur'an* (Koran), were made for the Islamic market. The Chinese began trading with the Middle East as early as the 10th century and designed and decorated porcelain specifically with that market in mind. Among the forms were large platters and bowls suitable for the communal banquets favored in that region; the decoration consisted mainly of floral designs and calligraphy, as Islamic law forbids the portrayal of human forms.[111]

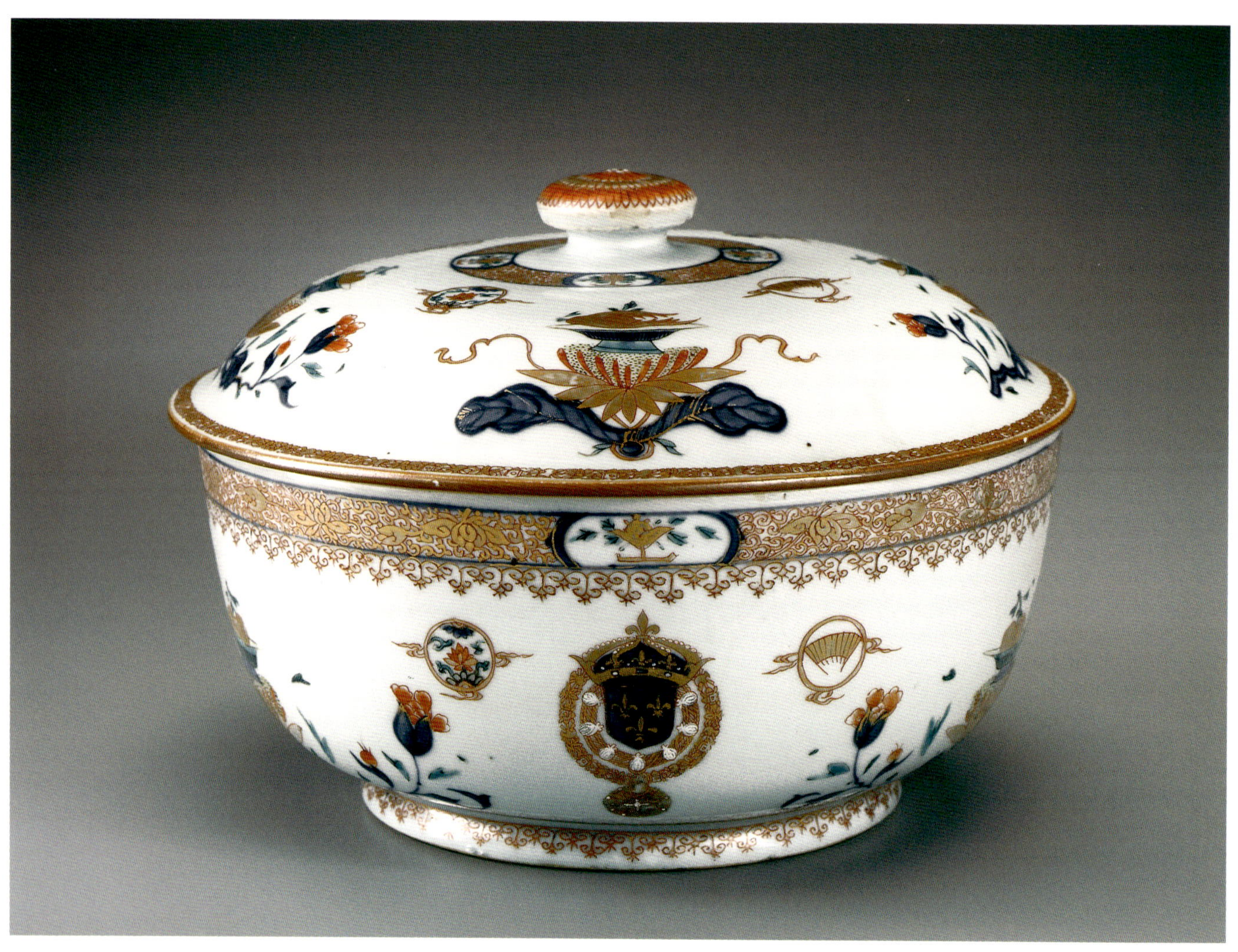

53 TUREEN

Jingdezhen, China; 1725–30
Diameter: 10.5 in. (267 mm)
L03.2775.84a,b

This soup tureen is part of a large and elaborate service decorated with the coat of arms of Louis XV. The service does not appear in the royal inventories of 1718, 1729, or 1775, suggesting it either was owned by the king and disposed of at some point before being inventoried or was bought as a gift for the king but never delivered. It may have been procured through Philippe d'Orléans, regent for Louis XV, who ordered a similar armorial service with his own arms. The French aristocracy had prized Chinese export porcelain since the 14th century, and armorial porcelain became especially popular in the early 1700s after Louis XIV ordered silver dinner services to be melted down during a financial crisis in 1709.[112]

Soup has been consumed since the beginning of time, but it was not until the 1650s that it appeared on fine dining tables. It was part of the first course of a multicourse meal, meant to take the edge off a diner's hunger, and tureens, introduced in the late 17th century, were the centerpiece of the table. One of the earliest references to tureens comes from 1710, when Patrick Lamb, author of *Royal Cookery,* described the vessel as "a terreyne dish, at court . . . made of silver, round and upright, holding about six quarts English measure . . . with the handles such as a small cistern." During this early period, tureens did not have ladles; diners used spoons to serve themselves, taking care to wipe the implements first on bread or a napkin if the utensils had already been used.[113]

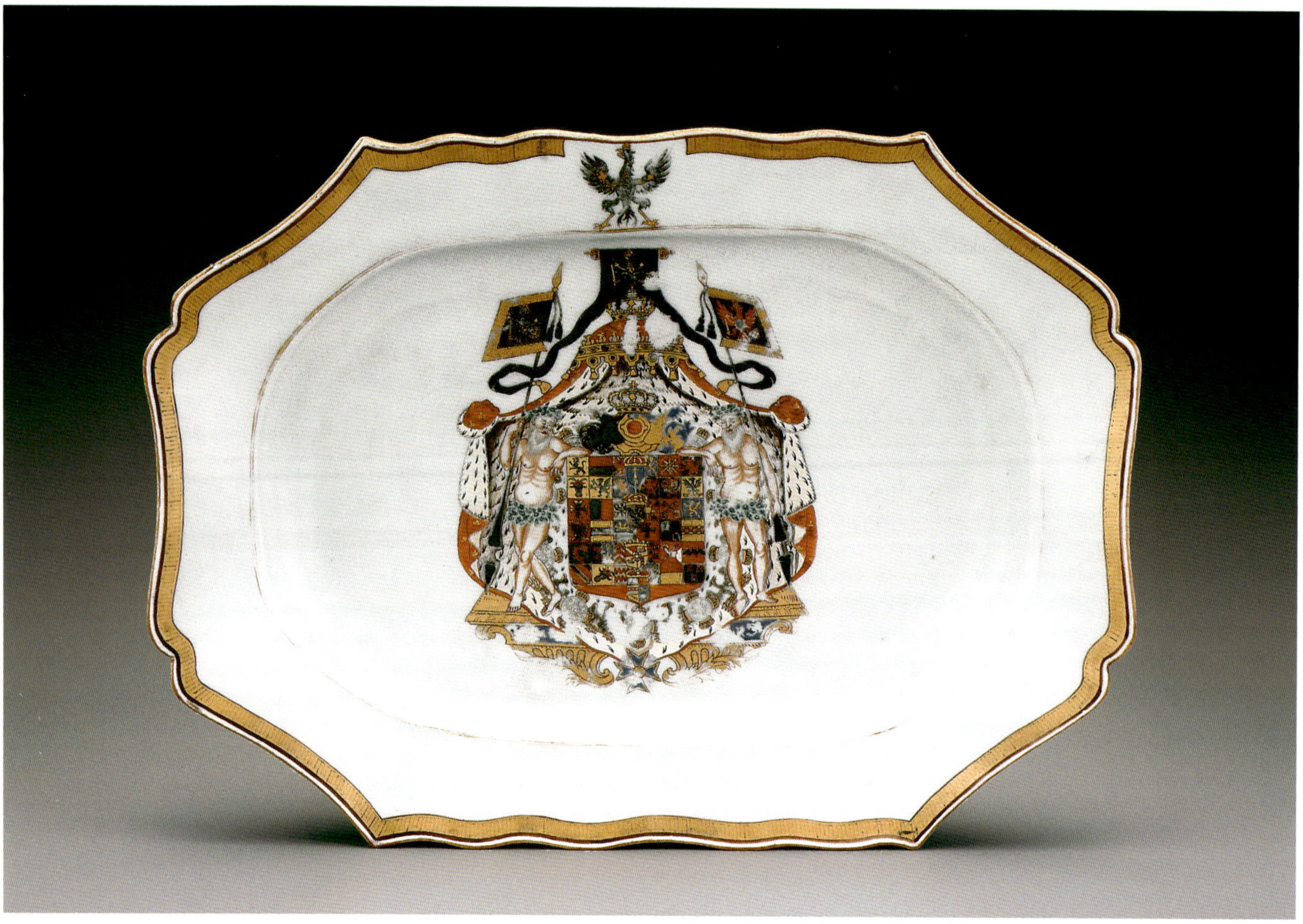

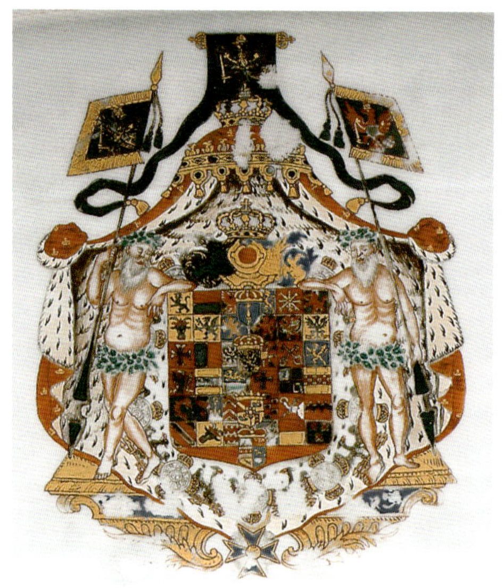

54 TUREEN STAND

Jingdezhen, China; 1750–55
Length: 14 in. (350 mm)
2000.61.38

The incredibly elaborate coat of arms in the center of this tureen stand belongs to Frederick the Great of Prussia. The forty shields represent the full heraldic history of the Hohenzollern family and are draped in an ermine-lined purple mantling and surmounted by a crown. The arms were copied from the original that served as the model for the Wappen Calendar of 1749.[114] The service is thought to have been commissioned by the Königliche Preussische Asiatische Companie zu Emden (Prussian East India Company) as a thank-you gift to the king, the company's founder.

The company might have hoped to find favor with the royal family in order to advance the popularity of export porcelain. Unfortunately, Frederick never enjoyed his porcelain. It was supposedly brought back on the *Prinz von Preussen,* which ran aground near her home port of Emden in 1755. The service was damaged and was therefore not presented to the king but instead was sold on the open market.[115]

LITERATURE
Howard, *Choice of the Private Trader,* pp. 110–11.

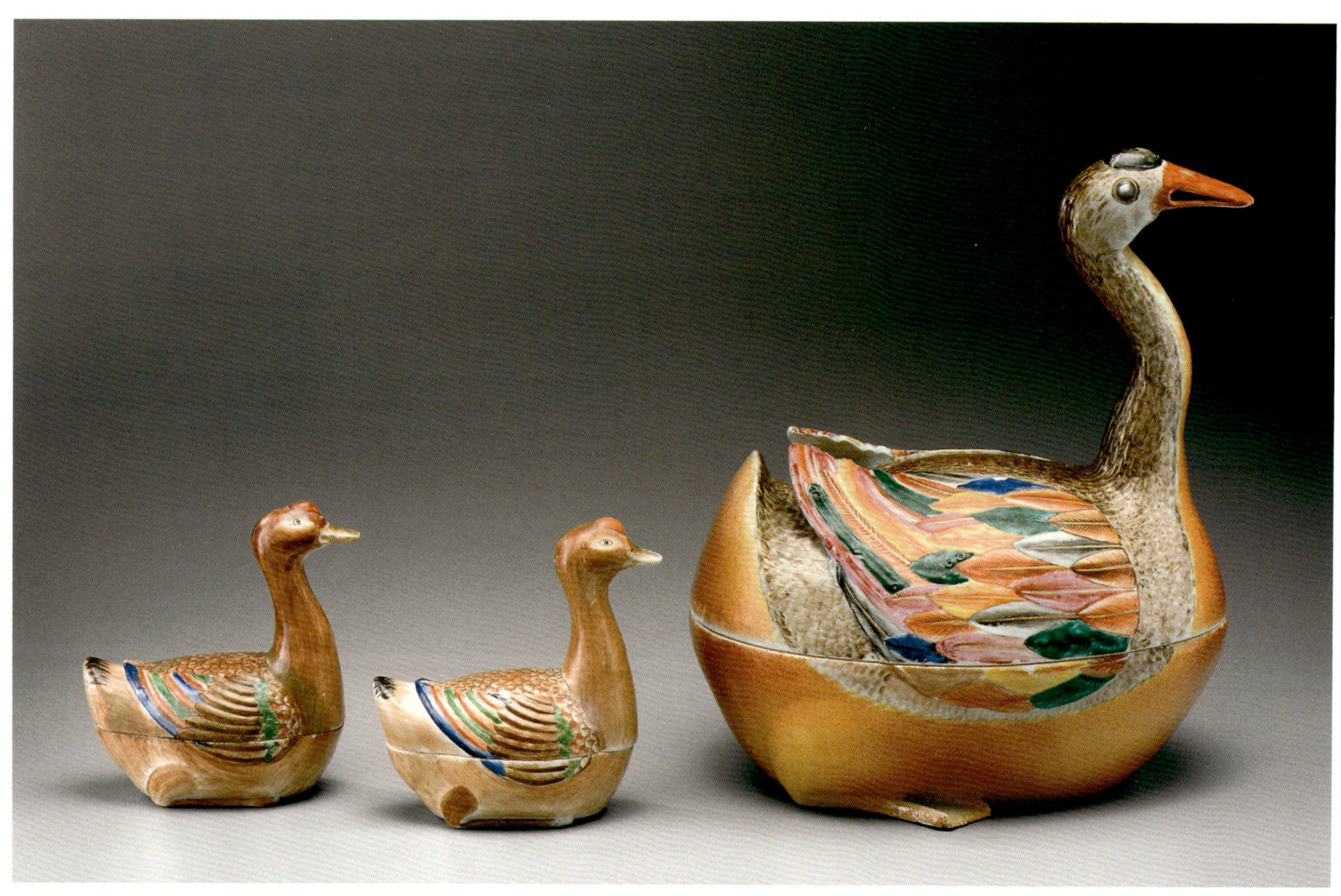

55 TUREEN AND SAUCE TUREENS

Jingdezhen, China; about 1760
Height (sauce tureens, each): 7.125 in. (182 mm), (tureen): 16 in. (406 mm)
2000.61.39, .40.1, .2

This magnificent tureen and accompanying sauce tureens in the shape of a goose and goslings are typical of the figural tureens that were popular in the mid-18th century. They most likely were copied from European examples, which were made by the Meissen factory in Germany, the Höchst faience factory in Germany, and the Strasbourg faience factory in France.[116]

Goose tureens were usually ordered as part of the Private Trade and seem to have been favored among Spanish and Portuguese families. In 1763, however, the Dutch East India Company ordered twenty-five "tureens in the form of a goose." These were already available in Canton, as supercargoes noted that "there were certainly more to be had, but the stands were not very well painted and yet the dealers were not willing to lower the price. We did not order these, because we were afraid that it would be impossible for this article to bring in a reasonable profit in view of the high purchase prices and great volume."[117]

LITERATURE

Howard, *Choice of the Private Trader,* pp. 112–13, 120.

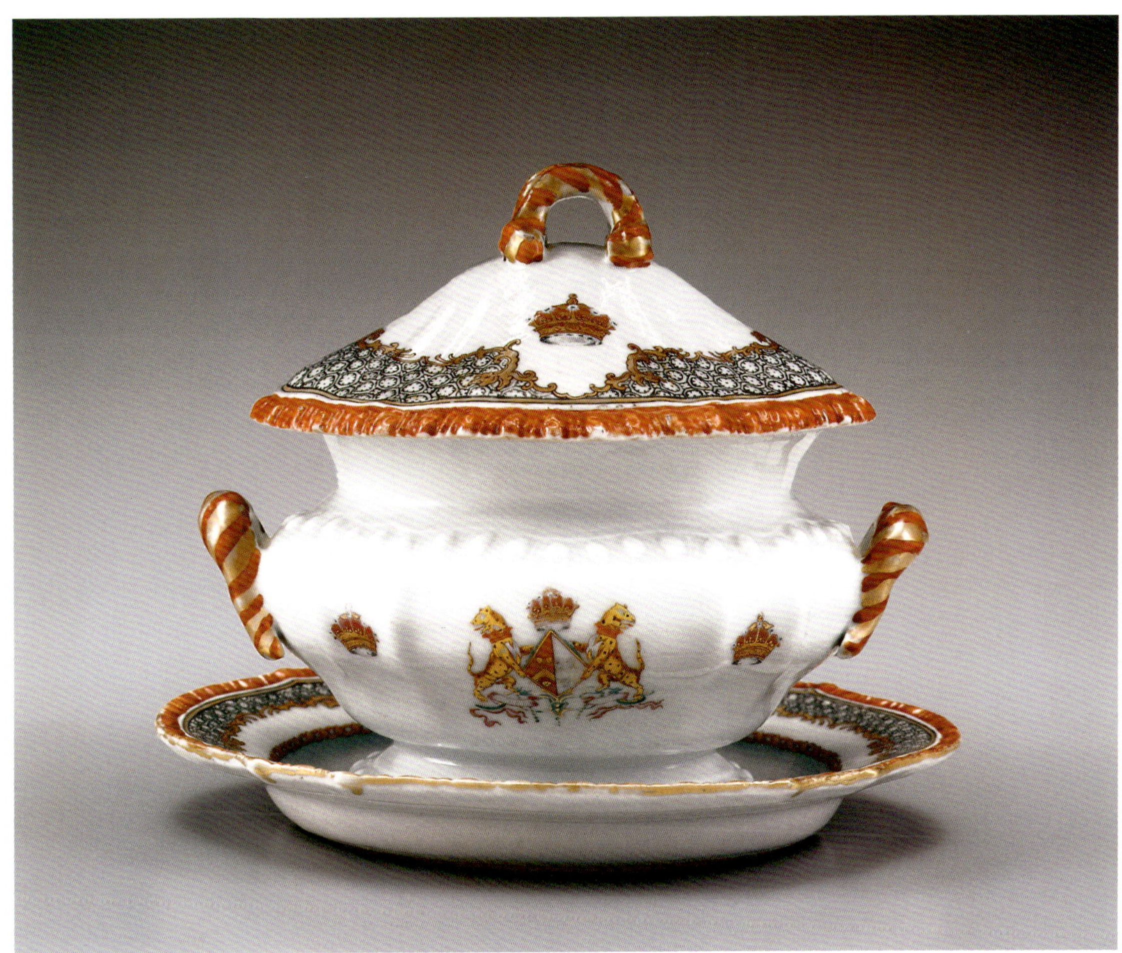

56 SAUCE TUREEN

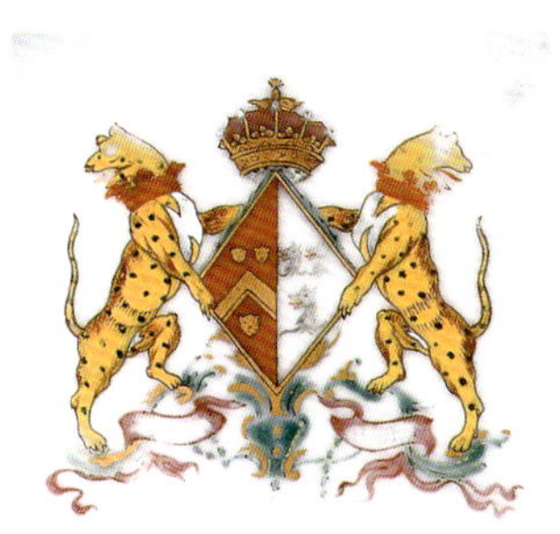

Jingdezhen, China; about 1765
Length (stand): 7.625 in. (194 mm)
L04.1026a–c

Part of a large and elaborate service made for Dorothy Nesbitt Parker, Countess of Macclesfield, this sauce tureen is based on an English creamware tureen that was copied from a silver example. Parker was a widow; her husband, George, the 2nd Earl of Macclesfield, died in 1764 without heirs, leaving the title to his wife.[118] This service was ordered sometime after his death because the impaled (joined) arms of Parker and Nesbitt are displayed in a lozenge, or diamond-shape shield, which was used by unmarried women and widows to display their coats of arms.

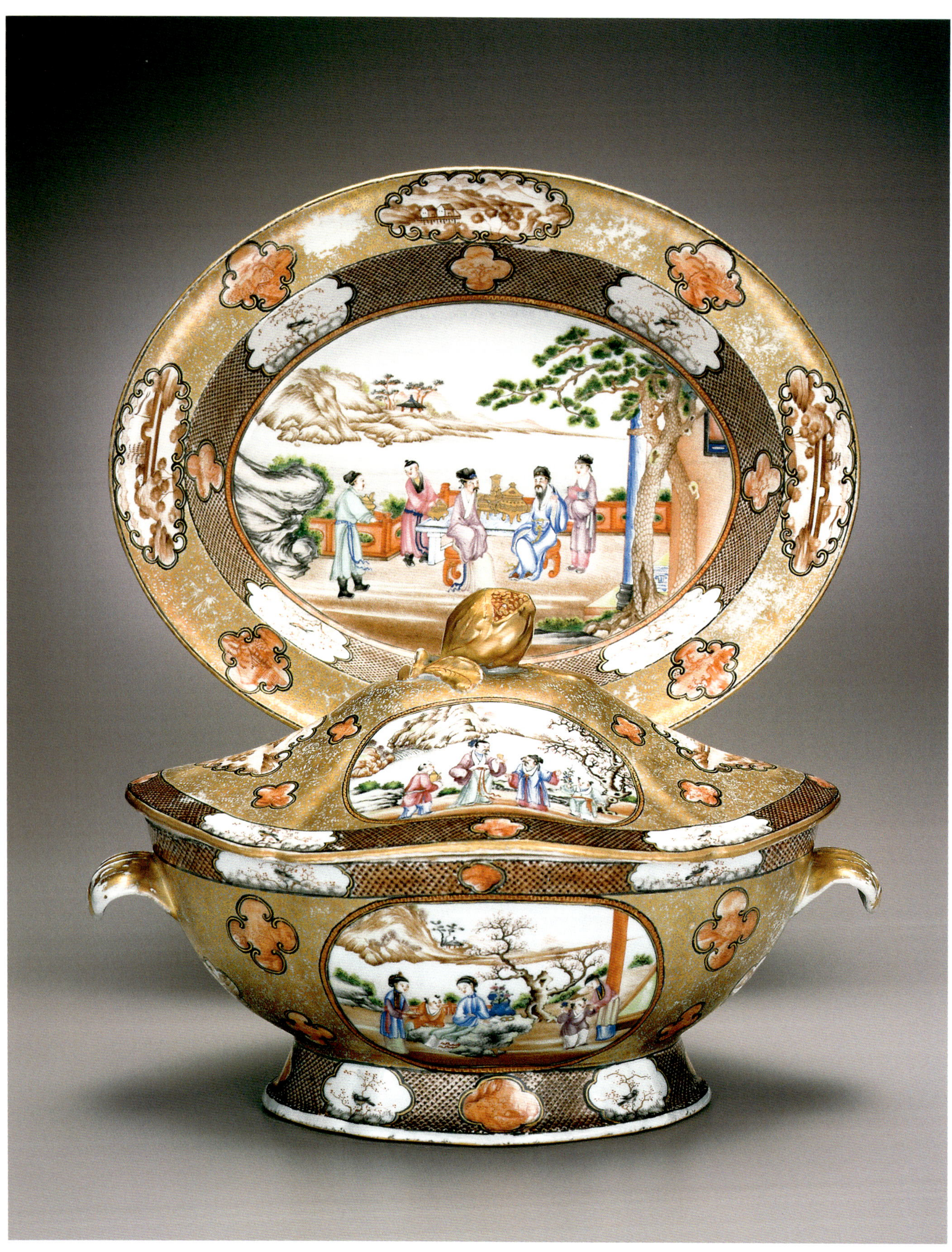

57 TUREEN AND STAND

Jingdezhen, China; 1795–1805
Length (stand): 15 in. (381 mm)
2003.47.18a–c

The decoration on this tureen, with its elaborate gold border and central panels containing finely painted scenes of Chinese courtiers, is known as palace ware. The name comes from the richness of the decoration and from the scenes of Chinese noblemen and noblewomen. Porcelain decorated with Chinese figures was especially popular with Europeans and Americans who were fascinated by the people, landscapes, and customs of China. An American, Robert Southey, wrote in 1807 that "plates and tea-saucers have made us better acquainted with the Chinese than we are any other people."[119]

By the time this tureen was made, European porcelain had replaced Chinese export as the most fashionable ceramic available. Rising import duties and declining demand even led the British East India Company to stop importing porcelain on its own account in 1791. However, extremely high-quality porcelain like this palace ware tureen continued to be commissioned by Private Traders, who no doubt could now acquire better quality at lower prices.[120]

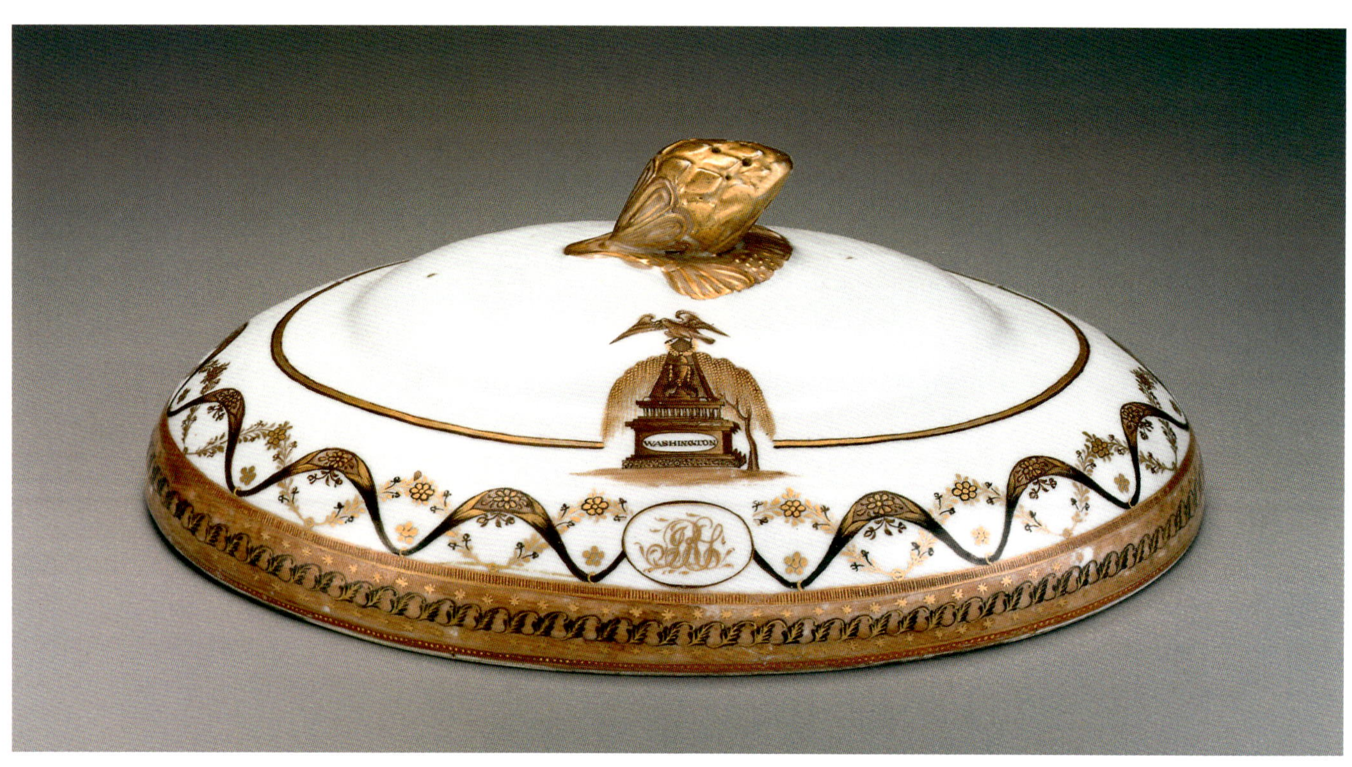
WASHINGTON

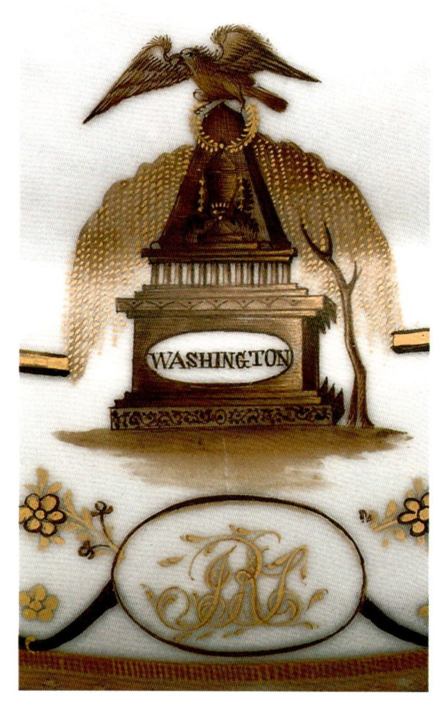
WASHINGTON

58 COVER FOR A TUREEN OR DISH

Jingdezhen, China; 1800–1805
Length: 11.75 in. (298 mm)
L03.2775.58

This cover comes from a dinner service made for Joseph and Rebecca Sims of Philadelphia and commemorates the death of George Washington. Sims was a wealthy China Trade merchant, and his federal-style home was described as "the finest house in town." Among the elegant furnishings was this dinner service. A visitor in 1824 noted that "all the china had the tomb of Washington in the center of every piece." The large service included such unusual forms as *pot-de-crème* cups, glaciers, and flowerpots.[121]

The Sims family clearly admired the president; in addition to their porcelain they also had blue, crimson, and yellow damask parlor curtains with a portrait of Washington woven into the design. Washington's death on December 14, 1799, led to a period of intense national mourning, which manifested itself in a proliferation of commemorative objects. Although the exact model for the obelisk seen here has not been found, prints, newspaper illustrations, temporary public monuments, and stage sets for eulogies that appeared in the months following Washington's death had similar examples. Obelisks, urns, and willow trees were used as symbols of grief and mourning in the late 18th and early 19th centuries and were popular elements for Washington memorials.[122]

LITERATURE

Illustrated in Howard and Ayers, *China for the West,* 2:494–95.

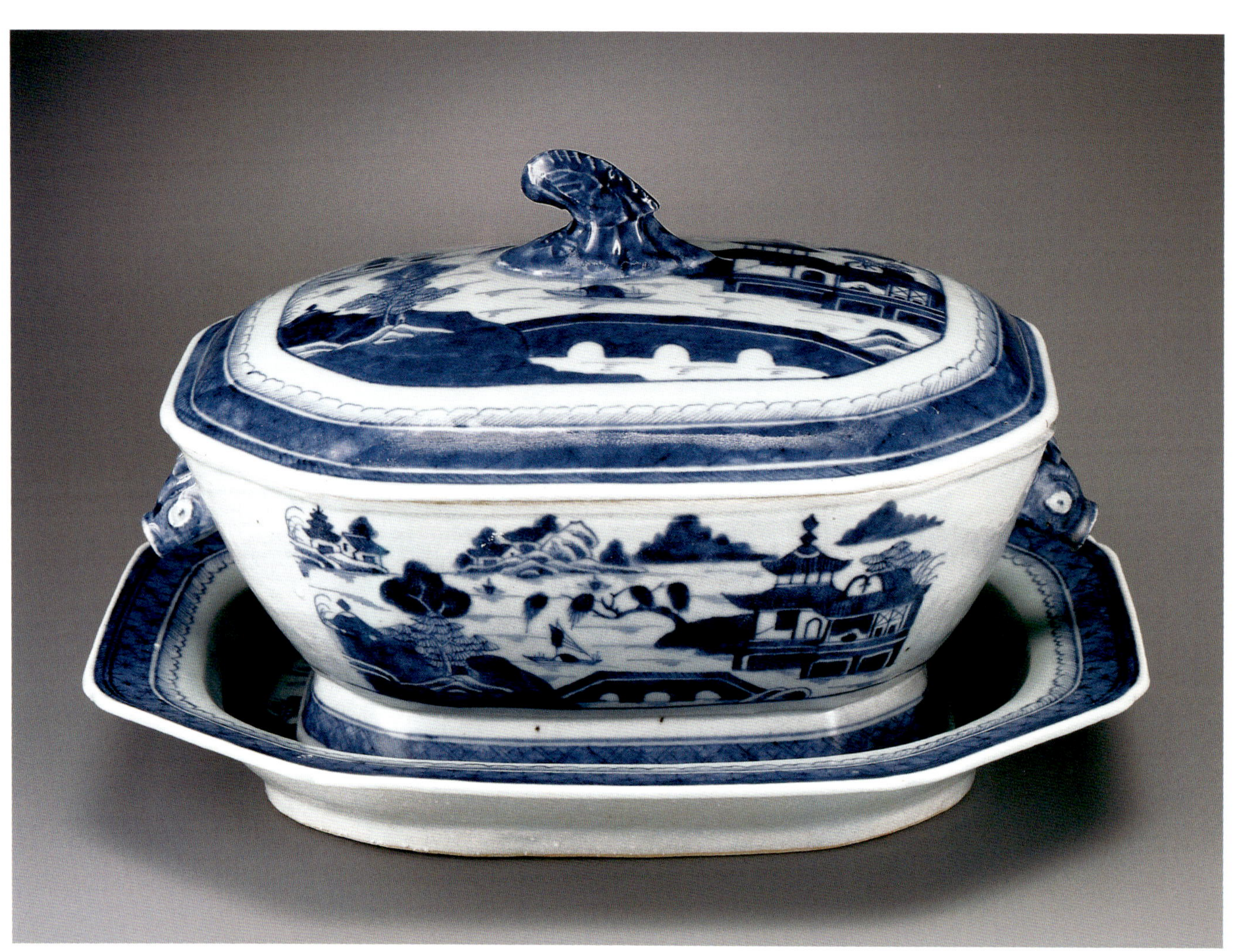

59 TUREEN AND STAND

Jingdezhen, China; about 1815
Length (stand): 14.125 in. (359 mm)
L03.2731.7a–c

This tureen and stand are decorated with the Canton pattern, which is a simple Chinese landscape and a latticework border with scalloped edge. Developed in the late 18th century, it was the most common design on Chinese export porcelain made during the 19th century and was especially popular in America.

Tureens such as the one seen here would have been part of a dinner service intended for a middle- or upper-class family. A typical example is the "Canton China Dinner Sett" bought in 1822 by Samuel Bailey of Wilmington, Delaware, for $38.00. It consisted of a soup tureen, 2 sauce tureens, 4 covered dishes, 12 platters, 1 salad bowl, 1 sauceboat, 2 pudding dishes, 12 custard cups, 36 dinner and luncheon plates, and 12 soup bowls.[123]

This tureen was part of the cargo of the *Diana,* which sank March 5, 1817, after striking a rock off the coast of Malaysia. The *Diana* was en route from Canton to the British city of Calcutta in India; she was carrying a cargo that included tea, sugar, sugar candy, spices, cotton and silk cloth, alum (used in dyeing fabric), white lead (used in paint), tutenag (zinc used in shipbuilding), and porcelain. The porcelain was probably destined for English settlers living in India.[124]

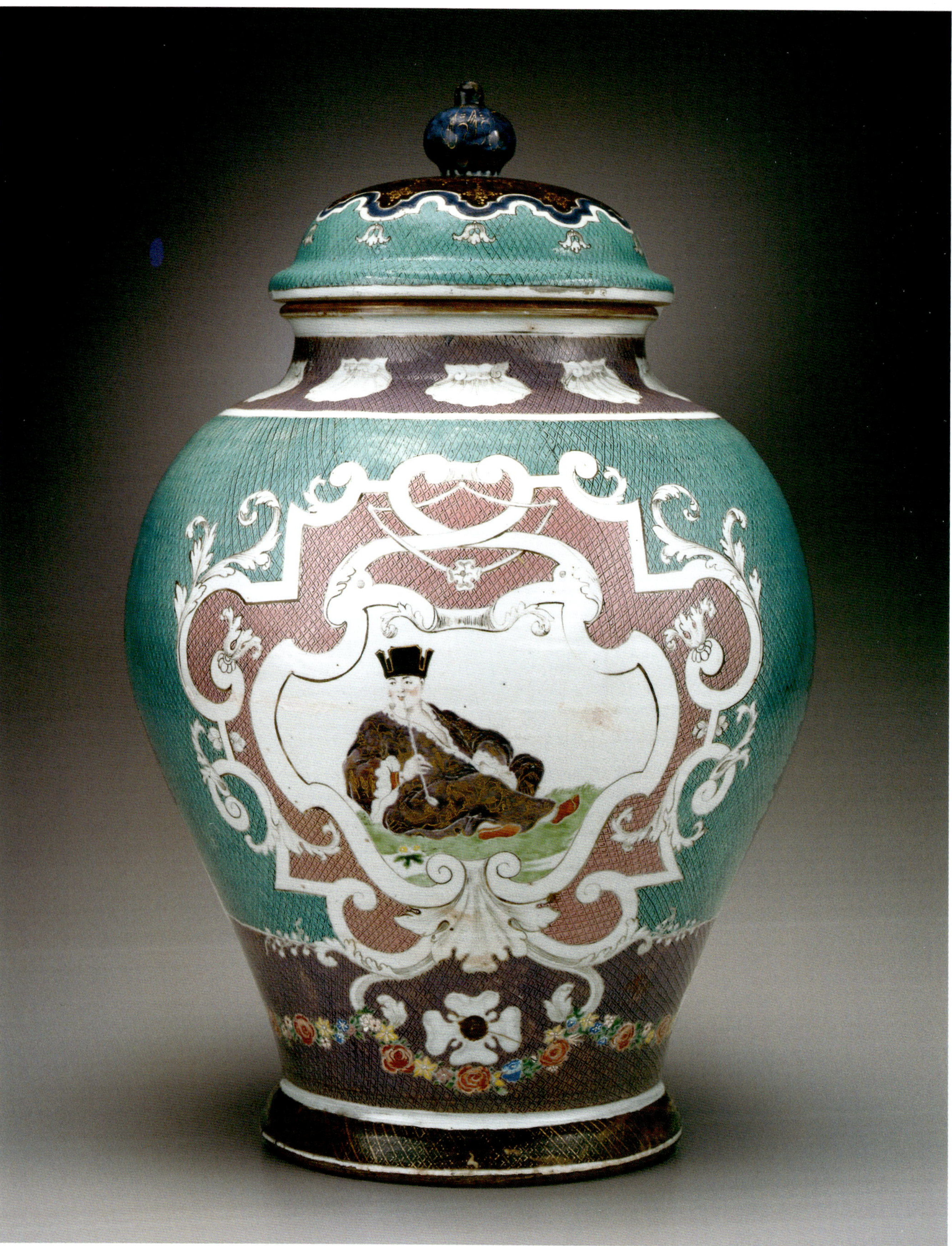

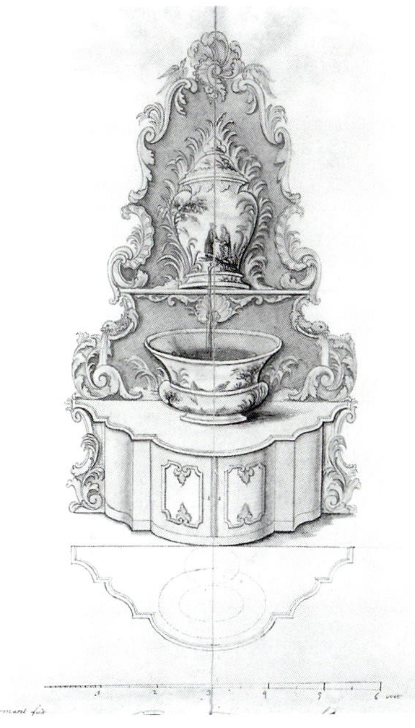

Pieter le Normant, design for a sideboard, Netherlands, about 1740. Pencil on paper; H. 16.5 in., W. 10 in. Photo, courtesy of the Historisch Museum, Rotterdam.

60 FOUNTAIN

Jingdezhen, China; 1734–40
Height: 21 in. (533 mm)
2000.61.85a,b

This large fountain, originally paired with an oval cistern, would have formed part of the fittings of an elegant European dining room in the mid-1700s. Used for washing hands or possibly for rinsing wineglasses, the fountain and cistern would have been installed in an alcove or on a specially designed sideboard similar to the one seen in the drawing by Amsterdam decorator and mirror-seller Pieter le Normant, from about 1740.

A reclining Turk smoking a pipe decorates the front of the fountain. Europeans of the 17th and 18th centuries were fascinated by Turkish and Islamic designs and customs. Images of Turks, often used to symbolize excess, are frequently depicted on decorative arts objects, either drinking coffee or smoking a pipe.[125] The design seen here, which is sometimes referred to as *The Potentate,* has often been attributed to Dutch artist Cornelis Pronk.

These large and expensive objects were first ordered in 1734, when the Dutch East India Company sent models of "water vases to set on sideboards in order to wash the hands, with the water bowls painted both inside and outside . . . on the foliage at the bottom of these vases is indicated a hole for applying a tap."[126]

LITERATURE
Illustrated in Howard, *Choice of the Private Trader,* pp. 240–41.

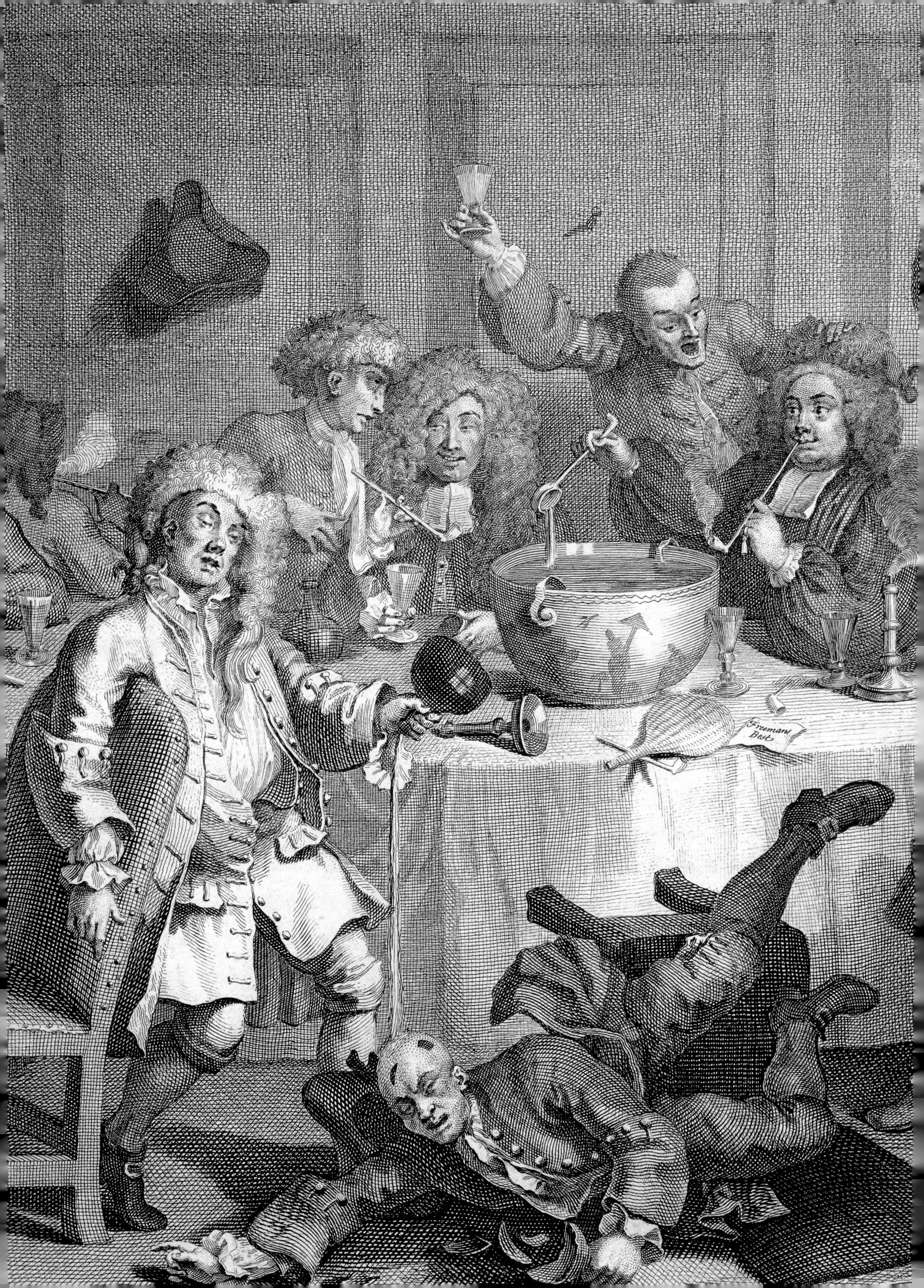
Fremans
Best

Drinking Wares

As drinking habits and patterns evolved from 1500 to 1850, so did the form and decoration of export porcelain drinking vessels. One of the most dramatic developments was the introduction of three exotic beverages: tea, coffee, and chocolate. These non-alcoholic stimulants were encountered by Europeans in the mid-16th century but did not become popular until a century later, probably when the widespread use of sugar made the bitter drinks more palatable.[127]

Coffee, chocolate, and especially tea were more than mere beverages, however. They provided a focal point for social activities and played a significant role in the ways that genteel people entertained one another. They also afforded the opportunity for displays of wealth and sophistication, an essential part of which were the appropriate cups, saucers, pots, and accoutrements. Chinese export porcelain was considered an especially appropriate medium for the beverages since it, like tea and coffee, came from the exotic and mysterious "Indies."

A complete tea service contained a teapot, milk jug, sugar bowl, slop bowl, tea caddy, spoon tray, and cups and saucers (usually twelve). Larger services included additional pots and cups for coffee and chocolate. Equipping a fashionable tea table was not an inexpensive undertaking, and families who could not afford porcelain for both the dinner and tea table often invested in porcelain for their tea service but purchased less expensive creamware for the dinner service. This was especially true in 18th-century America, where the "middling sort" aspired to a genteel lifestyle. But even the Assistant Keeper of the Wardrobe for Queen Charlotte of England wrote in 1783 that "our Tea and Coffee set were of common India china, our dinner service, of earthenware, to which, for our rank, was nothing superior."[128]

In addition to its use with tea, coffee, and chocolate, export porcelain could also hold a variety of other beverages. Porcelain jugs, mugs, and tankards allowed the wealthy to drink beer, ale, and cider in style. These traditional alcoholic beverages were joined by new ones, including distilled spirits such as gin. One new drink that included spirits was punch, which was consumed from bowls ranging in size from small, personal ones to enormous examples holding several gallons. Fitting its origins in Asia, where it was developed by China Trade merchants in the late 17th century, punch was commonly served in porcelain bowls.[129]

A large punch bowl is prominently featured at this 18th-century London drinking club. William Hogarth, *A Midnight Modern Conversation* (detail), London, England, after 1733. Etching on laid paper; H. 12.75 in., W. 17.75 in. 1975.219. Gift of Gordon Rust.

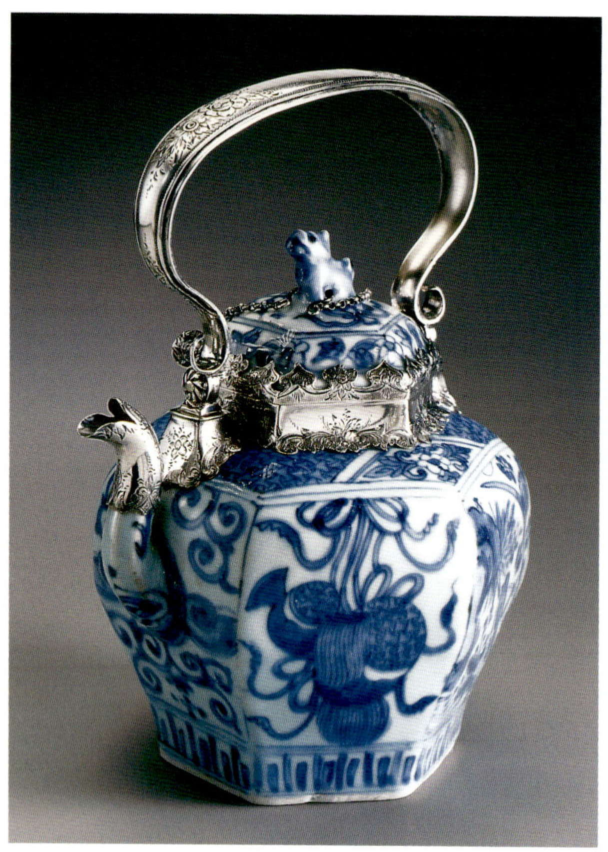

61 TEAPOT

Jingdezhen, China; 1575–1625
Height: 8.375 in. (213 mm)
L03.2775.43a,b

The silver handle and spout on this teapot or wine pot demonstrate the high regard with which Chinese export porcelain was held. The pot originally had a high, square porcelain handle and curved spout (see entry 62) that were damaged at some point and then replaced with silver mounts. The practice of mounting porcelain with precious metals began in the Middle Ages and continued through the 18th century. Silver, silver-gilt, and gilt-bronze mounts were used to repair damaged pieces, accentuate porcelain's exotic nature, and integrate it into high-style European interiors.[130]

This pot would have been used in Europe for tea or wine. The earliest recorded instance of tea in Europe occurs in 1610, with regular importation beginning in 1637. With those shipments came blue and white porcelain pots, which were first mentioned in the orders of the Dutch East India Company in 1639.[131]

LITERATURE
Illustrated in Howard and Ayers, *China for the West,* 1:55.

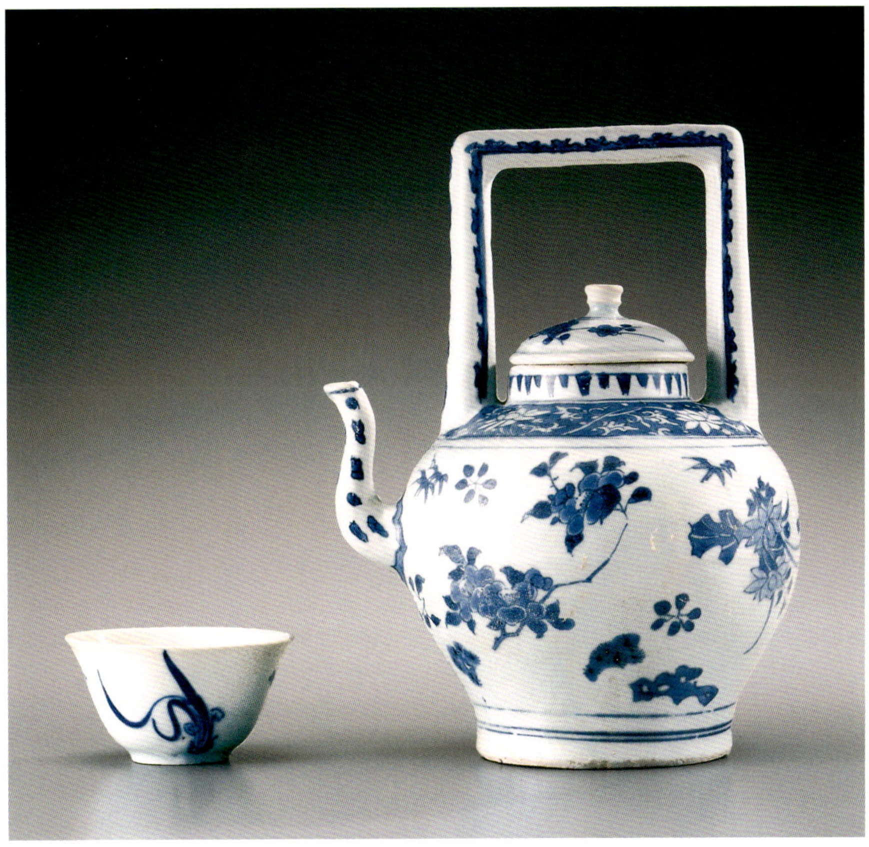

62 TEAPOT AND CUP

Jingdezhen, China; about 1640
Height (pot): 9.5 in., Diameter (cup): 3.5 in.
2000.61.49a,b, .60.1

This pot and cup would have been used in Europe for either wine or tea. Although wine had long been a popular drink among Europe's elite, tea was still a new beverage in 1640. These pieces were recovered from the wreck of a Chinese junk that sank in the South China Sea sometime around 1645. It was probably en route to the trading centers of Batavia or Bantam (in modern-day Indonesia), where the porcelain would have been bought by Chinese residents of Southeast Asia for their own use or by European traders for shipment to Europe.

LITERATURE

Illustrated in Howard, *Choice of the Private Trader,* pp. 142, 172.

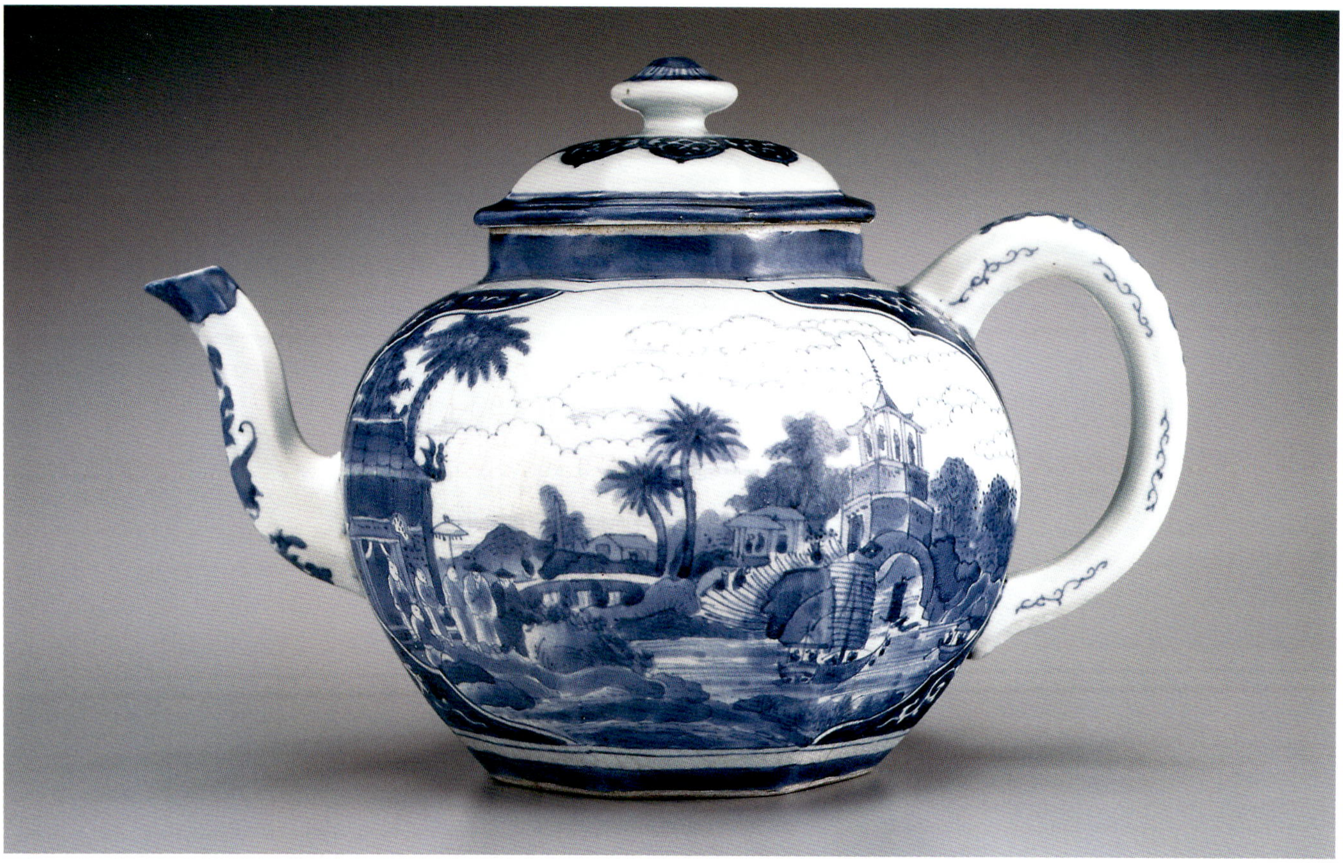

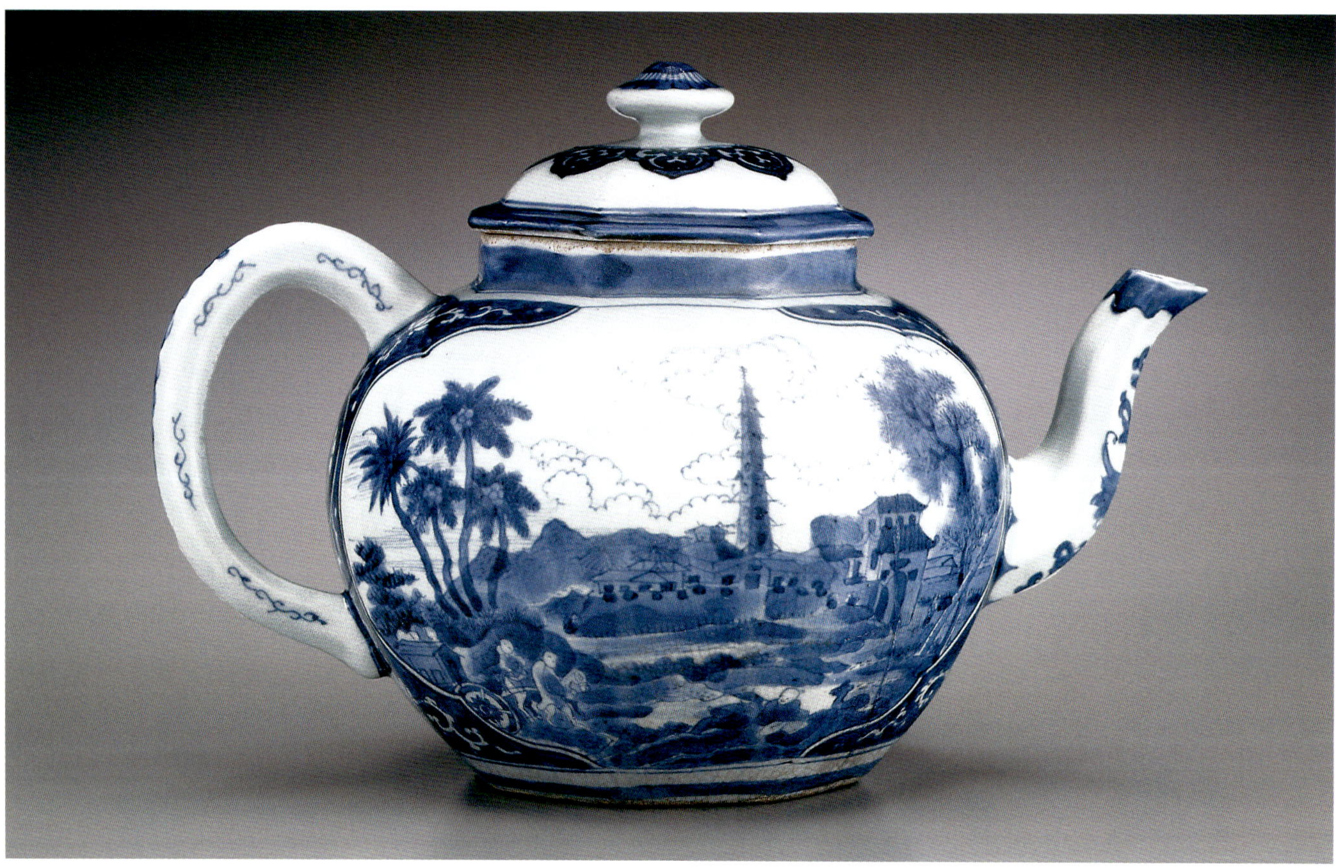

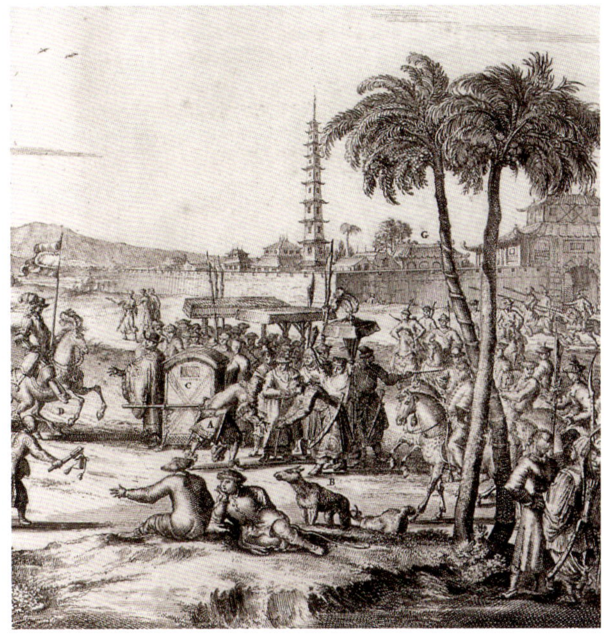

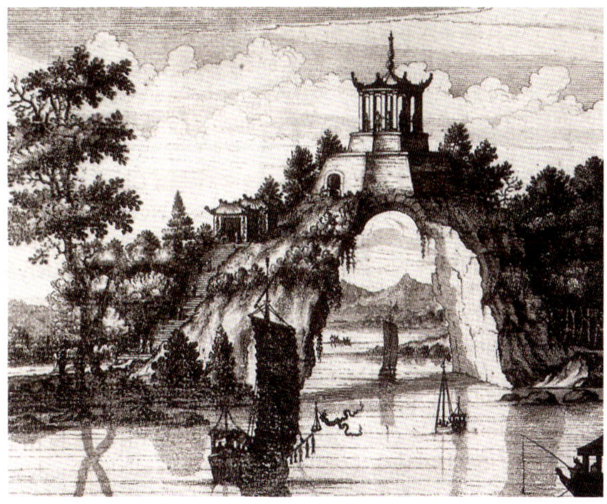

63 TEAPOT

Arita, Japan; 1700–1725
Height: 7.25 in. (184 mm)
2000.61.51a,b

Welcoming of the Ambassador (detail), from Arnoldus Montanus, *Atlas Chinensis* (London: Thomas Johnson, 1671). Printed Book and Periodical Collection, Winterthur Library.

Rock Bridge (detail), from Arnoldus Montanus, *Atlas Chinensis* (London: Thomas Johnson, 1671). Printed Book and Periodical Collection, Winterthur Library.

This pot represents the interaction of three cultures: Japanese, Chinese, and Dutch. It was made in Japan for export to the Netherlands; it imitates Chinese blue and white porcelain and is decorated with scenes of China copied from illustrations in a Dutch book.[132]

The scenes on the pot show the temple on the rock bridge between Gotanga and Quotinha and the welcoming of the Dutch ambassador, Joan van Hoorn, to the city of Beijing (then known as Peking). The scenes are from illustrations in Olfert Dapper's *Gedenkwaardig Bedryf der Nederlandsche,* which was published in Amsterdam in 1670 and in London the following year under the title *Atlas Chinensis: Being a Second Part of a Relation of Remarkable Passages in Two Embassies from the East-India Company of the United Provinces, to the Vice-Roy Singlamong and General Taising Lipovi, and to Kinghi, Emperor of China and East Tartary.*[133]

This pot is unusually large and may have held hot water to fill smaller teapots or may have been used at larger gatherings in a public coffeehouse. Generally, early teapots are small, in part because tea was so expensive.

LITERATURE

Illustrated in Howard, *Choice of the Private Trader,* pp. 144–45.

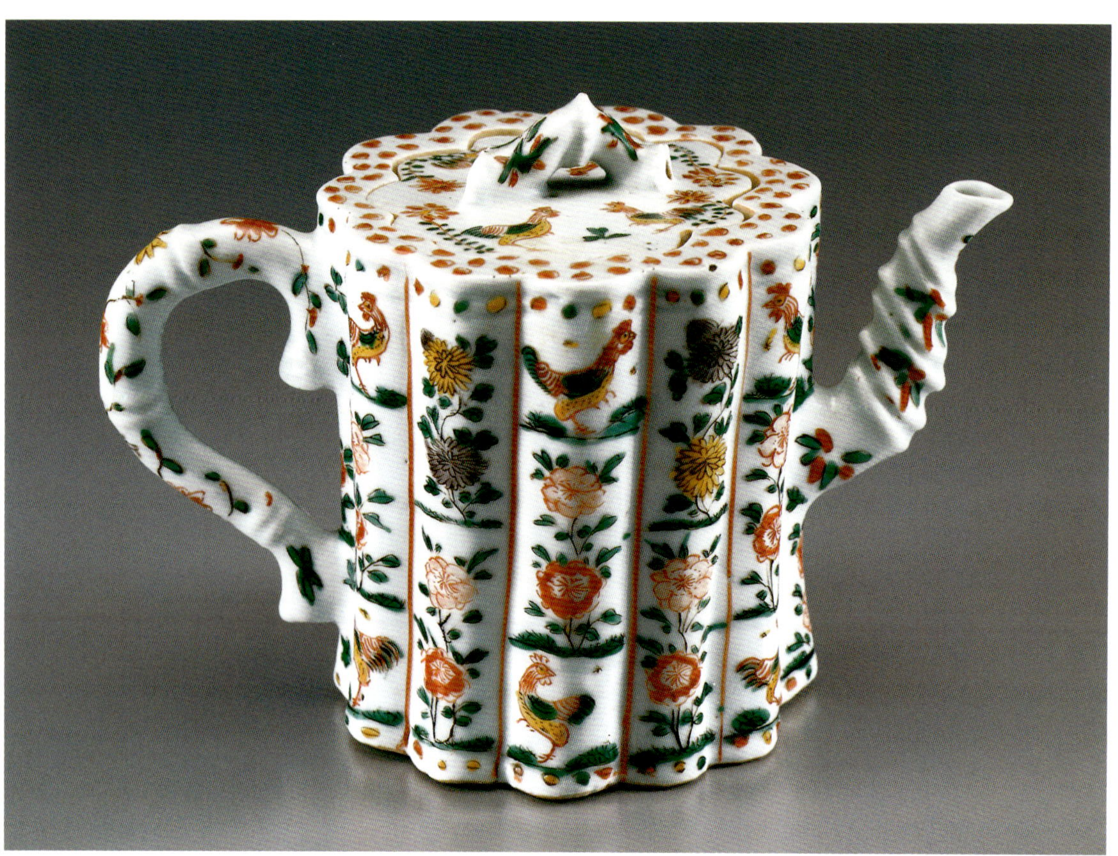

64 TEAPOT

Jingdezhen, China; 1700–1725
Height: 3.5 in. (89 mm)
2000.61.52a,b

Shaped like a bundle of bamboo, this teapot is typical of exotic and unusual pots in the forms of flower blossoms, fruit, and tree stumps that were popular in the first half of the 18th century. They were prized in Europe as curiosities, and an identical bamboo-shape pot was acquired by Augustus the Strong of Saxony for his collection by 1721. This particular pot may be a copy of a red stoneware teapot made in the Chinese city of Yixing.[134]

LITERATURE

Illustrated in Howard, *Choice of the Private Trader,* p. 146.

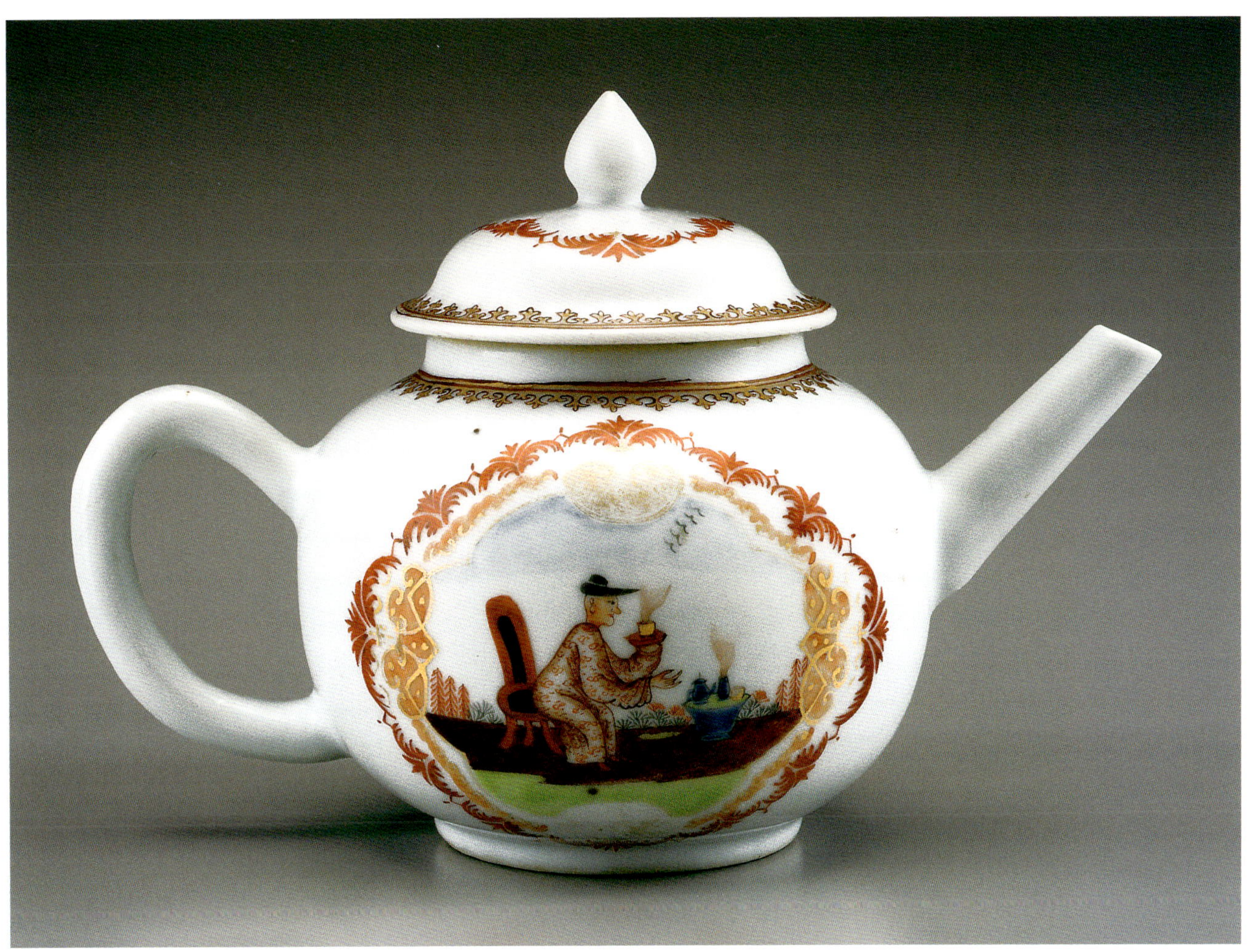

65 TEAPOT

Jingdezhen, China; about 1740
Height: 5 in. (127 mm)
L03.2775.31a,b

The scene on this teapot, that of a Chinese man enjoying a cup of hot tea, is actually European in origin. It is based on decoration found on Meissen porcelain of the 1720s and 1730s created by porcelain painter Johann Gregor Höroldt. Höroldt specialized in chinoiserie, which is a European interpretation of designs found on pieces of Chinese porcelain and lacquer.[135] By 1740 these European versions of Chinese designs were being sent to China to be reproduced on porcelain to be exported back to Europe.

The motivation behind producing export porcelain with Meissen-style chinoiserie may have been more than just an attempt to imitate a fashionable product; it may have been a move to promote tea drinking, which was becoming increasingly popular in the 1730s and 1740s.[136]

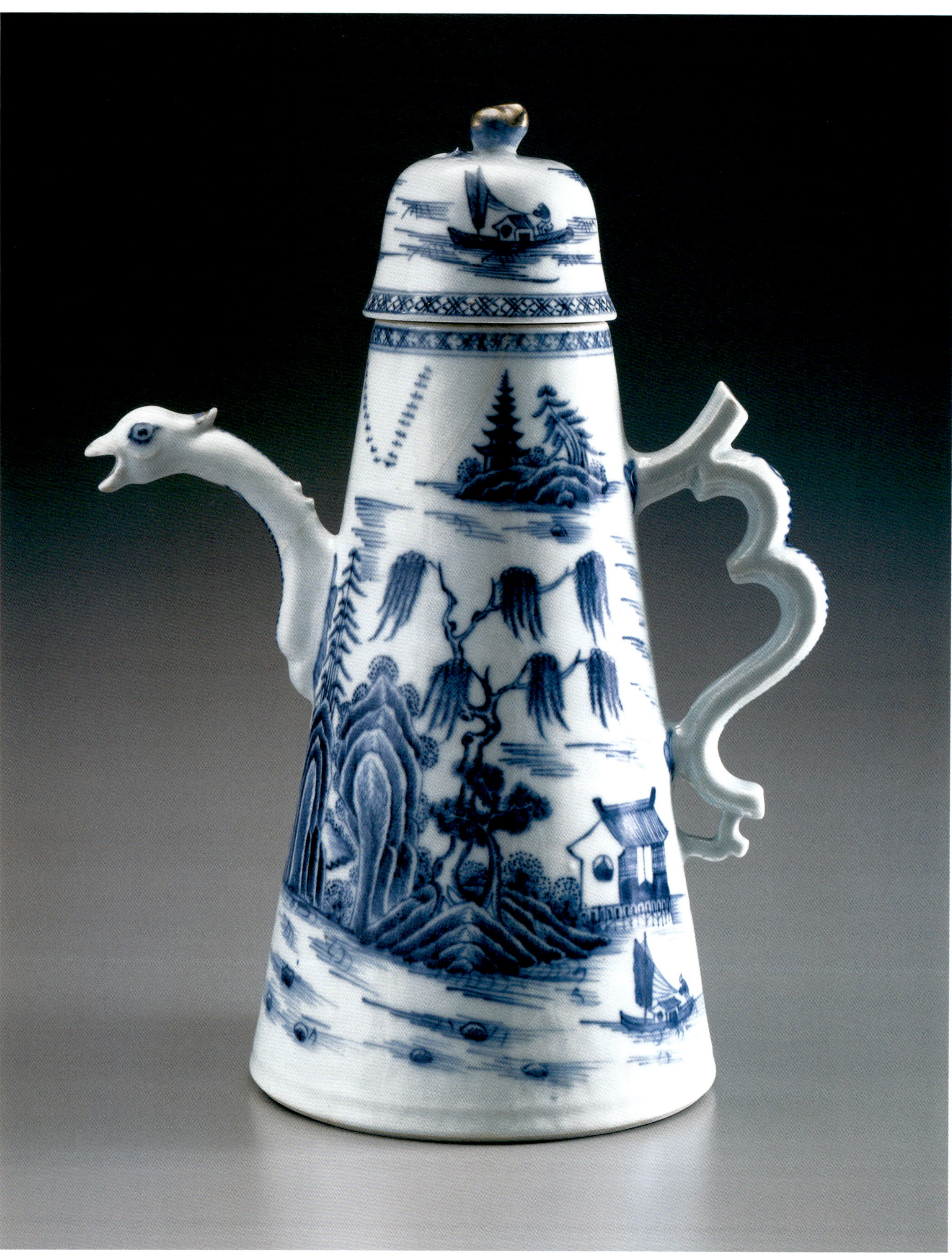

66 COFFEEPOT

Jingdezhen, China; about 1740
Height: 12.75 in. (324 mm)
L03.2775.75a,b

The form of this tall coffeepot, sometimes referred to as lighthouse shape, copies English silver pots made between 1680 and 1740. The bird-shape spout is probably inspired by those found on Meissen porcelain teapots and coffeepots from the 1720s and 1730s, although the Chinese are known to have used those spouts as well. Lighthouse-shape coffeepots continued to be made in porcelain into the early 1800s.[137]

Coffee was first encountered by Europeans traveling in the Middle East in the 16th century and was introduced to Europe in the 17th century. The drink quickly grew in popularity, no doubt because, as one early publication accurately recognized, coffee "will prevent *Drowsiness,* and make one fit for business, if one have occasion to *watch*." Although not quite as popular as tea, coffee was consumed in vast quantities throughout 18th-century continental Europe, Great Britain, and America. It was drunk at home, especially for breakfast, and also in public coffeehouses, which became important places to conduct business, exchange news, and gossip.[138]

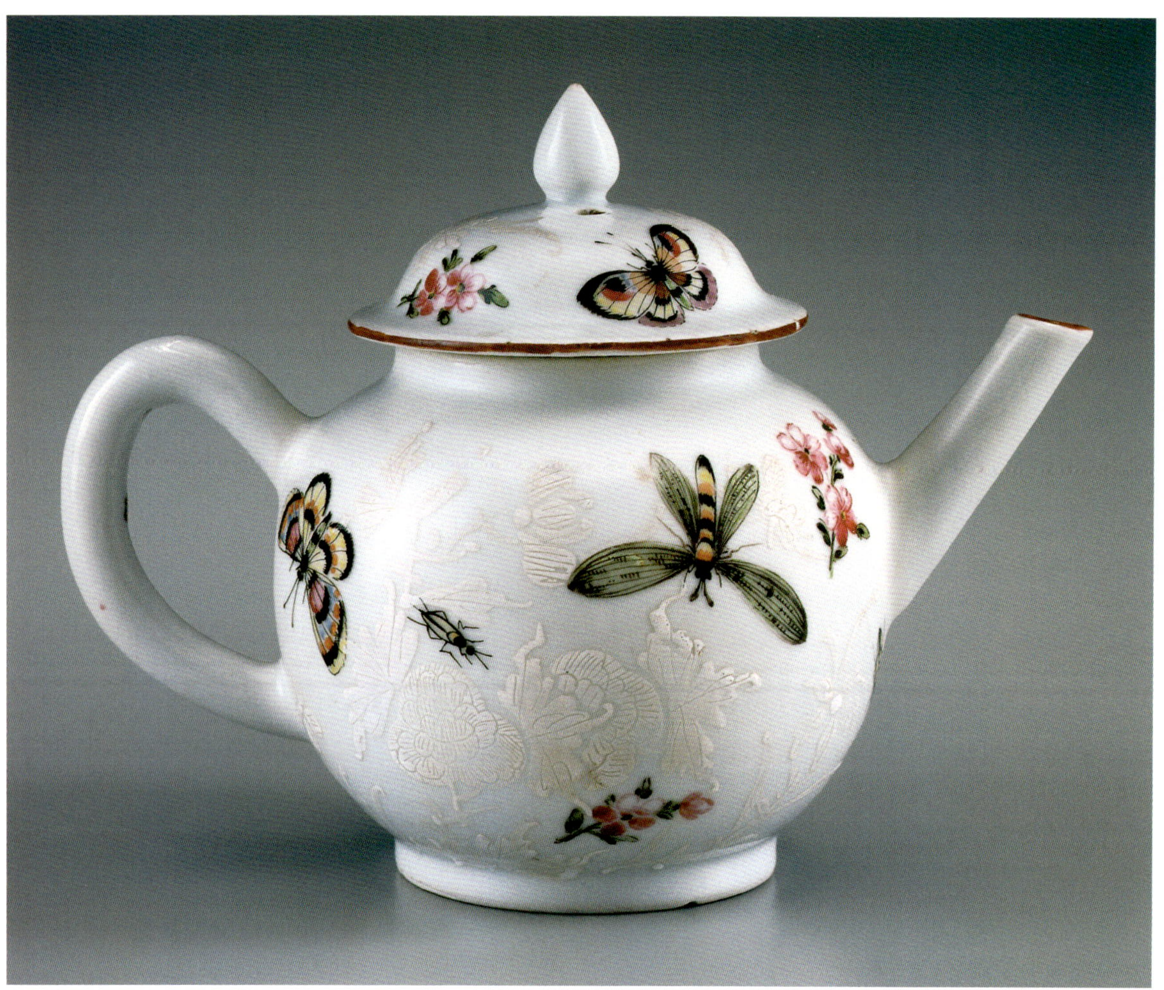

67 TEAPOT

Jingdezhen, China; about 1750
Decorated in London, England; 1750–70
Height: 5.25 in. (140 mm)
L03.2775.8a,b

Sometimes the Chinese decoration on export porcelain was just not enough for Western tastes, and so more decoration was added once an object reached Europe. Such was the case with this particular teapot, which was embellished with brightly colored flowers, butterflies, and insects in between and in some cases almost overtop the original, subtle, white-on-white floral design (known as *bianco-sopra-bianco*). The fact that the over-decoration seems to date to at least several years later than the pot suggests that it may have been added to an older piece to make it more attractive and marketable.[139]

LITERATURE
Illustrated in Howard, *Choice of the Private Trader,* p. 150.

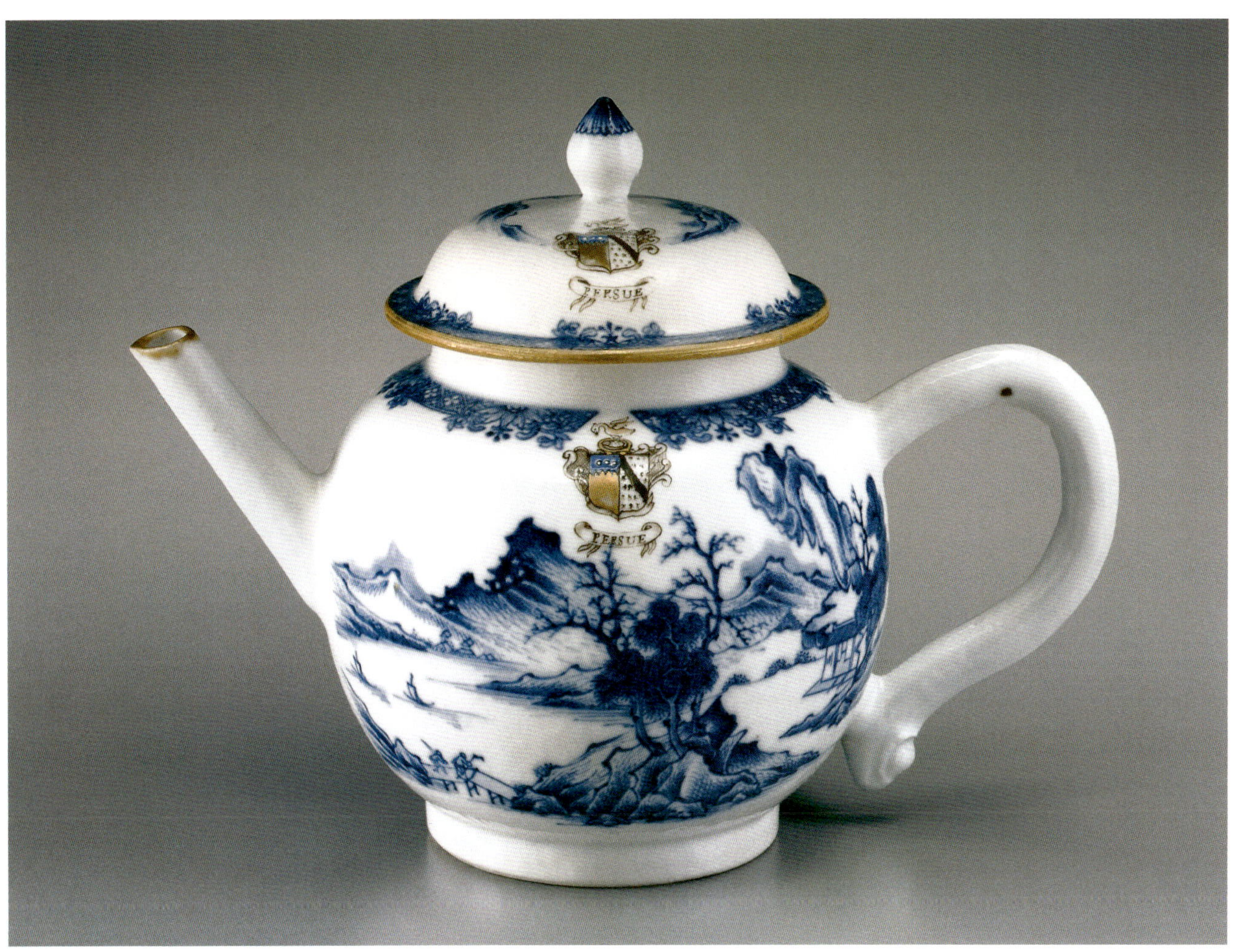

68 TEAPOT

Jingdezhen, China; about 1755
Height: 5.375 in. (137 mm)
L03.2775.76a,b

This teapot, with its bulbous body, straight spout, and ear-shape handle, is typical of mid-18th-century export porcelain teapots. It is decorated in underglaze blue with one of the most popular designs from the time: a Chinese landscape. The scene is carefully painted so as to leave a small space on the shoulder of the pot in which the arms of Latham impaling Kelsall are painted. The teapot is from one of two services made about the same time for Capt. Richard Latham of the British Royal Navy, who married Jane Kelsall about 1755.[140]

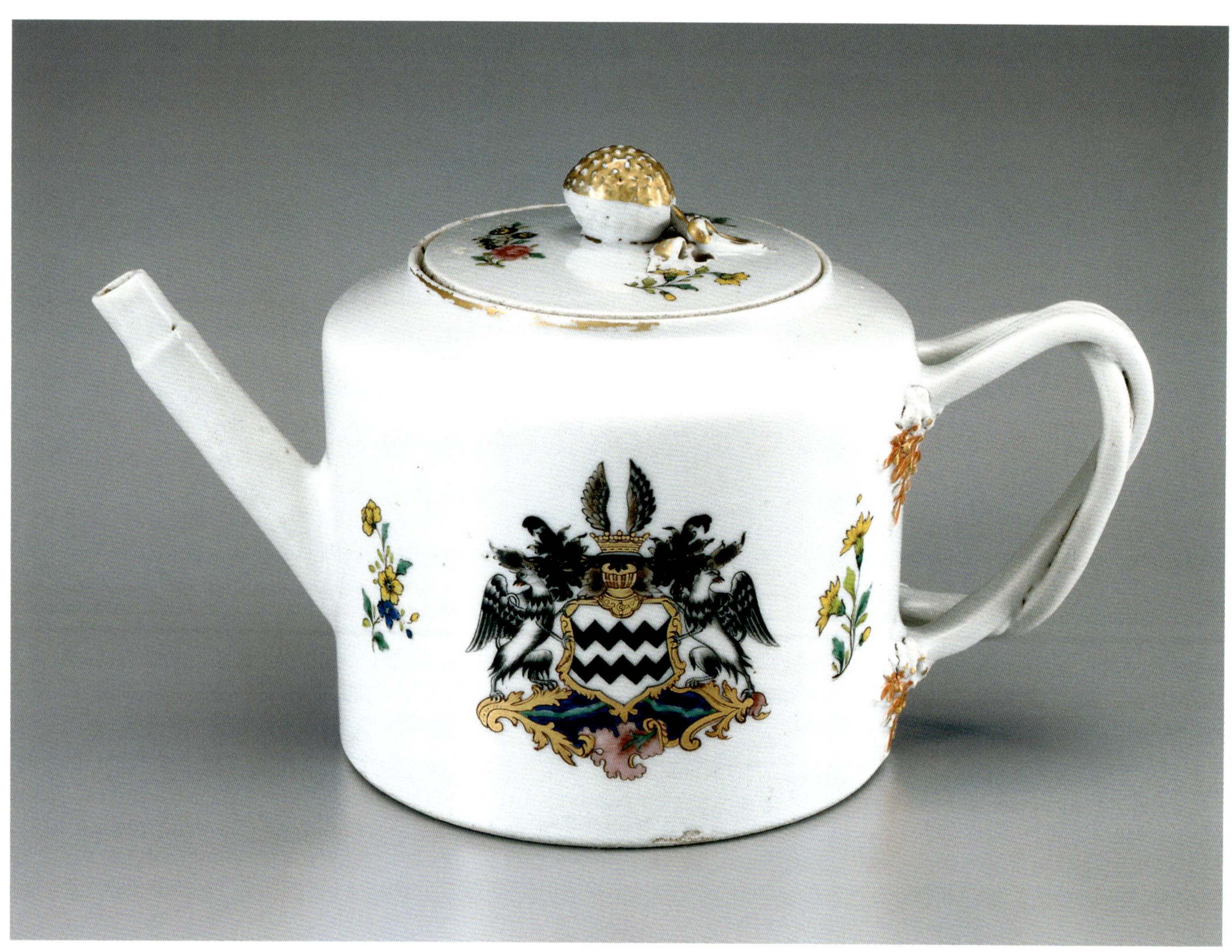

69 TEAPOT

Jingdezhen, China; about 1780
Height: 4.75 in. (122 mm)
2001.29.3a,b

This drum-shape teapot mimics silver examples made in the 1770s and reflects the new fashion for simpler forms inspired by classical Greek and Roman design. By the mid-1780s, globular and pear-shape teapots had been almost completely replaced by drum-shape pots, which remained in fashion through the 1820s. This particular example is from a tea service made for a member of the Ginkel family of Great Britain, probably Frederick Ginkel, the 5th Earl of Athlone, who also owned two earlier armorial porcelain dinner services.[141]

LITERATURE
Illustrated in Howard, *Choice of the Private Trader,* pp. 152–53.

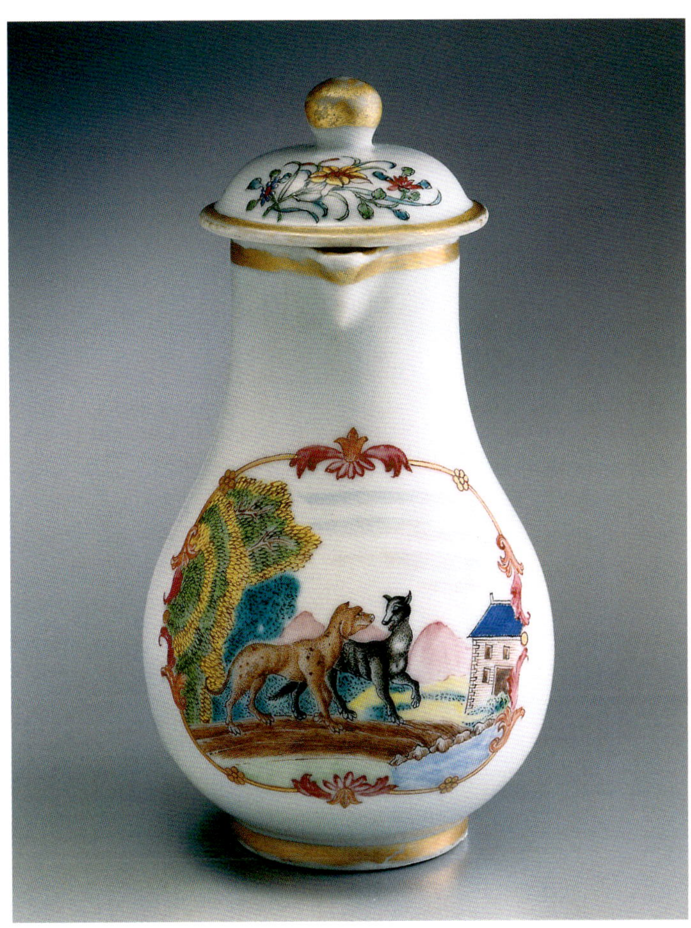

70 MILK JUG

Jingdezhen, China; about 1740
Height: 5 in. (127 mm)
L03.2775.38a,b

A scene from an Aesop's fable, "The House-dog and the Wolf," decorates this milk jug. In the story, a hound invites a wolf to his master's house, but the wolf declines, explaining he would rather have "a dry crust with liberty, against a king's luxury with a chain." The exact image on which this decoration is based has not been identified; it may be adapted from an illustration from an edition of *Aesop's Fables* published in London in 1666 by English engraver Francis Barlow. Although Chinese painters did replicate Western designs line for line, they often adapted them to fit on a particular piece of porcelain or to make them easier to copy.[142]

The Chinese did not take milk or cream with their tea or coffee, so Europeans had no Chinese prototypes to draw on as models for jugs. Instead they sent examples of their own metal, ceramic, and glass jugs to China, such as the "Glass pattern" milk pots requested by the British East India Company in 1712 or the 4,000 milk jugs copying English creamware models ordered by the Dutch East India Company in 1767.[143]

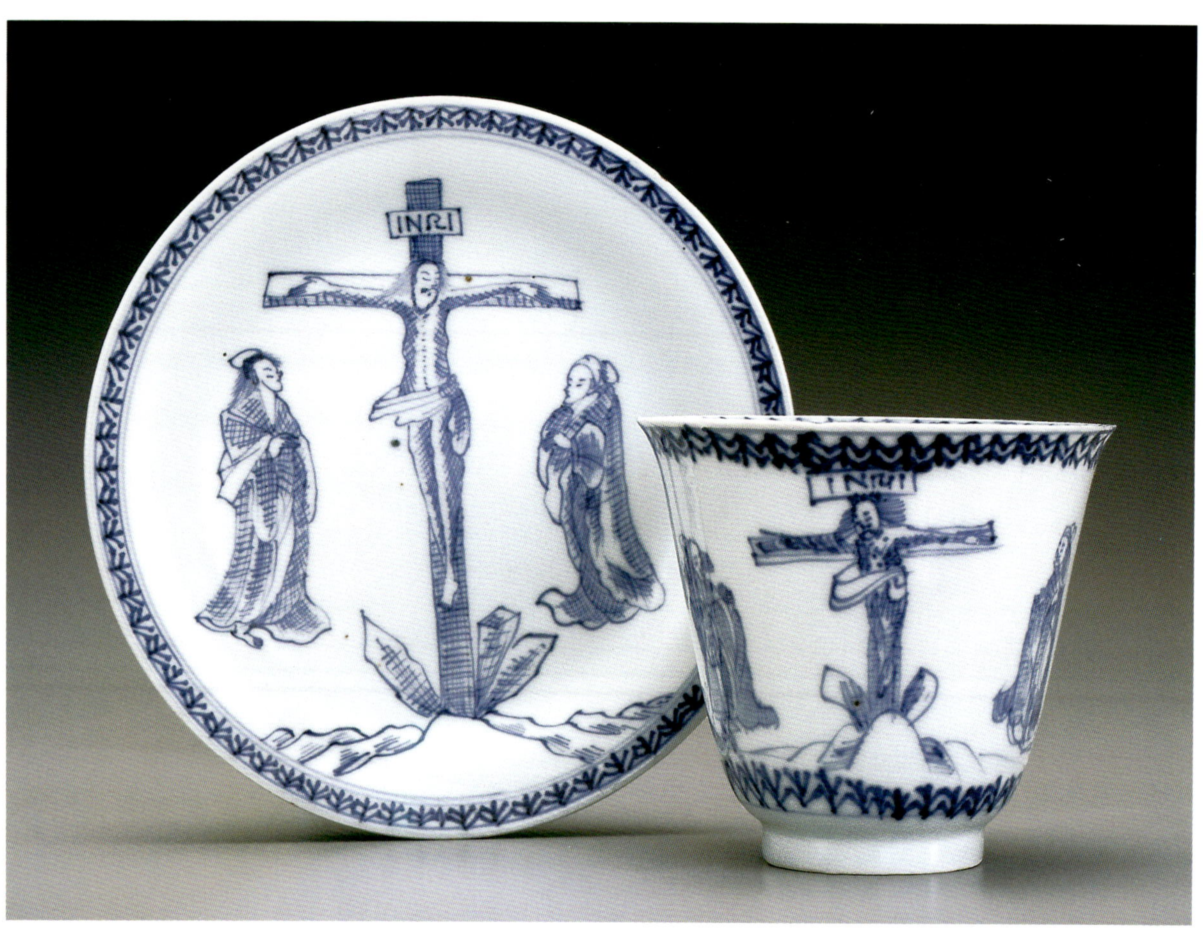

71 CUP AND SAUCER

Jingdezhen, China; 1690–1710
Diameter (saucer): 5.125 in. (130 mm)
L03.2731.10a,b

This cup and saucer are decorated with a scene of the crucifixion of Jesus. The design was probably copied from a painting, print, or even a needlework picture taken to China by Jesuit missionaries, who were active in Asia from the 16th century onward.[144]

Cups, saucers, plates, and jars are known to have been decorated with this image. Although suitable for European use, such pieces may in fact have been intended for Japanese or Chinese Christians interested in expressing their new-found faith. Père d'Entrecolles, a Jesuit missionary who toured the potteries of Jingdezhen, referred to a plate that must have been similar to this cup and saucer in decoration and date when he recounted how "they brought me from the Remains of a large Shop a small Plate, which I esteem more than that which was made a Thousand Years ago. There is painted at the bottom a Crucifix placed between the Virgin *Mary* and St. *John,* and it is said that they exported to *Japan* a great Quantity of this sort, but now there has been none made of it for sixteen or seventeen Years."[145]

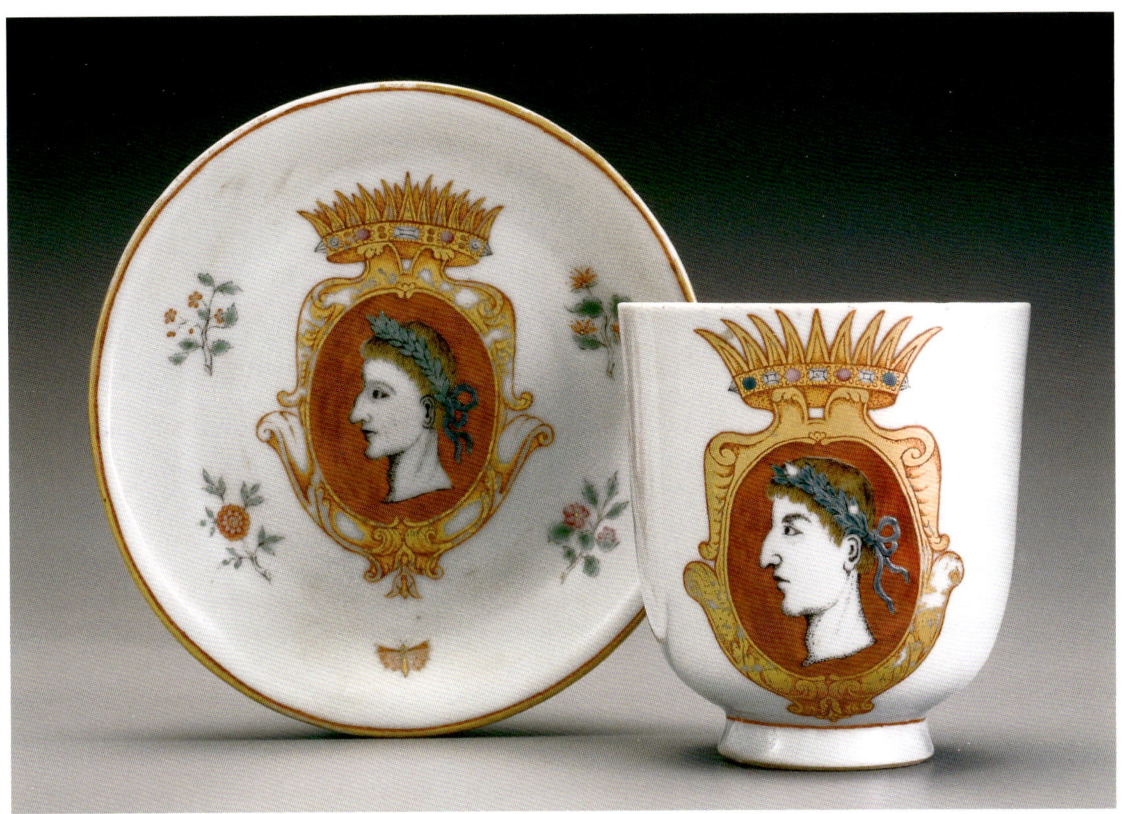

72 CUP AND SAUCER

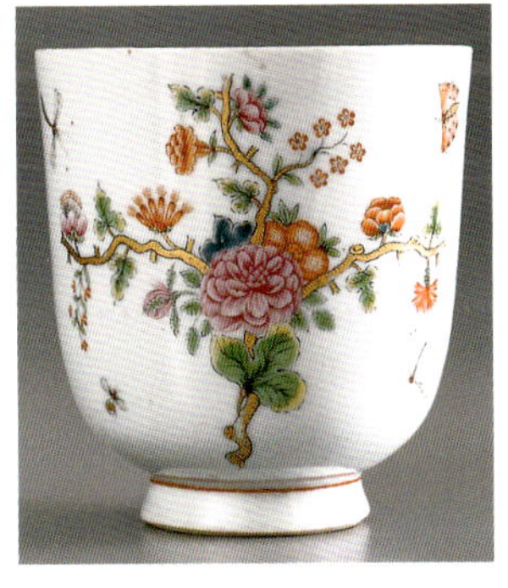

(reverse)

Jingdezhen, China; about 1725
Decorated in Europe, probably the Netherlands; about 1725
Diameter (saucer): 4.375 in. (111 mm)
2001.20.7a,b

This cup and saucer were imported into Europe as plain white porcelain and then embellished with delicate flowers and a medallion containing a classical bust. This process of over-decoration by European enamel painters was common throughout the 18th century. As much as 4 percent of the stock of one Amsterdam porcelain shop was plain white porcelain, no doubt intended to be over-decorated.[146]

The objects seen here are part of a distinctive group of porcelain characterized by rich colors and exceptionally fine painting that were probably done in the Netherlands in the mid-1720s. The flowers, painted in what is sometimes referred to as fine-line decoration, are similar to those created by German *hausmalers* (independent porcelain painters), which indicates that the artist who decorated this cup and saucer was from Germany or had trained there.[147]

LITERATURE

Illustrated in Howard and Ayers, *China for the West,* 1:258–59; Hervouët, Hervouët, and Bruneau, *La Porcelaine,* p. 220.

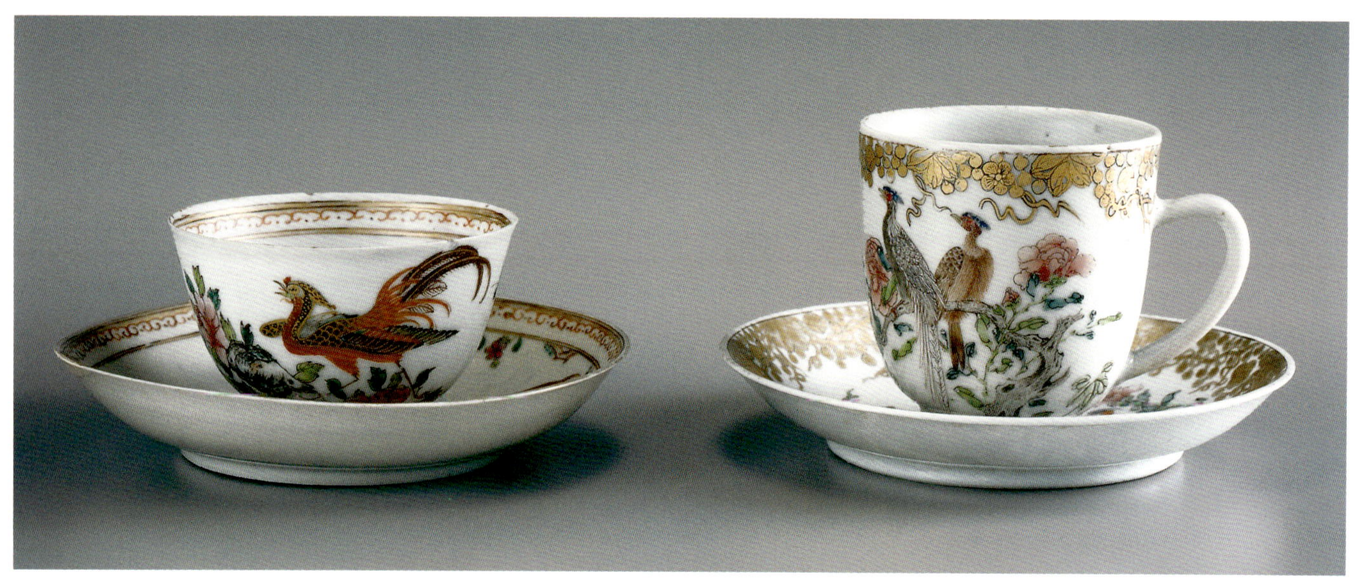

73 TEA BOWL AND SAUCER COFFEE CUP AND SAUCER

Jingdezhen, China; 1745–60
Diameter (saucers): 4.5 in. (114 mm)
2001.29.20a,b, .21a,b

As a general rule, for most of the 18th century, tea was drunk from low, wide, handleless bowls; coffee and chocolate called for taller, narrower cups with handles. Tea bowls were introduced to Europe from China in the mid-17th century, when tea was first imported in any quantity. The earliest large order for such bowls occurs in 1643, when 25,000 were requested. By the mid-18th century, two sizes of tea bowls were available, with the larger often described as "breakfast" cups. Handled cups may have originally been intended just for chocolate; purchasing records from the Dutch East India Company in the 1750s refer to handleless coffee cups and handled chocolate cups. By 1760, however, handled cups were in use for both beverages.[148]

Saucers, which were not used by the Chinese, were probably first made for the Turkish market in the mid-17th century and introduced to Europe a short while later.[149] Although not a pair, the cups and saucers seen here are decorated with exotic birds and flowers, which were popular motifs on export porcelain in the mid-18th century.

LITERATURE
Illustrated in Howard and Ayers, *China for the West,* 1:167–69.

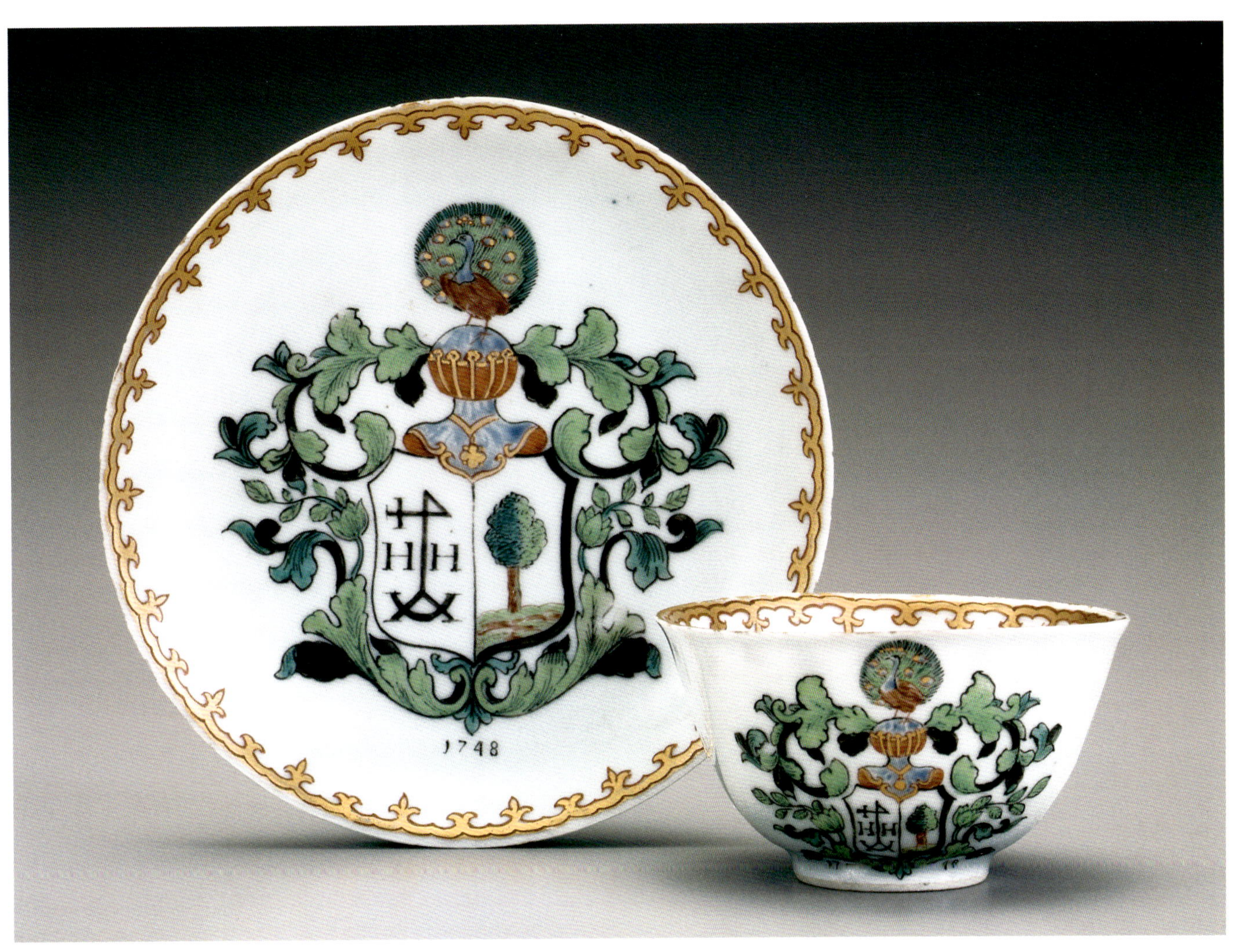

74 TEA BOWL AND SAUCER

Jingdezhen, China; 1748
Diameter (saucer): 4.5 in. (114 mm)
L03.2775.40a,b

This cup and saucer are decorated with an armorial that includes a merchant's mark and the arms of the Hesslink family of the Netherlands. Merchants' marks, which were branded or painted on crates and bundles, were a means of identification and served almost like shipping labels. This particular mark belonged to Hendrick Hesslink of the Netherlands.[150] Wealthy merchants who wanted armorial porcelain but lacked their own arms either borrowed arms from families with the same name or used their marks or trade cards to create pseudo-armorial porcelain.

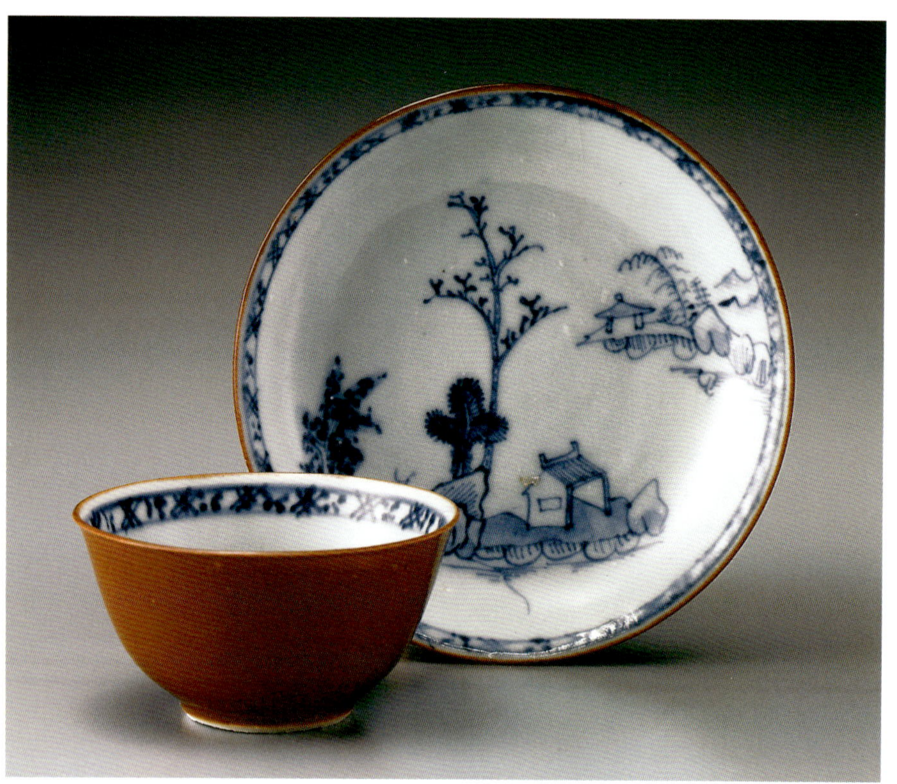

75 TEA BOWL AND SAUCER

Jingdezhen, China; about 1750
Diameter (saucer): 5.25 in. (135 mm)
2001.29.17a,b

Known as Batavian ware, after the Dutch trading center of Batavia (modern-day Jakarta, Indonesia), this tea bowl and saucer are decorated with an iron-brown wash that was popular on inexpensive export porcelain made from the late 17th through the mid-18th century. During the period, the color was described as "brown," "café-au-lait," "the colour of dead leaves," and even "cow dung."

These sturdy cups and saucers may be those referred to in Dutch East India Company records as "coffee house wares" intended for coffeehouses and taverns. In fact, this cup and saucer may have been used for coffee, not tea. They match the "double ordinary coffee cups and saucers" described as "brown with blue and white" that appear in the 1750 order thought to have been used for purchasing the porcelain that went down with the *Geldermalsen*. During the early and mid-18th century, both tea and coffee could be drunk from handleless bowls, while handled cups were used for coffee or chocolate.[151]

LITERATURE
Illustrated in Howard, *Choice of the Private Trader,* p. 181.

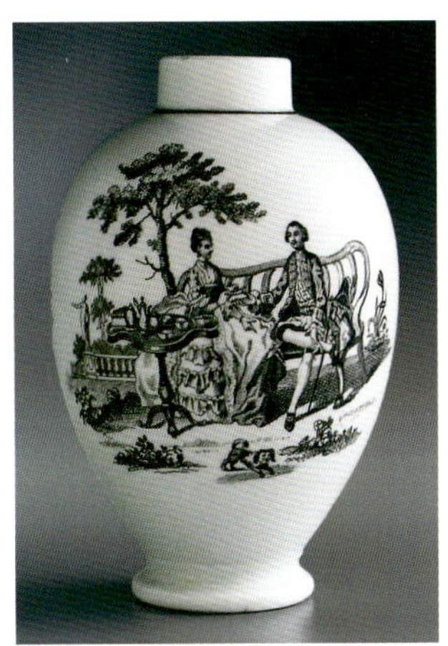

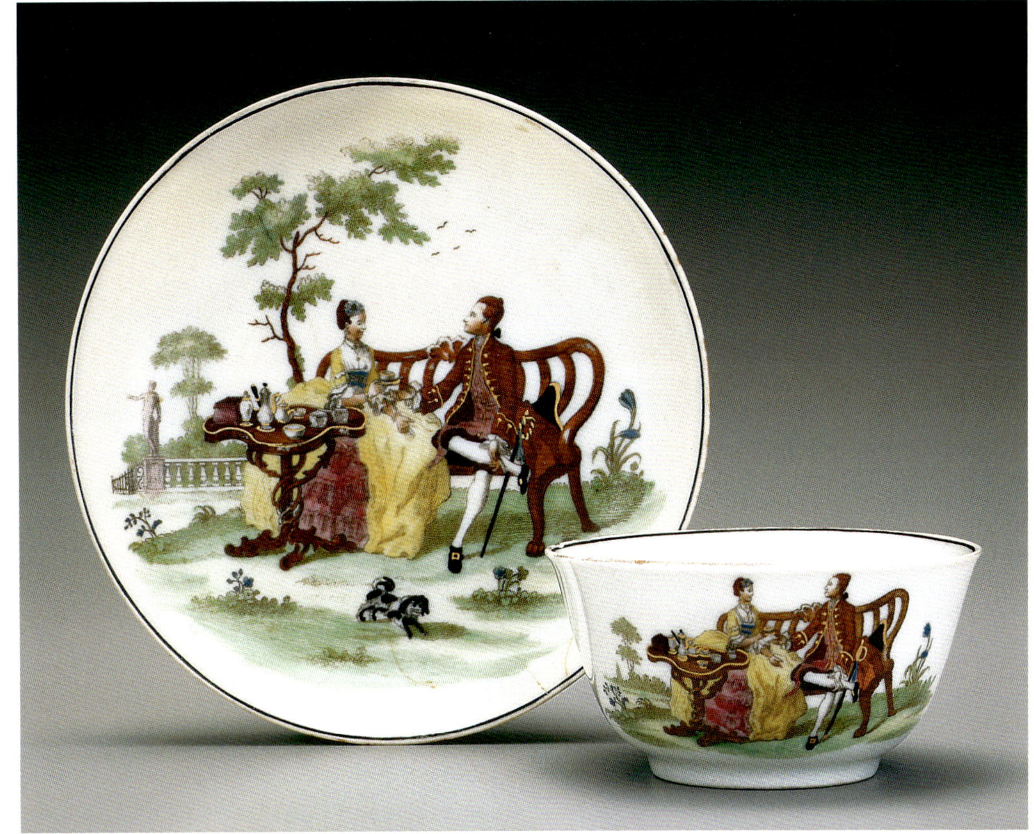

76 TEA BOWL AND SAUCER

Jingdezhen, China; 1755–70
Decorated in England; 1755–70
Diameter (saucer): 4.625 in. (117 mm)
L03.2775.61

The decoration on this tea bowl and saucer is unusual in that it is printed, not painted. The scene is known as *The Tea Party* and was designed by English engraver Robert Hancock, whose signature, *R. Hancock fecit,* appears on the tea bowl.[152]

The technique of transfer-printing on ceramics was developed in England in the early 1750s. Hancock helped perfect the process and supplied engraved copper plates to several porcelain factories, including that at Worcester. Most likely an independent decorator hoping to capitalize on the new fashion for printed porcelain purchased Hancock's plates in order to decorate export porcelain blanks. Although London was the location of many independent decorators, much early transfer-printing on porcelain was done in Birmingham and Worcester, so these pieces may have been decorated in one of those cities.[153]

Worcester Porcelain Factory, tea caddy transfer-printed with *The Tea Party* by Robert Hancock, Worcester, England, 1755–70. Porcelain; H. 5.125 in. L03.2775.60

LITERATURE

Illustrated in Howard and Ayers, *China for the West,* 2:544–45.

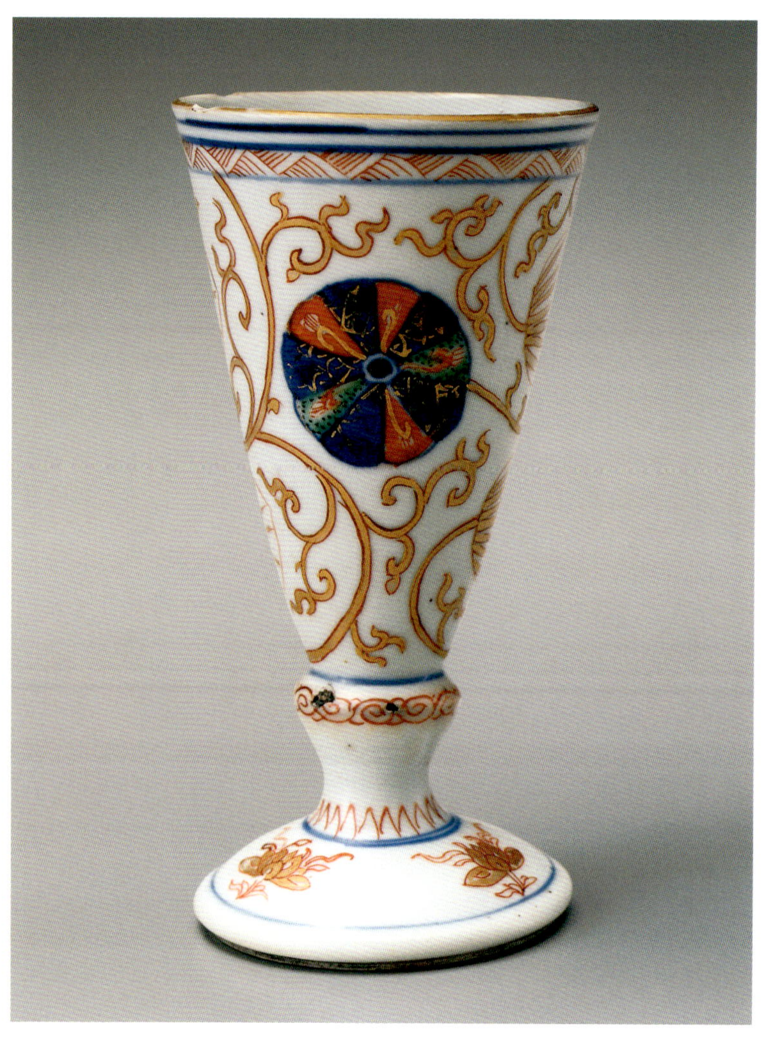

77 GOBLET

Jingdezhen, China; about 1710
Height: 5 in. (127 mm)
L03.2775.79

This goblet, with its conical bowl and domed foot, closely resembles glass goblets made in Europe and England during the last decades of the 17th century. Export porcelain goblets were probably commissioned in an attempt to compete with the growing European and British glass industry.[154]

The goblet would have been used primarily for wine. Typically in this period, wine was served to diners from a sideboard; a thirsty individual would request a glass, which would be brought full from the sideboard on a salver or tray, drunk, and then returned for washing and reuse.[155]

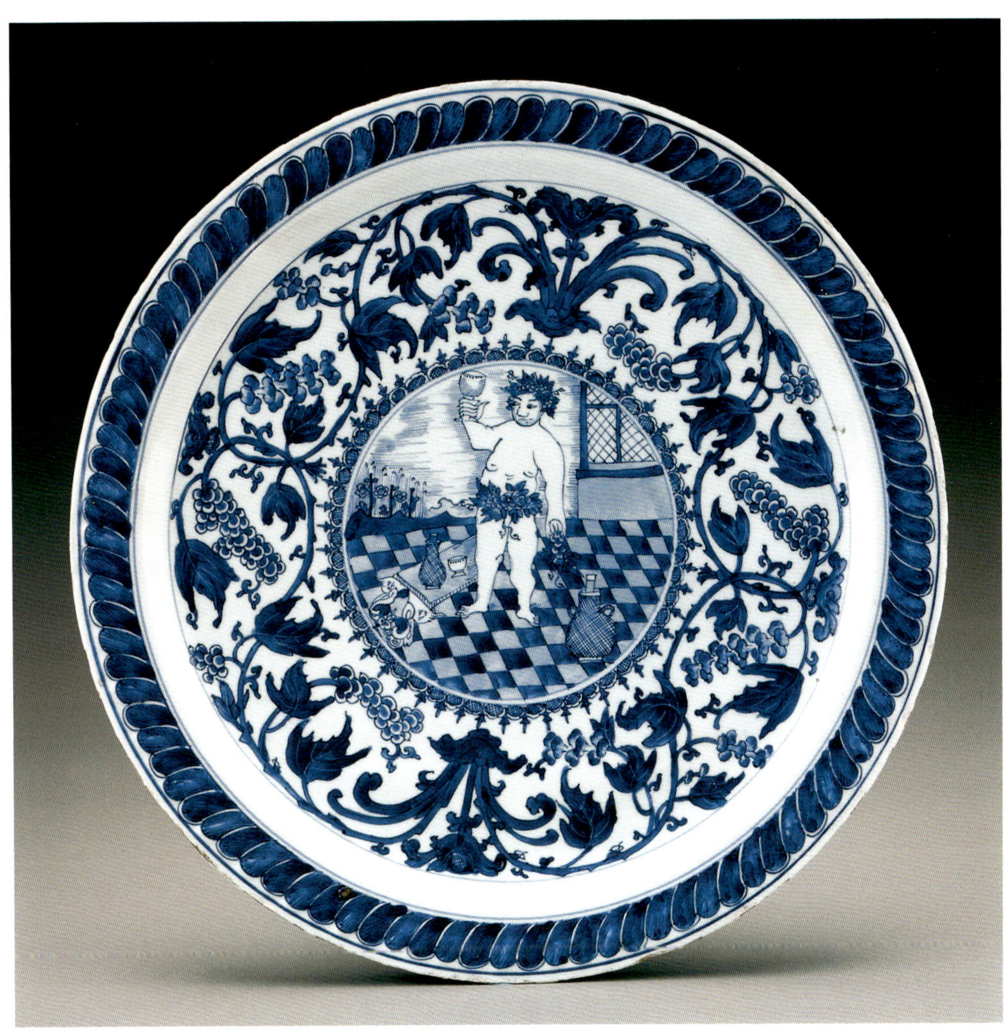

78 TRAY OR CHARGER

Jingdezhen, China; about 1700
Diameter: 14.75 in. (375 mm)
L03.2775.95

This tray, or charger, is decorated with a scene of Bacchus, the Roman god of wine. It was probably used for carrying goblets of wine from a sideboard to diners at the table. The scene of Bacchus in a Dutch-style interior with a tiled floor, diamond-pane window, and table set with a decanter and goblet is probably copied from the decoration on a Dutch delft dish; the gadrooned border copies those on silver and pewter plates.[156]

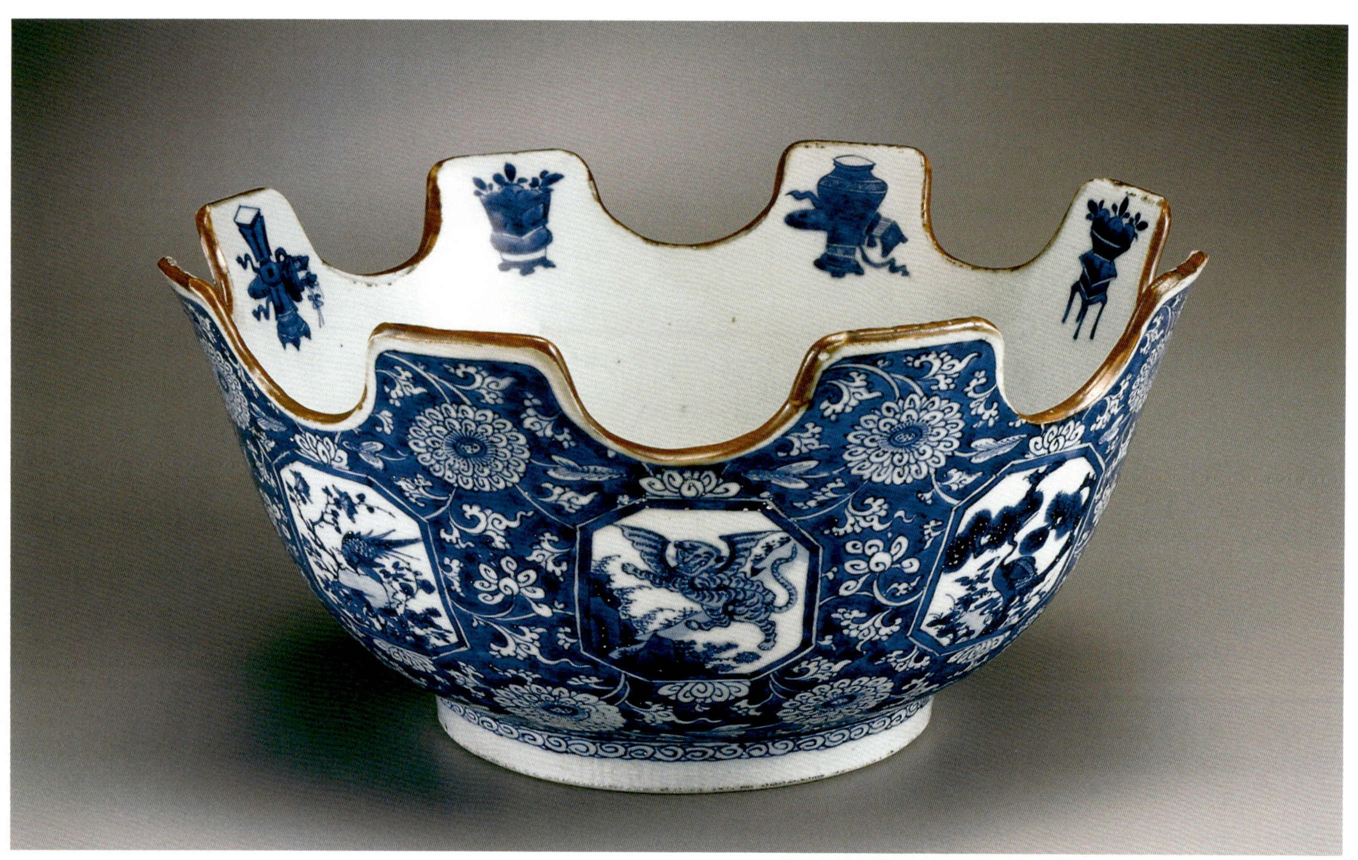

79 MONTEITH

Jingdezhen, China; 1700–1720
Diameter: 13 in. (330 mm)
2003.47.4

As described in a 1721 dictionary, a monteith is "a scallopt bason to cool glasses in."[157] In the 17th and early 18th centuries, wine was drunk chilled, which necessitated cool glassware.

English antiquarian Anthony à Wood recorded in his diary that

> This yeare in the Summer came up a vessel or bason notched at the brims to let drinking glasses hang there by the foot so that the body or drinking place might stand in the water to cool them. Such a basin was called a "Monteith" from a fantastical Scot called "Monsieur Monteith" who at that time or a little before wore the bottoms of his cloake or coate so notched UUUU.

Monteiths, also of silver, brass, tin-glazed earthenware, and glass, continued to be made until the late 1700s, although their popularity declined after the 1720s as chilled wines were replaced by fortified ones drunk at room temperature.[158]

LITERATURE
Illustrated in Howard, *Choice of the Private Trader,* p. 190.

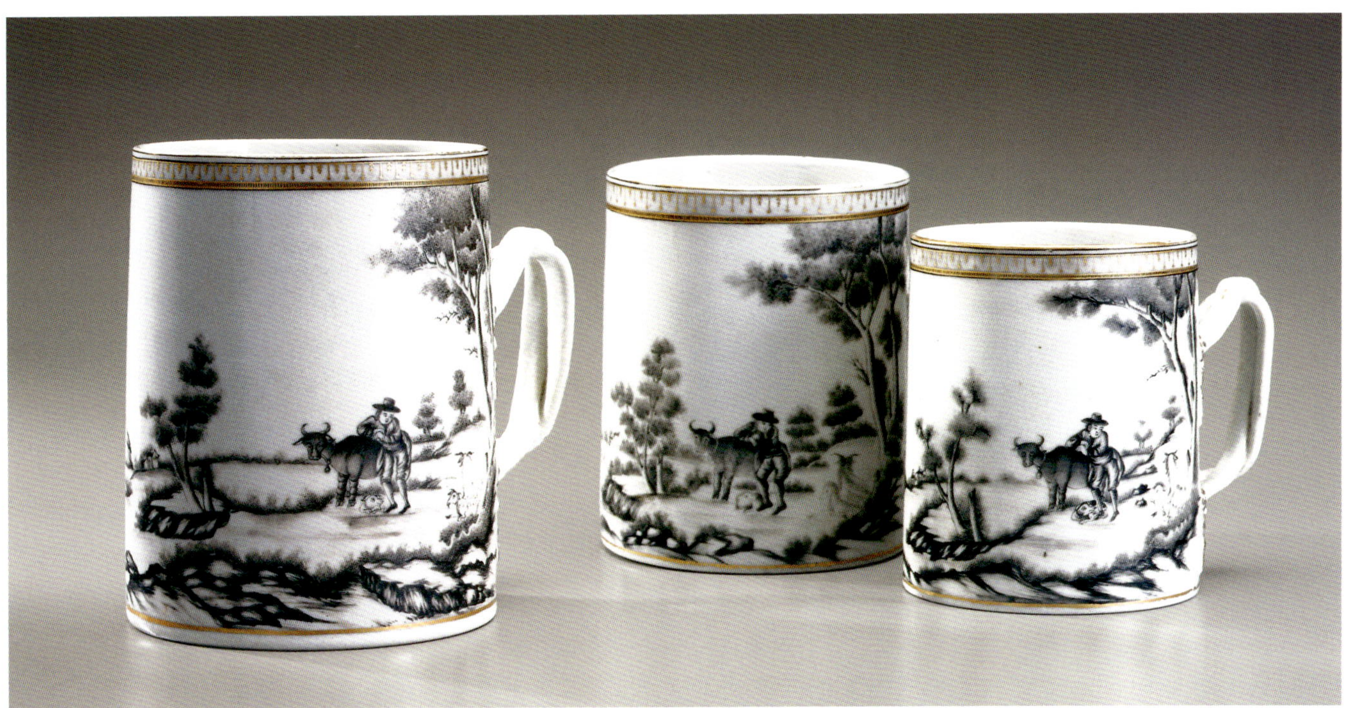

80 SET OF THREE MUGS

Jingdezhen, China; 1800–1810
Height (largest): 6 in. (152 mm)
2000.61.71.1–.3

The *grisaille* decoration on this set of mugs is known as the Quaker cow pattern, an attribution based on a surviving design thought to have been drawn by Philadelphia Quaker Mary Hollingsworth Morris and inscribed "Pattern for Set of China copied by Mary H. Morris Jan 7, 1797." Although the family history is not entirely correct, there is clearly some truth to the story, as a number of pieces in this pattern survive with Philadelphia histories. The design is also probably not original to the artist, whether Mary Morris or someone else, but was most likely inspired by a Dutch print.[159]

Used for beer, ale, or cider, mugs like these were typically ordered in graduated sets of three. Typical are the "best enameled mugs, 3 to a sett, 1 qt., 1 pt, 1 of ½ pint" that were bought for between $.75 and $1.00 by an unknown American China Trade merchant for export to America.[160]

LITERATURE
Illustrated in Howard, *Choice of the Private Trader,* p. 197.

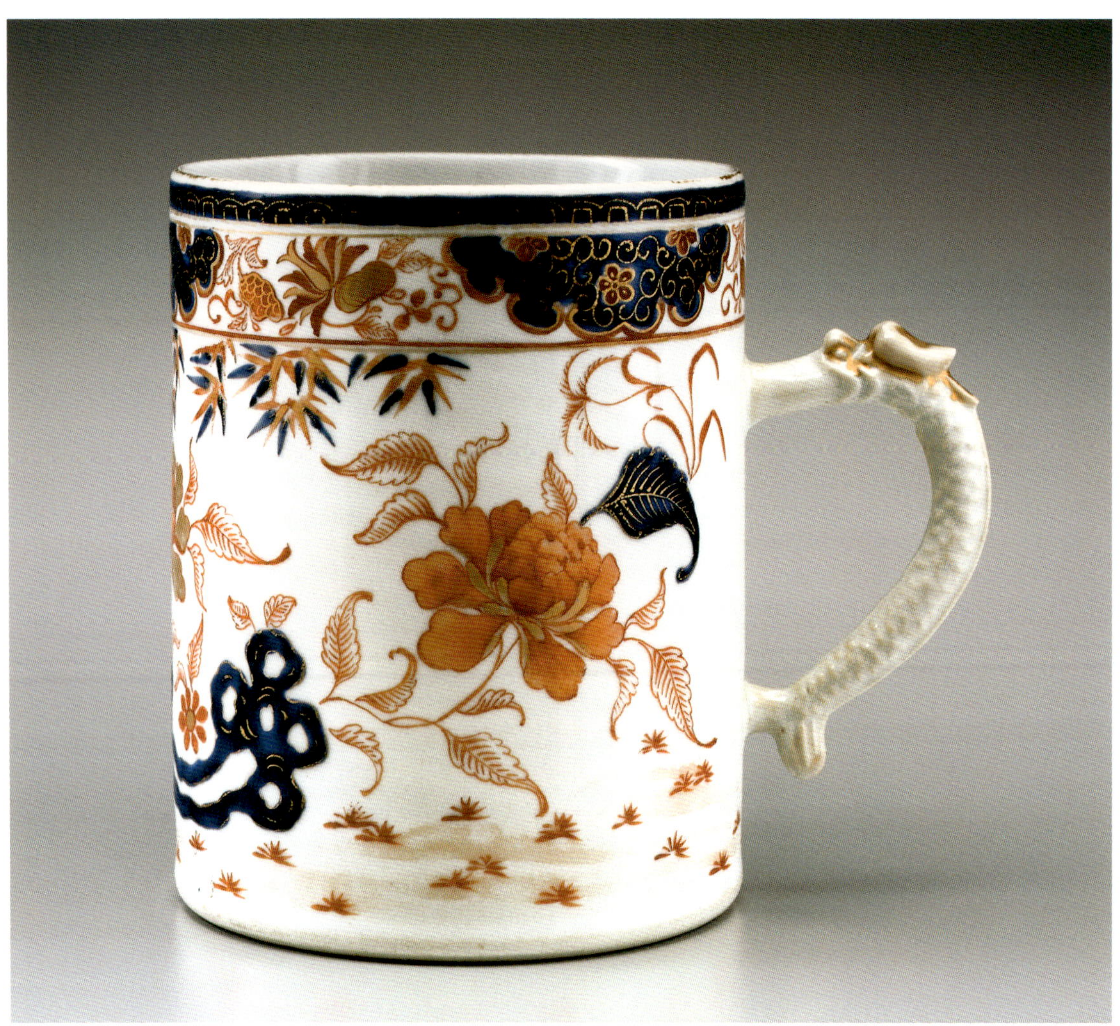

81 MUG

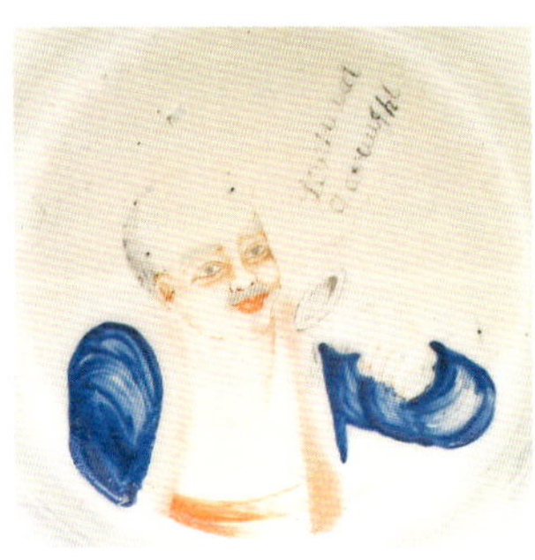

(interior)

Jingdezhen, China; about 1810
Height: 4.75 in. (121 mm)
L03.2775.86

The surprise in this mug lies on the inside; at the bottom is a picture of a man draining a mug and exclaiming, "Lord what a draught" (the word *what* has been incorrectly copied as a "u").[161] The scene would have been visible only after the beer, ale, or cider had been drunk. Several mugs with the same decoration are known—part of a long tradition of decorating the interiors of mugs and punch bowls with surprises such as figures of frogs and inscriptions that either make fun of the drinker or encourage further consumption.

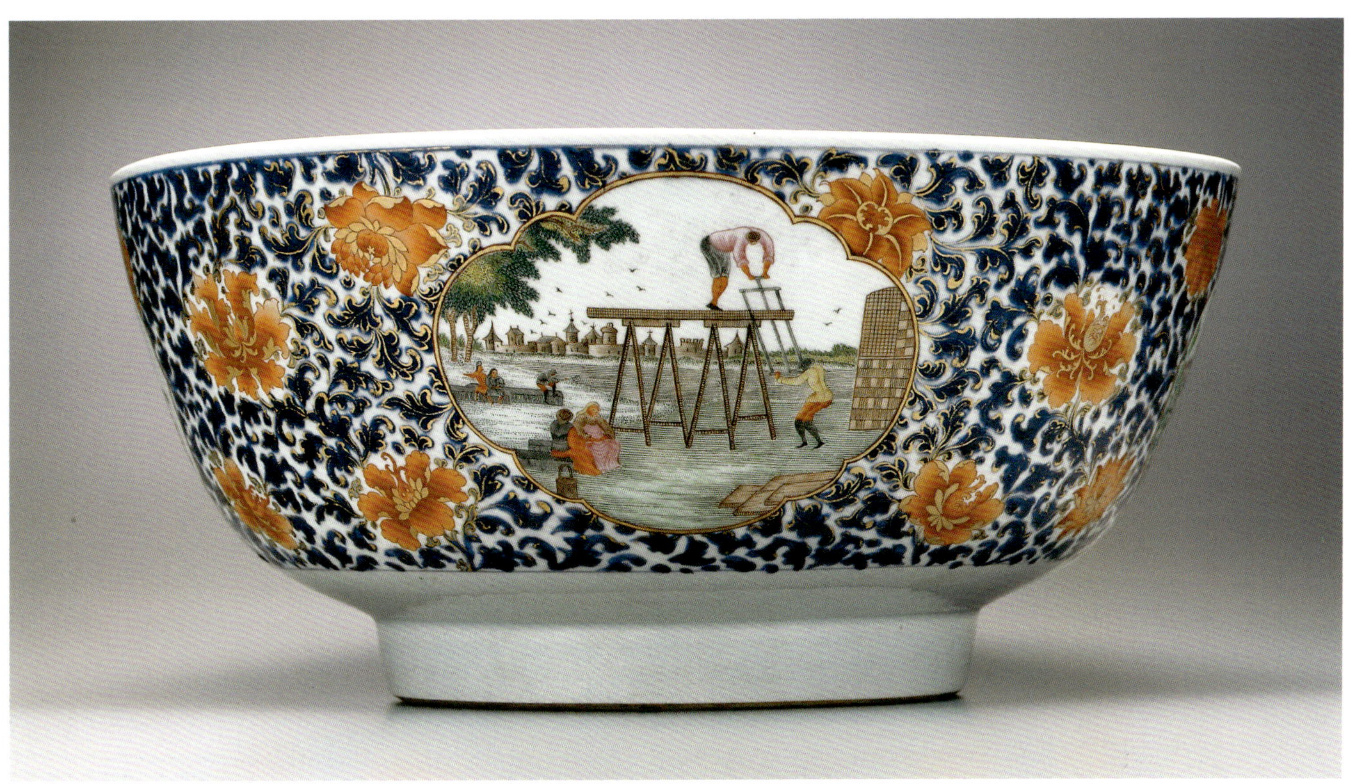

82 PUNCH BOWL

Jingdezhen, China; about 1745
Diameter: 16 in. (406 mm)
1.03.2775.87

This large punch bowl is decorated with panels containing a scene of sawyers cutting lumber supported on trestles. The design is inspired by Meissen porcelain of the 1720s and 1730s, which was often decorated with images of sailors, merchants, and laborers. Fragments of a tea service with identical decoration were recovered from the wreck of the *Götheborg,* which sank near her home port of Gothenburg, Sweden, in 1745.[162]

The word *punch* probably comes from the Persian *panj* or the Hindu *pànch,* both of which mean five. The drink is made of spirits, water, lemon or lime juice, sugar, and spices and was introduced to Europe by East India merchants. In 1664 English diarist John Evelyn recounted how he visited "an East India vessel that lay at Blackwall, where we had Entertainment. . . . Amongst other spirituous drinks as punch, etc. they gave us." The earliest known reference to export porcelain punch bowls occurs in 1696, when "8 Punch Bowles straw colour" were brought to England by the British East India Company.[163]

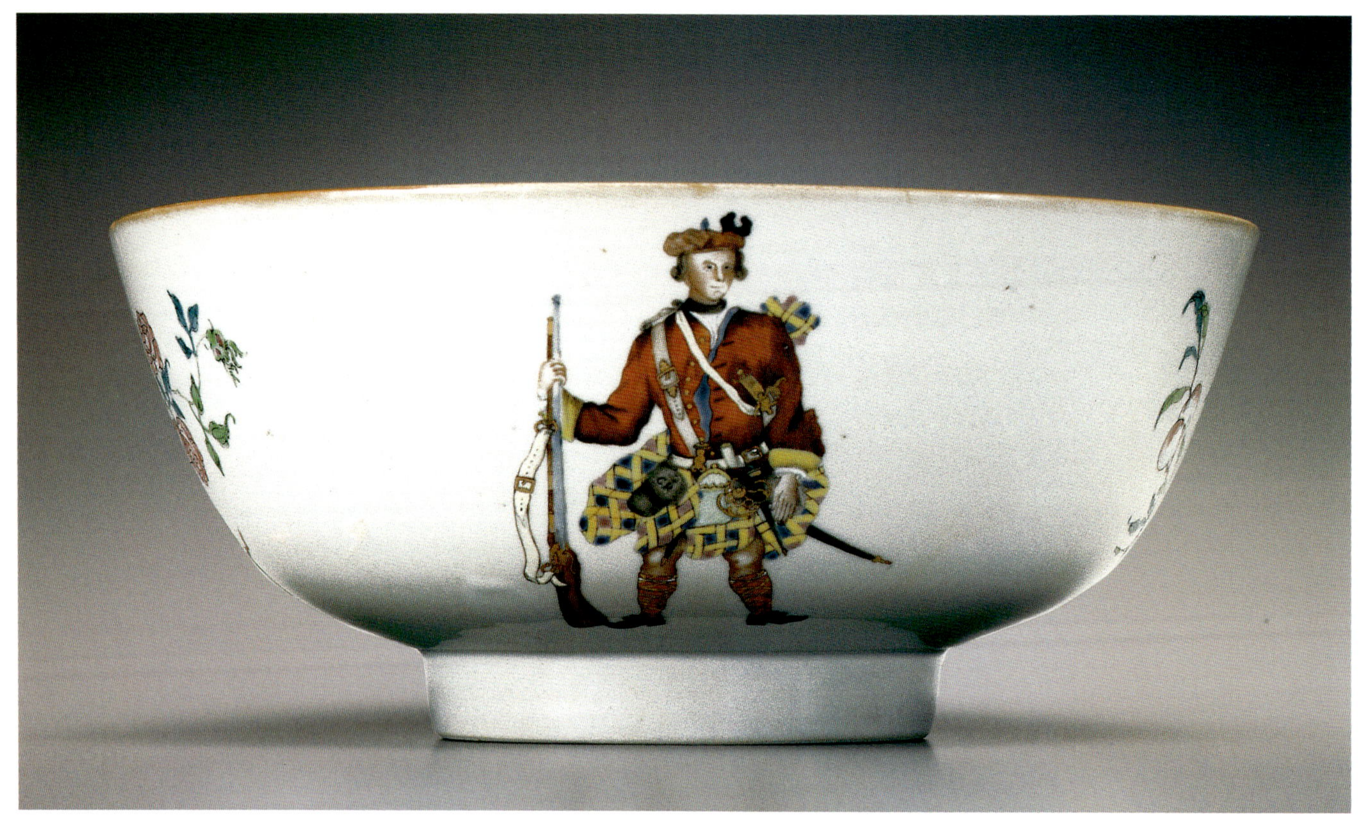

83 PUNCH BOWL

(interior)

Jingdezhen, China; about 1745
Diameter: 11.5 in. (292 mm)
L03.2731.5

The two Scotsmen painted on the exterior of this punch bowl are a piper and a private of the First Highland Regiment of the British Army, the 43rd Regiment of Foot, better known as the Royal Highland Regiment or Black Watch. Both images are copied from engravings by George Bickham and were included in a set of prints sold by dealer John Bowles of London. The piper also appeared as the frontispiece to *A Short History of the Highland Regiment,* published in London in 1743. The interior of the bowl is decorated with a medallion containing the portrait of an unidentified man who may be James Stuart, "The Old Pretender."[164]

A number of plates and a few punch bowls survive with this design. They may have been created for the general British market to satisfy a growing interest in Scotland or may have been for supporters of the Jacobite cause. Jacobites were followers of the Catholic James Stuart and his son Charles Edward Stuart (Bonnie Prince Charlie), who claimed the throne of England. Jacobites were active in Scotland, particularly during the mid-1740s, when several clans rose up in rebellion and marched south into England. They were ultimately driven back to Scotland and defeated at the Battle of Culloden, effectively ending Jacobite hopes for a return to the throne.[165]

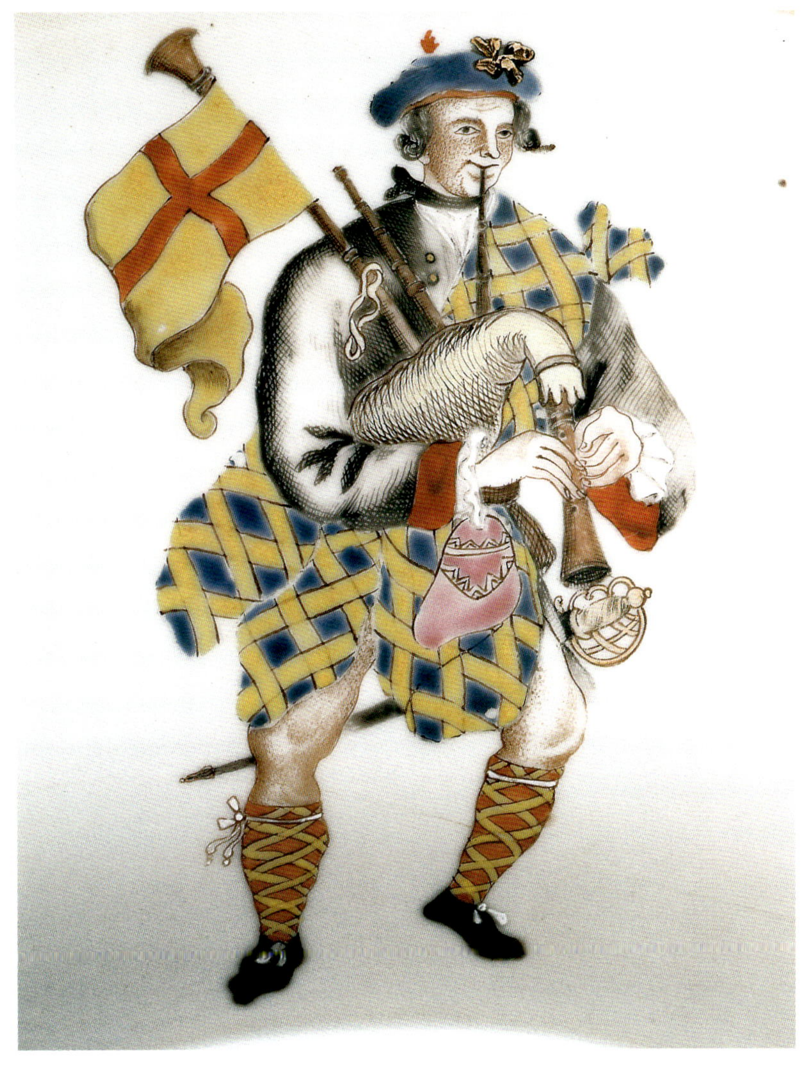

(reverse)

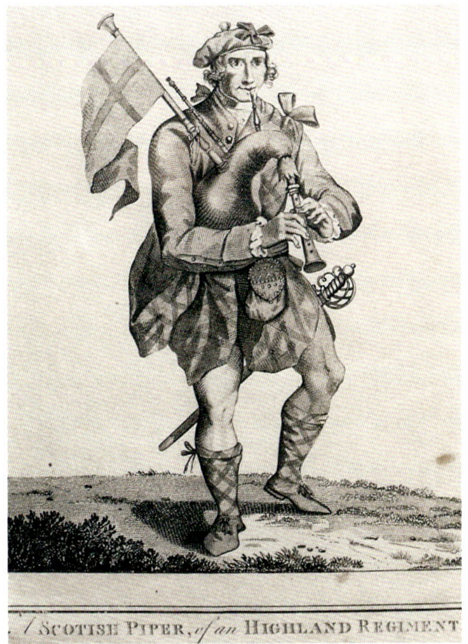

George Bickham, *A Scottish Piper, of an Highland Regiment,* London, England, about 1742. Engraving; H. 7.75 in., W. 8.5 in. Photo, courtesy of David S. Howard.

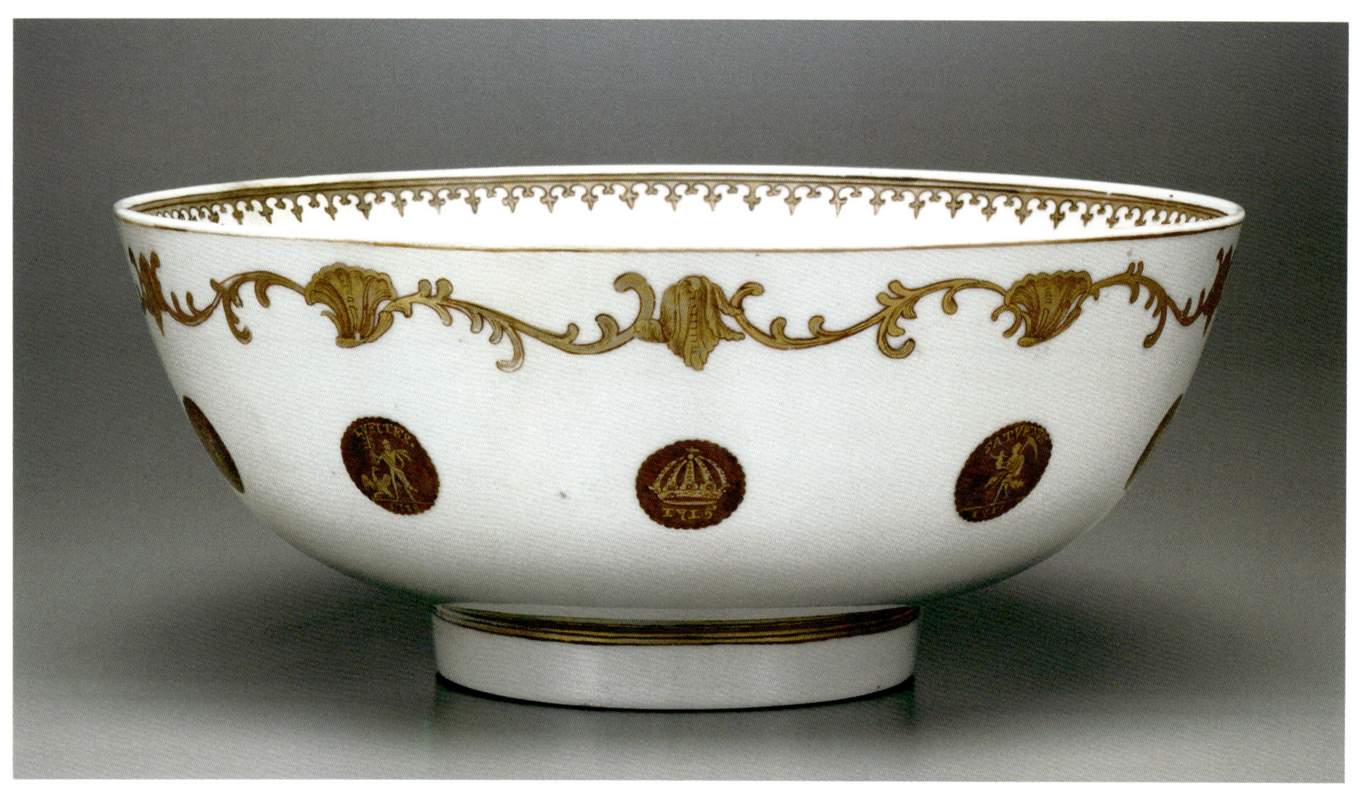

84 PUNCH BOWL

Jingdezhen, China; about 1750
Diameter: 10.25 in. (260 mm)
L03.2775.94

Ten Swedish copper coins served as the model for the decoration on this punch bowl. The coins were minted between 1715 and 1719 and were known as emergency or necessity dalers, which were issued to alleviate the shortage of silver coins during the Great Northern War between Sweden and Denmark, Poland, and Russia. The coins are decorated with a variety of emblems, including a crown; Roman gods such as Mars, Jupiter, and Saturn; and inscriptions such as *WETT OCH WAPPEN* (Wit and Weapons) and *FLINK OCH FARDIG* (Agile and Ready).[166]

Although prints and drawings were the most common sources of inspiration for designs on Chinese export porcelain, coins and medallions were also used. What is unusual is that the scroll and shell border dates this bowl to about 1750, approximately thirty years after the coins were minted. It is possible that the coins were issued to the Swedish East India Company for use in Asia after they had served their purpose in Sweden. There were currency shortages throughout the 18th century, and many nations issued tokens for use by their trading companies.[167]

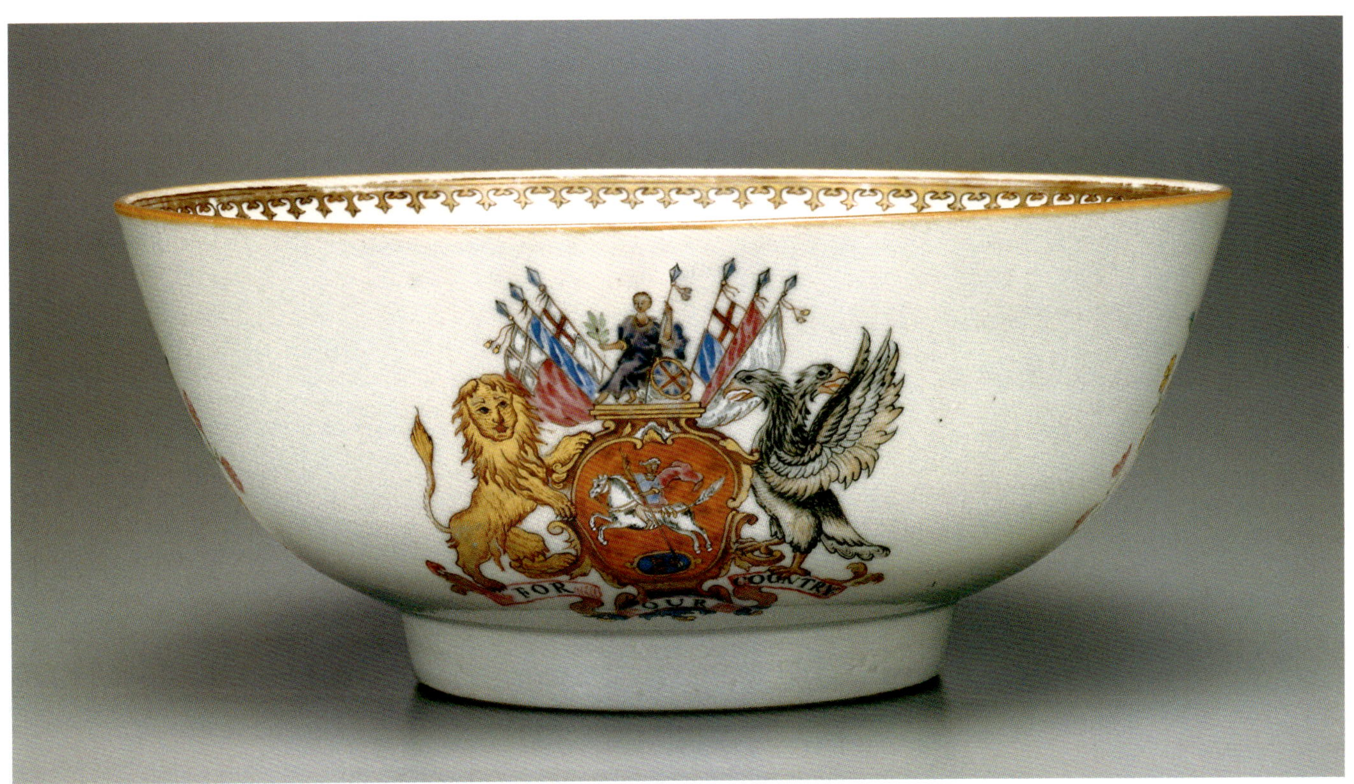

85 PUNCH BOWL

Jingdezhen, China; about 1755
Diameter: 9.125 in. (232 mm)
L03.2775.100

Movements to support local manufactures are nothing new. This punch bowl is decorated with the arms of the Anti-Gallican Society, which was founded in 1745 "to promote British Manufactures, extend the Commerce of England, and discourage the Introduction of French modes and the Importation of French commodities."[168]

France was the center of style and culture for much of the 17th and 18th centuries, but it was also England's traditional rival and enemy. Anti-French sentiment was especially strong during the mid-18th century, due partly to the failed Jacobite uprising, which was an attempt to restore the pro-French, Catholic Stuarts to the throne. So although some Englishmen and women readily adopted French fashion, cuisine, and styles of interior decoration, others lampooned them as foreign and dangerous.

The Anti-Gallican Society's coat of arms is full of nationalistic symbols, including the motto "For Our Country" as well as the patron saint of England, Saint George, who is dressed as King George II and shown spearing the coat of arms of France. A number of punch bowls with versions of the society's arms exist, no doubt designed for use during their social gatherings.

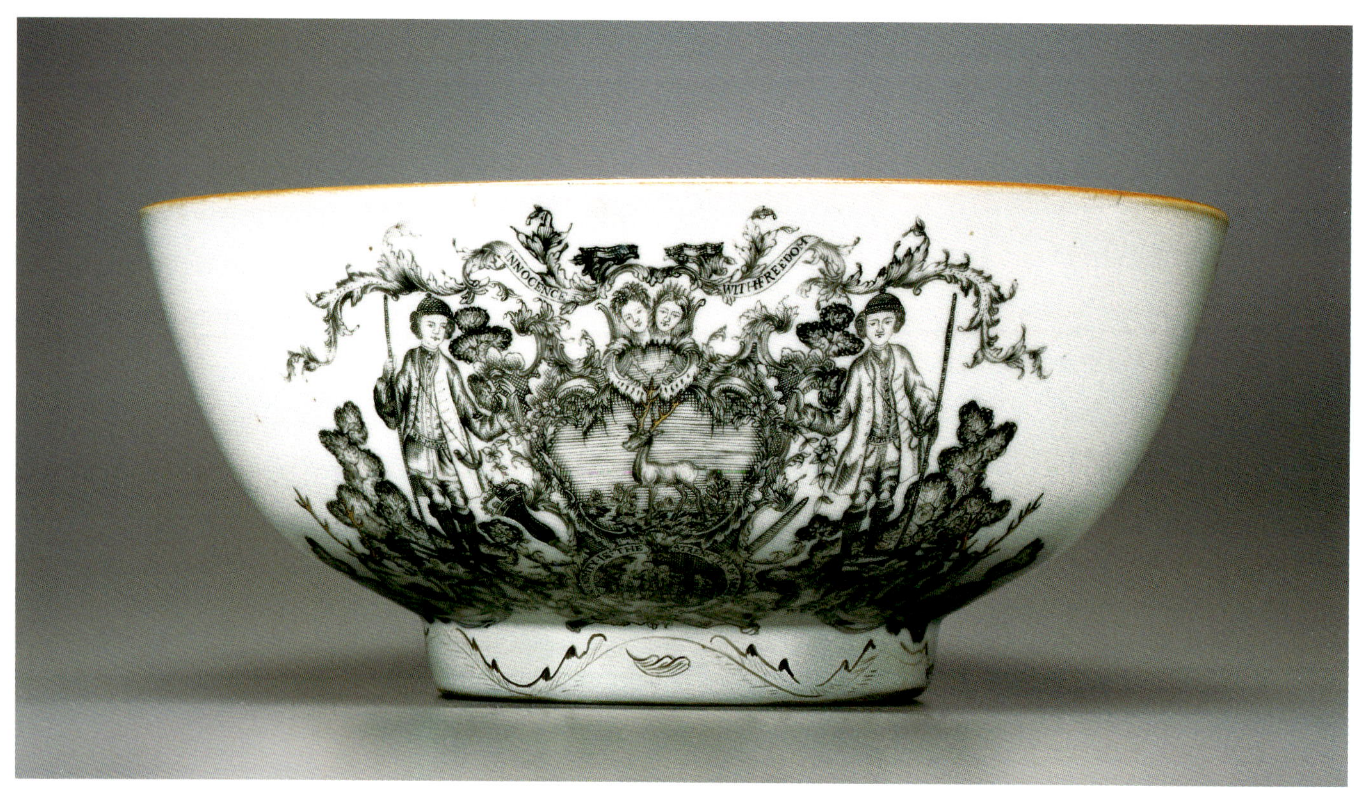

86 PUNCH BOWL

Jingdezhen, China; about 1760
Diameter 10.375 in. (264 mm)
2003.47.11

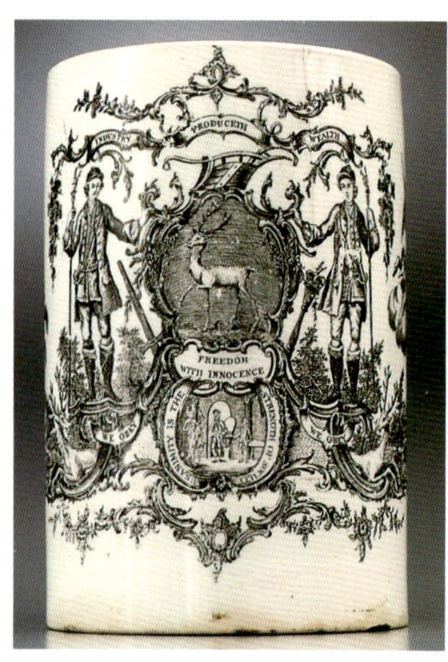

Mug, transfer-printed with the arms of the Society of Bucks, Staffordshire, England, about 1760. Creamware; H. 5 in. 2003.47.10.

This export porcelain punch bowl is decorated with the arms of the Society of Bucks, an English social organization similar to the Masons. The arms are copied directly from a piece of English transfer-printed creamware or porcelain, such as the creamware mug shown here.

The Society of Bucks was founded probably in the 1720s. Although the society's papers refer to principles of Nimrodism (based on the teachings of Nimrod, the ancient king of Assyria, who was a mighty hunter), the main purpose of the group was most likely social. Drinking was clearly a popular activity, and a large number of mugs, jugs, and punch bowls decorated with the arms of the society survive. The heyday of the Bucks seems to have been in the 1760s and 1770s; by 1770 there were at least nineteen lodges throughout Britain. The society died out probably between 1820 and 1830.[169]

LITERATURE

Illustrated in Howard and Ayers, *China for the West,* 2:426.

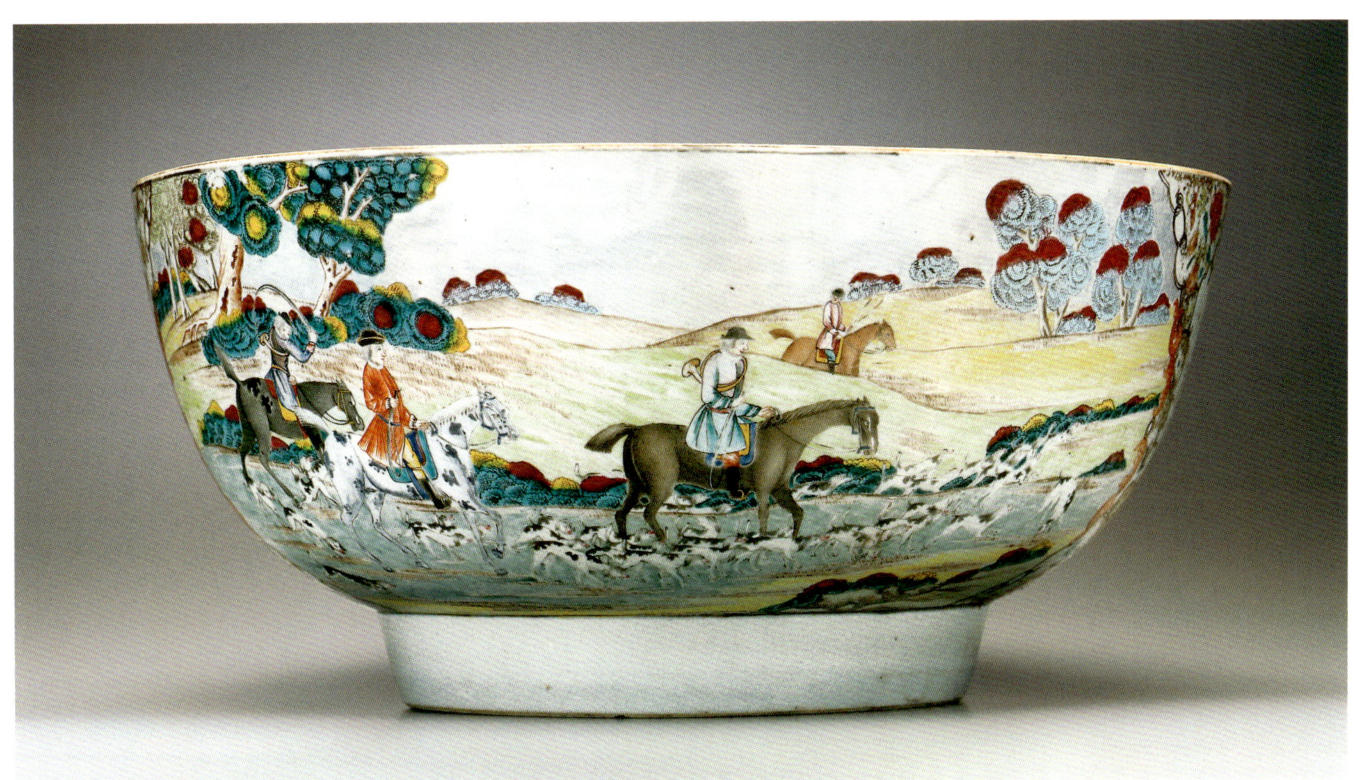

87 PUNCH BOWL

Jingdezhen, China, about 1760
Diameter: 15.5 in. (392 mm)
L03.2775.11

Elaborately painted scenes of one of 18th-century England's favorite sports, foxhunting, decorate the exterior of this punch bowl. The images are copied from English prints, most likely Pierre-Charles Canot's *Brushing into Cover* and Thomas Burford's *Beating and Trailing for a Hare,* which were based on works by English artist James Seymour.[170] Punch bowls decorated with foxhunting scenes were popular in 18th-century Britain and America, where they were no doubt used during festivities before and after hunts.

LITERATURE
Illustrated in Howard, *Choice of the Private Trader,* pp. 198–99.

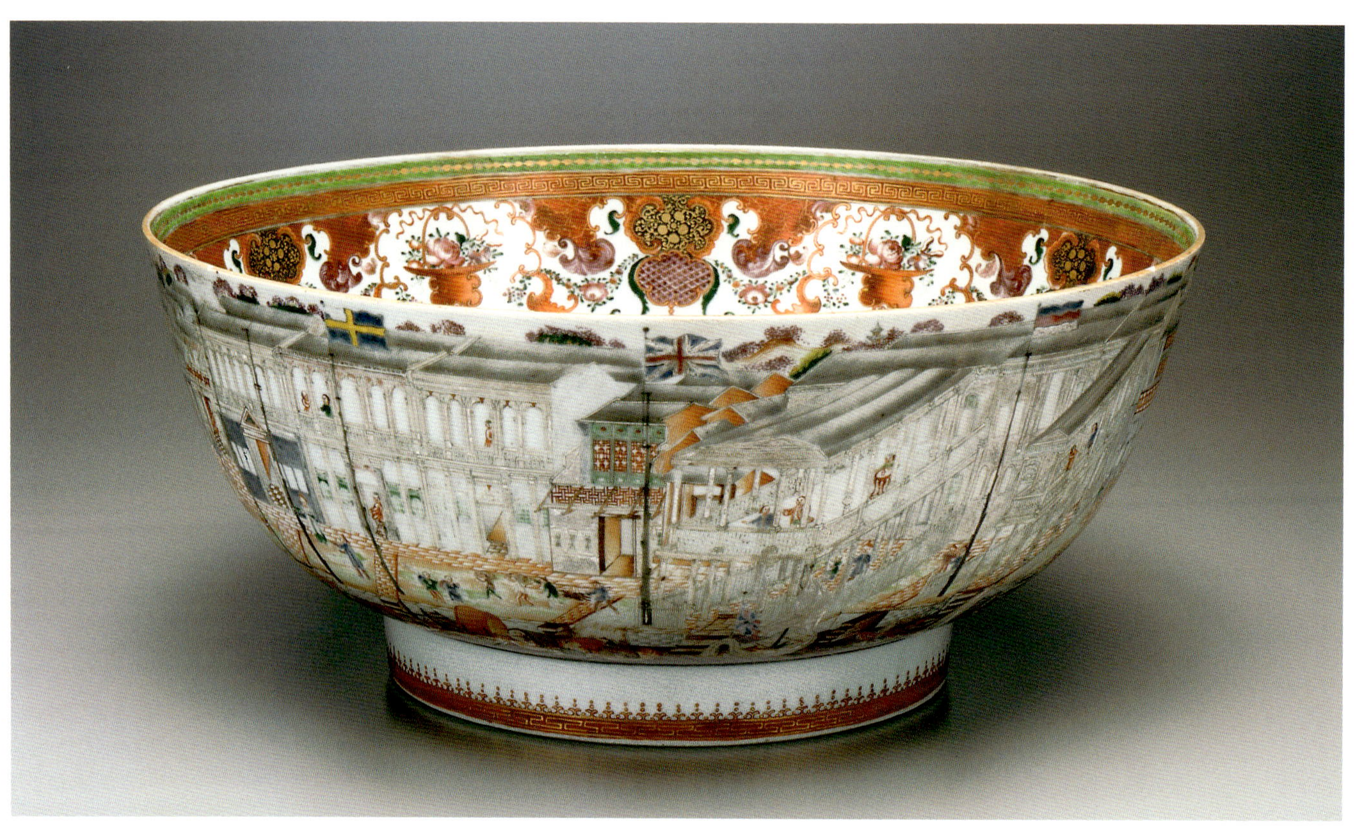

88 PUNCH BOWL

Jingdezhen, China; 1780–90
Diameter: 10.25 in. (360 mm)
2000.61.73

A panoramic view of the European trading offices, or hongs, in Canton is seen on this punch bowl. Hongs were long, narrow buildings on the foreshore of the Pearl River, outside the city walls, where European and American merchants lived, worked, and stored their merchandise. The buildings, owned by Chinese merchants and rented by Western traders, were usually identified by national or company flags flown in front. The hongs were rebuilt several times over the course of the 18th and 19th centuries, with this particular view showing them as they existed in the late 18th century.

The image was probably inspired by traditional Chinese hand scrolls and represents an interesting blending of Chinese painting convention—which tends to view a landscape as a progression through nature with no fixed focal point—and Western, one-point perspective. Bowls decorated with images of the hongs were probably first made in the late 1760s. The earliest known order dates to 1779, when the Dutch East India Company requested bowls decorated with the "town of Canton with the ships on the roadstead."[171]

Hong bowls were among the most popular souvenirs brought back by traders. In 1785 John Green, captain of the *Empress of China,* which was the first American ship to trade directly with China, purchased four "Factory painted Bowles" for $5.50 apiece—a large sum of money at the time.[172]

LITERATURE
Illustrated in Howard, *Choice of the Private Trader,* pp. 200–201.

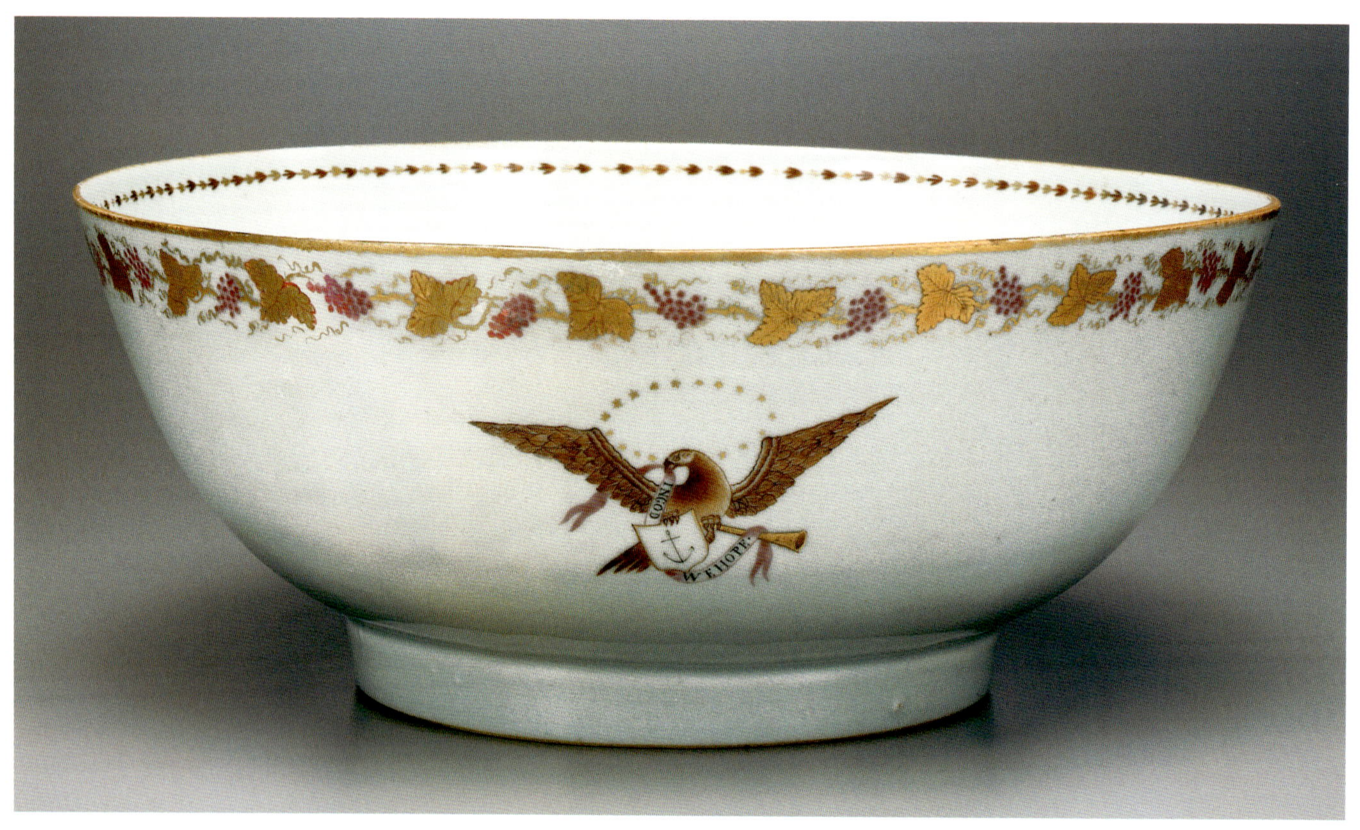

89 PUNCH BOWL

Jingdezhen, China; 1802–6
Diameter: 11.25 in. (286 mm)
L03.2775.34

This punch bowl is decorated with an American eagle holding a shield bearing a foul anchor (an anchor entangled by its rope), a trumpet of fame, and a banner inscribed *IN GOD WE HOPE*—all symbols that represented the state of Rhode Island in the late 18th and early 19th centuries. The design is based on the masthead that appeared between February 13, 1802, and June 19, 1805, on the *Rhode-Island Republican,* a newspaper published by Oliver Farnsworth in Newport.[173]

A number of different pieces, including tea sets, vases, cider jugs, and plates, are known with this design, some of which descended in the family of New York importer and merchant Jesse Baldwin. How these objects created for Rhode Islanders landed in the hands of New Yorkers is not known. There were close trading ties between the two states, so it is not unreasonable to assume that the pieces could have been ordered by a New York merchant for sale in Rhode Island.[174]

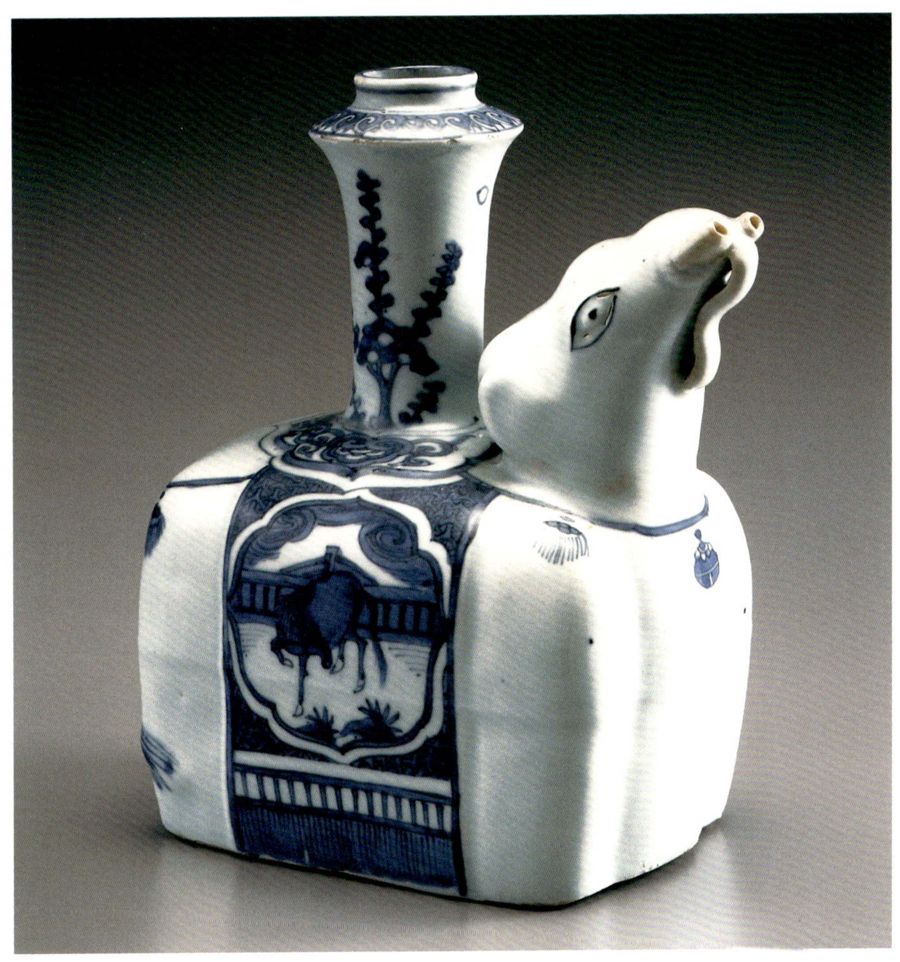

90 KENDI IN THE SHAPE OF AN ELEPHANT

Jingdezhen, China; 1575–1600
Height: 7.25 in. (184 mm)
L03.2775.93

Kendis are water vessels used primarily in Southeast Asia, where they have both practical and religious functions. The form, which may have been developed in India as early as 2000 B.C., was produced by the Chinese for export since at least the Tang Dynasty (618–906). Simple, bulbous forms were the most common, but zoomorphic kendis like this one were also made in the late 16th and early 17th centuries. Elephant-shape kendis were prized outside Southeast Asia; a number were in the collections of the sultans of the Ottoman Empire; another belonged to Philip II of Spain; and one was given pride of place in a 17th-century still life painting by Dutch artist Wilhelm Kalf.[175]

LITERATURE
Illustrated in Howard and Ayers, *China for the West,* 1:50.

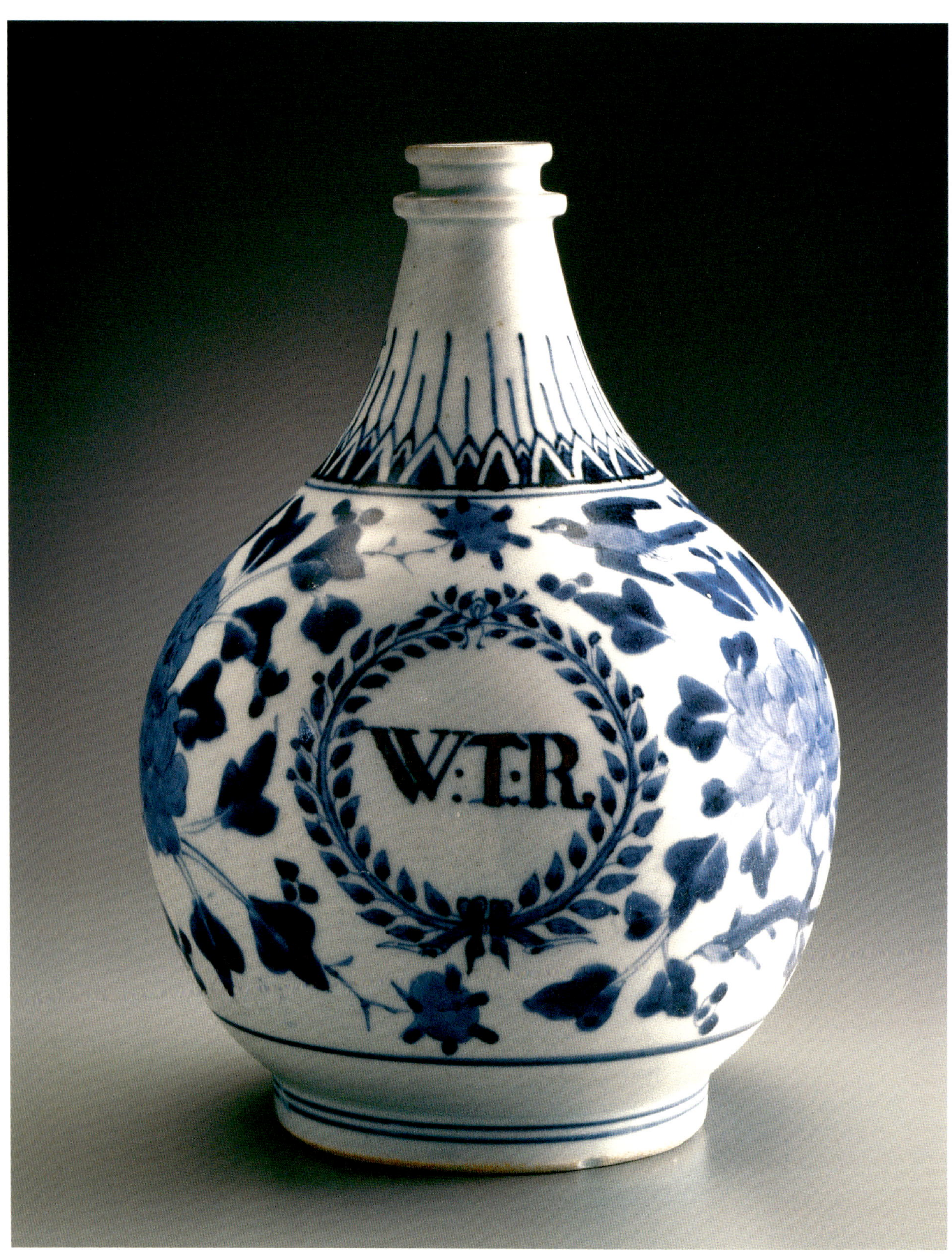
W:T:R

91 BOTTLE

Arita, Japan; 1670–1700
Height: 10 in. (255 mm)
L03.2775.9

Known today as apothecary bottles, porcelain vessels such as the one seen here could have been used for medicine or wine. Their shape is based on that of 17th-century European glass bottles. Many of the export bottles have initials on them, which may refer to either their contents or their original owners. It has been suggested that the initials are those of high-ranking Dutch East India Company officials based in Asia; the initials "W:T:R" on this bottle may be those of Willem ten Rhijne, a surgeon who worked at Deshima, the Dutch East India Company trading settlement in Japan, between 1674 and 1676.[176]

It is also possible that a few of these inscribed bottles were intended for a Japanese rather than Dutch market. Such bottles, if filled with wine, may have been gifts from the Dutch to Japanese merchants or officials, or they may have been bought by Japanese individuals who prized Western objects as exotic curiosities, just as Asian objects were prized in Europe.[177]

LITERATURE
Illustrated in Howard, *Choice of the Private Trader,* pp. 204–5.

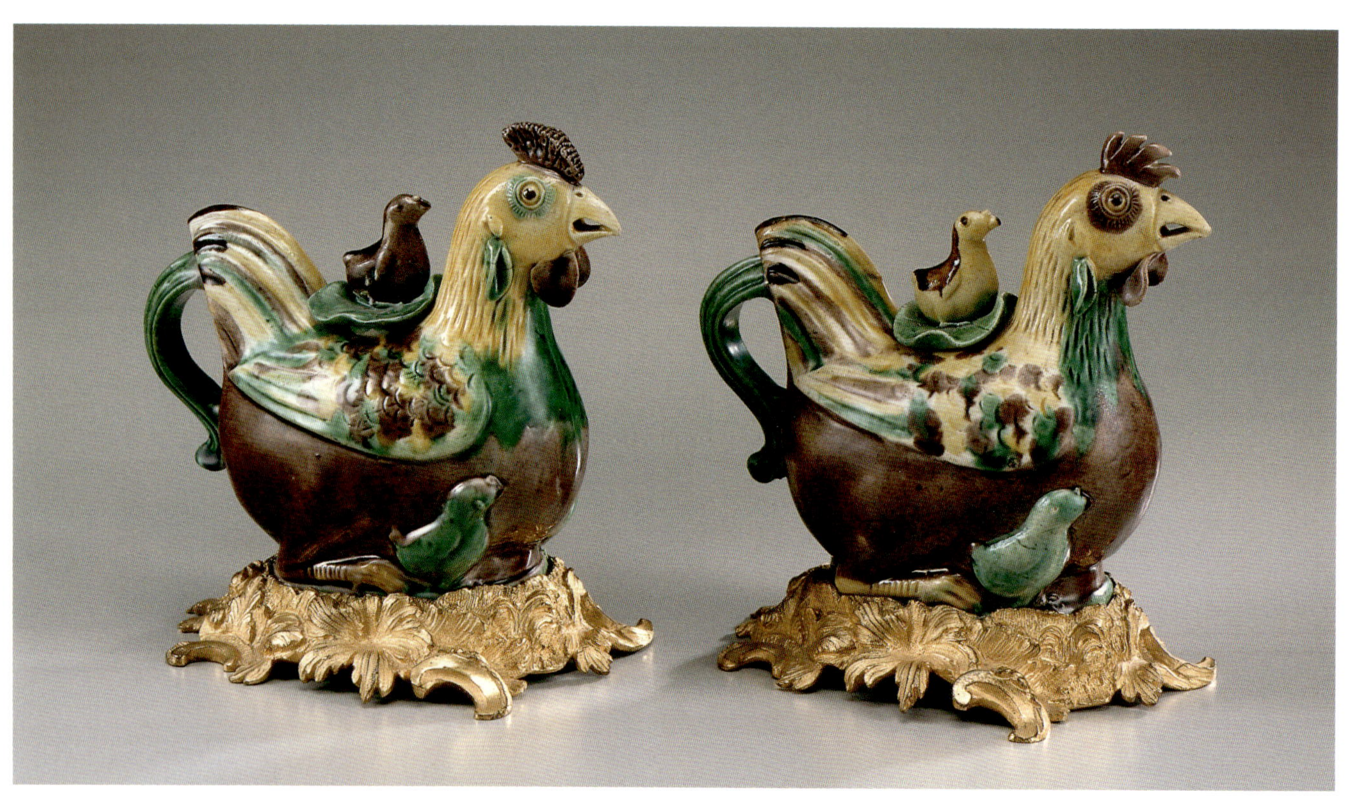

92 PAIR OF EWERS IN THE FORM OF A HEN

Jingdezhen, China; about 1700
Gilt-bronze mounts added in Europe; probably late 1800s
Height (each): 6 in. (152 mm)
2001.15.8.1, .2

Resembling nesting hens, these ewers would have been prized in Europe as curiosities. Animal-shape ewers emerged late in the Ming Dynasty (1368–1644) and reached their peak of popularity during the Kangxi Period (1662–1722), when vessels in the form of cocks, hens, parrots, fish, deer, and monkeys were manufactured. Those in the shape of a hen seem to have been particularly popular and were even copied in Meissen porcelain.[178]

These ewers are decorated with *famille verte* enamels applied directly to an unglazed porcelain body, known as biscuit. The ewers have been embellished with rococo-style gilt-bronze mounts, which were probably added in the late 19th century. Metal mounts were often appended to export porcelain as a way of accentuating its preciousness and to better integrate the objects into European interiors. Gilt-bronze mounts were especially popular in mid-18th-century France, and the style was revived in the late 19th century.[179]

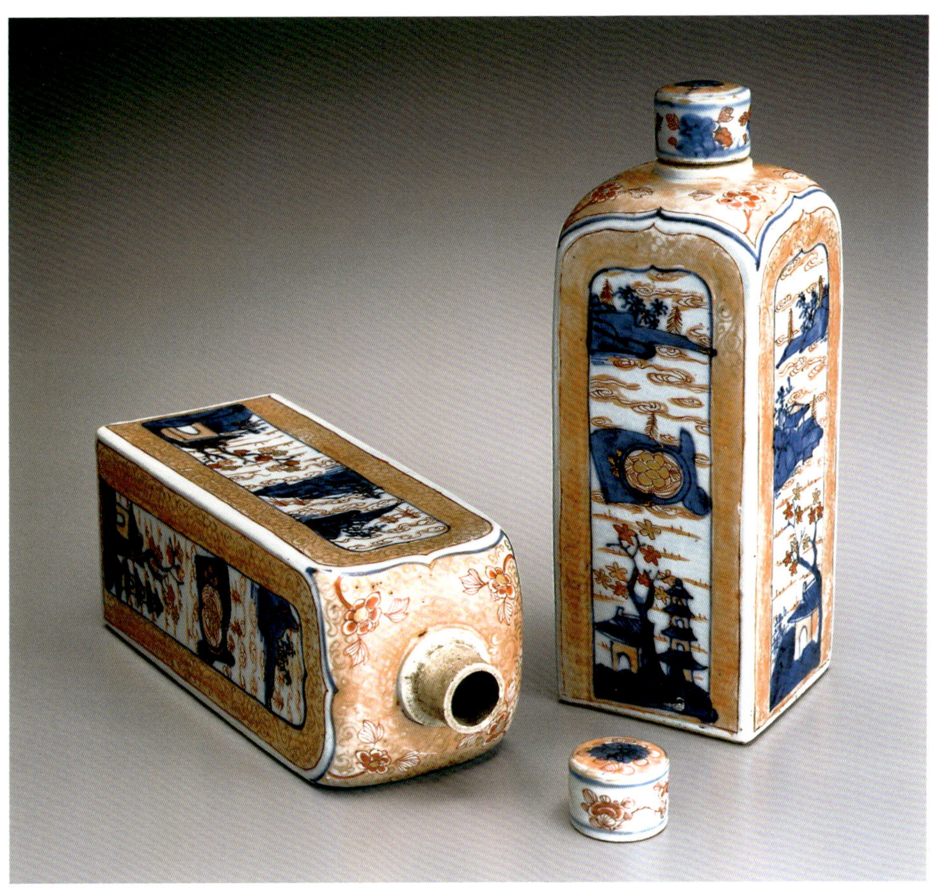

93 PAIR OF BOTTLES

Jingdezhen, China; about 1725
Height (each): 10 in. (254 mm)
L03.2775.78.1, .2

The shape of this pair of square bottles is based on that of European case bottles. Case bottles, whether of glass or export porcelain, usually came in sets of six, nine, or twelve and were designed to fit into partitioned wooden boxes.

Case bottles were also known as gin bottles, after their most common contents. Gin, a distilled spirit flavored with juniper berries, was developed by the Dutch in the mid-17th century. Its low price and high alcoholic content (in comparison to beer) made it especially popular, and gin consumption and its abuse grew tremendously during the 18th century. In 1733 eleven million gallons were distilled in London alone, increasing to an incredible twenty million gallons in 1742. English artist William Hogarth produced a print, *Gin Lane,* in 1751 documenting in graphic detail how gin led to "Idleness, Poverty, misery and ruin."[180]

Though most commonly associated with spirits, these bottles had other, more innocent uses. Several 18th-century colonial Mexico paintings show square porcelain bottles filled with flowers on altars.[181]

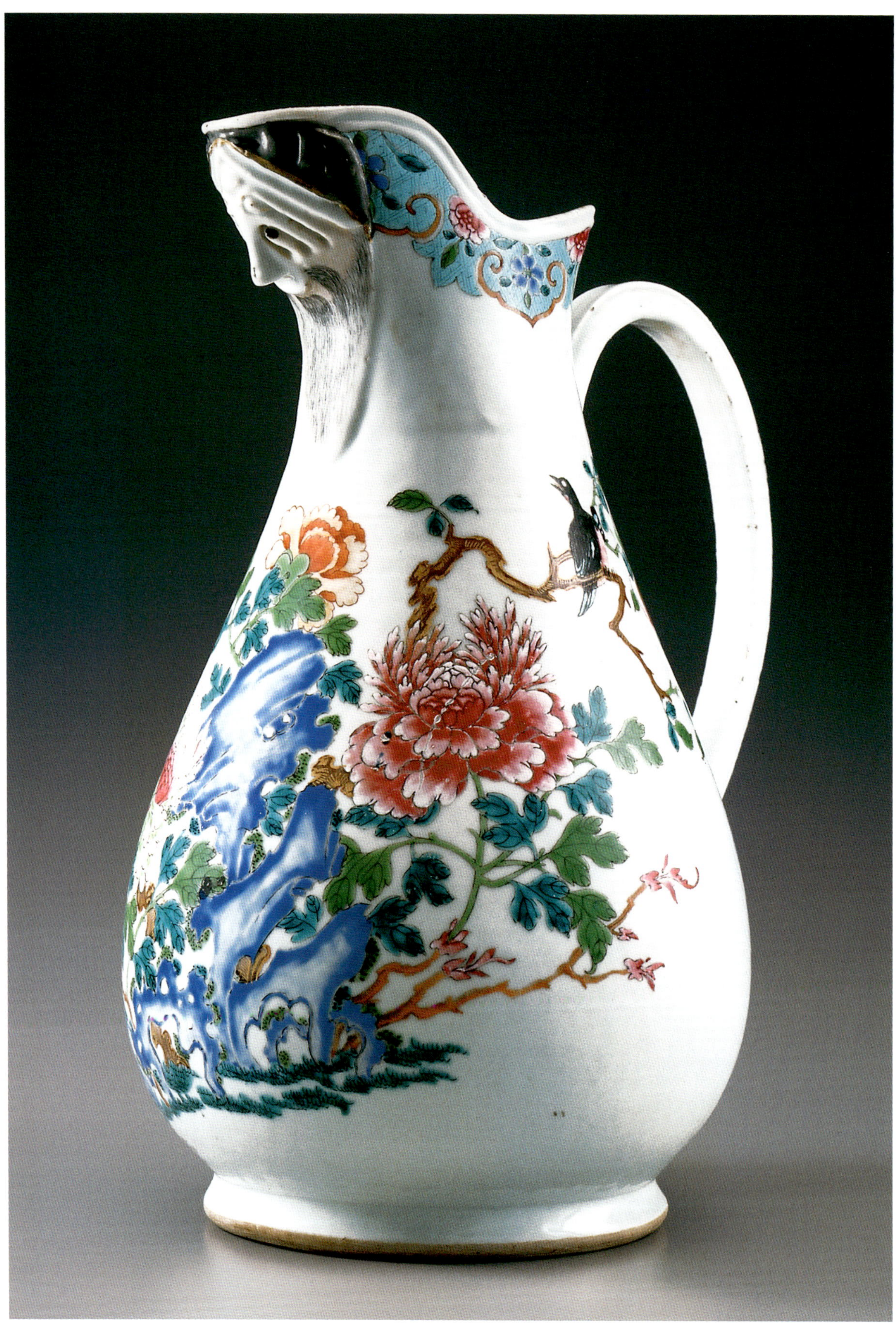

94 JUG

Jingdezhen, China; about 1750
Height: 13.75 in. (348 mm)
2001.20.19

This jug is decorated with vibrantly painted *famille rose* peonies and Chinese rockwork. The shape of the jug, with its molded mask on the spout, is probably based on 17th- and early 18th-century European silver and tin-glazed earthenware forms. These jugs were also produced in blue and white porcelain.[182]

Often referred to today as beer jugs, these vessels held any number of alcoholic beverages, including ale, beer, cider, and punch. One Englishman, while traveling in Southeast Asia in 1665, noted how "I never came ashore, but I drank very immoderately of Punce, Rack, Tea, &, which was brought up in great China-jugs holding at least two Quarts."[183]

LITERATURE

Illustrated in Howard, *Choice of the Private Trader,* p. 212; Brown, *Come Drink the Bowl Dry,* p. 76.

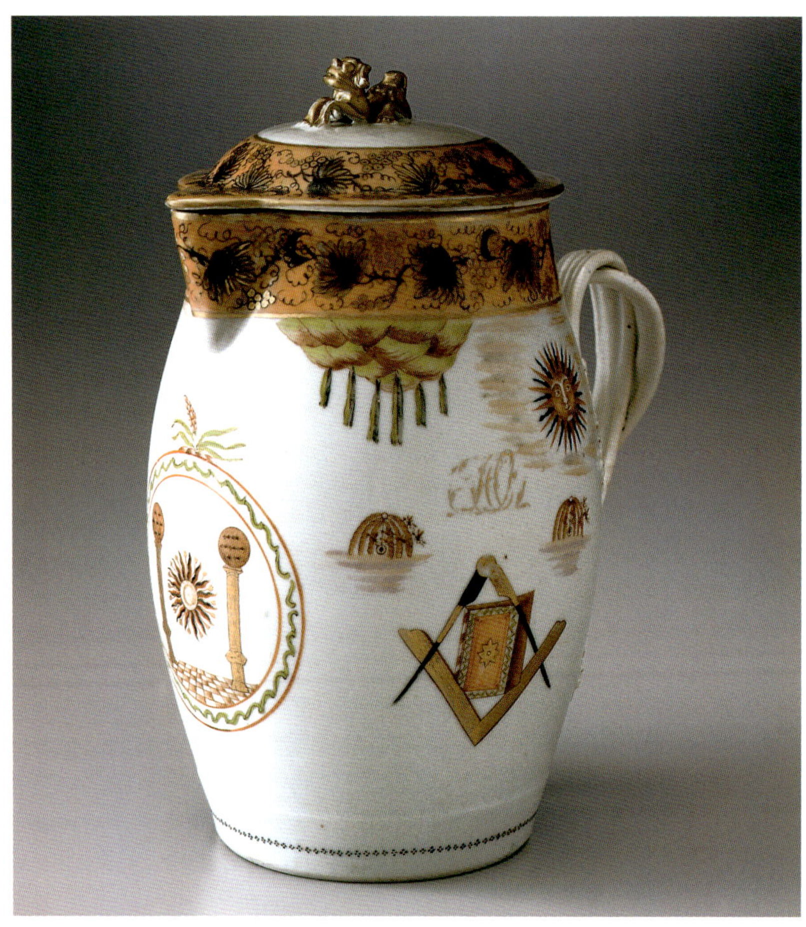

95 CIDER JUG

Jingdezhen, China; 1800–1820
Height: 10.25 in. (260 mm)
L03.2775.32a,b

As personalized porcelain became more common during the 18th century, people began to commission pieces decorated with not only their coats of arms and initials but also the emblems of organizations with which they were affiliated. This jug, decorated with Masonic symbols, was probably made for an American Mason.

The Freemasons, a semi-secret fraternal society that developed in England in the early 17th century, was especially popular in 18th-century Great Britain and America. The Masons had an elaborate system of rituals and symbols, many of which were derived from the practices and tools of medieval stonemasons. Among the symbols were two columns, representing King Solomon's Temple; the letter "G" in a starburst, referring to either God or geometry; and the builder's square and compass with the Bible, meaning reason and faith.[184]

Masonic symbols can be found on a wide range of silver, glass, and ceramic objects. The earliest export porcelain so decorated is dated 1755, and it continued to be made into the 19th century.[185]

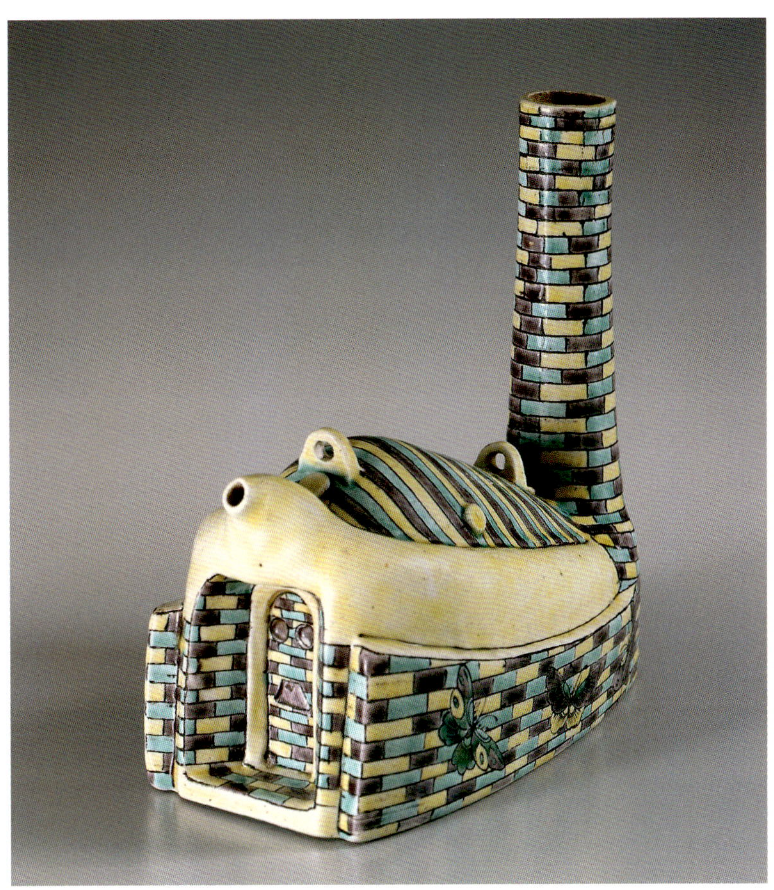

96 VESSEL IN THE SHAPE OF A KILN

Jingdezhen, China; late 1800s
Height: 6.125 in. (156 mm)
103.2775.51

This unusual vessel is in the form of an egg-shape kiln, the type most commonly used in Jingdezhen to produce export porcelain. Such kilns were developed toward the end of the Ming Dynasty (1368–1644) and were usually twenty to thirty feet long, with a door and firebox at one end and a chimney at the opposite end.[186]

The Chinese have a tradition of making vessels in the shapes of animals, plants, and other objects, which were prized in the West as exotic curiosities.[187] This example is made of biscuit, or unglazed, porcelain decorated with *famille verte* enamels. "Enamel on biscuit" figures were especially popular in the late 17th and early 18th centuries. Interest in biscuit faded around 1725 but was revived in the late 1800s, when this piece was made.

LITERATURE
Illustrated in Howard and Ayers, *China for the West,* 1:121.

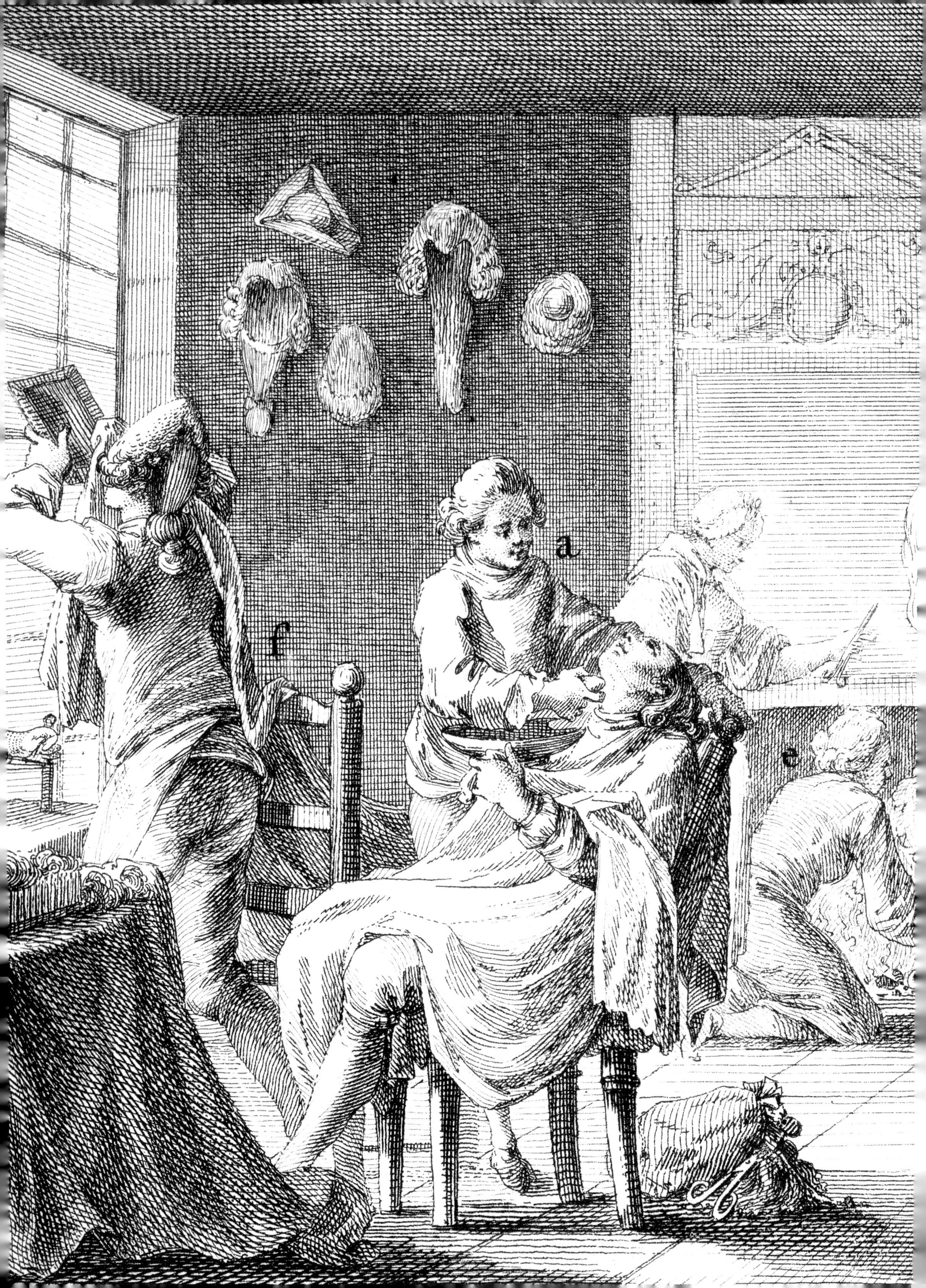
a
f
e

Utensils

In addition to dining, drinking, and decorative wares, a wide range of miscellaneous export porcelain objects could be found throughout well-furnished European and American households from the 17th to the 19th century. Candlesticks, wash basins, shaving bowls, drug jars, inkwells, and even fireplace tiles were produced. In fact, candlesticks, one of the earliest Western forms made in export porcelain, were ordered as early as 1639 by the Dutch East India Company.[188]

Wash basins, ewers, shaving bowls, and chamber pots were items commonly found in the bedroom. These were made to be both functional and decorative, as bedchambers were often used for entertaining during the 17th and 18th centuries. Less common were other objects for personal use, such as inkwells, cane handles, and snuffboxes. Like most export porcelain wares, these were based on European ceramic, glass, and metal examples.

Ceramic shaving bowls were a necessity in the well-equipped 18th-century barbershop. *Perruquier-Barbier,* from Denis Diderot, *Recueil des planches sur les sciences, les arts libéraux, et les arts mécaniques avec leur explication* (Paris: Chez Briasson, 1762–72). Printed Book and Periodical Collection, Winterthur Library.

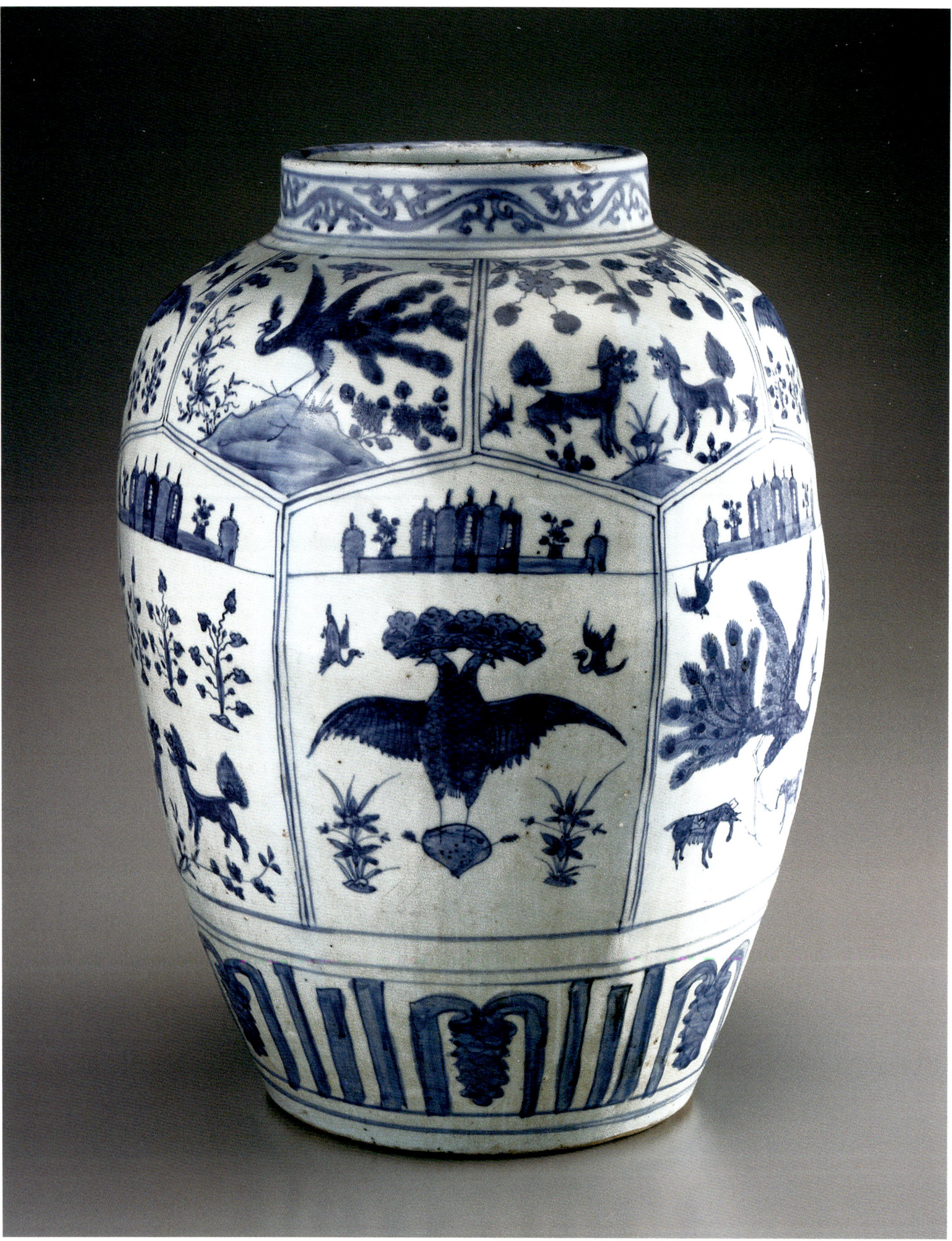

97 JAR

Jingdezhen, China; about 1590
Height: 16 in. (407 mm)
2000.61.81

This massive jar is decorated with one of the earliest Western designs to appear on export porcelain—a crowned, double-headed eagle clutching a heart pierced by two arrows. The design was used by the Augustinians (a Catholic monastic order based on the teachings of Saint Augustine).

Philip II of Spain granted this emblem to the Augustinians of the Philippine Islands following the discovery of the Holy Child of Cebu, a miraculous image left by explorer Ferdinand Magellan in 1521. The emblem combines the double-headed eagle of the Hapsburgs (the royal family of Philip II) and the Sacred Heart of Jesus. The Augustinians founded missions in Spanish colonies in Mexico and Asia and in 1589 opened a monastery in the Portuguese settlement of Macao. This jar was probably ordered for that monastery, although similar jars have also been found in Mexico, suggesting they were used by Augustinian settlements throughout Asia and the New World. In addition to jars (both ovoid and hexagonal in shape), dishes decorated with the same emblem were ordered by the Augustinians. The jars may have been decorative, but it is more likely that they were used for storing wine, food stuffs, or other commodities and probably had fitted covers.[189]

LITERATURE

Illustrated in Howard, *Choice of the Private Trader,* p. 231.

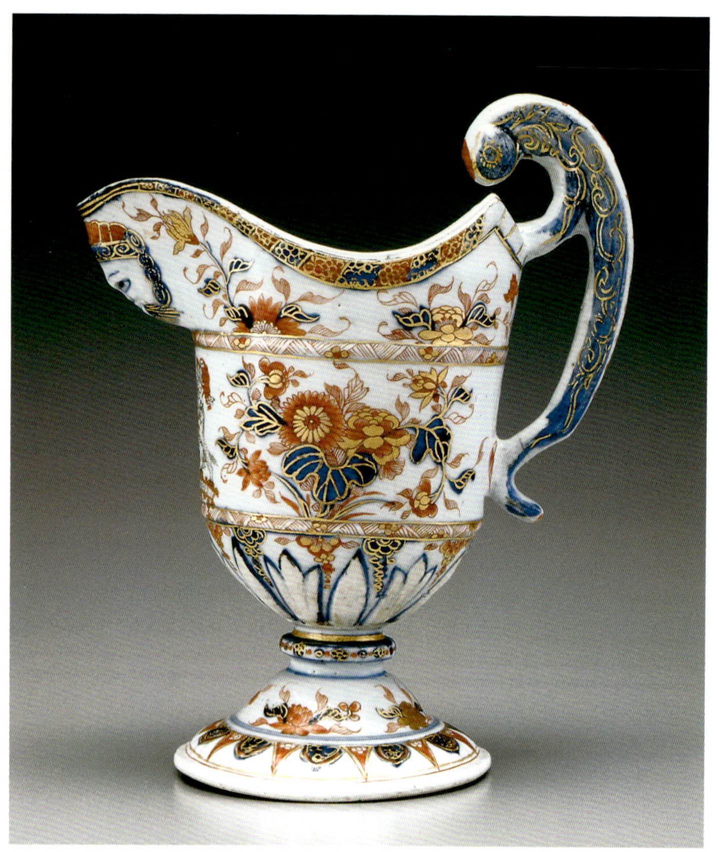

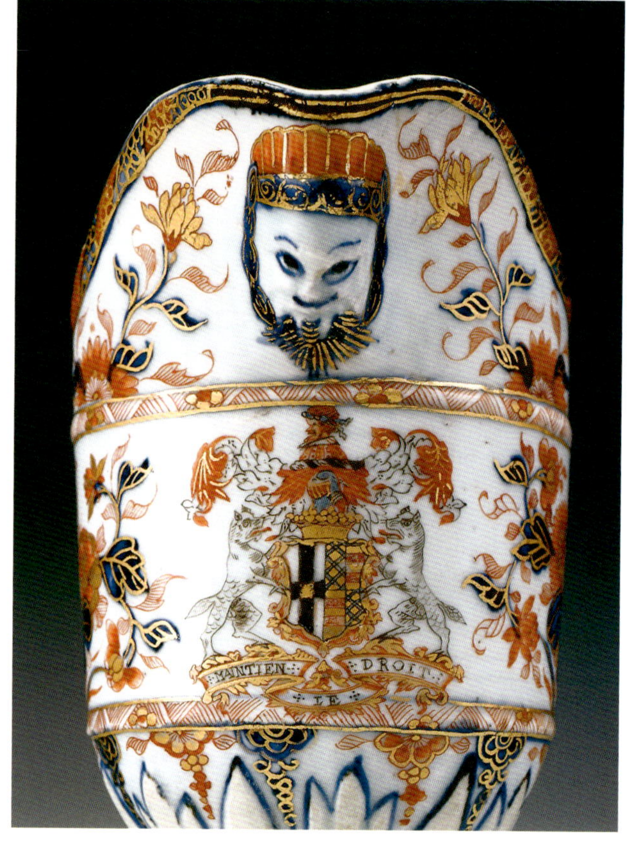

98 EWER

Jingdezhen, China; 1720–25
Height: 9.875 in. (251 mm)
2003.47.13

This helmet-shape ewer is based on silver forms developed in France in the 1680s and then copied in Dutch and French tin-glazed earthenware (delftware). Originally it would have been paired with a basin and used for washing, in either the dining room or bedchamber. The ewer bears the arms of James Brydges, the first Duke of Chandos, of Canons, England. Known as princely Chandos, he lived lavishly, especially after being elevated to the dukedom in 1719. The large and elaborately decorated service from which this ewer comes is just one example of his luxurious lifestyle.[190]

Hand washing was an important part of fine dining before the widespread use of forks, and a dictionary compiled in the 1680s described ewers like this one as "a vessell of much honor, and is used at all great feasts to wash withall, after eating tyme is finished." Even when forks became common in the late 17th century, ewers and basins continued to be made in silver, brass, and porcelain for display on elaborate sideboards. Ewers were also one of the key components of toilet sets used in the bedchamber. Porcelain toilet sets became increasingly popular during the first half of the 18th century, replacing silver examples.[191]

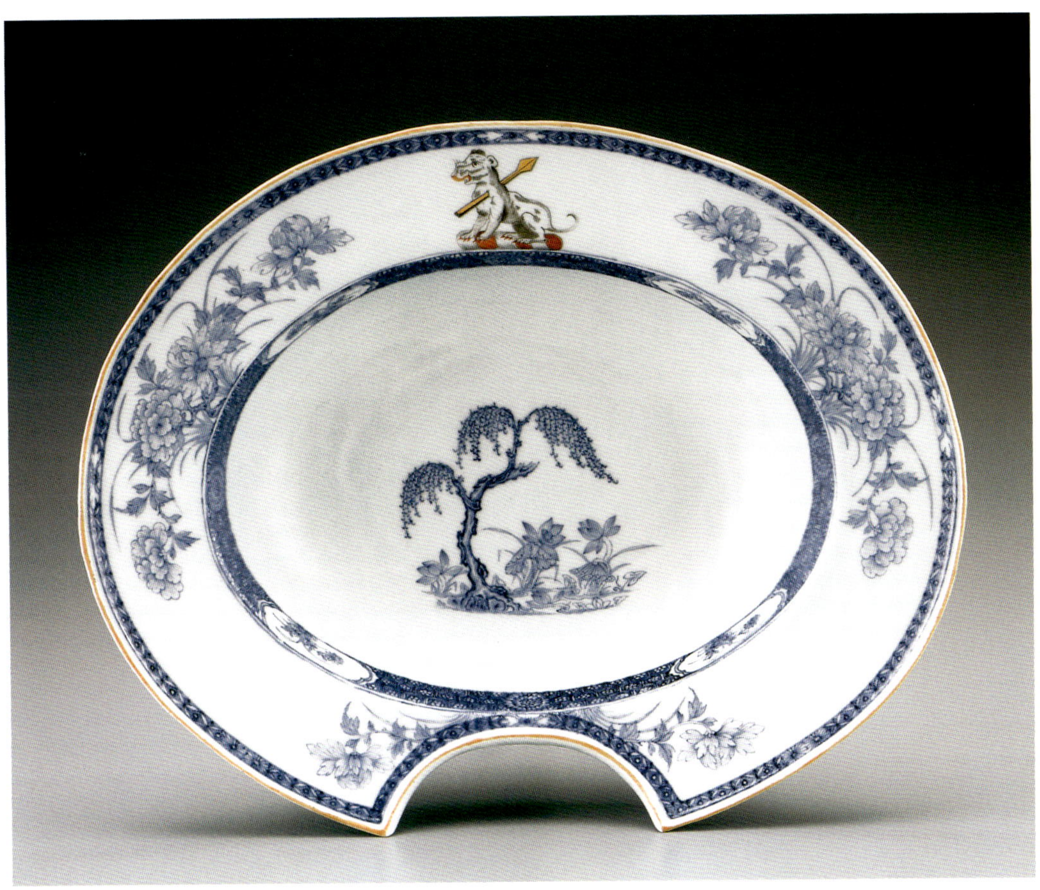

99 SHAVING BOWL

Jingdezhen, China; about 1730
Length: 13.75 in. (349 mm)
L03.2775.107

Shaving bowls were described in one late 17th-century dictionary as a "barbers Washing Bason or Trimming Bason [which] generally have rounds cut in the rim or edge therof, to compass about a mans Throat or Neck." Such items could be found at home and in barbershops, for which an 18th-century French guide lists "a basin for the Beard of tin or china" as one of the most necessary pieces of equipment.[192]

Circular and oval basins were made in export porcelain in the 17th and 18th centuries. The one seen here bears the crest of the Nicholson family of Ireland and was probably made for Christopher Nicholson, who was high sheriff of County Meath in 1735.[193]

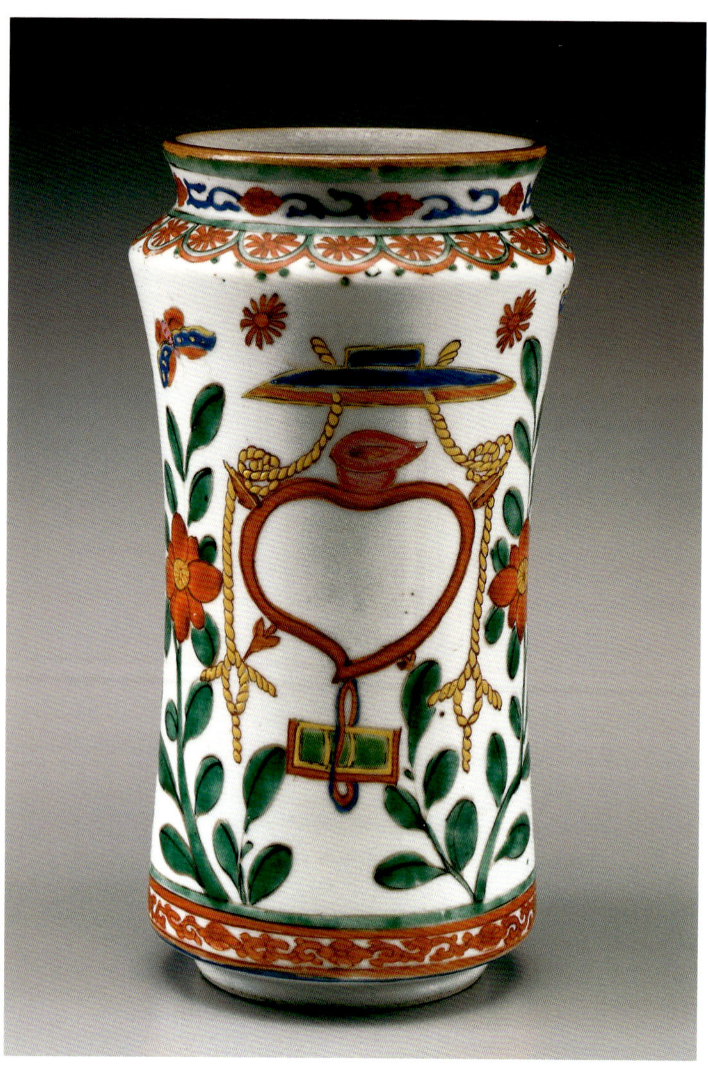

100 DRUG JAR

Jingdezhen, China; about 1735
Height: 8.5 in. (216 mm)
L03.2775.115

The form of this jar is based on an Italian or Spanish tin-glazed earthenware drug jar known as an *albarello*. The wide mouth suggests that the vessel was for dry, rather than wet, drugs, and the heart-shape panel on the side provides a space where the name of the contents could be written. Part of a much larger set, the jar was designed to outfit an apothecary shop. Its quality as well as the image of the bishop's hat with tassels suggest that the set was to be used at a monastery.[194]

LITERATURE

Illustrated in Howard and Ayers, *China for the West,* 2:560.

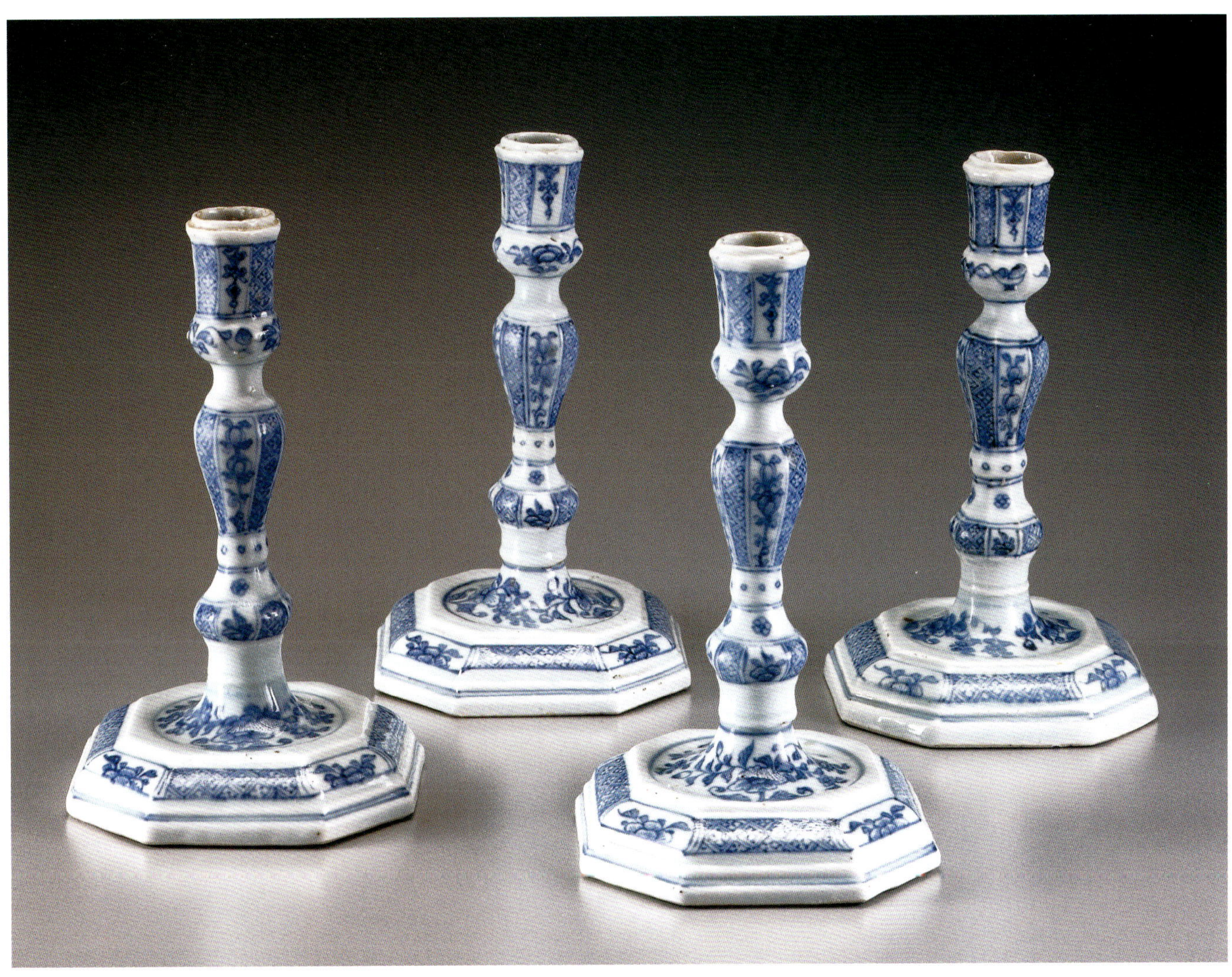

101 SET OF FOUR CANDLESTICKS

Jingdezhen, China; about 1740
Height (each): 7.5 in. (190 mm)
L03.2775.72.1–.4

The baluster shape of these candlesticks is closely based on English or European baroque-style silver or brass candlesticks made between 1700 and 1740. Despite the fact that export porcelain candlesticks were ordered by the Dutch East India Company in 1639—making them among the earliest European objects reproduced in porcelain—they were still relatively uncommon in the 18th century. Candlesticks could be ordered individually through the Private Trade or as part of large dinner services. Four were a component of a 161-piece service ordered by the Dutch in 1750, and twelve were included in an enormous 525-piece service sold in 1764.[195]

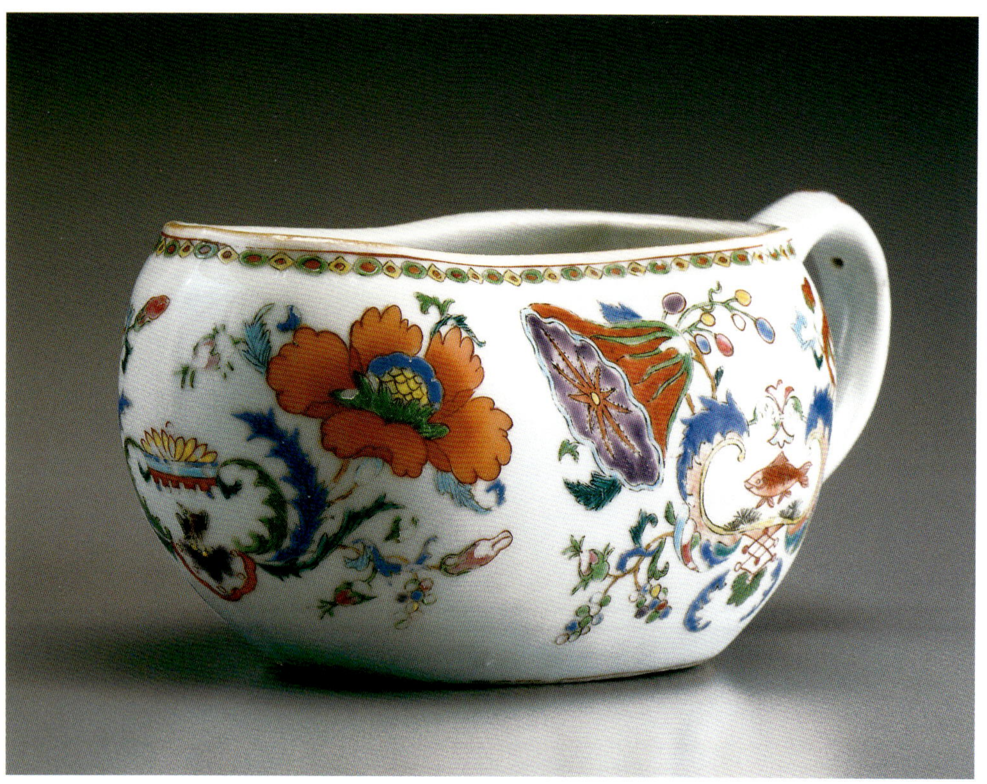

102 BOURDALOUE

Jingdezhen, China; about 1745
Length: 10.5 in. (267 mm)
L03.2775.12

A *bourdaloue* is a woman's chamber pot that could be transported as needed. The form seems to have been developed in the early 18th century, but the exact origin of the name is unknown. It may come from the French Provençal word for refuse, *bourdallo,* or from the name of French Jesuit priest Père Louis Bourdaloue, who was known for delivering extremely long sermons.[196]

This *bourdaloue,* which would have had a cover, is decorated with what is sometimes referred to as the Pompadour pattern, after Madame de Pompadour, mistress of Louis XV of France. The design was almost certainly not created specifically for Madame de Pompadour, but the connection comes from the fish—perhaps representing her maiden name, Poisson, which means fish—and the crowned eagles, representing Louis XV.[197]

LITERATURE
Illustrated in Howard, *Choice of the Private Trader,* p. 229.

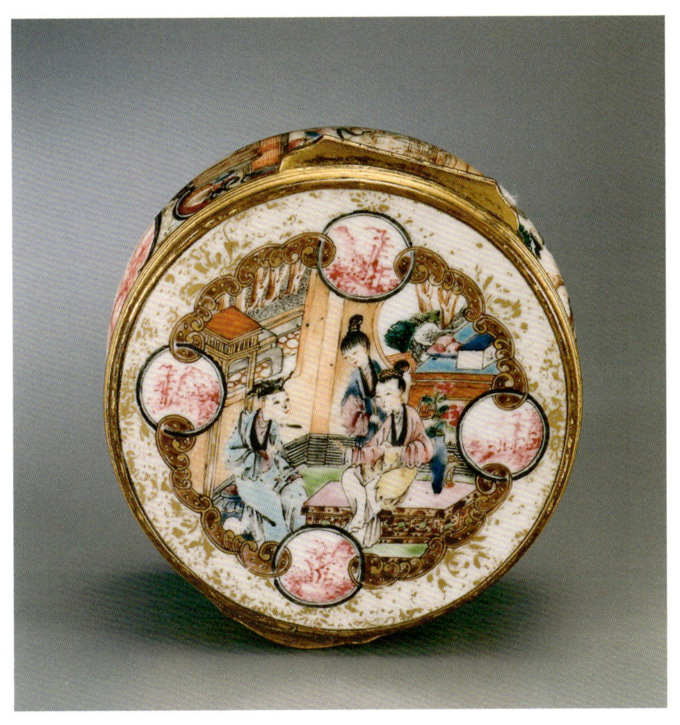

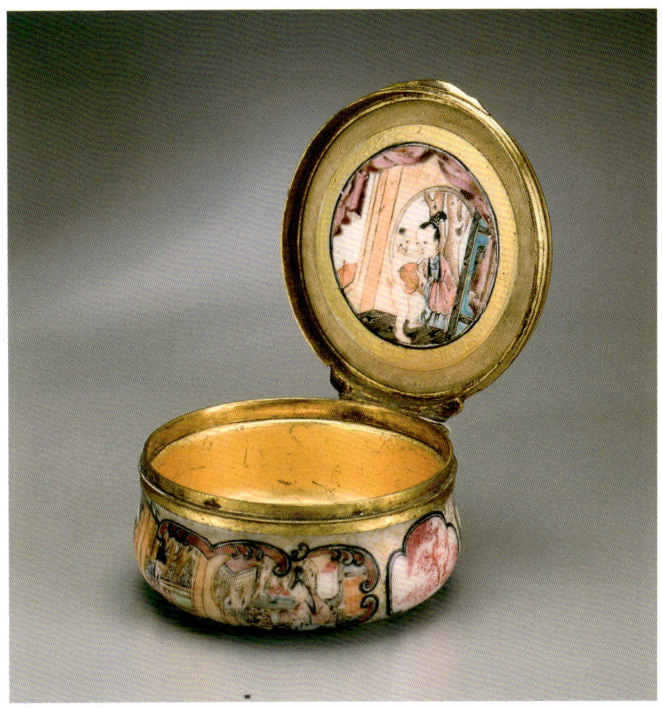

103 SNUFFBOX

Jingdezhen, China; about 1740
Diameter: 2.75 in. (70 mm)
L03.2775.101

Delicately painted Chinese scenes, including a portrait of a mother and child on the interior of the cover, decorate this snuffbox. Inspired in part by Meissen examples, the design of this precious object required careful coordination among the China Trade merchant who ordered it, the Chinese potters and painters who made the porcelain body and cover, and the European metalsmiths who crafted the ormolu mounts that hold the box together.[198]

Snuff, which is powdered tobacco that is inhaled through the nostrils, was popular in the 18th century. Snuff-taking was an important social ceremony among the aristocracy, and finely decorated snuffboxes of gold, silver, porcelain, or other materials were a necessary accessory for any stylish gentleman or lady. Etiquette manuals instructed readers to offer their open snuffboxes to others before partaking themselves, giving ample opportunity for the workmanship on the box to be admired, which is no doubt why they are so lavishly decorated, especially on the interiors.[199]

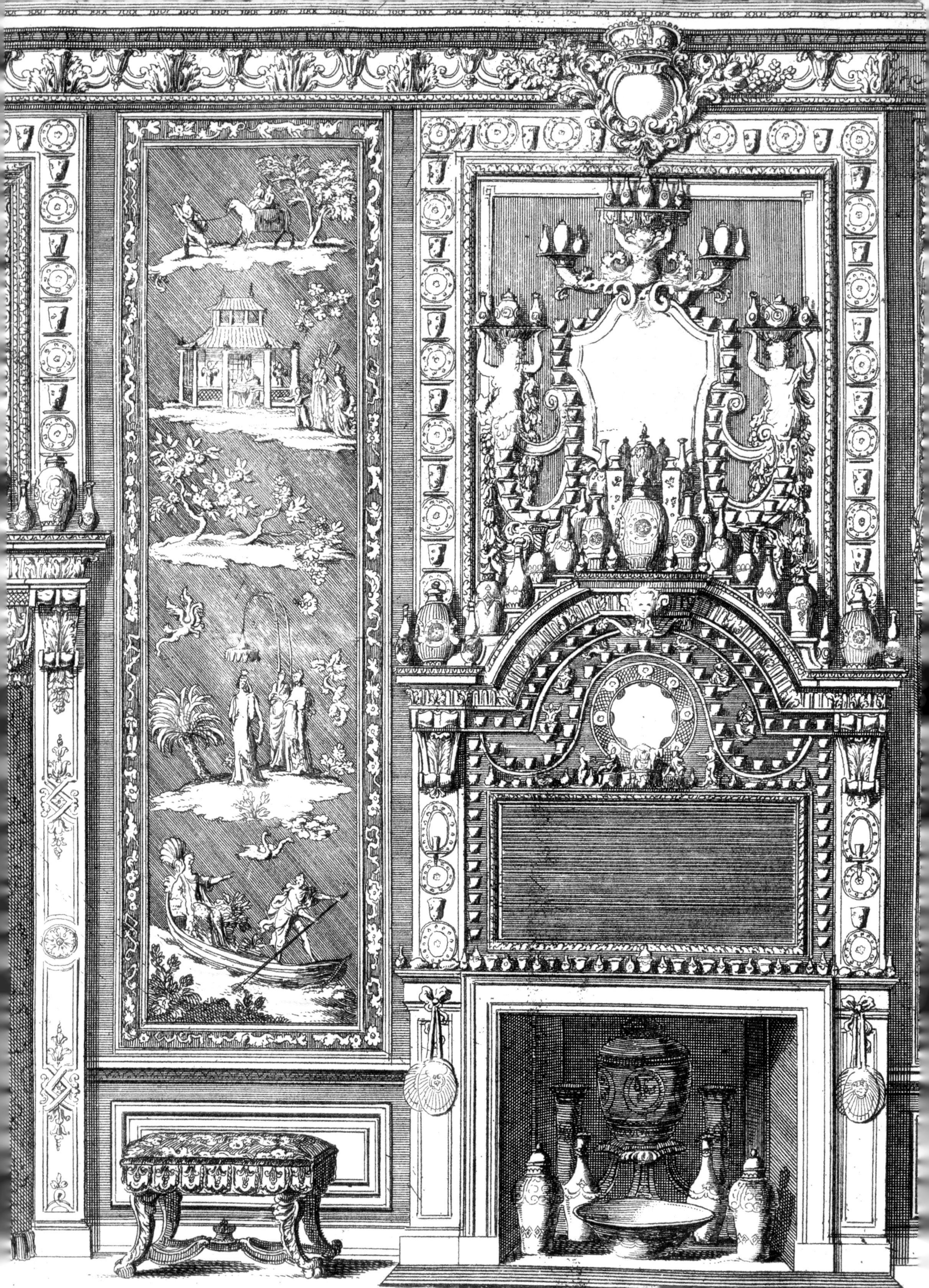

Decorative Wares

According to English satirist Daniel Defoe, Queen Mary II of England introduced

> the custom or humour of furnishing houses with China-ware, which spread to lesser mortals and increased to such a strange degree afterwards, piling their china upon the tops of cabinets, scrutores and every chimney-piece . . . till it became a grievance in the expense of it and even injurious to their families and estates.

Although Queen Mary owned more than 800 pieces of export porcelain—one of the largest collections of her day—she was far from the first European to use porcelain for decoration. The earliest pieces to arrive in Europe, in the 15th and 16th centuries, were extremely rare and were treasured as art objects. They were often made even more precious with gold, silver, and jeweled mounts, like the ornamental "suite of Porcellane sett in silver and gylt" that Sir Walter Raleigh left to his friend Robert Cecil in 1597.[200]

By the late 17th century, porcelain had become an important component of well-decorated European interiors. Vases and figures were imported in great quantities; the cargo of one Chinese junk that sank about 1695 was made up almost entirely of porcelain vases destined for the European market. Porcelain items ornamented chimneypieces, cornices, and cupboards and were even used to create "porcelain chambers," entire rooms decorated with porcelain set on specially constructed wall brackets, mantelpieces, and cornices. In at least one instance, even the ceiling of a chamber was covered with porcelain plates. Displays were not restricted to Europe; in 1686, Charleston, South Carolina, merchant Paul Grimball owned a collection of "Toyes of chainy," which were probably small porcelain figures.[201]

As the fashion for all things Chinese peaked in the 1730s, 1740s, and 1750s, porcelain could be found in nearly every genteel interior in Europe and America. George Washington ordered several sets of vases to decorate the mantelpieces at Mount Vernon, and his neighbor George Mason fitted out his parlor with chinoiserie brackets for displaying porcelain vases or figures.[202] Although the popularity of Chinese porcelain faded in the late 18th century, figures and vases continued to be imported throughout the 19th century.

Garnitures and porcelain vases cover virtually every inch of this early 18th-century chimneypiece. Plate 52 from Daniel Marot, *Werken van D. Marot* (Amsterdam, 1707). Printed Book and Periodical Collection, Winterthur Library.

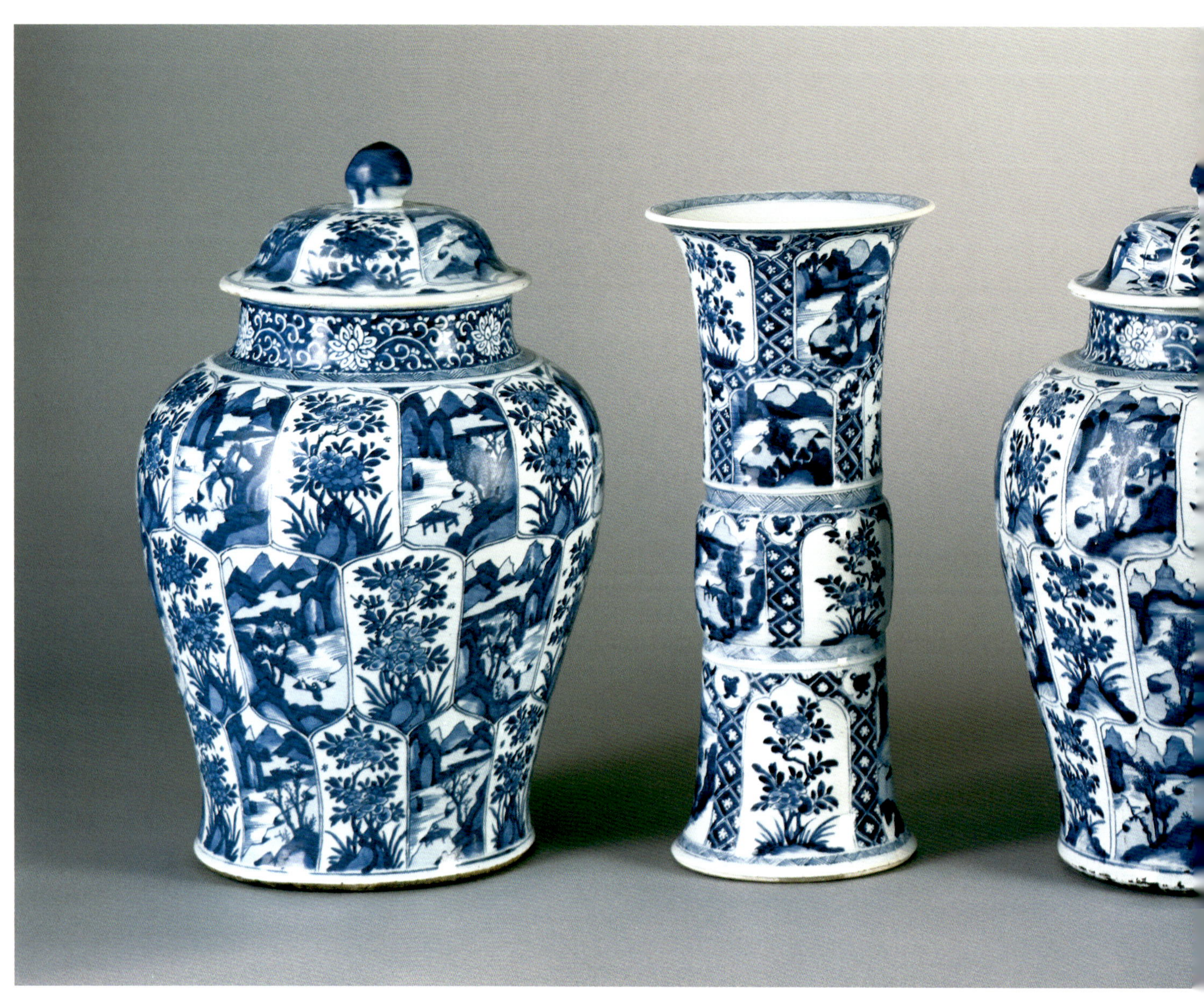

104 GARNITURE

Jingdezhen, China; 1690–1710
Height (tallest vase): 22.25 in. (565 mm)
2003.47.16.1–.5

These massive objects make up what is known as a garniture, which is a combination of matching beakers and covered vases. The fact that the borders and other decorative elements on these vases are similar but not identical suggests that the pieces may not have been made together.

Garnitures seem to have been developed about 1680. Although their shapes were inspired by traditional Chinese forms, the concept of the set was probably created by Dutch merchants who were looking for "porcelain

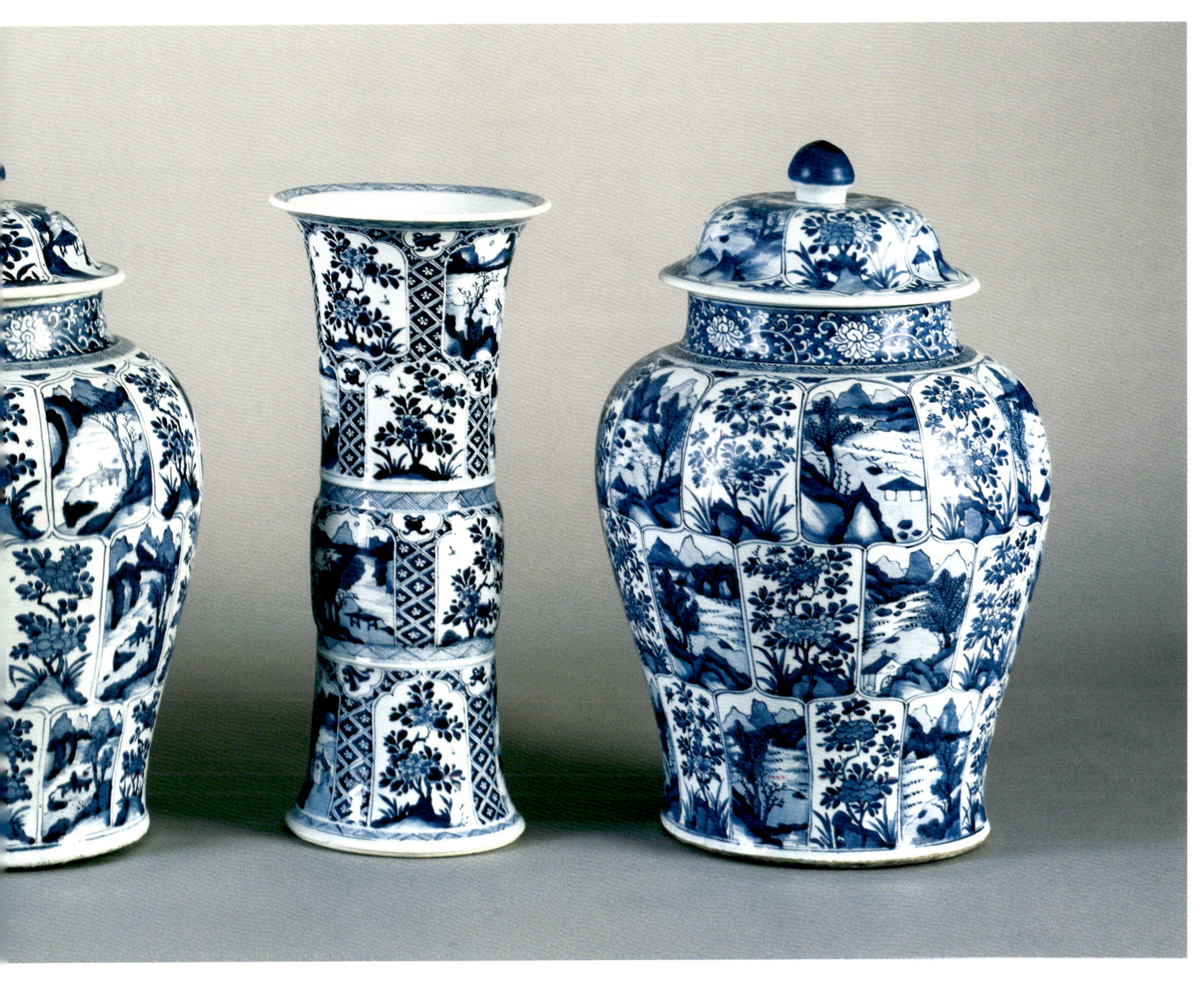

of the new inventions" with which to tempt the fickle tastes of wealthy Europeans. Any number of vases could make up a garniture, but the most common combination was two beakers and three covered vases. Garnitures were purely decorative; they were designed to be displayed on cabinets, mantelpieces, or cornices over doorways. Such a massive grouping as the one seen here would have been placed in a grand public room of a British or continental European mansion.[203]

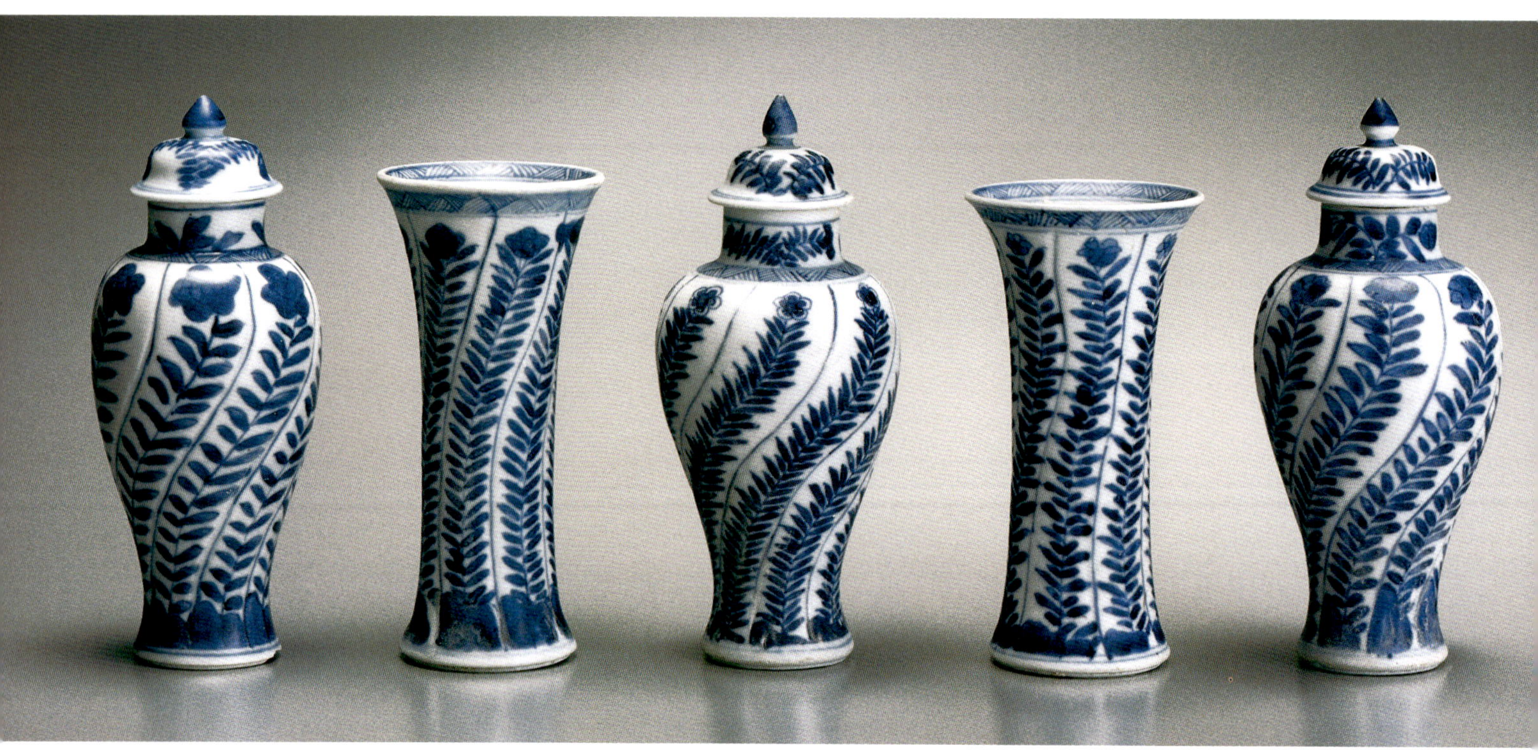

105 GARNITURE

Jingdezhen, China; 1690–1700
Height (tallest vase): 6.5 in. (165 mm)
2000.61.83.1–.5

This small garniture was part of the cargo of a Chinese junk that sank off the coast of Vietnam in the 1690s. The ship carried mainly vases, which were no doubt intended to satisfy the demand for decorative porcelain in Europe in the late 17th and early 18th centuries. The limited number of forms and design motifs found on the vases suggests that the cargo may have been the stock of a single Chinese merchant, perhaps even the output of a single kiln in Jingdezhen.[204]

The junk, probably en route from China to the Dutch trading center of Batavia (modern-day Jakarta, Indonesia), was part of an extensive maritime trading network active throughout Southeast Asia. Run by Chinese merchants operating out of southern China, the junk trade transported Chinese goods to local populations and Chinese communities throughout Southeast Asia as well as to European trading posts that were collecting points for Asian goods destined for Europe or America. The trade was crucial to the success of the Dutch East India Company, supplying it a wide range of goods far more efficiently and cheaply than the company could have by sending its own ships directly to China.[205]

LITERATURE
Illustrated in Howard, *Choice of the Private Trader,* pp. 236–37.

106 PAIR OF VASES

Jingdezhen, China; 1710–25
Height: 10.125 in. (257 mm)
L03.2775.90.1, .2

This pair of vases reflects the wide range of influences that affected the design of Chinese export porcelain. The bulbous shape with a bulge at the neck was inspired by Persian metal and ceramic vases. The unusual spiral decoration is not typical of Chinese design but was a fashionable element of the European baroque style, which was popular at the time these vases were made. The spiral was probably inspired by 17th-century Venetian *latticino* glassware, in which opaque white enamel threads are applied to a colorless glass vessel while the glass is still malleable and then twisted to produce the spiral design. An identical pair of vases graced the massive porcelain collection of Augustus the Strong of Saxony and was included in the 1721 inventory of his collection.[206]

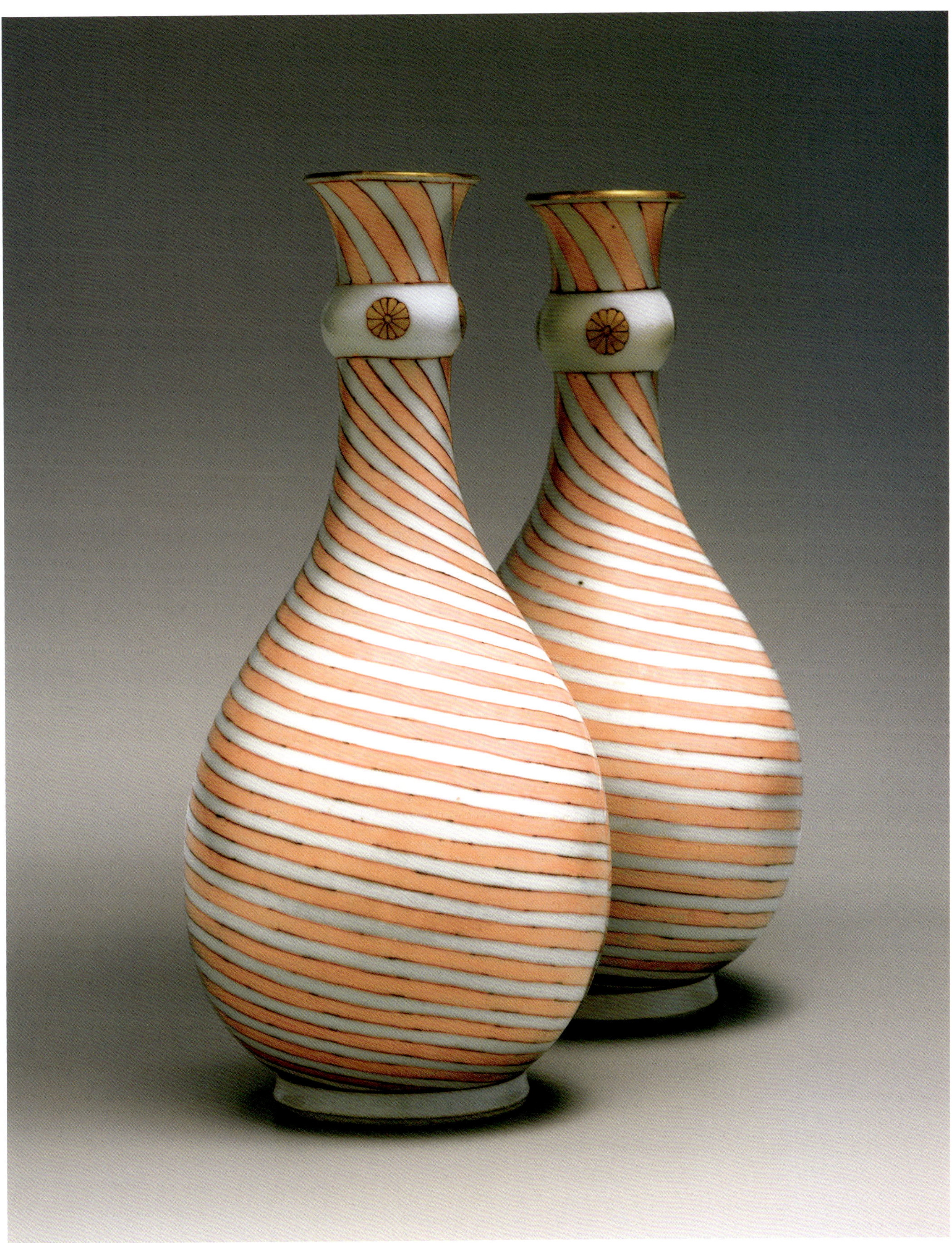

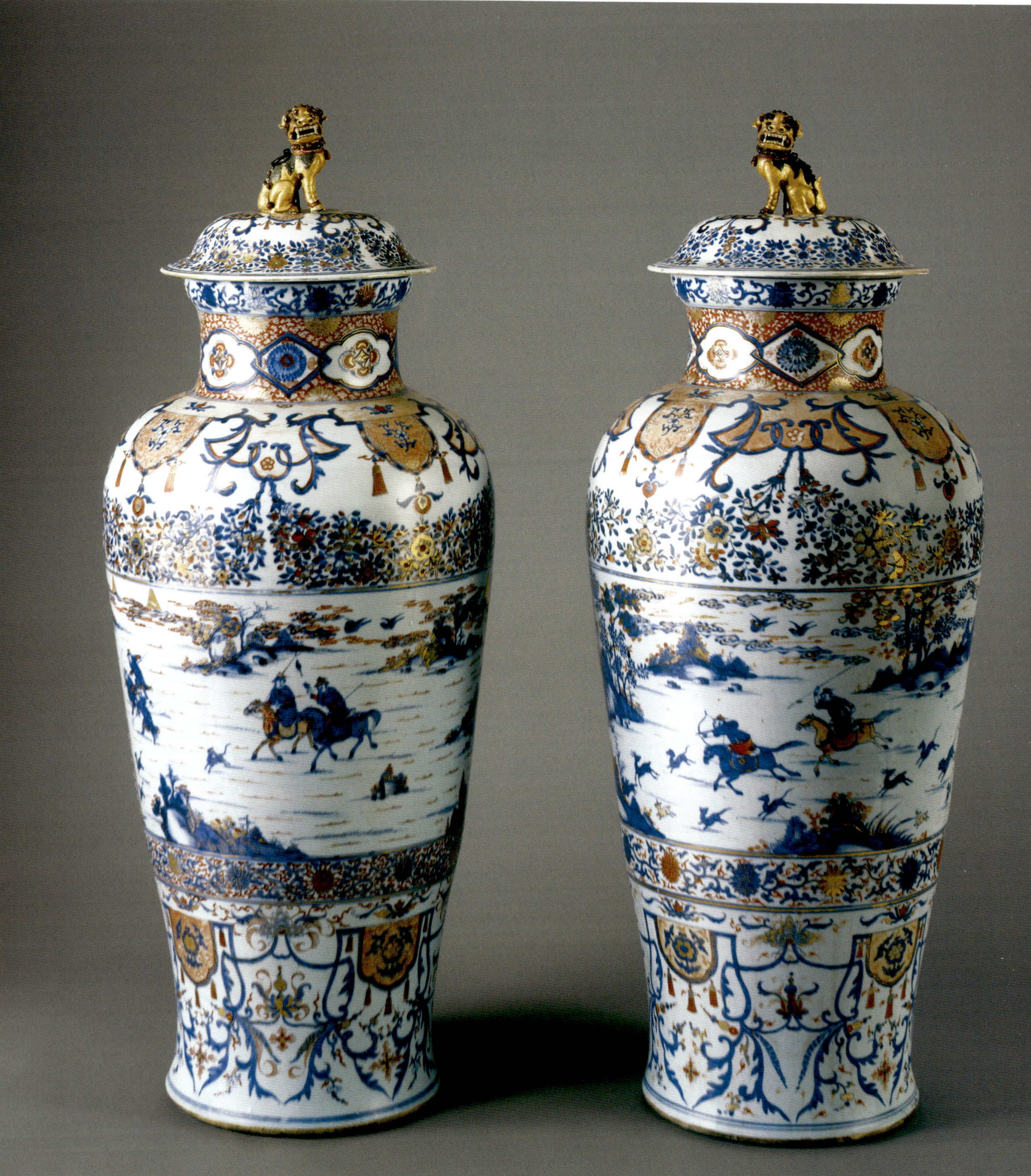

107 PAIR OF SOLDIER VASES

Jingdezhen, China; about 1720
Height (each): 50.375 in. (1280 mm)
2003.47.15.1, .2

Vases of this great size are known as soldier or dragoon vases. In 1717 Augustus the Strong of Saxony traded 600 soldiers from his army for 151 pieces of Chinese export porcelain that belonged to Friedrich Wilhelm I of Prussia. Among that collection were a number of massive, baluster-shape vases similar to this pair, thus explaining the unusual name. Augustus was obsessed with porcelain, acquiring some 24,000 pieces and even starting the renovations on a palace in Dresden, the Japanische Palais, specifically to house the collection.[207]

These vases represent the great esteem afforded export porcelain and the skills of the Chinese potters. Père d'Entrecolles, a Jesuit missionary who toured China in 1712 and 1722, described vases like these with awe when he wrote that he had "seen Designs executed which were said to be impracticable; these were Urns above three Foot high without the Lid, which rose like a Pyramid a Foot high; these Urns were made of three Pieces, but joined together so neatly that the Place of their Union could not be discover'd; I was told at the same time that out of twenty-four eight only succeeded: These Works were bespoke by the Merchants of *Canton* for the *European* trade."[208]

Typical for export porcelain, the decoration on these vases blends Chinese and European design. The scrollwork and tassels are part of the European baroque style while the panoramic hunting scene is Chinese. Hunting scenes and other images of horsemen became popular in China in the 17th century; the new Manchu rulers of China (who overthrew the Ming Dynasty in 1644) were descended from Tartar horsemen and preferred popular scenes derived from Chinese history, literature, and mythology rather than more formal designs. Hunting scenes were specifically ordered by China Trade merchants throughout the 17th and 18th centuries; in 1756 the Dutch East India Company requested porcelain decorated "with Chinese figure work, either hunts or other subjects in which there is much movement."[209]

108 COVERED JAR

Jingdezhen, China; 1720–30
Height: 34 in. (864 mm)
2003.47.12a,b

This type of massive jar is sometimes known as a ginger jar, a reference to its original function as a food-storage vessel. In the West, baluster-shape jars were used almost exclusively for decoration and could be found singly, in pairs, or with trumpet-shape vases to form a garniture. Single jars of this size are known to have ornamented side tables, staircases, and even the interiors of fireplaces during the summer months.

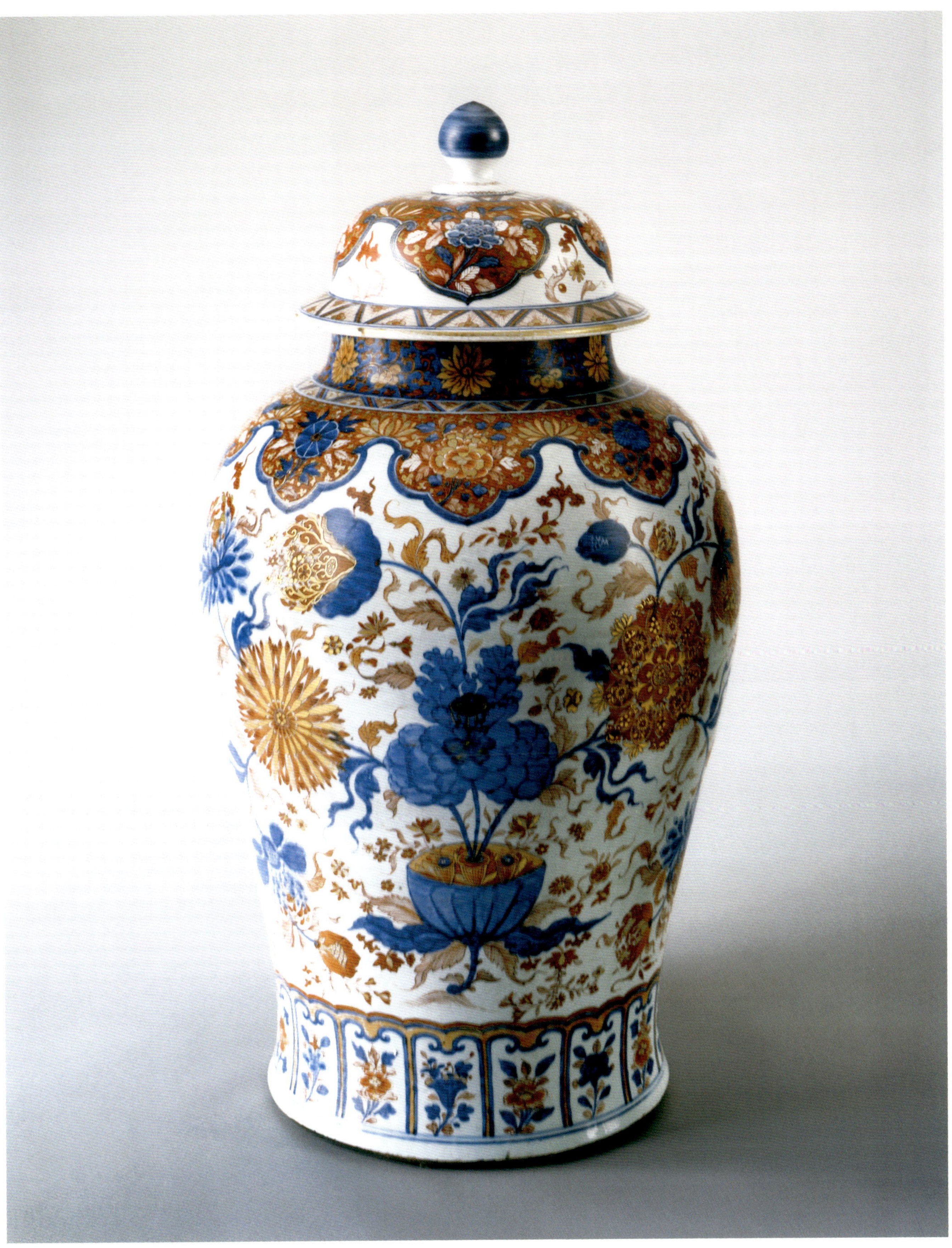

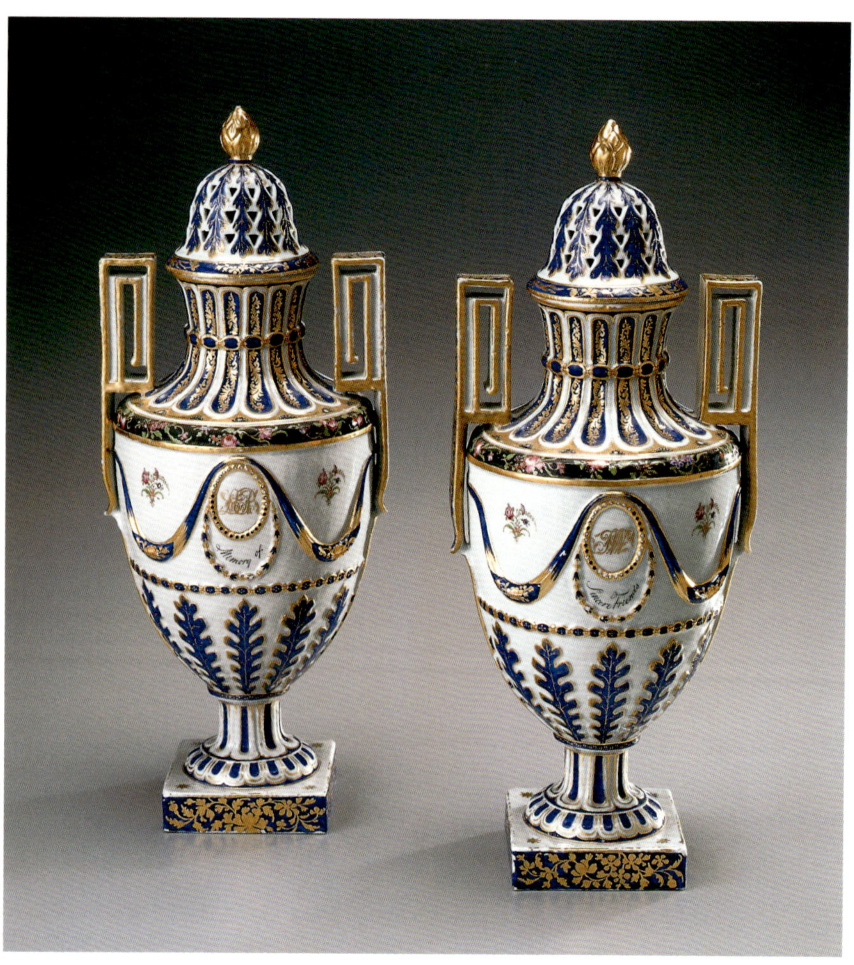

109 PAIR OF VASES

Jingdezhen, China; 1800–1810
Height (each): 17.33 in. (440 mm)
2000.61.86.1, .2

This pair of vases is in the shape of classical urns, which were among the most popular symbols of mourning in the late 18th and early 19th centuries. The presence of the initials "LCB" and "TW" and the inscription "Memory of Sincere Friends" (which is divided between the two vases) makes it clear that they were meant to be a memorial.[210]

Starting about 1760, designs based on the art and architecture of ancient Greece and Rome became fashionable. "Vases were all the cry," wrote English potter Josiah Wedgwood in 1769, acknowledging the popularity of these ultimate symbols of the classical style. China Trade merchants were quick to capitalize on this growing "vase madness," commissioning export porcelain vases and urns modeled after antique examples.[211]

LITERATURE

Illustrated in Howard, *Choice of the Private Trader,* p. 245.

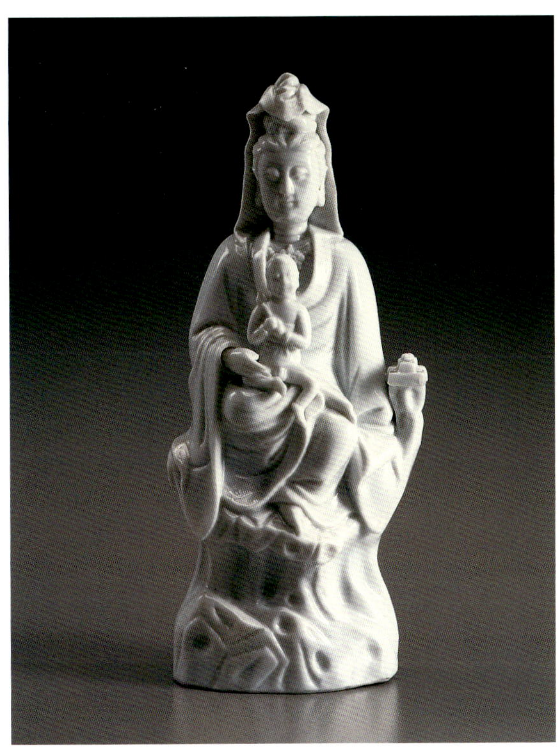

110 FIGURE OF GUANYIN

Dehua, China; 1680–1720
Height: 10.25 in. (262 mm)
2000.61.89

This *blanc-de-chine* figure depicts Guanyin, the Buddhist goddess of compassion and mercy. She was one of the most popular deities in China, partly because of her role as a fertility goddess with the power to grant sons and protect women during pregnancy and childbirth. Figures such as the one seen here were for devotional use, probably for the altar in a private home.

Figures of Guanyin were often known in the West as Sancta Marias (Sacred Marys) because of their resemblance to the Virgin Mary. The production of Guanyin figures in the 17th century was possibly stimulated by ivory figures of the Virgin made by Chinese craftsmen for the Portuguese and Spanish markets. There is some thought that Guanyin was named the goddess of mercy by Jesuit missionaries working in China in the 16th and 17th centuries.[212]

Guanyin figures were avidly collected in the West. Queen Mary II of England is known to have owned at least two, and Augustus the Strong of Saxony owned four. The figures even reached the American colonies; one descended in the Brewton family of Charleston, South Carolina, and another was recovered from Port Royal, a port in Jamaica destroyed during an earthquake in 1692.[213]

LITERATURE
Illustrated in Howard, *Choice of the Private Trader,* pp. 250–51.

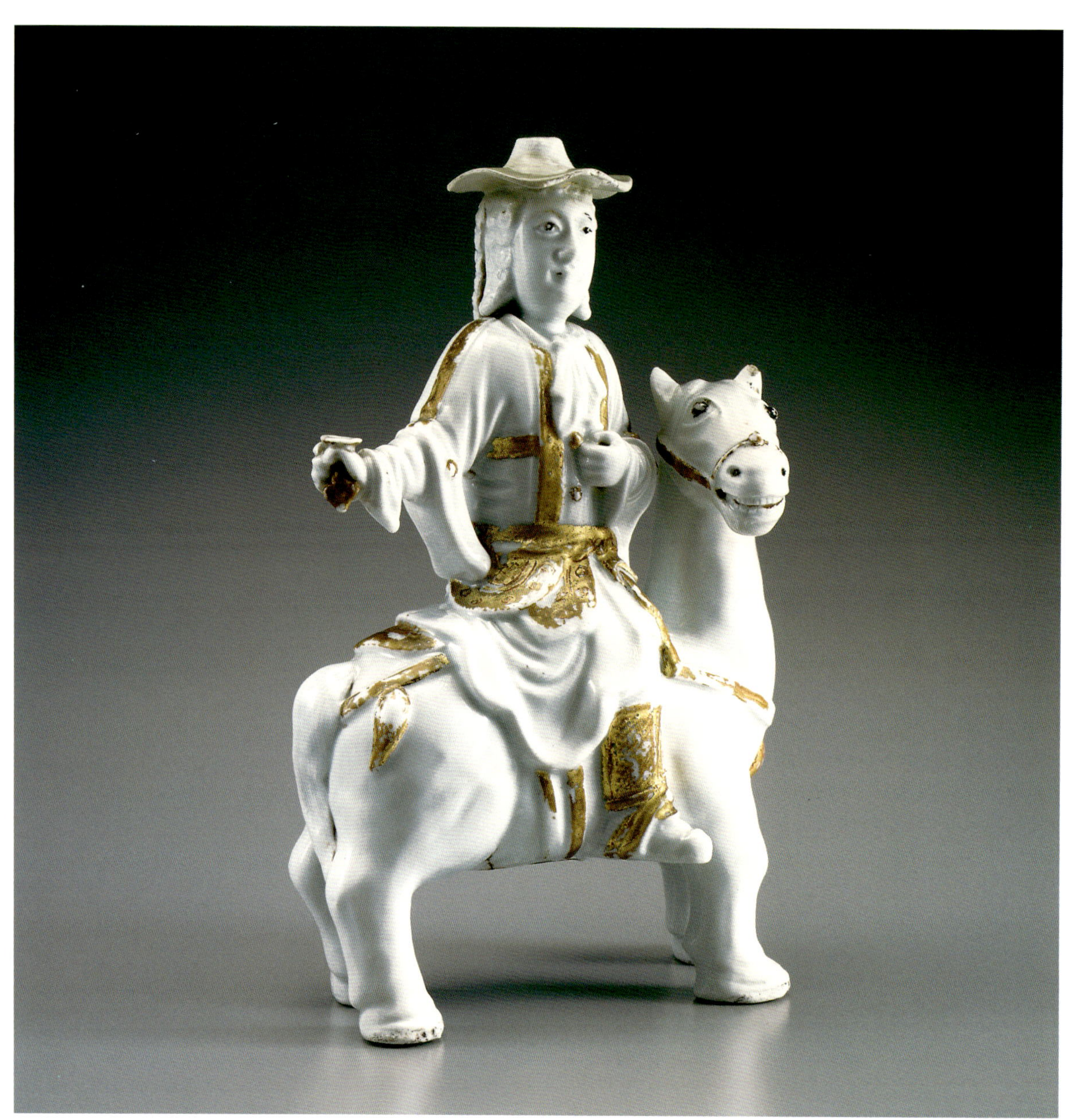

111 FIGURE OF A EUROPEAN ON HORSEBACK

Dehua, China; 1700–1720
Height: 11.75 in. (298 mm)
L03.2775.48

This figure of a horseman holding aloft his sword (now lost) was made in Dehua, a city in southern China known for producing finely modeled figures. The porcelain from Dehua was created for the domestic market as well as export to Japan, Southeast Asia, and Europe. In the late 17th century, as trade with Europeans increased through the nearby port of Amoy, Dehua potters added a number of European subjects to their repertoire to suit the needs of these new consumers. This figure may be the same as the "2 Men on horses" sold by the British East India Company in London in 1703 for two shillings apiece, wholesale, or the "2 Horsemen" sold in 1706 for four shillings apiece, wholesale.[214]

Shipping records document that "painted" and "white and gold" figures were imported directly from China, and it is also known that undecorated *blanc-de-chine* figures were enameled in Europe.[215]

LITERATURE
Illustrated in Howard and Ayers, *China for the West,* 1:96.

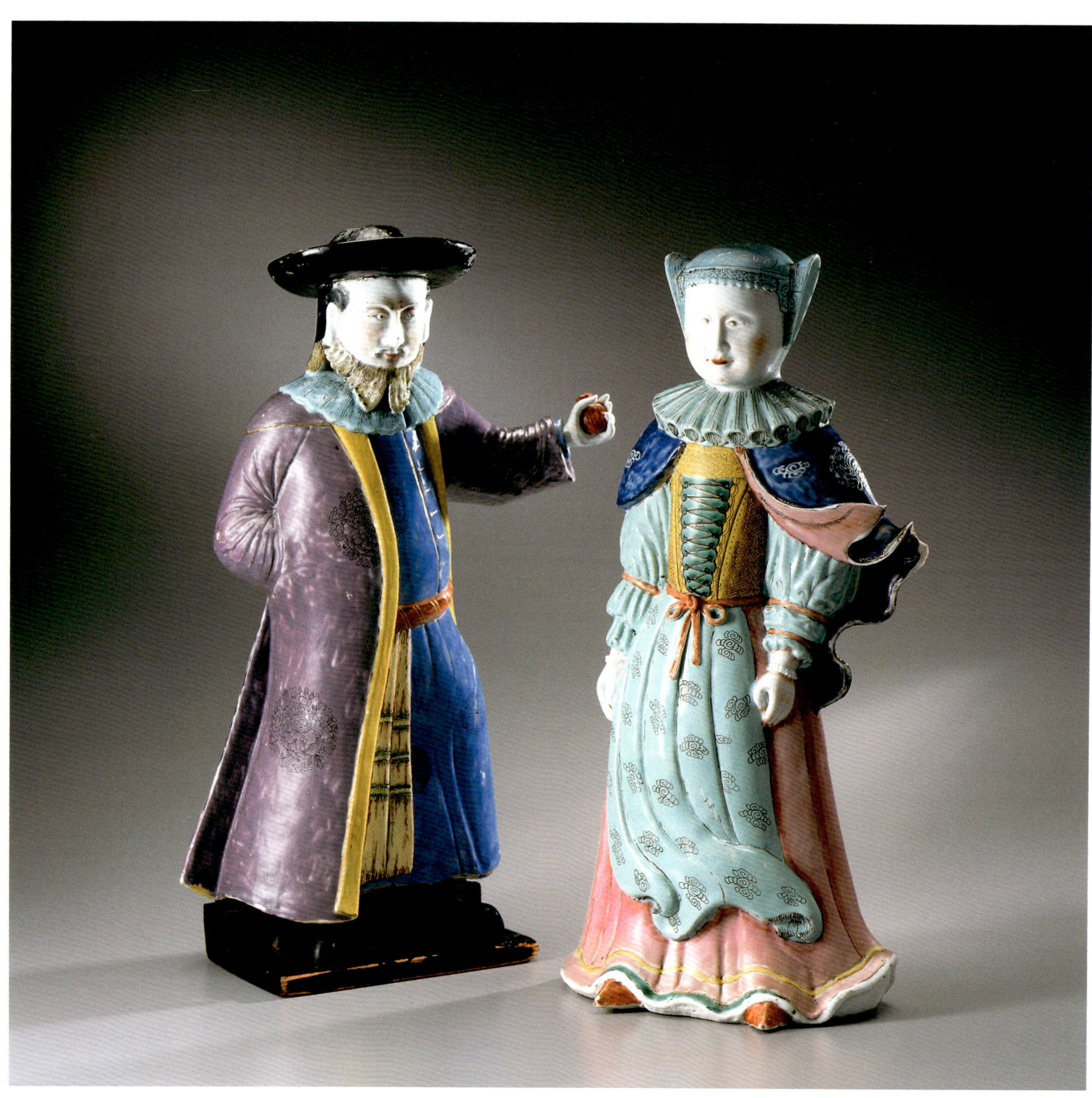

112 FIGURES OF A EUROPEAN MERCHANT AND LADY

Jingdezhen, China; about 1740
Height (man): 16.75 in. (425 mm), (lady): 16.625 in. (421 mm)
2000.61.90, .91

These are the largest export porcelain figures of Europeans known to have been made. Fewer than two dozen of these rare figures survive, many of which appear to be from the same molds, suggesting they were part of one large, special order for the Private Trade.[216]

Traditionally thought to represent a Dutch merchant and lady, no exact design source has yet been identified for the figures. It is likely that they were based on European printed images or on images of Europeans made by the Chinese for their own education and entertainment. Whether they represent a Dutch man and woman is debatable; the man does resemble mid-18th-century Chinese woodcuts of Dutchmen, but the woman is similar to one on a print of a "Swabian peasant" (Swabia is a region in southwestern Germany).[217]

The figure of the merchant once had a label stating that it was one of two Dutch merchants that belonged to John Byng, an admiral in the British Navy and a passionate collector of Chinese export porcelain. Byng was court-martialed and shot for failing to prevent the French from capturing the island of Minorca in 1755 during the Seven Years' War. Though probably innocent of the charges of cowardice and negligence, he was depicted in cartoons as being more interested in his porcelain than in national defense—giving the order to flee the French while sitting in a ship's cabin luxuriously decorated with porcelain vases and figures.[218]

LITERATURE

Illustrated in Howard, *Choice of the Private Trader,* pp. 252–53.

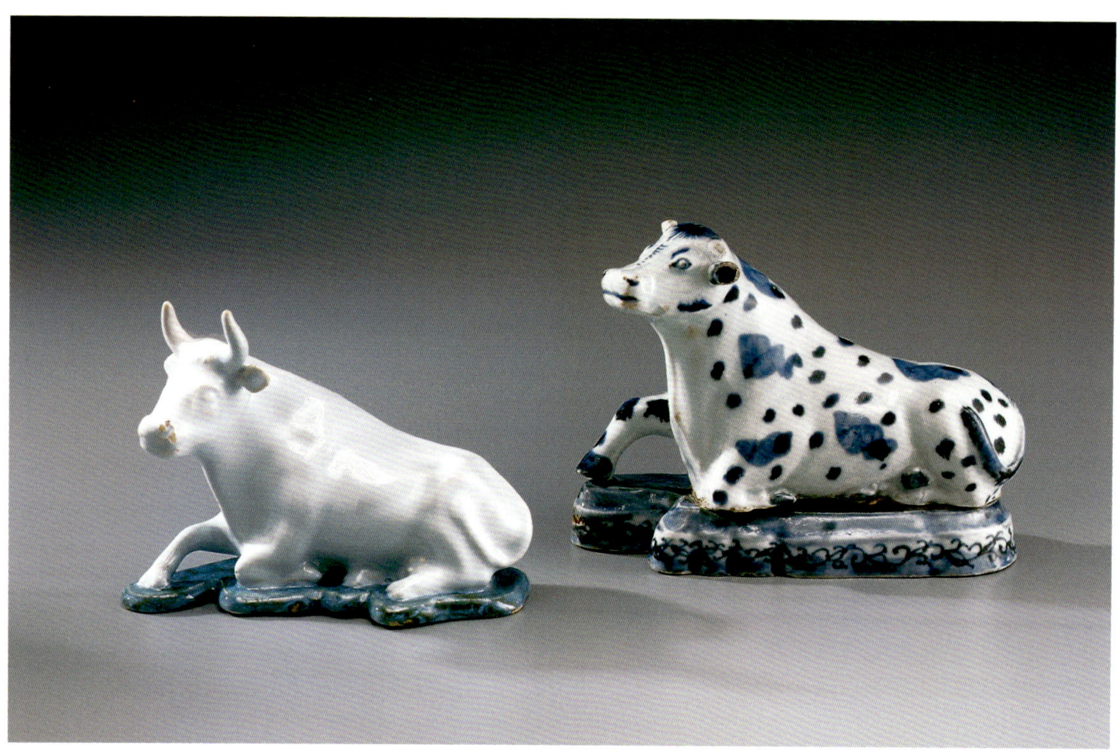

113 FIGURES OF COWS

Holland; 1730–70 *(left)*
Arita, Japan; 1740–70 *(right)*
Length: 5.75 in. (146 mm), 6.5 in. (165 mm)
L03.2775.52, .53

European ceramic figures were often sent to Asia to be copied. In many cases, the European model is not known, but in this case it is fairly certain that a Dutch tin-glazed earthenware figure of a cow similar to the example on the left was sent to Japan, where it was copied in export porcelain. Figures of cows were also sent to China, such as those in the 1746 request of the Dutch East India Company for "Cows, each pair with the heads facing each other, white grounds some with brown, some with blue spots, according to sample." Dutch tin-glazed figures of standing cows and recumbent horses were also reproduced in Japanese export porcelain.[219]

LITERATURE

Illustrated in Howard and Ayers, *China for the West,* 1:127.

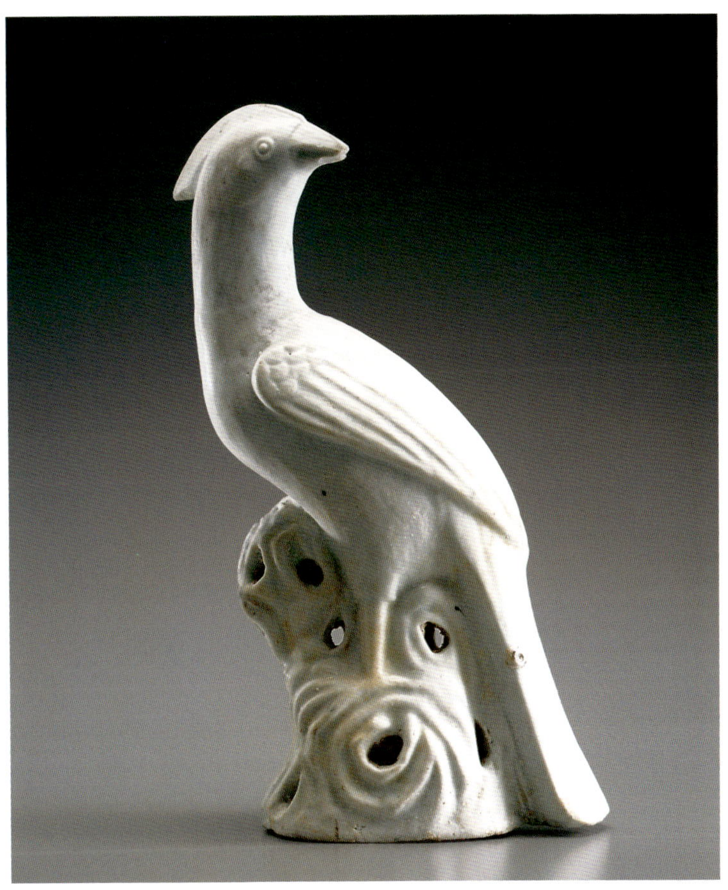

114 FIGURE OF A PHEASANT

Jingdezhen, China; about 1750
Height: 10.25 in. (262 mm)
L03.2775.2

One of two pheasant figures recovered from the wreck of the *Geldermalsen*, a Dutch East India Company ship that sank in 1752, this figure was originally brightly decorated with overglaze enamels. After more than two centuries under water, however, those colors have been lost.[220]

Figures were expensive and usually formed part of the Private Trade. This pheasant and other figures recovered do not appear on the cargo manifest of the *Geldermalsen* and were probably in one of the "permitted small boxes" of Private Trade goods known to have been on board. The loss of the enamel decoration and the damage to other figures probably occurred because the Private Trade shipments were packed higher up in the ship than the bulk porcelain in the bottom of the hold and so were more affected as the ship sank and broke apart.[221]

LITERATURE

Illustrated in Howard, *Choice of the Private Trader,* p. 264; Sheaf and Kilburn, *Hatcher Porcelain Cargoes,* p. 158; Jörg, *Geldermalsen,* p. 100.

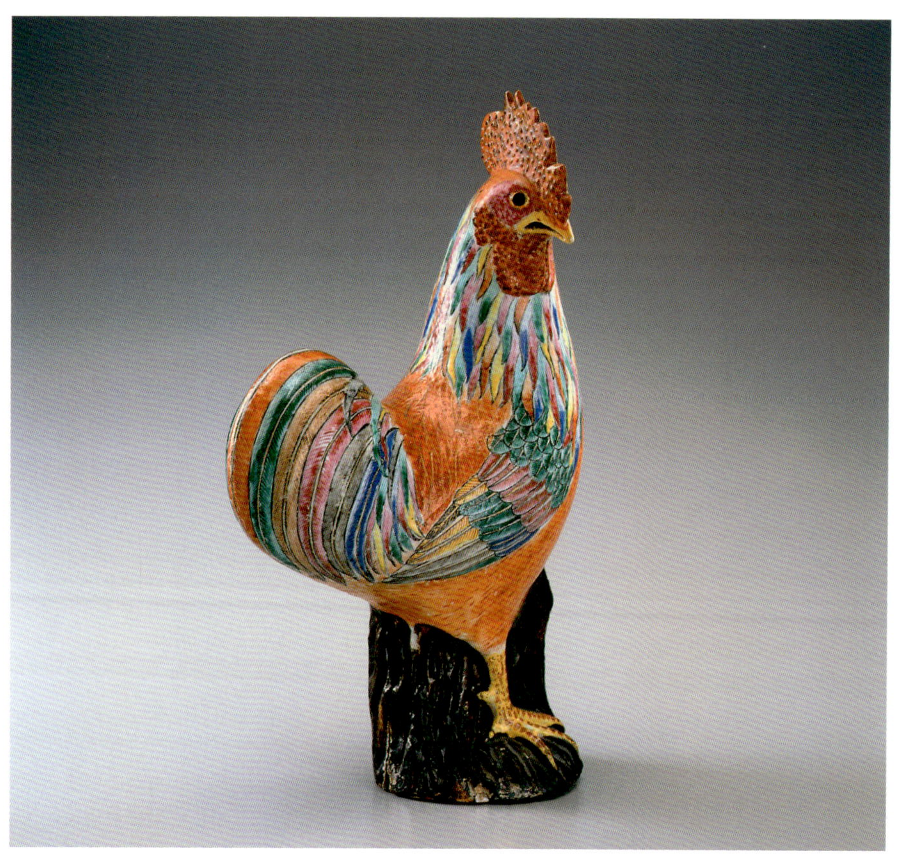

115 FIGURE OF A ROOSTER

Jingdezhen, China; about 1750
Height: 12.625 in. (320 mm)
2000.61.97

This magnificent figure of a rooster, a popular item for export throughout the 18th century, is naturalistically modeled and colorfully painted. Roosters, displayed singly or in pairs, were favored among wealthy Europeans. Similar figures are known to have been sold by Parisian merchant Lazare Duvaux to members of the French aristocracy, including Madame de Pompadour, and no fewer than six pairs ornamented the library in the Chinese Pavilion on the grounds of Drottningholm Palace in Sweden. Depictions of roosters were also found in China as a symbol of courage, benevolence, and faithfulness; the homophone *ji* means both rooster and fortunate.[222]

LITERATURE
Illustrated in Howard, *Choice of the Private Trader,* p. 263.

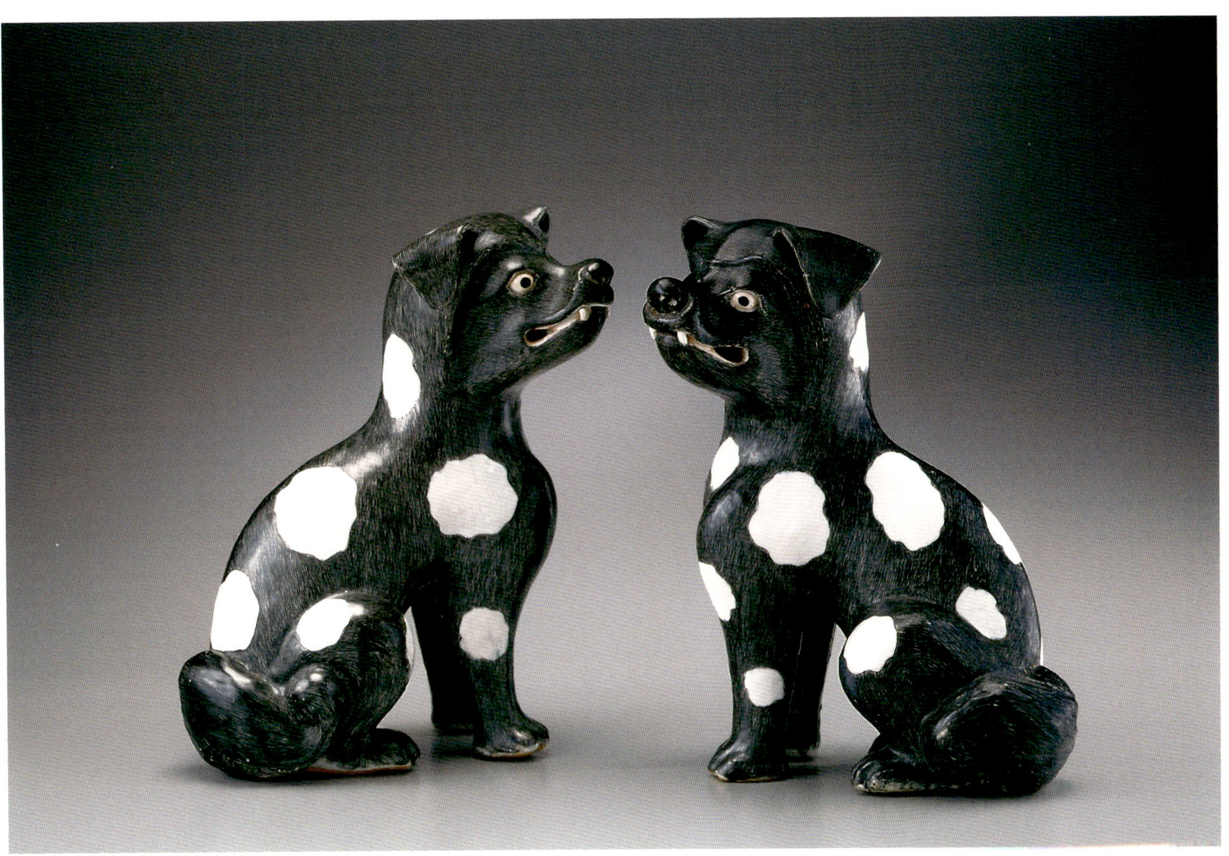

116 FIGURES OF DOGS

Jingdezhen, China; about 1770
Height (each): 11.75 in. (300 mm)
2000.61.126.1, .2

Figures of dogs were popular in both China and the West, where they were symbols of fidelity. Chinese hounds and European spaniels and pugs (the latter two probably based on European porcelain or earthenware figures) were the most common types of dogs reproduced in export porcelain. The pair seen here may be a breed known as Tibetan mastiff.[223]

LITERATURE
Illustrated in Howard, *Choice of the Private Trader,* p. 276.

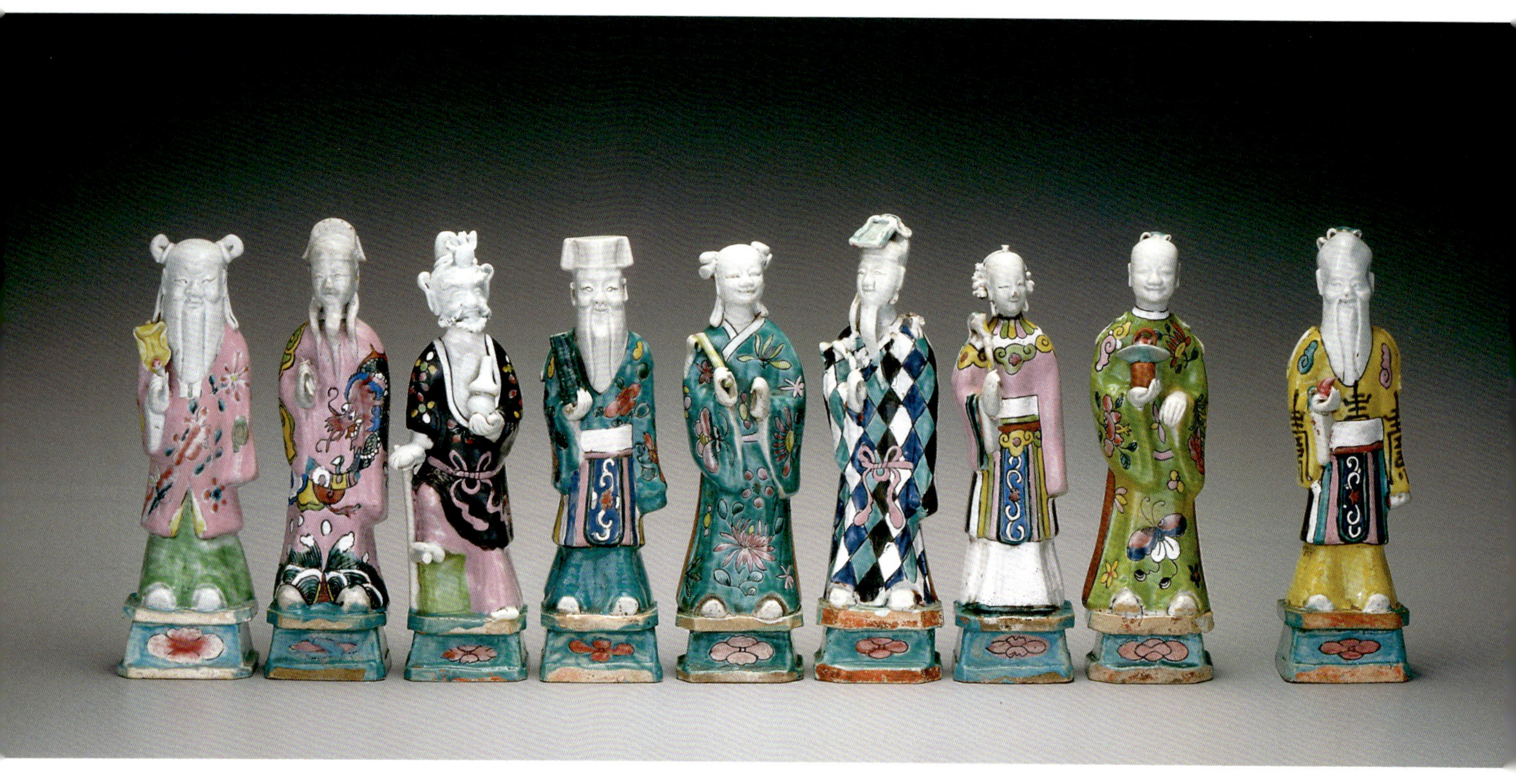

117 FIGURES OF THE EIGHT IMMORTALS AND SHOULOU

Jingdezhen, China; 1775–1800
Height (tallest): 9 in. (229 mm)
L03.2775.112.1–.9

The Eight Immortals are the gods of Daoism, one of the primary philosophical and religious systems in China. As seen here, they are *(left to right)* Zhongli Quan, chief of the Immortals, shown with a fan; Cao Guojiu, seen with wooden clappers; Li Tieguai, shown as a crippled beggar; Zhang Guolao, identified by a bamboo tube with two sticks; Han Xiangzi, seen with a bamboo flute and a boy's topknot; Lü Dongbin, who carries a fly whisk; He Xiangu, a female with a lotus bud; and Lan Caihe, seen with a flower basket. The Immortals are joined by Shoulou, the god of longevity. The Eight Immortals have individual attributes but collectively represent long life, prosperity, and hope for children.[224]

Figures of the Immortals are known to have been collected in the West since the 1750s, when a number were lost with the sinking of the *Geldermalsen*.[225] It is almost certain that the identities of these gods were unknown to their Western owners, who would have viewed them simply as mysterious characters.

Appendix 1: Achievement of Arms

An achievement of arms, more loosely and commonly called a *coat of arms,* was a symbol of individual identity that became a mark of status and rank among those directly descended from the original man to whom the arms had been granted (the grantee). Developed in the 12th century and called *Heraldry,* because the heralds were called upon to authorize and regulate the system, arms were first used by knights to confirm identification in battle but increasingly became accepted as a decorative indication of a family's identity and position in society.

FULL ACHIEVEMENT

The term refers to a shield bearing an individual's *coat,* which is surmounted by a helmet (referred to as a *helm*) on which is placed a *crest*—usually a bird or beast but also any other device. The crest sits on a *wreath* of twisted cloth originally designed to secure it to the helm. *Mantling* is often part of a full achievement and, although now largely decorative, was originally a cloak designed to protect the wearer from the heat of the sun beating on the helmet. A scroll bearing a family or personal motto is usually displayed beneath the shield, but this was a matter of personal choice and could vary among different family members (in Scotland, the motto is frequently displayed above the crest).

Mottoes themselves may derive from battle cries, a play on words of the family name, or from a conviction or faith. *Supporters* are figures that stand on either side of a shield to support it; these were granted to noblemen (a duke, marquess, earl, viscount, or baron), Scottish clan chieftains, and, at a later date, a baronet or senior member of an order. Noblemen also bore a *coronet* of a particular design and helm, each indicating his rank. (On the continent of Europe, some countries also permit coronets to be used by "untitled noblemen," being senior military commanders or "burgrafs" [civic titles such as mayor], but this does not occur in Britain.)

BLAZON

This term applies to the official wording—largely Norman French of the 12th and 13th centuries—used to describe (or *blazon*) a grant of arms so that it is different in some respect from any other armorial and therefore recognizable and unique. The grant was authorized by the heralds; the depiction and arrangement of arms is controlled by the College of Arms in London (which granted arms to English and Irish families and, later, those living abroad, including many in America) and by the Lord Lyon Court in Edinburgh (which granted arms to Scottish families).

TINCTURES ETC.

argent (silver or white)

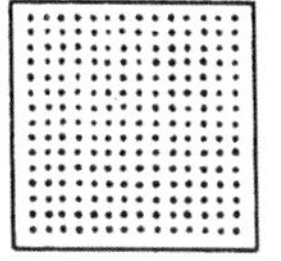
or (gold)

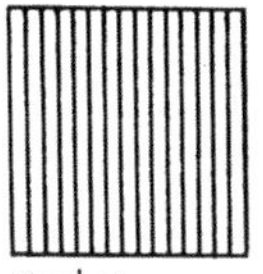
gules (red)

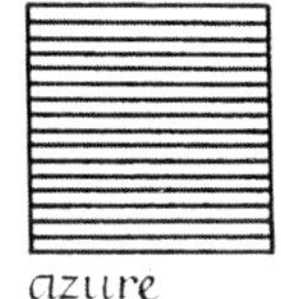
azure (blue)

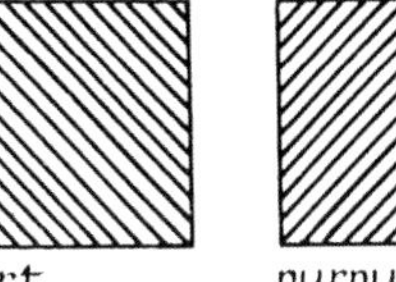
vert (green)

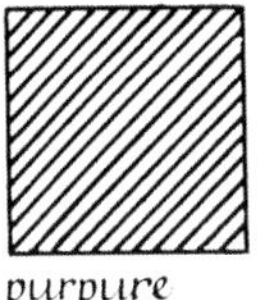
purpure (purple)

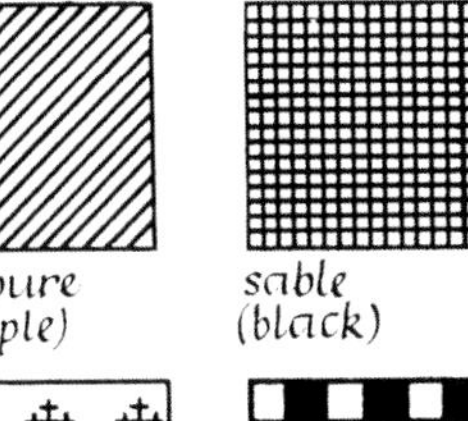
sable (black)

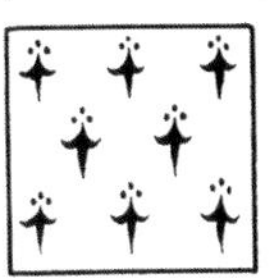
ermine (white, black tufts)

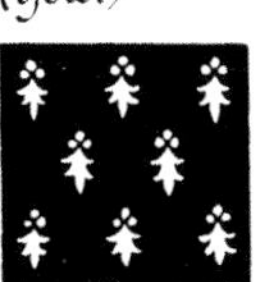
ermines (black, white tufts)

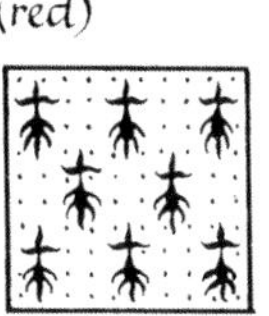
erminois (gold, black tufts)

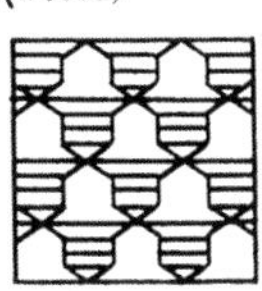
vair

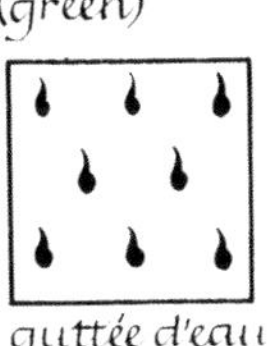
guttée d'eau (d'or etc.)

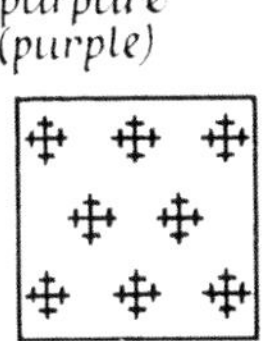
semée of crosses crosslet

chequy

ORDINARIES (and Subordinaries)

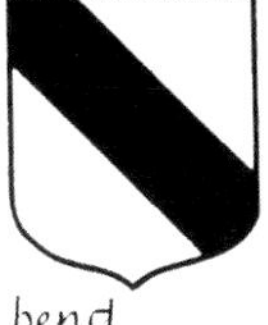
bend

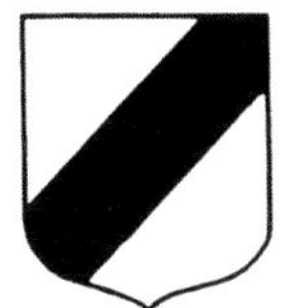
bend sinister

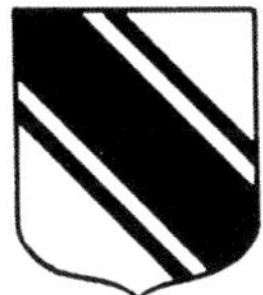
bend cotised

baton

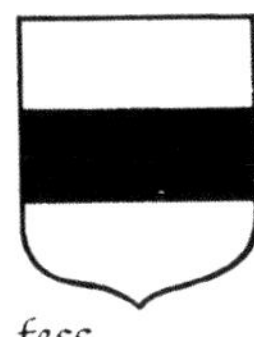
fess

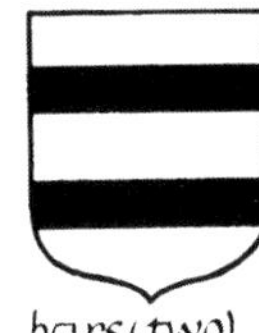
bars (two)

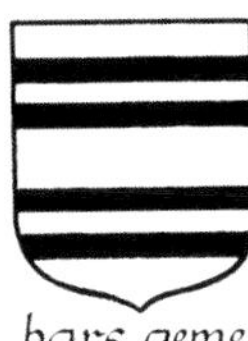
bars gemel (two)

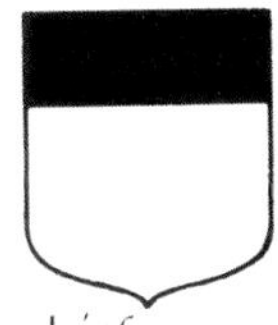
chief

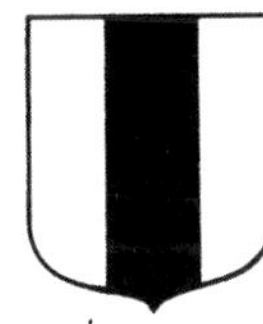
pale

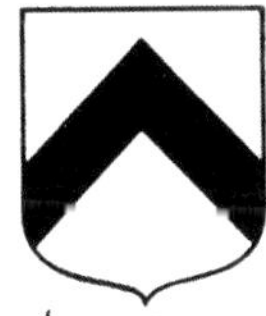
chevron

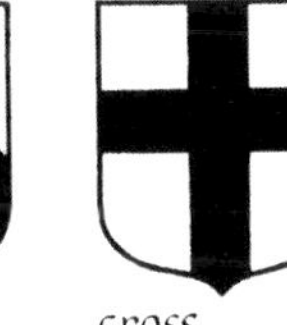
cross

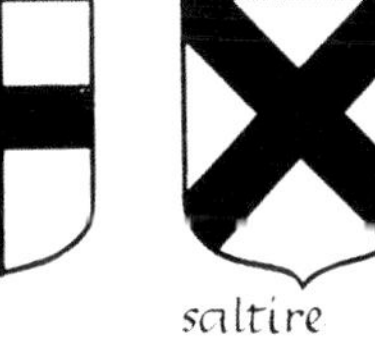
saltire

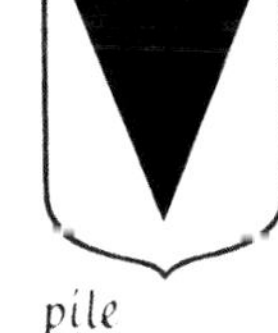
pile

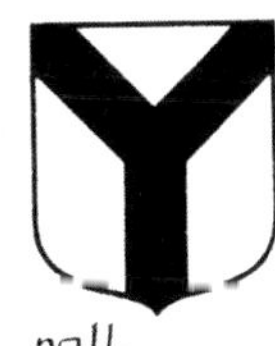
pall

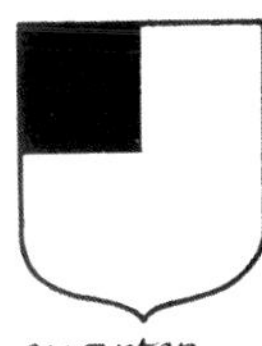
quarter

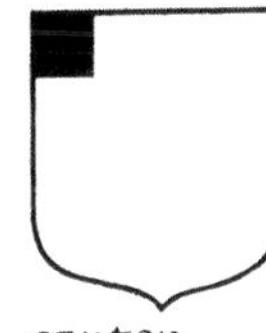
canton

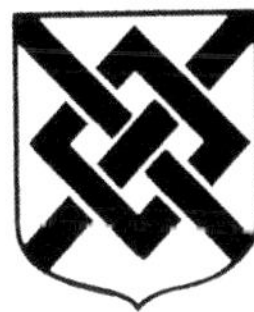
fret

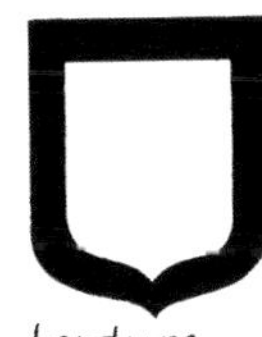
bordure

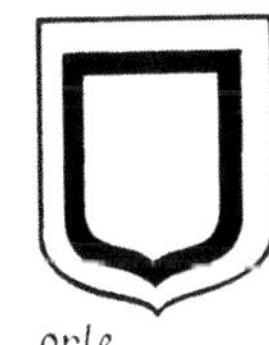
orle

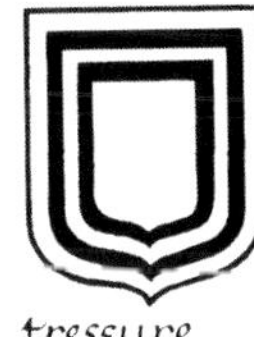
tressure

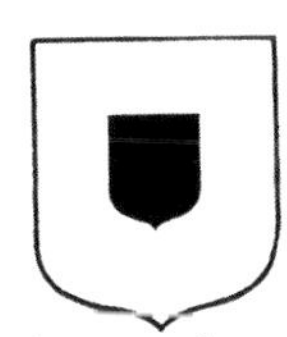
inescutcheon

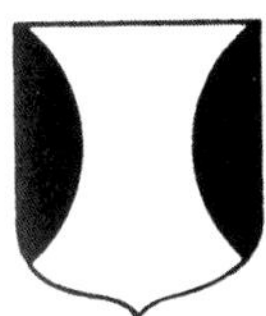
flaunch (two)

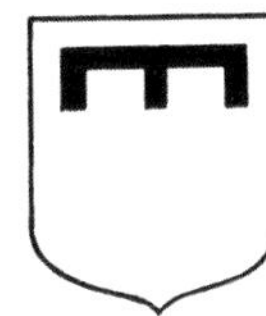
label

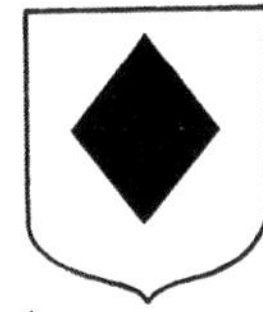
lozenge

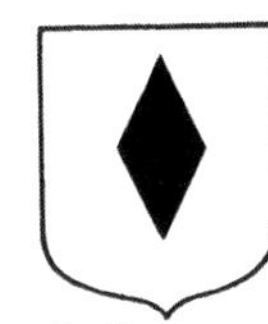
fusil

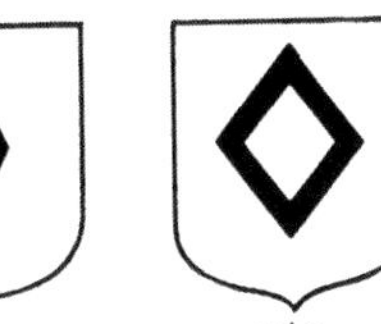
mascle

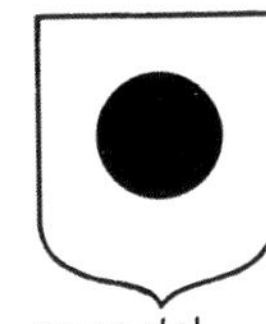
roundel

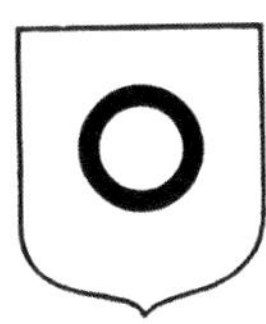
annulet

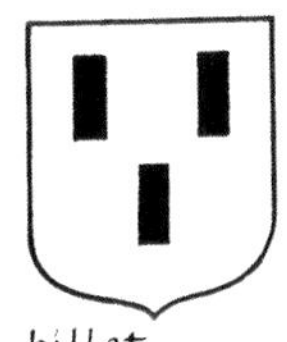
billet (three)

mullet

pierced mullet

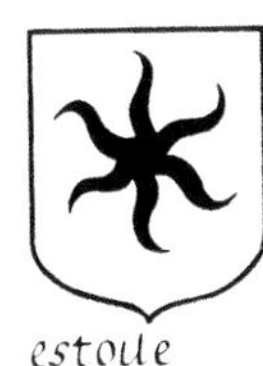
estoile

PARTITION LINES

engrailed
invected
wavy
nebuly
embattled
ragully

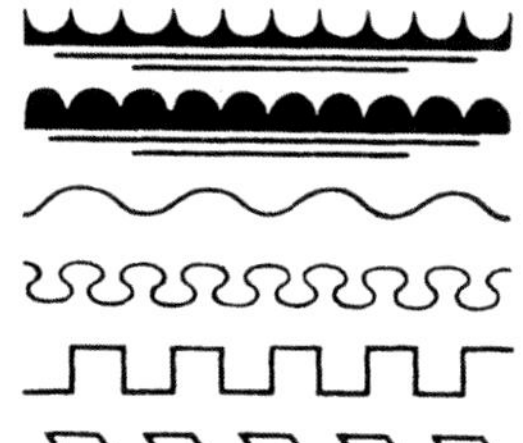

indented
dancetté
dovetailed
potent
rayonné
flory counterflory

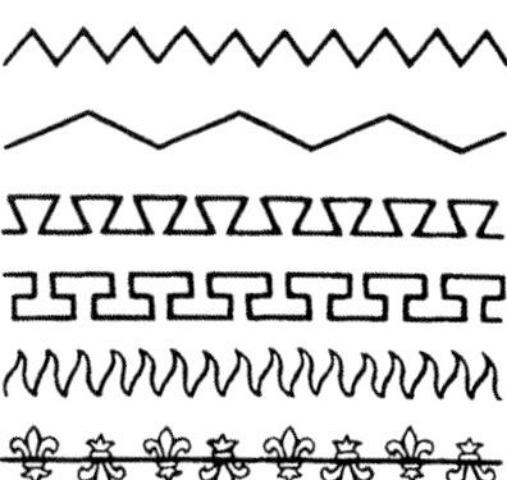

METHODS OF PARTITION

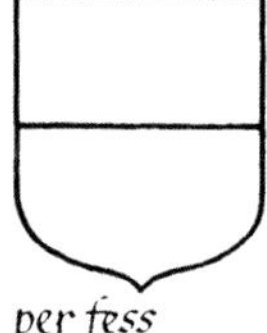
per fess

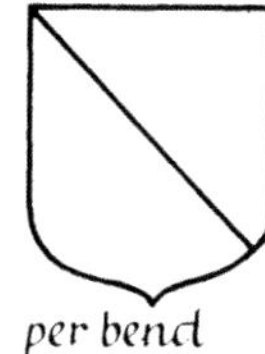
per bend

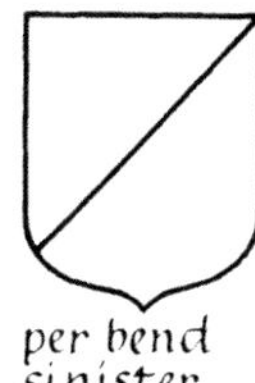
per bend sinister

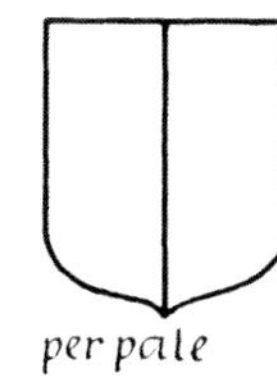
per pale

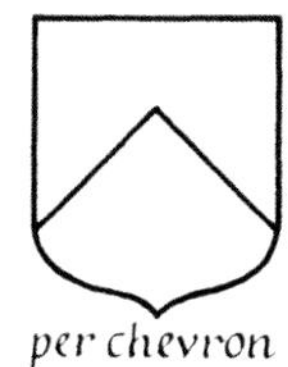
per chevron

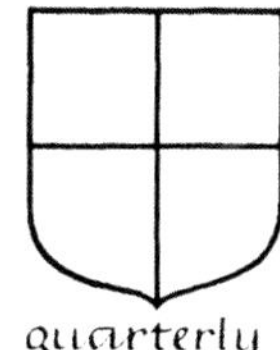
quarterly

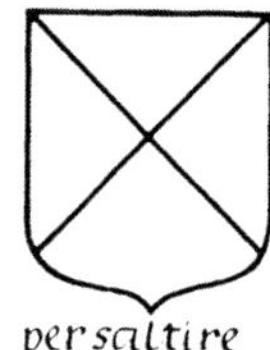
per saltire

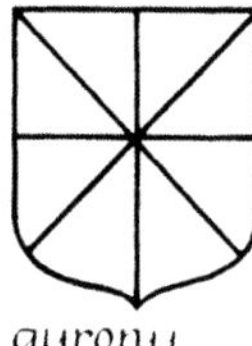
gyrony

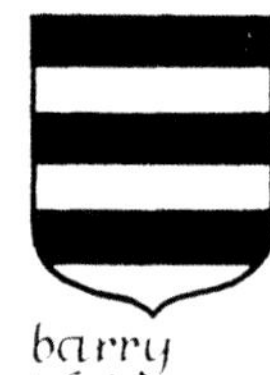
barry (of six)

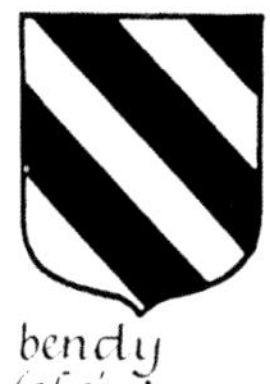
bendy (of six)

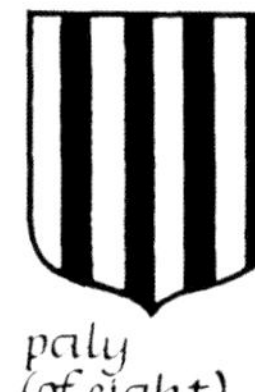
paly (of eight)

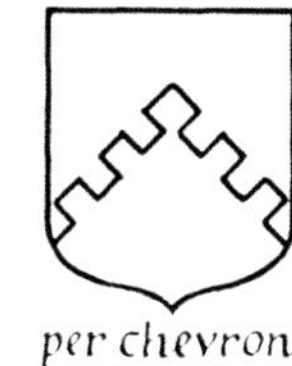
per chevron embattled

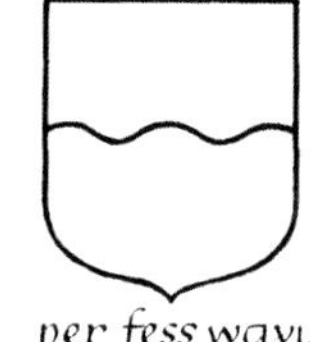
per fess wavy

ROUNDELS

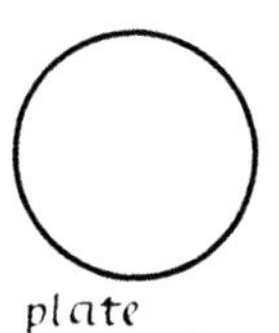
plate (argent)

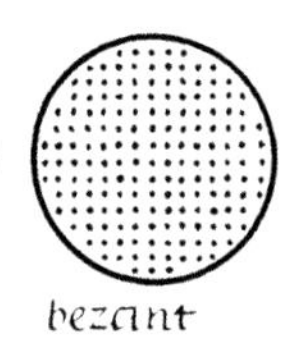
bezant (or)

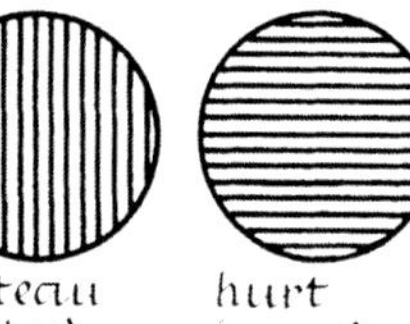
torteau (gules)

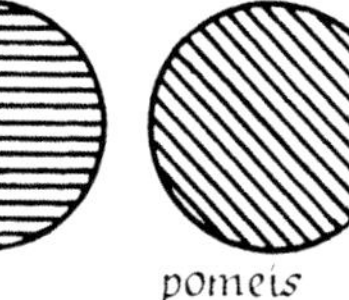
hurt (azure)

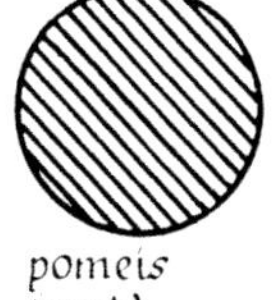
pomeis (vert)

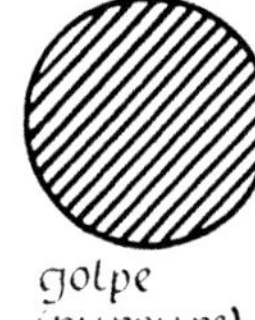
golpe (purpure)

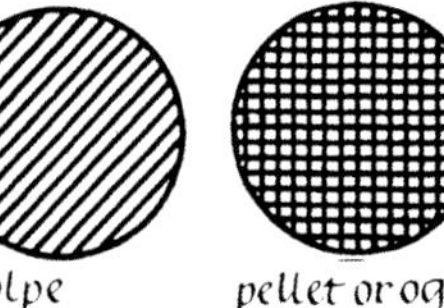
pellet or ogress (sable)

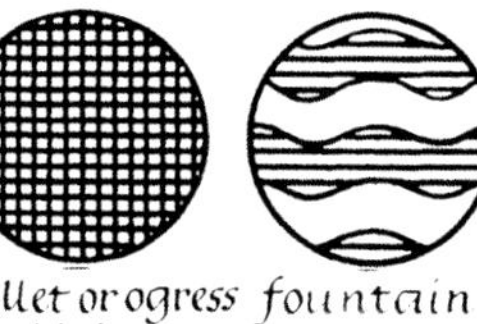
fountain

CROSSES

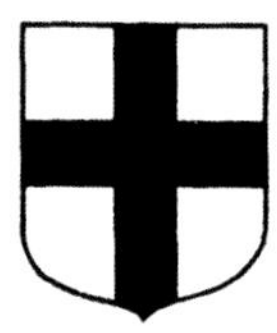
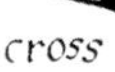
cross

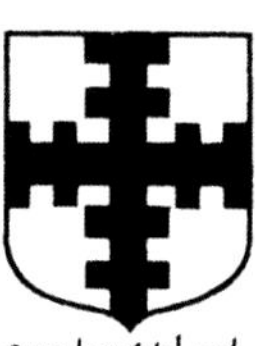
embattled

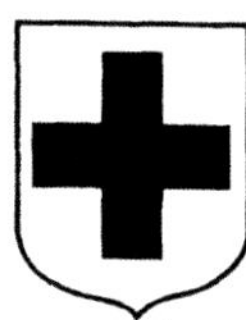
couped

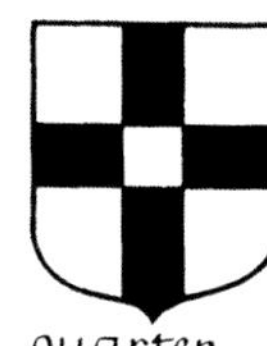
quarter pierced

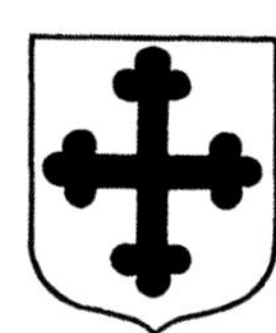
botonny

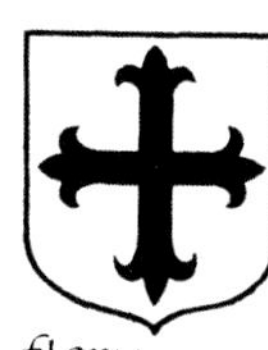
flory

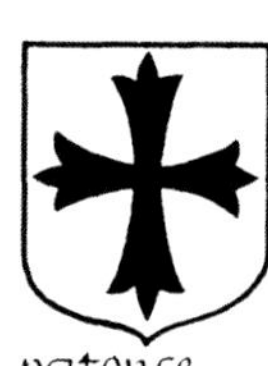
patonce

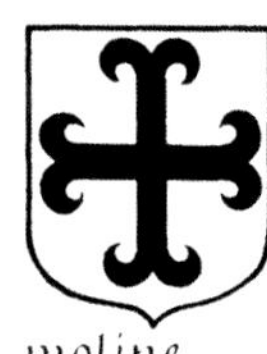
moline

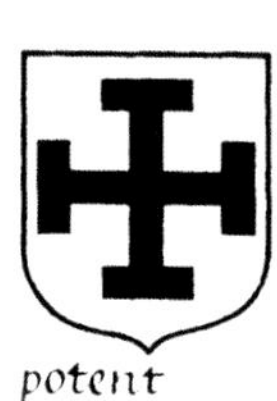
potent

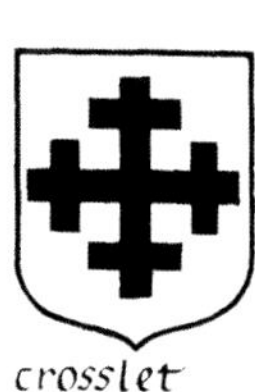
crosslet

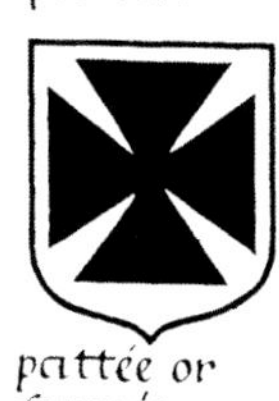
pattée or formée

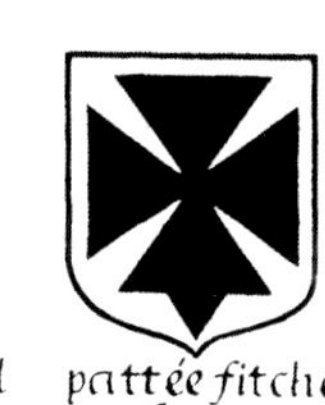
pattée fitched

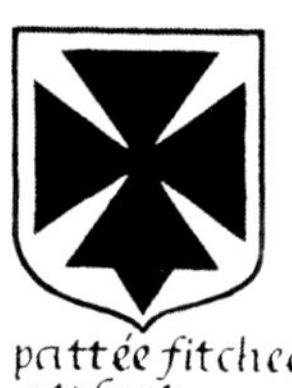
pattée fitched at foot

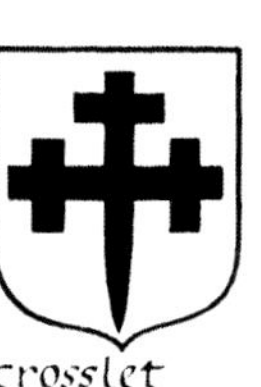
crosslet fitched

The senior herald in England is called *Garter King of Arms* (because he is responsible for the senior order of chivalry of that name), and in Scotland the senior herald is *Lord Lyon King of Arms.* Although the exact subject and colors (correctly called *tinctures*) of each armorial were closely controlled, there was considerable artistic license as to how these could be displayed on shields, seals, cloths, furniture, silver, porcelain, and other objects.

COAT OF ARMS

The name refers to charges such as chevrons, bars, crosses, animals, birds, and other devices. Some smaller charges were laid over larger basic ones (called *ordinaries*), but all were arranged so that, in conjunction with the crest, they created a unique design representing one person and his descendants only.

Women were entitled to display coats of arms if their fathers or husbands were armigerous (arms-bearing). In some circumstances, they could display these arms as their own if they had no brother or if he and his descendants were dead (in both cases, being known as an *heraldic heiress*). An unmarried lady or widow would, however, only display her arms on a *lozenge* (diamond shape) and not on a shield (because she did not fight). For the same reason, ladies did not display a crest (because they did not have helmets).

CREST

This terms refers only to the device on a wreath (or helmet); it is never to be used to describe a full coat of arms.

IMPALEMENT

If both a husband and wife have the right to bear arms, the shield (or lozenge) may be divided vertically—called *impaled*—displaying his arms on the left (as viewed) and hers on the right.

Confusingly, these are always, in heraldry, referred to as if held by the bearer. Thus, the left side as viewed (the husband's coat) is actually the bearer's right and is called the *dexter.* The right side as viewed (the wife's coat) is actually the bearer's left and is called the *sinister.* Unless a mother inherited the right to her father's arms (which she could only do if she had no surviving brothers who left no male heirs), her children could bear only their father's armorials. If she did have brothers but all her brothers' lines subsequently died out, then the descendants of that lady could claim the arms as *eventual heirs,* as if they had been entitled to them in the first place.

IN PRETENCE

A lady with no brothers who has inherited her father's arms may, before marriage, display these on a lozenge. When married, her husband would display her arms *in pretence* (on an escutcheon of pretence, which is a small shield in the center of the husband's coat) instead of impaling them. This also indicates that in due course their children may *quarter* their mother's armorials with their father's if they wish.

ARMS ACCOLLÉE

Two shields may sometimes be illustrated leaning against each other, known as *arms accollée*. This indicates almost the same thing as "arms impaled" but serves an additional purpose. Where a man may be the recipient of an order or knighthood, which is not conferred on his wife, and he wishes to indicate this in his armorials, he may only do so on his arms and not on his impaled arms. It is thus necessary to find an arrangement that enables him to display his own coat with his order and yet show his marriage (this idea appears to have been adopted by British heraldry from the Continent, where the arrangement is more usual).

QUARTERING

This is an arrangement of coats displaying the shields of as many ancestors as a descendant may be entitled to (and wishes to) through the male and various female lines, provided the latter are through an heraldic heiress. These are shown from top left to bottom right in the order that they joined the male line—the older being shown first. In order to balance the display, coats may be repeated once (as when they are "quarterly of four" showing just the father's and mother's arms). In more complex cases where quarters "of eight," "of sixteen," or more are involved, it is possible that maternal coats may appear more than once where cousins have married in the past.

It is not permitted to select at random some particularly illustrious ancestor unless all the intermediate quarterings are also shown. In a small number of cases, this has led to exceptionally complex shields in excess of 300 quarterings, but such instances are rare. At any time a descendant may revert to the simple single coat of his male ancestor if he wishes.

POSITIONS OF BEASTS & MONSTERS

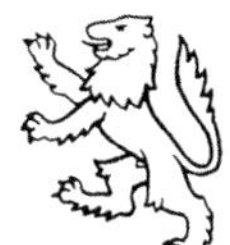
rampant

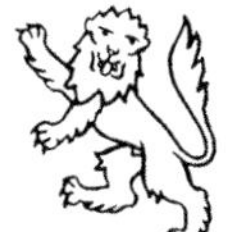
rampant gardant

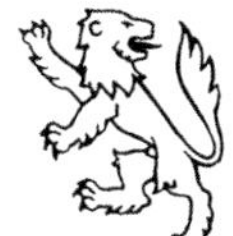
rampant regardant

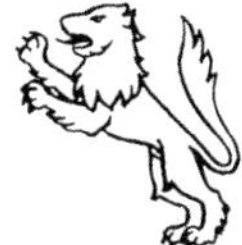
salient

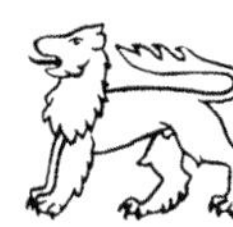
statant

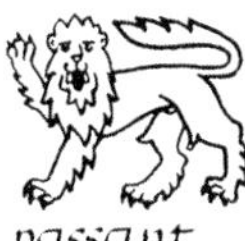
passant gardant

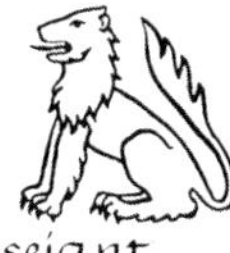
sejant

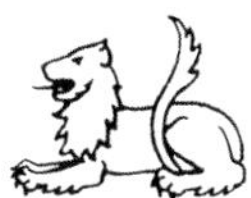
couchant

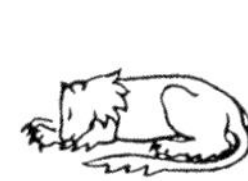
dormant

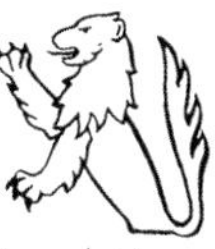
demi lion rampant

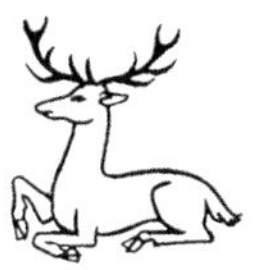
stag lodged

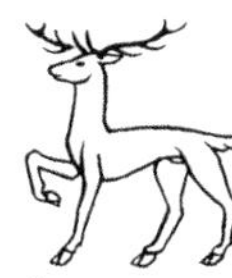
stag trippant

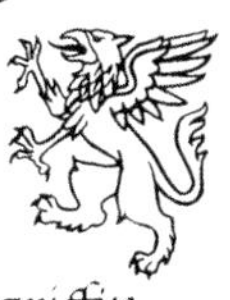
griffin segreant

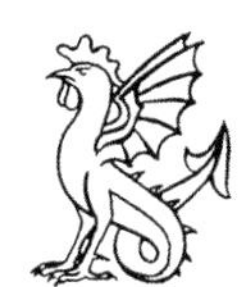
cockatrice

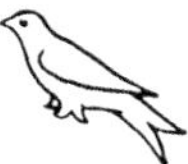
martlet

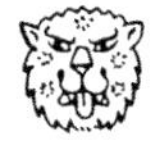
leopard's face

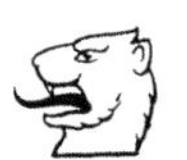
lion's head couped

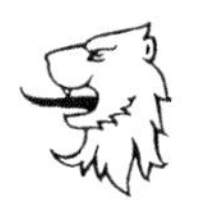
lion's head erased

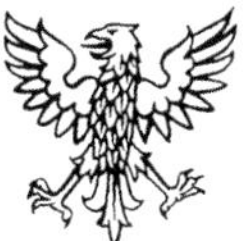
eagle displayed

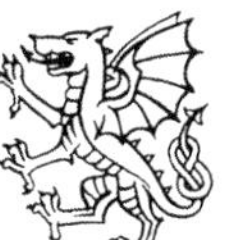
dragon tail nowed

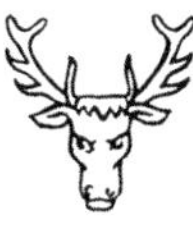
stag's head cabossed

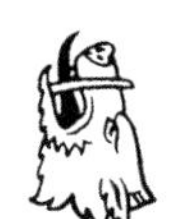
boar's head erased and erect

MARKS OF CADENCY

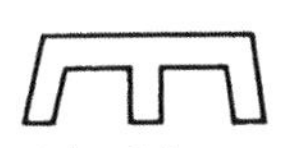
Heir, eldest son label

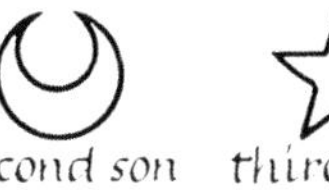
second son crescent

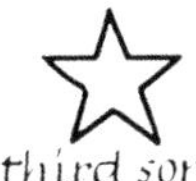
third son mullet

fourth son martlet

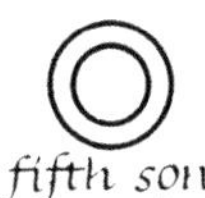
fifth son annulet

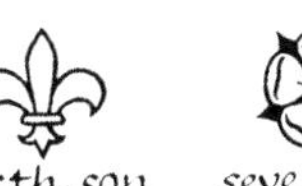
sixth son fleur de lis

seventh son rose

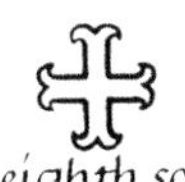
eighth son cross moline

THE HELM

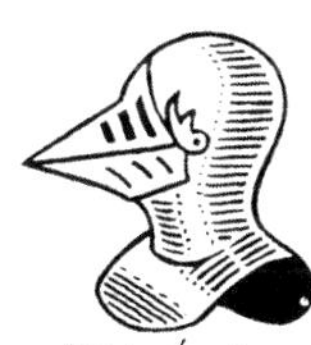
Esquire

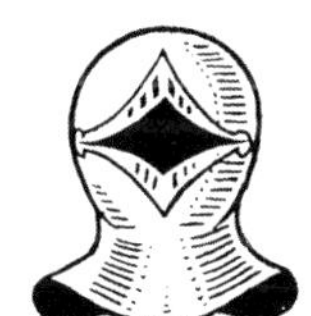
Knight & Baronet

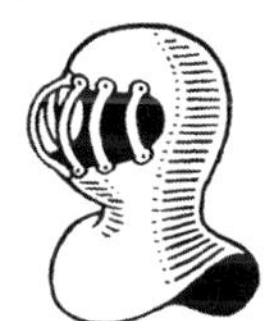
Peer, below the rank of Duke

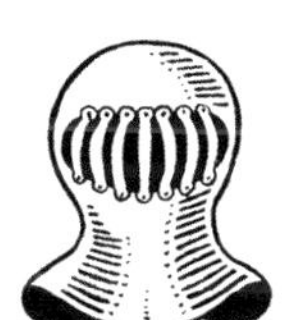
Royal Prince & Duke

CORONETS

duke's coronet

marquis's coronet

earl's coronet

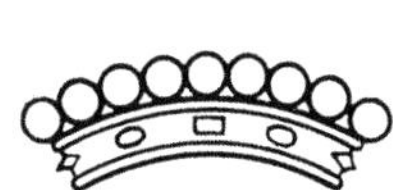
viscount's coronet

baron's coronet

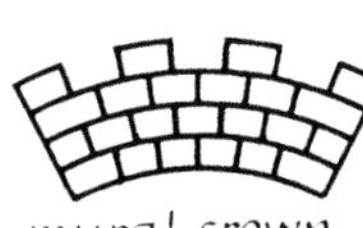
mural crown

naval crown

eastern crown

cap of maintenance

BARONET'S BADGES

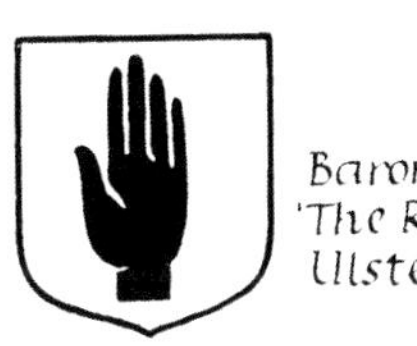
Baronet of England 'The Red hand of Ulster'

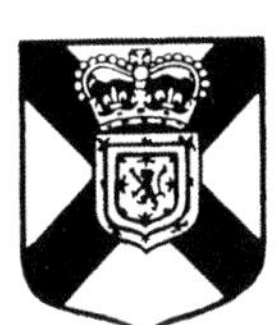
Baronet of Nova Scotia The arms of Scotland regally crowned on a cross of St. Andrew

MARSHALLING OF ARMS

The plain coat of a man and his male descendants (he being a second son).

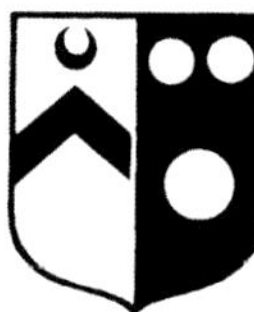

The impaled coat of a man and his wife (not borne by his descendants).

The coat of a man with that of his wife 'in pretence' – she an heraldic heiress.

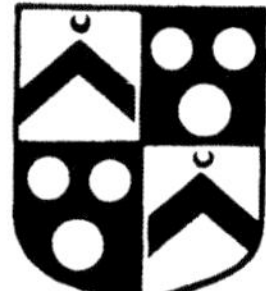

The male descendants of the man and his heiress wife – the coat 'quarterly'.

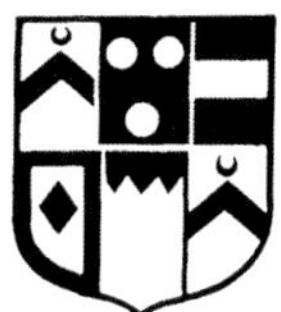

The male descendants of a later generation after a further marriage or marriages with an heiress or heiresses – the coat 'quarterly of six'.

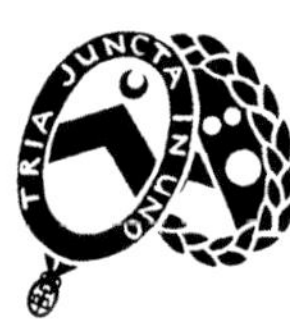

Arms accollée.

The unmarried daughter.

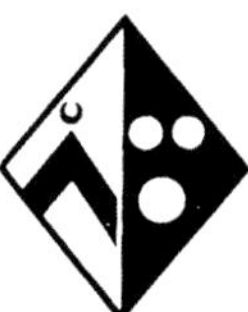

The widow.

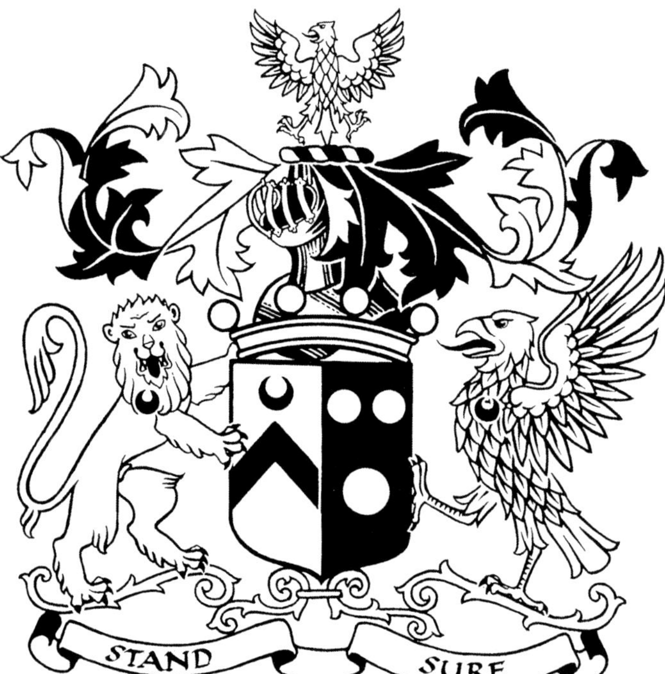

THE FULL ACHIEVEMENT
of a Baron

Arms: 'Argent a chevron (gules), a crescent for difference' impaling '(Azure) three plates'. Crest: 'An eagle displayed (or)'. Supporters: 'A lion rampant gardant (argent) and an eagle (or) each charged with a crescent'. Motto: 'Stand Sure'.

MARKS OF CADENCY

In order to differentiate among brothers and their respective lines, a system of *marks of difference* (a label of three points for the eldest son, a crescent for a second, a martlet for a third, etc.) may be used. This can carry down into subsequent generations and indicate a different branch of the family. In Scotland, it is more usual to use different *bordures* (or borders) to indicate "difference."

DISTINCTION

This term, paradoxically, is only used to indicate illegitimacy and is sometimes shown by the use of a *bend sinister* (a bar from top right to bottom left of the shield, in French, *barre sinister*). In Scotland the usual method is a *bordure wavy.*

RANKS AND ORDERS

As is mentioned above, coronets and helms of different patterns indicate the rank of a nobleman. A baronet's badge—Scotland differing from the rest of the United Kingdom—is placed on the arms of an actual baronet. Members of an order indicate this with a chain or circular motto scroll of the order round the shield of the recipient only. This sometimes requires the arms to be *accollée.*

Text (adapted) and images are from David S. Howard, *Chinese Armorial Porcelain,* vol. 2 (Chippenham, England: Heirloom and Howard, 2003).

Appendix II: Chinese Dynasties and Reigns
(covered in this book)

TANG DYNASTY	(618–906)
THE FIVE DYNASTIES	(907–960)
LIAO DYNASTY	(907–1125)
SONG DYNASTY	(960–1279)
JIN DYNASTY	(1115–1234)
YUAN DYNASTY	(1279–1368)
MING DYNASTY	(1368–1644)
Hongwu	1368–1398
Jianwen	1399–1402
Yongle	1403–1424
Hongxi	1425
Xuande	1426–1435
Zhengtong	1436–1449
Jingtai	1450–1457
Tianshun	1457–1464
Chenghua	1465–1487
Hongzhi	1488–1505
Zhengde	1506–1521
Jiajing	1522–1566
Longqing	1567–1572
Wanli	1573–1619
Taichang	1620
Tianqi	1621–1627
Chongzhen	1628–1644
QING DYNASTY	(1644–1911)
Shunzhi	1644–1661
Kangxi	1662–1722
Yongzheng	1723–1735
Qianlong	1736–1795
Jiaqing	1796–1820
Daoguang	1821–1850
Xianfeng	1851–1861
Tongzhi	1862–1874
Guangxu	1875–1908
Xuantong	1909–1911

Endnotes

1. The earliest documented piece of Chinese export porcelain to reach Europe is the so-called Fonthill Vase, made about 1300 and known to have been in Europe by 1381, when it was given silver and gilt mounts. It is illustrated in Emerson, Chen, and Gates, *Porcelain Stories,* p. 25.
2. Ricci, *China in the Sixteenth Century,* pp. 14–15.
3. The word *kaolin* comes from *Gaoling,* the name of the mountain in southern China where some of the finest china clay was mined. The term *petunsc* comes from *baidunzi,* the Chinese word for the small, white bricks of processed porcelain stone used by potters; Pierson, *Earth, Fire, and Water,* pp. 9–12.
4. Emerson, Chen, and Gates, *Porcelain Stories,* p. 25.
5. Du Halde, *General History of China,* 2:321.
6. Savage and Newman, *Illustrated Dictionary of Ceramics,* pp. 108, 208, 303–4; Kingery and Vandiver, "Eighteenth-Century Change," pp. 369–73.
7. Du Halde, *General History of China,* 2:323.
8. "Letters of Père d'Entrecolles," p. 60.
9. Medley, *Chinese Potter,* pp. 232–33; Pierson, *Earth, Fire, and Water,* p. 13.
10. Ayers et al., *Porcelain for Palaces,* pp. 15–34.
11. De Matos, "Chinese Porcelain," pp. 115, 111.
12. Phillips, *China-Trade Porcelain,* p. 21.
13. Volker, *Porcelain and the Dutch East India Company,* pp. 42, 24.
14. Howard, *Choice of the Private Trader,* p. 15; Le Corbeiller, *China Trade Porcelain,* p. 4.
15. Mézin, *Cargaisons de Chine,* pp. 14–25; Roth, *Chinese Porcelain,* pp. 5–8; Howard, *Chinese Armorial Porcelain,* 2:50–59; Parnetier, *Tea Time in Flanders,* pp. 14–15; Scheurleer, *Chinese Export Porcelain,* p. 119.
16. Quincy, *Journals of Samuel Shaw,* p. 183.
17. Staunton, *Authentic Account of an Embassy,* 2:527.
18. Quincy, *Journals of Samuel Shaw,* pp. 178–79; Phillips, *China-Trade Porcelain,* p. 32.
19. Quincy, *Journals of Samuel Shaw,* p. 180; Jörg, *Porcelain and the Dutch China Trade,* pp. 77, 217–20.
20. Jörg, *Geldermalsen,* pp. 59, 115–16.
21. Howard, *Choice of the Private Trader,* p. 23.
22. Jörg, *Geldermalsen,* p. 59; Howard, *Choice of the Private Trader,* p. 24; John Latimer to Ann Latimer, October 19, 1815, Latimer Family Papers, University of Delaware Library, Newark, Del.
23. Howard, *Choice of the Private Trader,* pp. 18–28.
24. Yam Shinqua trade label, 58 x 33, Downs Collection, Winterthur Library; Mudge, *Chinese Export Porcelain for the American Trade,* p. 78.
25. Rawson and Portal, "Luxuries for Trade," p. 277.
26. Volker, *Porcelain and the Dutch East India Company,* p. 37; Jörg, *Porcelain and the Dutch China Trade,* pp. 94–112; Howard, *Tale of Three Cities,* p. 55; Quincy, *Journals of Samuel Shaw,* p. 199; Howard, *Chinese Armorial Porcelain,* 2:15–18.
27. Frei Bartolomeu dos Mártires to Pope Paul IV (1563) in De Matos, "Chinese Porcelain," p. 115; Loys Guyon in Phillips, *China-Trade Porcelain,* p. 42.
28. Harrison-Hall, "Export Porcelain from the British Museum," pp. 4–11; Finlay, "Pilgrim Art," p. 72.

29. Labaree, *Autobiography of Benjamin Franklin,* p. 145; Howard, *Chinese Armorial Porcelain,* 2:9.
30. Detweiler, *George Washington's Chinaware,* p. 31.
31. Le Corbeiller and Frelinghuysen, *Chinese Export Porcelain,* p. 34.
32. Finlay, "Pilgrim Art," pp. 169–70.
33. Glanville and Young, *Elegant Eating,* pp. 42–67; forks were in use in Italy as early as 1023 and in Europe in the 16th century.
34. Strong, *Feast,* p. 165; Woolley, *Queene-like Closet,* p. 341.
35. Glanville and Young, *Elegant Eating,* p. 60; Canton Journal, Oriental and India Office Collections, R/10/4, p. 42, British Library.
36. Kawahara, *Ko-sometsuke,* p. 238.
37. Impey, *Early Porcelain Kilns of Japan,* p. 26.
38. Similar dishes are illustrated in Le Corbeiller, *China Trade Porcelain,* p. 19; Brawer, *Chinese Export Porcelain,* p. 95; and Litzenburg and Bailey, *Reeves Center Collection,* p. 26.
39. Kyushu Ceramic Museum, *Voyage of Old-Imari,* pp. 37–38; Jörg, *Fine and Curious,* pp. 210, 225.
40. Le Corbeiller, *China Trade Porcelain,* pp. 31–32.
41. For a similar plate with the medal, see Scheurleer, *Chinese Export Porcelain,* pls. 131–32; Le Corbeiller, *China Trade Porcelain,* p. 32; Jörg, "To the Highest Bidder," p. 63.
42. Krahl and Harrison-Hall, *Ancient Chinese Trade Ceramics,* p. 54.
43. Jörg, *Fine and Curious,* pp. 232–33.
44. Krahl and Harrison-Hall, *Ancient Chinese Trade Ceramics,* p. 44; Howard and Ayers, *China for the West,* 1:83.
45. Howard, *Chinese Armorial Porcelain,* 1:164, 176; Howard and Ayers, *China for the West,* 1:83.
46. Howard, *Chinese Armorial Porcelain,* 1:177–78; Howard, *Tale of Three Cities,* p. 97.
47. Howard, *Chinese Armorial Porcelain,* 1:188, 2:33.
48. Howard, *Chinese Armorial Porcelain,* 2:135.
49. Jörg and van Campen, *Collection of the Rijksmuseum,* p. 148; Howard, *Chinese Armorial Porcelain,* 1:189.
50. Matt. 3:16 (King James Version).
51. Brawer, *Chinese Export Porcelain,* p. 118; Howard and Ayers, *China for the West,* 1:312–13; Litzenburg and Bailey, *Reeves Center Collection,* p. 198.
52. I Sam. 10:1 (King James Version).
53. Howard and Ayers, *China for the West,* 1:309; Viega, *Chinese Export Porcelain,* p. 138; Hervouët, Hervouët, and Bruneau, *La Porcelaine,* p. 399.
54. Howard and Ayers, *China for the West,* 1:234–35; Le Corbeiller, *China Trade Porcelain,* pp. 42–43.
55. Howard, *Chinese Armorial Porcelain,* 2:131.
56. Howard, *Chinese Armorial Porcelain,* 1:172.
57. Howard, *Chinese Armorial Porcelain,* 2:142.
58. Howard, *Chinese Armorial Porcelain,* 2:142.
59. Jörg and van Campen, *Collection of the Rijksmuseum,* p. 306.
60. Kühne-van Diggelen, "Armorial Services of Jan Albert Sichterman," pp. 2–11, 44; correspondence with Johan de Haan, Groningen, November 2003.
61. Jörg, *Porcelain and the Dutch China Trade,* p. 102.
62. Du Halde, *General History of China,* 2:326.
63. Howard, *Chinese Armorial Porcelain,* 1:234; Howard and Ayers, *China for the West,* 2:408; Le Corbeiller, *China Trade Porcelain,* pp. 50–51.
64. The original receipt as well as pieces from the service are illustrated in Le Corbeiller, *China Trade Porcelain,* pp. 52–53.
65. Howard, *Chinese Armorial Porcelain,* 1:174; invoices cited in Krahl and Harrison-Hall, *Ancient Chinese Trade Ceramics,* p. 224; Howard and Ayers, *China for the West,* 2:408; Howard, *Choice of the Private Trader,* p. 67.
66. Communication with David Howard, November 2003.
67. Howard, *Chinese Armorial Porcelain,* 2:50–59.
68. Cohen and Cohen, *After You!,* pp. 22–24.
69. Howard, *Chinese Armorial Porcelain,* 2:265.
70. Howard, *Chinese Armorial Porcelain,* 1:394.
71. Choi, "Hong Bowls," pp. 42–43.
72. Howard, *Chinese Armorial Porcelain,* 1:227, 235, 329; Howard, *Choice of the Private Trader,* p. 68.
73. Jörg, *Pronk Porcelain,* p. 49.

74. Jörg, *Pronk Porcelain,* pp. 14–26; Howard, *Choice of the Private Trader,* p. 73.
75. Le Corbeiller, *China Trade Porcelain,* p. 87.
76. Howard, *Choice of the Private Trader,* pp. 78–79, 211; Le Corbeiller, *China Trade Porcelain,* p. 87.
77. Howard and Ayers, *China for the West,* 2:414; for the plate and pattern, see Howard and Ayers, *China for the West,* 2:414; and Howard, *Tale of Three Cities,* p. 57; Howard, *Choice of the Private Trader,* pp. 80, 67.
78. Howard and Ayers, *China for the West,* 2:414.
79. Howard, *Choice of the Private Trader,* p. 83; for other dishes with the same design as well as the print source, see Scheurleer, *Chinese Export Porcelain,* pls. 206–7.
80. Jörg, "Pattern of Exchange," pp. 171–74.
81. Jörg, "Pattern of Exchange," p. 175.
82. Jörg, *Chinese Export Porcelain,* p. 222; for a plate with an identical central design but a different border, see Howard and Ayers, *China for the West,* 2:522; and Scheurleer, *Chinese Export Porcelain,* pl. 249.
83. Howard and Ayers, *China for the West,* 2:400–401; Christie's catalogue, New York, January 21, 2003, no. 284.
84. Howard, *Chinese Armorial Porcelain,* 1:46–48, 327.
85. Howard, *Chinese Armorial Porcelain,* 2:238.
86. Thanks to Ann Wagner, McNeill Fellow, Winterthur Program in Early American Culture, for providing this information.
87. Howard, *Tale of Three Cities,* p. 61.
88. Howard, *Chinese Armorial Porcelain,* 2:387.
89. Howard and Ayers, *China for the West,* 2:389; Howard, *Choice of the Private Trader,* p. 85.
90. Detweiler, *George Washington's Chinaware,* pp. 24–36.
91. Howard and Ayers, *China for the West,* 1:281–83.
92. Howard, *Choice of the Private Trader,* p. 99.
93. Krahl and Harrison-Hall, *Ancient Chinese Trade Ceramics,* p. 68; Akveld and Jacobs, *Colourful World of the VOC,* p. 15; Jörg, *Geldermalsen,* p. 48.
94. Howard and Ayers, *China for the West,* 1:222; Jörg, *Porcelain and the Dutch China Trade,* pp. 146–47.
95. Jörg and van Campen, *Collection of the Rijksmuseum,* p. 310; Jörg, *Chinese Export Porcelain,* pp. 240–41.
96. Howard, *Chinese Armorial Porcelain,* 1:414.
97. Howard, *Chinese Armorial Porcelain,* 1:404; Howard and Ayers, *China for the West,* 2:428–29.
98. Howard, *Tale of Three Cities,* pp. 127–29.
99. Howard, *Chinese Armorial Porcelain,* 1:51–54, 973.
100. Howard, *Chinese Armorial Porcelain,* 1:741; Phillips, *China-Trade Porcelain,* p. 27; Howard and Ayers, *China for the West,* 2:436–37; Litzenburg and Bailey, *Reeves Center Collection,* p. 141; Brawer, *Chinese Export Porcelain,* p. 57; Palmer, *Winterthur Guide,* p. 30.
101. Howard and Ayers, *China for the West,* 1:202; Howard, *Chinese Armorial Porcelain,* 2:435.
102. Howard and Ayers, *China for the West,* 1:229.
103. Howard, *Chinese Armorial Porcelain,* 2:702.
104. Hartop, *Huguenot Legacy,* p. 140; Alcorn, *English Silver,* 2:53.
105. Paston-Williams, *Art of Dining,* p. 189.
106. Glanville and Young, *Elegant Eating,* p. 60; Volker, *Porcelain and the Dutch East India Company,* p. 25.
107. Glanville and Young, *Elegant Eating,* pp. 60–62; Hartop, *Huguenot Legacy,* p. 154.
108. Paston-Williams, *Art of Dining,* p. 171; Glanville and Young, *Elegant Eating,* p. 60; Hartop, *Huguenot Legacy,* p. 206.
109. Jörg, *Geldermalsen,* pp. 57–61.
110. Jörg, *Geldermalsen,* pp. 59, 62–63; Sheaf and Kilburn, *Hatcher Porcelain Cargoes,* pp. 157–58.
111. Rawson and Portal, "Luxuries for Trade," p. 275; communication with Dr. Rudi Matthee, University of Delaware, August 2004.
112. Lebel, "Royal China," pp. 88–91; Beurdeley, *Chinese Trade Porcelain,* p. 106.
113. Glanville and Young, *Elegant Eating,* pp. 62, 7; Strong, *Feast,* p. 141.
114. Howard, *Choice of the Private Trader,* pp. 110–11.
115. Krahl and Harrison-Hall, *Ancient Chinese Trade Ceramics,* p. 278.

116. Calvão, *Porcelain Route,* pp. 268–69.

117. Jörg, *Porcelain and the Dutch China Trade,* p. 190; for similar tureens, see Palmer, *Winterthur Guide,* p. 57; Howard, *Tale of Three Cities,* p. 140; Howard and Ayers, *China for the West,* 2:590–91; Sargent, *Copeland Collection,* pp. 200–201; Beurdeley, *Porcelain of the East India Companies,* p. 85.

118. Howard, *Chinese Armorial Porcelain,* 1:261; Cohen and Cohen, *School's Out,* p. 34.

119. The pattern is also referred to as the Rockefeller pattern, as a large service was collected by John D. Rockefeller Jr.; Rockefeller, *David and Peggy Rockefeller Collection,* no. 241, pp. 233–34; Southey and Simmons, *Letters from England,* p. 191.

120. Howard, *Tale of Three Cities,* p. 47.

121. Wainwright, *Philadelphia Perspective,* p. 125; Sims went bankrupt, and the house and contents were auctioned in January 1824; see "Ewing Papers," p. 43 (with thanks to Statia Norman, Historic Kenmore, Fredericksburg, Va.).

122. Wick, *George Washington,* pp. 138–42.

123. Receipt, R. Tyndale to Samuel Bailey, Philadelphia, Pa., March 4, 1822, Latimer Papers, Downs Collection, Winterthur Library.

124. Ball, *Diana Adventure,* pp. 29–86.

125. Known as *turquerie,* Islamic designs and images of Turks were adapted by Europeans as exotic ornament, just as Chinese designs were adapted to create European chinoiserie; Schnyder, "Influence of Turkey," pp. 23–28.

126. Jörg, *Pronk Porcelain,* p. 51; for similar fountains, see Jörg and van Campen, *Collection of the Rijksmuseum,* pp. 285–86; Scheurleer, *Chinese Export Porcelain,* pp. 122–23.

127. Mintz, *Sweetness and Power,* p. 108.

128. Jörg, *Porcelain and the Dutch China Trade,* p. 188; Martin, "'Fashionable Sugar Dishes, Latest Fashion Ware,'" p. 183.

129. Oxford English Dictionary (1933), s.v. "punch."

130. Rinaldi, *Kraak Porcelain,* pp. 182–84; Watson, Chinese *Porcelain in European Mounts,* pp. 9–21.

131. Volker, *Porcelain and the Dutch East India Company,* p. 43.

132. For similar or related pots, see Jörg, *Oosters Porselein,* pp. 103–4; Jörg, *Fine and Curious,* pp. 250–51; and Impey, *Japanese Export Porcelain,* p. 226.

133. Dapper, *Gedenkwaardig Bedryf der Nederlandsche,* pp. 346–47, 289; Montanus, *Atlas Chinensis,* pp. 318–19, 265.

134. Loesch, *Pietsch, and Reichel, Porcelain Collection Dresden,* p. 47; Valfré, *Yixing,* p. 227; for similar bamboo-shape pots, see Litzenburg and Bailey, *Reeves Center Collection,* p. 59; Ströber, *"La maladie de porcelaine,"* p. 119.

135. Den Blaauwen, Meissen *Porcelain in the Rijksmuseum,* p. 37.

136. Howard, *Chinese Armorial Porcelain,* 2:12–13; for other pieces that are possibly from this service, see Antunes, *Porcelanas da China,* p. 34.

137. Schroder, *English Domestic Silver,* p. 137; for similar pots with famille rose decoration, see Jörg, *Collection of Oriental Ceramics,* pp. 134–35; Jörg, *Chinese Export Porcelain,* pp. 84–85; Howard, *Tale of Three Cities,* p. 123; and Krahl, *Chinese Ceramics,* p. 1106; Cummer Gallery of Art, Wark Collection, no. 254, p. 339.

138. Brown, *In Praise of Hot Liquors,* pp. 12, 38–49; Paston-Williams, *Art of Dining,* p. 223.

139. Young, "Eighteenth-Century English Decorators," pp. 18–22; Howard, *Choice of the Private Trader,* p. 150.

140. Howard, *Chinese Armorial Porcelain,* 1:586, 2:212.

141. Howard, *Chinese Armorial Porcelain,* 1:406.

142. Mézin, *Cargaisons de Chine,* p. 129; for pieces with the same decoration, see Howard and Ayers, *China for the West,* 1:342–43; Mézin, *Cargaisons de Chine,* p. 129; Litzenburg and Bailey, *Reeves Center Collection,* p. 182.

143. Orders for the Loyal Bliss, 1712, quoted in Howard, *Choice of the Private Trader,* p. 23; Jörg, *Porcelain and the Dutch China Trade,* p. 180.

144. Howard and Ayers, *China for the West,* 1:317; Litzenburg and Bailey, *Reeves Center Collection,* p. 198; Scheurleer, *Chinese Export Porcelain,* nos. 235–36; Hervouët, Hervouët, and Bruneau, *La Porcelaine,* p. 265.

145. Du Halde, *General History of China,* 2:353.
146. Jörg, "To the Highest Bidder," p. 66.
147. Manners, "Dutch 'Fine Line' and German Schwartzlot," pp. 138–41.
148. Sheaf and Kilburn, *Hatcher Porcelain Cargoes,* p. 111; Jörg, *Geldermalsen,* pp. 67–69; Volker, *Porcelain and the Dutch East India Company,* pp. 34, 48–49; Jörg, *Porcelain and the Dutch China Trade,* p. 165.
149. Jörg and Flecker, *Porcelain from the Vung Tau,* p. 56.
150. Howard and Ayers, *China for the West,* 2:402; Palmer, *Winterthur Guide,* p. 101; Williamson, *Book of Famille Rose,* pl. 37.
151. York Co., Virginia, Wills, Inventories, Judgments & Orders, no. 19, 1740–46, pp. 163–66; Jörg, *Porcelain and the Dutch China Trade,* p. 166; Sheaf and Kilburn, *Hatcher Porcelain Cargoes,* pp. 111–14; Jörg, *Geldermalsen,* p. 114.
152. For other pieces from this tea service, see Phillips, *China-Trade Porcelain,* p. 155; Hervouët, Hervouët, and Bruneau, *La Porcelaine,* p. 371.
153. Young, "Eighteenth-Century English Decorators," pp. 17–22; Godden, "Chinese Porcelain," pp. 58–65; Godden, *Oriental Export Market Porcelain,* pp. 373–74.
154. Howard and Ayers, *China for the West,* 1:140; for similar goblets, see Howard and Ayers, *China for the West,* 1:140; Howard, *Tale of Three Cities,* p. 93; and Litzenburg and Bailey, *Reeves Center Collection,* p. 216.
155. Hartop, *Huguenot Legacy,* p. 34.
156. For similar or related examples, see Howard, *Choice of the Private Trader,* p. 40; Howard and Ayers, *China for the West,* 1:76; Krahl and Harrison-Hall, *Ancient Chinese Trade Ceramics,* p. 41; Hervouët, Hervouët, and Bruneau, *La Porcelaine,* p. 294.
157. McNab, "Legacy of a Fantastical Scot," p. 174.
158. Lee, *British Silver,* p. 10; Brown, *Come Drink the Bowl Dry,* p. 63; for similar or related examples, see Litzenburg and Bailey, *Reeves Center Collection,* p. 217; Le Corbeiller, *China Trade Porcelain,* pp. 36–37; and Clunas, *Chinese Export Art and Design,* pp. 58–59.
159. Lee, *Philadelphians and the China Trade,* p. 74; for objects with the same decoration, see Lee, *Philadelphians and the China Trade,* pp. 73–74; Litzenburg and Bailey, *Reeves Center Collection,* p. 273; Palmer, *Winterthur Guide,* p. 89; and Hervouët, Hervouët, and Bruneau, *La Porcelaine,* p. 85.
160. Notebook of an unknown American China trader, 1798–1809, p. 50, Rhode Island Historical Society.
161. Howard, *Chinese Armorial Porcelain,* 2:635.
162. Wästfelt, Gyllensvärd, and Weibull, *Porcelain from the East Indiaman Götheborg,* pp. 278–79; for pieces with the same decoration, see Hervouët, Hervouët, and Bruneau, *La Porcelaine,* p. 352.
163. Oxford English Dictionary (1933), s.v. "punch"; Brown, *Come Drink the Bowl Dry,* p. 47.
164. Howard, "Chinese Porcelain of the Jacobites," pp. 243–44.
165. Le Corbeiller, *China Trade Porcelain,* pp. 94–95.
166. Mottahedeh, "Numismatic Sources," pp. 113–16; for similar punch bowls, see Howard and Ayers, *China for the West,* 1:238; Wirgin, *Från Kina till Europa,* p. 192; and Hervouët, Hervouët, and Bruneau, *La Porcelaine,* p. 227.
167. Howard and Ayers, *China for the West,* 1:238–39.
168. Howard, *Chinese Armorial Porcelain,* 2:173; for other objects with the arms of the Anti-Gallican Society, see Howard, *Chinese Armorial Porcelain,* 1:370, 390, 487, 945, 2:173; Howard and Ayers, *China for the West,* 1:243; Krahl and Harrison-Hall, *Ancient Chinese Trade Ceramics,* pp. 104–7; and Hervouët, Hervouët, and Bruneau, *La Porcelaine,* p. 331.
169. Wyman, "Society of Bucks," pp. 293–304.
170. Howard and Ayers, *China for the West,* 1:282–83; Krahl and Harrison-Hall, *Ancient Chinese Trade Ceramics,* pp. 110–11; Litzenburg and Bailey, *Reeves Center Collection,* p. 169.
171. Choi, "Painting and Porcelain," pp. 38–68; Jörg, *Porcelain and the Dutch China Trade,* pp. 108, 182.
172. Smith, *Empress of China,* p. 294.
173. Sharpe, "Chinese Export Porcelain," p. 247.
174. Sharpe, "Chinese Export Porcelain," p. 250.

175. Adhyatman, *Kendi,* pp. 5–10; Krahl, *Chinese Ceramics,* pp. 460, 729–30; Pope, *Chinese Porcelains,* pl. 97; Shulsky, "Philip II of Spain," p. 51; Scheurleer, *Chinese Export Porcelain,* p. 211.
176. Jörg, "Japanese Apothecary Bottles," p. 6; Dumbrell, *Understanding Antique Wine Bottles,* p. 152; Jörg, "Japanese Apothecary Bottles," pp. 4–5.
177. Jörg, *Fine and Curious,* p. 221.
178. Howard and Ayers, *China for the West,* 2:582; for similar ewers, see Howard and Ayers, *China for the West,* 2:582; Howard, *Tale of Three Cities,* p. 91.
179. Watson, *Chinese Porcelain in European Mounts,* pp. 9–21.
180. Hume, *If These Pots Could Talk,* p. 302; Brown, *Come Drink the Bowl Dry,* p. 18; Shesgreen, *Engravings by Hogarth,* pls. 75–76.
181. Kuwayama, *Chinese Ceramics in Colonial Mexico,* p. 38.
182. For jugs with similar decoration, see Welsh, *Western Orders,* pp. 38–39; Calvão, *Porcelain Route,* pp. 274–75; Antunes, *Porcelanas da China,* p. 51.
183. Brown, *Come Drink the Bowl Dry,* pp. 75–76; Oxford English Dictionary (1933), s.v. "punch."
184. Scottish Rite Masonic Museum, *Material Culture of the American Freemasons,* pp. 47–52.
185. Krahl and Harrison-Hall, *Ancient Chinese Trade Ceramics,* pp. 102–3.
186. Vainker, *Chinese Pottery and Porcelain,* pp. 222–23.
187. Examples include kendis in the shape of ducks, fish, elephants, and squirrels and teapots in the shape of melons, trees, and bundles of bamboo.
188. Volker, *Porcelain and the Dutch East India Company,* p. 43.
189. De Matos, "Christian Iconography in Chinese Porcelain," p. 29; for similar or related objects, see Calvão, *Porcelain Route,* pp. 156–57; Kuwayama, *Chinese Ceramics in Colonial Mexico,* pp. 28–29; and De Castro, *Chinese Porcelain,* p. 29.
190. Howard and Ayers, *China for the West,* 1:117, 143.
191. Holme, *Academy of Armory,* 1:2; Hartop, *Huguenot Legacy,* pp. 404, 415.
192. Holme, *Academy of Armory,* 1:438; Fennimore, *Metalwork in Early America,* p. 339.
193. Howard, *Chinese Armorial Porcelain,* 2:131.
194. Howard and Ayers, *China for the West,* 2:560.
195. Jörg, *Porcelain and the Dutch China Trade,* p. 172.
196. Lambton, *Chambers of Delights,* p. 52.
197. Howard, *Choice of the Private Trader,* pp. 88, 229.
198. Howard, *Choice of the Private Trader,* p. 221.
199. Schivelbusch, *Tastes of Paradise,* pp. 131–32.
200. Cocks, "Nonfunctional Use of Ceramics," p. 196; Impey, "Eastern Trade," p. 180.
201. Jörg and Flecker, *Porcelain from the Vung Tau;* the ceiling of the porcelain room in the Santos Palace in Lisbon, Portugal, is covered entirely in export porcelain dishes; illustrated in Rinaldi, *Kraak Porcelain,* pp. 63–64; Leath, "'After the Chinese Taste,'" p. 50.
202. Detweiler, *George Washington's Chinaware,* p. 169.
203. Jörg, "Porcelain for the Dutch," pp. 194–96; Cocks, "Nonfunctional Use of Ceramics," pp. 195–216.
204. Jörg and Flecker, *Porcelain from the Vung Tau,* pp. 36–37.
205. Jörg and Flecker, *Porcelain from the Vung Tau,* pp. 18–27.
206. Jörg and Flecker, *Porcelain from the Vung Tau,* p. 39; Ströber, *"La maladie de porcelaine,"* pp. 84–85; for similar vases, see Le Corbeiller and Frelinghuysen, *Chinese Export Porcelain,* p. 11.
207. Ströber, *"La maladie de porcelaine,"* p. 46.
208. Du Halde, *General History of China,* 2:349.
209. Ferguson, *Cobalt Treasures,* p. 20; Jörg, *Porcelain and the Dutch China Trade,* p. 156.
210. For vases of this identical shape, see Wirgin, *Från Kina till Europa,* p. 168; similar vases with pistol handles were also popular, and a number of examples were made for American families, including ones for the Duane and Greenwood families of New York; Howard, *Chinese Armorial Porcelain,* 2:651; Howard, *New York and the China Trade,* p. 93.
211. Euphemia, *Letters of Josiah Wedgwood,* 1:261.
212. Rawson and Portal, "Luxuries for Trade," p. 278; Kerr and Ayers, *Blanc de Chine,* no. 8.

213. Godden, *Oriental Export Market Porcelain,* p. 257; Ströber, "*La maladie de porcelaine,*" pp. 114–15; Leath, "'After the Chinese Taste,'" p. 51; DeWolf, "Chinese Porcelain," p. 96.
214. Emerson, Chen, and Gates, *Porcelain Stories,* p. 156; for similar figures, see Ayers, *Blanc de Chine,* p. 108; Beurdeley, *Chinese Trade Porcelain,* p. 32; and Godden, *Oriental Export Market Porcelain,* pp. 266, 270, 277.
215. Godden, *Oriental Export Market Porcelain,* p. 277.
216. Howard, *Choice of the Private Trader,* pp. 15–16, 252–53; there are more figures of women than men, suggesting that they may not originally have been created as pairs; for similar figures, see Howard and Ayers, *China for the West,* 2:612–13; Sargent, *Copeland Collection,* pp. 112–14; Antunes, *Porcelanas da China,* p. 37; Williamson, *Book of Famille Rose,* pl. 41; and Beurdeley, *Chinese Trade Porcelain,* p. 91.
217. Howard and Ayers, *China for the West,* 2:613.
218. Howard, *Choice of the Private Trader,* pp. 15–16, 252–53.
219. Jörg, *Fine and Curious,* p. 287; Jörg, *Porcelain and the Dutch China Trade,* pp. 175–76; Howard and Ayers, *China for the West,* 1:127.
220. Sheaf and Kilburn, *Hatcher Porcelain Cargoes,* p. 154.
221. Jörg, *Geldermalsen,* pp. 98–100; Sheaf and Kilburn, *Hatcher Porcelain Cargoes,* p. 153.
222. Sargent, *Copeland Collection,* pp. 141–42; Setterwall, Fogelmark, and Gyllensvärd, *Chinese Pavilion,* pp. 165, 293, 295–96; for similar figures, see Howard and Ayers, *China for the West,* 2:584; Sargent, *Copeland Collection,* pp. 144–45; and Antunes, *Porcelanas da China,* pp. 118–20.
223. Howard, *Choice of the Private Trader,* p. 276.
224. Communication with John R. Finlay, Curator of Chinese Art, Norton Museum of Art, April 2004; Viega, *Chinese Export Porcelain,* pp. 144–45; Rawson, *British Museum Book,* p. 164; for a similar set of figures, see Viega, *Chinese Export Porcelain,* pp. 144–45.
225. Sheaf and Kilburn, *Hatcher Porcelain Cargoes,* p. 152.

Bibliography

Adhyatman, Sumarah. *Kendi.* Jakarta: Himpunan Keramik Indonesia, 1987.

Akveld, Leo, and Els Jacobs. *The Colourful World of the VOC.* Bussum, Neth.: THOTH Publishers, 2002.

Alcorn, Ellenor. *English Silver in the Museum of Fine Arts, Boston.* 2 vols. Boston: By the museum, 1993.

Antunes, Mary. *Porcelanas da China: The Collection of Ricardo do Espírito Santo Silva.* Lisbon: Ricardo do Espírito Santo Silva Foundation, 2000.

Ayers, John. *Blanc de Chine: Divine Images in Porcelain.* New York: China Institute, 2002.

Ayers, John, Oliver Impey, J.V. G. Mallet, Anthony du Boulay, and Lawrence Smith. *Porcelain for Palaces: The Fashion for Japan in Europe, 1650–1750.* London: Oriental Ceramics Society, 1990.

Ball, Dorian. *The Diana Adventure.* Groningen, Neth.: Kemper Publishers, 1995.

Beurdeley, Michel. *Chinese Trade Porcelain.* Rutland, Vt.: Charles E. Tuttle, 1962.

———. *Porcelain of the East India Companies.* London: Barrie and Rockliff, 1962.

Brawer, Catherine. *Chinese Export Porcelain from the Ethel (Mrs. Julius) Liebman and Arthur L. Liebman Porcelain Collection.* Madison: University of Wisconsin–Madison, 1992.

Brown, Peter. *Come Drink the Bowl Dry: Alcoholic Liquors and Their Place in 18th-Century Society.* York, Eng.: Fairfax House, 1996.

———. *In Praise of Hot Liquors: The Study of Chocolate, Coffee, and Tea-Drinking, 1600–1850.* York, Eng.: Fairfax House, 1995.

Calvão, João Rodrigues, ed. *The Porcelain Route: Ming and Qing Dynasties.* Lisbon: Fundação Oriente, 1999.

Carswell, John. *Blue and White: Chinese Porcelain and Its Impact on the Western World.* Chicago: University of Chicago Press, 1985.

Choi, Kee Il, Jr. "Hong Bowls and the Landscape of the China Trade." *The Magazine Antiques* 156, no. 4 (October 1999): 500–509.

———. "Painting and Porcelain: Design Sources for Hong Bowls." In *A Tale of Three Cities: Canton, Hong Kong, and Shanghai,* edited by Caroline Block. London: Sotheby's Publications, 1997.

Clunas, Craig. *Chinese Export Art and Design.* London: Victoria and Albert Museum, 1987.

Cocks, Anna. "The Nonfunctional Use of Ceramics in the English Country House during the Eighteenth Century." In *The Fashioning and Functioning of the British Country House,* edited by Gervase Jackson-Stops. Washington, D.C.: National Gallery of Art, 1989.

Cohen Michael, and Ewa Cohen. *After You!* London: Cohen and Cohen, 2002.

———. *School's Out.* London: Cohen and Cohen, 2001.

Cook, Cyril. *The Life and Work of Robert Hancock.* London: Chapman and Hall, 1948.

Cummer Gallery of Art. *The Wark Collection: Early Meissen Porcelain.* Jacksonville, Fla.: By the gallery, 1984.

Dapper, Olfred. *Gedenkwaardig Bedryf der Nederlandsche Oost-Indische Maetschapye: op de Kuste en in het Keizerrijk van Taising of Sina.* Amsterdam, 1670.

de Castro, Nuno. *Chinese Porcelain and the Heraldry of the Empire.* Barcelos, Port.: Américo Fraga Lamares, 1988.

de Matos, Maria Antónia Pinto. *Chinese Export Porcelain from the Museum of Anastácio Gonçalves, Lisbon.* London: Philip Wilson, 1996.

———. "Chinese Porcelain: From Royal Gifts to Commercial Products." In *The Porcelain Route: Ming and Qing Dynasties,* edited by João Rodrigues Calvão. Lisbon: Fundação Oriente, 1999.

———. *Chinese Porcelain in the Calouste Gulbenkian Collection.* Lisbon: Fundação Calouste Gulbenkian, 2003.

———. "Christian Iconography in Chinese Porcelain." *Oriental Art* 47, no. 5 (2001): 27–34.

den Blaauwen, Abraham. *Meissen Porcelain in the Rijksmuseum.* Amsterdam: By the museum, 2000.

Detweiler, Susan. *George Washington's Chinaware.* New York: Harry N. Abrams, 1982.

DeWolf, Helen. "Chinese Porcelain and Seventeenth-Century Port Royal, Jamaica." Ph.D. Diss., Texas A&M University, 1998.

du Halde, Jean-Baptiste. *The General History of China.* 4 vols. London: John Watts, 1736.

Dumbrell, Roger. *Understanding Antique Wine Bottles.* Woodbridge, Eng.: Antique Collectors' Club, 1983.

Emerson, Julie, Jennifer Chen, and Mimi Gardner Gates. *Porcelain Stories: From China to Europe.* Seattle: University of Washington Press, 2000.

Euphemia, Katherine, ed. *Letters of Josiah Wedgwood.* 3 vols. Barlaston, Eng.: Wedgwood Museum, 1973.

"The Ewing Papers—Part Two." *The American Magazine* 3, no. 2 (Autumn–Winter 1987–88): 43.

Faulkner, Rupert, ed. *Tea: East and West.* London: V&A Publications, 2003.

Feller, John Quentin. *Chinese Export Porcelain in the 19th Century: The Canton Famille Rose Porcelains from the Alma Cleveland Porter Collection in the Peabody Museum of Salem.* Salem, Mass.: Peabody Museum of Salem, 1982.

Fennimore, Donald. *Metalwork in Early America: Copper and Its Alloys from the Winterthur Collection.* Wilmington, Del.: Henry Francis du Pont Winterthur Museum, 1996.

Ferguson, Patricia. *Cobalt Treasures: The Bell Collection of Chinese Blue and White Porcelain.* Toronto: Gardiner Museum of Ceramic Art, 2003.

Finlay, Robert. "The Pilgrim Art: The Culture of Porcelain in World History." *Journal of World History* 9, no. 2 (Fall 1998): 141–87.

Glanville, Philippa, and Hilary Young. *Elegant Eating: Four Hundred Years of Dining in Style.* London: V&A Publications, 2002.

Godden, Geoffrey. "Chinese Porcelain, Transfer Printed in England." *Transactions of the English Ceramic Circle* 4, pt. 2 (1957): 58–67.

———. *Oriental Export Market Porcelain and Its Influence on European Wares.* London: Granada, 1979.

Harrison-Hall, Jessica. "Export Porcelain from the British Museum." *Oriental Art* 40, no. 2 (1994): 5–11.

Hartop, Christopher. *The Huguenot Legacy: English Silver, 1680–1760, from the Alan and Simone Hartman Collection.* London: Thomas Heneage & Co., 1996.

Hervouët, François, Nicole Hervouët, and Yves Bruneau. *La Porcelaine des Compagnies des Indes: À Décor Occidental.* Paris: Flammarion, 1986.

Holme, Randle. *The Academy of Armory.* 2 vols. 1688. Reprint, London: Roxburghe Club, 1905.

Howard, David S. *Chinese Armorial Porcelain.* 2 vols. London: Faber and Faber, 1974; Chippenham, Eng.: Heirloom and Howard, 2003.

———. "Chinese Porcelain of the Jacobites: I." *Country Life,* January 25, 1973, pp. 243–44.

———. *The Choice of the Private Trader: The Private Market in Chinese Export Porcelain Illustrated from the Hodroff Collection.* London: Zwemmer, 1994.

———. *New York and the China Trade.* New York: New-York Historical Society, 1984.

———. *A Tale of Three Cities: Canton, Shanghai, and Hong Kong.* London: Sotheby's Publications, 1997.

Howard, David S., and John Ayers. *China for the West: Chinese Porcelain and Other Decorative Arts for Export Illustrated from the Mottahedeh Collection.* 2 vols. New York: Sotheby Parke Bernet, 1978.

Hume, Ivor Noël. *If These Pots Could Talk: Collecting 2,000 Years of British Household Pottery.* Milwaukee: Chipstone Foundation, 2001.

Impey, Oliver. *The Early Porcelain Kilns of Japan.* Oxford, Eng.: Clarendon Press, 1996.

———. "Eastern Trade and the Furnishing of the British Country House." In *The Fashioning and Functioning of the British Country House,* edited by Gervase Jackson-Stops. Washington, D.C.: National Gallery of Art, 1989.

———. *Japanese Export Porcelain: Catalogue of the Ashmolean Museum, Oxford.* Amsterdam: Hotei Publishing, 2002.

Jackson-Stops, Gervase, ed. *The Fashioning and Functioning of the British Country House.* Washington, D.C.: National Gallery of Art, 1989.

Jörg, Christiaan. *Chinese Export Porcelain: Chine de Commande from the Royal Museums of Art and History in Brussels.* Hong Kong: Urban Council, 1989.

———. *Fine and Curious: Japanese Export Porcelain in Dutch Collections.* Amsterdam: Hotei Publishing, 2003.

———. *The Geldermalsen: History and Porcelain.* Groningen, Neth.: Kemper Publishers, 1986.

———. *Jan Menze van Diepen Stichting: Selections from the Collection of Oriental Ceramics.* Slochteren, Neth.: By the museum, 2002.

———. "Japanese Apothecary Bottles with Initials." *The "Hyakunenan" Journal of Porcelain Study* 7 (Summer 1991): 1–26.

———. *Oosters Porselein Delfts Aardwerk.* Groningen, Neth.: Kemper Publishers, 1983.

———. "A Pattern of Exchange: Jan Luyken and *Chine de Commande* Porcelain." *Metropolitan Museum Journal* 37 (2002): 171–76.

———. *Porcelain and the Dutch China Trade.* The Hague: Martinus Nijhoff, 1982.

———. "Porcelain for the Dutch in the Seventeenth Century: Trading Networks and Private Enterprise." In *The Porcelain of Jingdezhen,* edited by Rosemary Scott. London: Percival David Foundation of Chinese Art, 1993.

———. *Pronk Porcelain: Porcelain after Designs by Cornelis Pronk.* Groningen, Neth.: Groninger Museum, 1980.

———. "To the Highest Bidder: The Auction of a Porcelain Shop in Amsterdam in 1778." *Transactions of the Oriental Ceramics Society* 65 (2000–2001): 61–72.

Jörg, Christiaan, and Michael Flecker. *Porcelain from the Vung Tau Wreck: The Hallstrom Excavation.* London: Sun Tree Publications, 2001.

Jörg, Christiaan, Tatsuya Shimokawa, Hisako Oyagi Matsushita, Miho Moriya, and Minako Kito. *Ceramics Crossed Overseas: Jingdezhen, Imari, and Delft from the Collection of the Groninger Museum.* Groningen, Neth.: By the museum, 1999.

Jörg, Christiaan, and Jan van Campen. *Chinese Ceramics in the Collection of the Rijksmuseum, Amsterdam: The Ming and Qing Dynasties.* London: Philip Wilson, 1997.

Kawahara, Masahiko. *Ko-sometsuke.* Kyoto: Kyoto Shoin Co., 1977.

Kerr, Rose. *Chinese Ceramics: Porcelain of the Qing Dynasty, 1644–1911.* London: Victoria and Albert Museum, 1998.

Kerr, Rose, and John Ayers. *Blanc de Chine: Porcelain from Dehua.* Chicago: Art Media Resources, 2002.

Kingery, W. D., and P. B. Vandiver. "The Eighteenth-Century Change in Technology and Style from the Famille-Verte Palette to the Famille-Rose Palette." In *Ceramics and Civilization,* edited by W. D. Kingery. Columbus, Ohio: American Ceramic Society, 1986.

Krahl, Regina. *Chinese Ceramics in the Topkapi Saray Museum, Istanbul.* London: Sotheby's Publications, 1986.

Krahl, Regina, and Jessica Harrison-Hall. *Ancient Chinese Trade Ceramics from the British Museum.* Taipei: National Museum of History, 1994.

Kühne-van Diggelen, Wiet. "The Armorial Services of Jan Albert Sichterman." Translated by Patricia Wardle. *Vormen uit Vuur* 176 (2001): 44.

Kuwayama, George. *Chinese Ceramics in Colonial Mexico.* Los Angeles: LACMA, 1997.

Kyushu Ceramic Museum. *The Voyage of Old-Imari Porcelains.* Arita, Japan: By the museum, 2000.

Labaree, Leonard, ed. *The Autobiography of Benjamin Franklin.* New Haven: Yale University Press, 1964.

Lambton, Lucinda. *Chambers of Delights.* London: Gordon Fraser Gallery, 1983.

Leath, Robert. "'After the Chinese Taste': Chinese Export Porcelain and Chinese Design in Eighteenth-Century Charleston." *Historical Archaeology* 33 (1999): 48–61.

Lebel, Antoine. "Royal China: Chinese Porcelain Commissioned by the French Royal Family in the 18th Century." *Christie's Magazine* 20, no. 1 (January–February 2003): 88–91.

Le Corbeiller, Clare. *China Trade Porcelain: Patterns of Exchange.* New York: Metropolitan Museum of Art, 1974.

Le Corbeiller, Clare, and Alice Cooney Frelinghuysen. *Chinese Export Porcelain.* New York: Metropolitan Museum of Art, 2003.

Lee, Georgina. *British Silver Monteith Bowls: Including American and European Examples.* Byfleet, Eng.: Manor House Press, 1978.

Lee, Jean Gordon. *Philadelphians and the China Trade, 1784–1844*. Philadelphia: Philadelphia Museum of Art, 1984.

Leiper, Susan. *Precious Cargo: Scots and the China Trade*. Edinburgh: National Museums of Scotland, 1997.

"The Letters of Père d'Entrecolles." In Robert Tichane, *Ching-te-chen: Views of a Porcelain City*. Painted Post, N.Y.: New York State Institute for Glaze Research, 1983.

Little, Robert. *Oriental Export Porcelain from the Collection of the Montreal Museum of Fine Arts*. Montreal: By the museum, 1992.

Litzenburg, Thomas V., Jr., and Ann T. Bailey. *Chinese Export Porcelain in the Reeves Center Collection at Washington and Lee University*. London: Third Millennium Publishing, 2003.

Loesch, Anette, Ulrich Pietsch, and Fridrich Reichel. *Porcelain Collection Dresden*. Dresden: Staatliche Kunstsammlungen Dresden, 1998.

Manners, Erol. "Dutch 'Fine Line' and German Schwartzlot Decoration." *Transactions of the Oriental Ceramics Society* 65 (2000–2001): 135–42.

Martin, Anne Smart. "'Fashionable Sugar Dishes, Latest Fashion Ware': The Creamware Revolution in the Eighteenth-Century Chesapeake." In *Historical Archaeology of the Chesapeake*, edited by Paul Shackel and Barbara Little. Washington, D.C.: Smithsonian Institution Press, 1994.

McNab, Jessie. "The Legacy of a Fantastical Scot." *Metropolitan Museum of Art Bulletin* (February 1961): 172–80.

Medley, Margaret. *The Chinese Potter: A Practical History of Chinese Ceramics*. London: Phaidon, 1989.

Mézin, Louis. *Cargaisons de Chine*. Lorient, Fr.: Musée de la Compagnie des Indes, 2002.

Mintz, Sidney. *Sweetness and Power: The Place of Sugar in Modern History*. New York: Penguin Books, 1985.

Montanus, Arnoldus. *Atlas Chinensis: Being a Second Part of a Relation of Remarkable Passages in Two Embassies from the East-India Company of the United Provinces, to the Vice-Roy Singlamong and General Taising Lipovi, and to Konghi, Emperor of China and East Tartary*. London: Thomas Johnson, 1671.

Mottahedeh, Suzanne. "Numismatic Sources of Chinese Export Porcelain Decorations." *The Connoisseur* 172, no. 692 (October 1969): 111–18.

Mudge, Jean McClure, ed. *Chinese Export Porcelain for the American Trade, 1785–1835*. Newark: University of Delaware Press, 1981.

———. *Chinese Export Porcelain in North America*. New York: Riverside Book Company, 2000.

Nadler, Daniel. *China to Order: Focusing on the 19th Century and Surveying Polychrome Export Porcelain Produced during the Qing Dynasty*. Paris: Vilo International, 2001.

Palmer, Arlene. *A Winterthur Guide to Chinese Export Porcelain*. New York: Rutledge Books, 1976.

Parnetier, Jan. *Tea Time in Flanders: The Maritime Trade between the Southern Netherlands and China in the 18th Century*. Ghent, Belg.: Ludion Press, 1996.

Paston-Williams, Sarah. *The Art of Dining: A History of Cooking and Eating*. London: National Trust, 1993.

Phillips, John. *China-Trade Porcelain*. Cambridge: Harvard University Press, 1956.

Pierson, Stacey. *Earth, Fire, and Water: Chinese Ceramic Terminology*. London: Percival David Foundation of Chinese Art, 1996.

Pope, John. *Chinese Porcelains from the Ardebil Shrine*. Washington, D.C.: Smithsonian Institution Press, 1956.

Quincy, Josiah. *The Journals of Major Samuel Shaw*. Boston: W. Crosby & H. P. Nichols, 1847.

Rawson, Jessica, ed. *The British Museum Book of Chinese Art*. London: Thames and Hudson, 1992.

Rawson, Jessica, and Jane Portal. "Luxuries for Trade." In *The British Museum Book of Chinese Art*, edited by Jessica Rawson. London: Thames and Hudson, 1992.

Ricci, Matteo. *China in the Sixteenth Century: The Journals of Matthew Ricci, 1583–1610*. New York: Random House, 1953.

Rinaldi, Maura. *Kraak Porcelain: A Moment in the History of Trade*. London: Bamboo Publishing, 1989.

Rockefeller, David. *The David and Peggy Rockefeller Collection: Volume IV, Decorative Arts*. New York: By the author, 1992.

Roth, Stig. *Chinese Porcelain Imported by the Swedish East India Company*. Gothenburg, Swed.: Gothenburg Historical Museum, 1965.

Sargent, William. *The Copeland Collection: Chinese and Japanese Ceramic Figures*. Salem, Mass.: Peabody Museum of Salem, 1991.

Savage, George, and Harold Newman. *An Illustrated Dictionary of Ceramics*. London: Thames and Hudson, 1985.

Scheurleer, D. F. Lunsingh. *Chinese Export Porcelain*. London: Faber and Faber, 1974.

Schivelbusch, Wolfgang. *Tastes of Paradise: A Social History of Spices, Stimulants, and Intoxicants*. New York: Pantheon Books, 1992.

Schnyder, Rudolf. "The Influence of Turkey and the Near East on 18th-Century European Ceramics." In *The International Ceramics Fair and Seminar.* London: By the seminar, 1990.

Schroder, Timothy. *English Domestic Silver, 1500–1900.* London: Penguin Books, 1988.

Scott, Rosemary, ed. *The Porcelain of Jingdezhen.* London: Percival David Foundation of Chinese Art, 1993.

Scottish Rite Masonic Museum of Our National Heritage. *Material Culture of the American Freemasons.* Lexington, Mass.: By the museum, 1994.

Setterwall, Åkel, Stig Fogelmarck, and Bo Gyllensvärd. *The Chinese Pavilion at Drottningholm.* Malmö, Swed.: Allhem, 1974.

Sharpe, Elizabeth. "Chinese Export Porcelain with Arms of Rhode Island." *The Magazine Antiques* 139, no. 1 (January 1991): 246–55.

Sheaf, Colin, and Richard Kilburn. *The Hatcher Porcelain Cargoes: The Complete Record.* Oxford, Eng.: Phaidon Christie's, 1988.

Shesgreen, Sean, ed. *Engravings by Hogarth.* New York: Dover, 1973.

Shulsky, Linda. "Philip II of Spain as Porcelain Collector." *Oriental Art* 44, no. 2 (1998): 51–54.

Smith, Philip. *The Empress of China.* Philadelphia: Philadelphia Maritime Museum, 1984.

Southey, Robert, and Jack Simmons, eds. *Letters from England.* London: Cresset Press, 1951.

Staunton, George. *An Authentic Account of an Embassy from the King of Great Britain to the Emperor of China.* 3 vols. London: Printed by W. Bulmer for G. Nicol, 1797.

Ströber, Eva. *"La maladie de porcelaine": East Asian Porcelain from the Collection of Augustus the Strong.* Berlin: Edition Leipzig, 2001.

Strong, Roy. *Feast: A History of Grand Eating.* Orlando, Fla: Harcourt, 2002.

Tichane, Robert. *Ching-te-chen: Views of a Porcelain City.* Painted Post, N.Y.: New York State Institute for Glaze Research, 1983.

Vainker, S.J. *Chinese Pottery and Porcelain from Prehistory to the Present.* London: British Museum Press, 1991.

Valfré, Patrice. *Yixing: Teapots for Europe.* Poligny, Fr.: Exotic Line, 2000.

van den Bossche, Willy. *Antique Glass Bottles: Their History and Evolution, 1500–1850.* Woodbridge, Eng.: Antique Collectors' Club, 2001.

van der Pijl-Ketel, C.L., ed. *The Ceramic Load of the Witte Leeuw.* Amsterdam: Rijksmuseum, 1982.

Viega, Jorge. *Chinese Export Porcelain in Private Brazilian Collections.* London: Han-Shang, 1989.

Volker, T. *Porcelain and the Dutch East India Company.* Leiden, Neth.: E.J. Brill, 1971.

Wainwright, Nicholas. *A Philadelphia Perspective: The Diary of Sidney George Fisher Covering the Years 1834–1871.* Philadelphia: Historical Society of Pennsylvania, 1967.

Wästfelt, Berit, Bo Gyllensvärd, and Jörgen Weibull. *Porcelain from the East Indiaman Götheborg*, translated by Jeanne Rosen. Denmark: Wiken, 1990.

Watson, Francis. *Chinese Porcelain in European Mounts.* New York: China Institute in America, 1980.

Welsh, Jorge. *Western Orders of Chinese Porcelain.* London: Jorge Welsh Oriental Porcelain and Works of Art, 2001.

Wick, Wendy. *George Washington: An American Icon.* Washington, D.C.: Smithsonian Institution Press, 1982.

Williamson, George. *The Book of Famille Rose.* Rutland, Vt.: Charles E. Tuttle, 1970.

Wirgin, Jan. *Från Kina till Europa.* Stockholm: Östasiatiska Museum, 1998.

Woolley, Hannah. *The Queene-like Closet; or, Rich Cabinet: Stored with All Manner of Rare Receipts.* London: Printed for R. Chiswel and T. Sawbridge, 1681.

Wyman, Colin. "The Society of Bucks." *Transactions of the English Ceramic Circle* 10, no. 5 (1980): 293–304.

Yeo, S.T., and Jean Martin. *Chinese Blue and White Ceramics.* Singapore: Arts Orientalis, 1978.

Young, Hilary. "Eighteenth-Century English Decorators of Chinese Porcelain." *Apollo* 156, no. 490 (November 2002): 17–22.

Index

Note: Page numbers in italics denote illustrations.